Graphical User Interface Programming

Graphical User Interface Programming

Steve Rimmer

WINDCREST®/McGRAW-HILL

FIRST EDITION
FIRST PRINTING

© 1992 by **Windcrest Books**, an imprint of TAB Books.
TAB Books is a division of McGraw-Hill, Inc.
The name "Windcrest" is a registered trademark of TAB Books.

Library of Congress Cataloging-in-Publication Data

Rimmer, Steve.
    Graphical user interface programming / by Steve Rimmer.
      p.   cm.
    Includes index.
    ISBN 0-8306-2475-9   ISBN 0-8306-2472-4 (pbk.)
     1. User interfaces (Computer systems) 2. Computer graphics.
    I. Title.
QA76.9.O83R55 1991
006.6′6—dc20   91-21760
                                    CIP

TAB Books offers software for sale. For information and a catalog, please
contact TAB Software Department, Blue Ridge Summit, PA 17294-0850.

Acquisitions Editor: Stephen Moore
Book Editor: David M. McCandless
Production: Katherine G. Brown
Book Design: Jaclyn J. Boone
Paperbound Cover: Sandra Blair Design,
   and Brent Blair Photography, Harrisburg, PA   EL1

This one's for Megan as well, and also for
Dreadlord Octavius Murphy,
who learned for himself that a hundred-
pound dog can sleep nearly
anywhere it wants to.

Contents

An easily understood, workable falsehood is more useful than a complex, impenetrable truth.

Murphy's Laws of Computers

Introduction

THE USER INTERFACE OF MOST APPLICATIONS REPRESENTS ABOUT THREE quarters of the work involved in getting the whole effort up and running. In those cases where this isn't true, it's usually pretty obvious that it should've been. Software that functions but is difficult or confusing to use rarely actually gets to do anything.

One of the powerful aspects of writing applications for the PC environment is that a PC doesn't presuppose very much. It doesn't include a built-in user interface that your programs can call up, and as such, you're free to construct your software as you see fit. Of course, one could argue that this is more of an omission than a feature; it gives you the freedom to roll on whatever wheels you like but still insists that you re-invent them for every application you start.

Graphical user interfaces (GUIs)—menus, mouse buttons, and dialog boxes— are a serious effort to invent. Big ones like Microsoft Windows require teams of programmers to write them, as well as teams of pizza delivery people to feed the programmers. Unfortunately, big user interfaces usually presuppose pretty elaborate programs to run under them. Applications written for Windows frequently call for almost as many programmers and easily as much pizza as writing Windows itself did.

This book will provide you with the code for a graphical user interface of a manageable scope. You will be able to understand its functions to a degree sufficient to modify it if you want to. You'll certainly have no difficulty in writing programs to use it. Requiring no more pizza than you'd require to get through an average weekend, you should be able to construct medium-to-large applications using the interface in this book. Unless you greatly want to modify the user interface, you shouldn't have to re-invent anything.

In addition, by virtue of their all calling a common user GUI library, your programs will have a consistent user interface. People who know how to run one of them will be well on their way to using anything else you write.

Lore of the Macintosh

There are quite a few references to the Apple Macintosh in this book—and a few ideas borrowed from it. Advocates of the Mac will read this and no doubt wonder aloud why people who want to write Macintosh-like applications don't simply go buy Macintoshes.

The philosophical basis of the ongoing media skirmishes of Macintosh and PC proponents is beyond me—I'm inclined to feel that there are things each system does well, and people for whom each is suited. One can envision a latter day Socratic debate between Apple and PC owners over the relative merits of their systems, the hills ringing with shouts of "Oh, yeah?", "Sez you!", and "But can it multitask?"

The Mac is based on some very good thinking and is a conception of a user interface that takes into account a great deal about the way inexperienced users deal with their computers. It would be a shame to ignore the Mac's virtues merely so you could claim that your work is wholly without derivation.

Besides, aside from the most passionate system owners, people usually discuss the results of the software they use rather than the computer it runs on. If you produce a workable plan to save the rain forests, eliminate global warming, get four hundred miles to a gallon of regular gas, and eliminate commercial television in our lifetime, one of the questions that the reporters pushing microphones and lenses in your face *won't* ask you will be "Did you do this on a Macintosh or a PC?"

There's a distinction between learning from the general concepts of the Macintosh and deliberately emulating its details. Setting out to create PC software cosmetically indistinguishable from that of a Macintosh would be unethical—as well as being a bit foolhardy. It would also be a handicap for most programmers. As you develop applications with the graphical user interface in this book, you'll no doubt have original ideas to bring to your programming projects, ones that might not have occurred to the authors of Mac applications.

Also, those aspects of this book that lean on the Mac do so more for programming concepts rather than aspects of the appearance or operation of the software resulting from said programming.

The paint program

You can't develop a user interface in isolation—at least, you can't expect to get all the bugs out of it if you try. In addition to writing the code to be discussed in this book, I wrote Desktop Paint, an application to run under the user interface. It was released as shareware several months before the completion of this book, and its users have been instrumental in suggesting improvements both to it and to the code here. Aside from helping to kill the few bugs remaining in the initial release version of the user interface, they've helped to make it more intuitive and user-friendly.

Desktop Paint itself appears frequently throughout this book, as bits of its workings serve as good examples of the sorts of things you'll probably want to use the graphical user interface library for, even if you never touch a paint program. In addition, all the illustrations in this book were created with Desktop Paint. While perhaps not as slick as the output of a drawing package might have been, they're authentic.

There is a companion source code disk set available for this book including the executable files for Desktop Paint as well as the C and assembler files for the user interface library discussed herein. You'll find that a paint program of some sort is all but essential for creating several aspects of graphical user interface based programs, and Desktop Paint's features make it ideal for this task. Alternately, you can find Desktop Paint on most computer bulletin boards and in the graphics support conference of CompuServe.

Finally, I should note that several aspects of the graphical user interface entail dealing with bitmapped image files, specifically PCX files. While this book discusses them insofar as they pertain to the user interface code, you might want to know more about them. In this case, you'll find that my book *Bitmapped Graphics*, also published by TAB Windcrest (TAB Book #3558), includes a much more complete treatment of the subject.

I hope you have as much fun creating your applications with the graphical user interface as I did when writing it. It will allow you to do in hours what might have taken weeks to write from scratch. It's very satisfying to be able to thumb your nose at all the grunt work normally accompanying the onset of a new programming project.

Steve Rimmer
CIS: 70451,2734
BDS: 14167294609

I'm not bad. I'm just drawn that way.
Jessica Rabbit

Basic GUI concepts

GRAPHICAL USER INTERFACES AREN'T NEW. YOU CAN FIND THEM ON THE walls of caves in southern France, in the pyramids of Egypt, and on the walls of most countries in which spray paint is readily available. Far more universal than words, pictures are easily understood even by people for whom the equivalent words would mean nothing.

Pictographic communication is typically found among people who haven't developed anything better, among those who want their words to transcend the boundaries of language, and among computer companies whose demographic research reveals that most of their users don't—or can't—read manuals.

In its simplest sense, a written phonetic language—such as English—is a code. The marks on this page represent sounds, not meanings, with the individual sounds themselves remaining meaningless in isolation. Only someone who knows the key (i.e., speaks the language) can read the text and make sense of it.

This also applies to subsets of English, such as that used to define computer terms. People otherwise fluent in conversational English may feel it forgivable not to know what a serial port is.

This situation becomes easier to comprehend if you don't understand the code. Figure 1-1 is an example of perfectly respectable, readable phonetic communication.

A few thousand years ago, this inscription would've been readable by most upper class Egyptians, who no doubt would've sneered at your inability to understand it. Figure 1-2 offers a translation.

1-1 An older graphical user interface.

As an aside, hieroglyphs historically were among the most difficult of ancient writings to decipher because they're only phonetic some of the time—and, of course, they look to be pictographic. Names are written phonetically, but everything else is expressed pictographically. In addition, you should note that the translation in Fig. 1-2 is only approximate, because phonetic hieroglyphs represented a set of phonetics different from our own. (For example, Egyptian hieroglyphs lacked true vowels.)

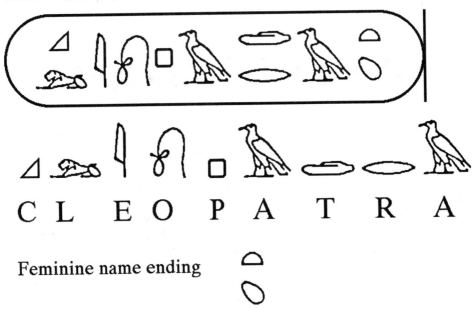

C L   E O   P A   T   R   A

Feminine name ending

1-2 An older graphical user interface with text alternatives.

Pictures would seem to be far more universal than phonetics, at least if they're applied properly. However, in dealing with computer-related concepts, a software designer is frequently confronted with two problems in this respect: many ideas related to computers don't lend themselves to visual representations; and, for those that do, many of the better pictures have already been copyrighted by the Apple Computer company.

Communicating with graphics also has another potential drawback. You might consider that the interpretations of graphics are usually somewhat culturally biased. For example, to us, the little trash can icon on a Macintosh screen suggests the disposal of things. However, to an Egyptian living three thousand years ago, it would probably resemble a pot for keeping things in—quite the opposite function.

A *graphical user interface* is the real time application of visual representations of otherwise information-based phenomena relating to the operation of computers. Graphical user interfaces traditionally annoy programmers, who see all those graphics as merely tying up both useful memory and processor time and doing no real good except for allowing someone to operate the machine without typing. However, for the rest of the planet, a graphical user interface makes a computer look more like something familiar—a desktop, perhaps, or a trash can.

The unfortunate reality of microcomputers at the moment is that most people using them really believe that the computer actually contains desktops and trash cans. Graphical user interfaces have done for computers what Masterpiece Theater did for literature—many more people use computers than would if they were all forced to type DOS commands, but few people actually understand much of what's going on.

All this being the case, applications destined for mass consumption fairly cry out for mice, menus, and all the other trappings of a user-friendly graphical interface. Programmers working in the Macintosh environment have little difficulty in implementing this, as it's hard-wired into the computer and all but impossible to avoid. The situation differs on the PC, however: it has no inherent higher level graphics. When taken out of the box, a PC doesn't know how to draw menus, open windows, or drive a mouse.

In writing a program with a graphical user interface on a PC, one is confronted with a number of potential catches. Some first generation PCs still exist, and they're very slow. Most newer machines have at least some extended or expanded memory, but it's probably not a good idea to assume that they all do. Some machines have fairly standardized EGA or VGA display cards, but many have older style monochrome boards—the mythical Hercules graphics card, or clones thereof. Most users have machines with hard drives, but others—especially the owners of lower-end laptop machines—still deal only with floppies. Finally, the 8086 series of processors are fast at many things, but the sort of operations cropping up when doing graphics aren't among them.

While the PC doesn't have a built-in graphical user interface per se, numerous canned third-party graphical user interface packages to which you can attach your code are available. The most commonly encountered of these is unquestionably Windows 3, which also offers such things as multitasking, peripheral management, and so on. However, Windows is enormous; and if you write a program to run under Windows, you must presuppose that everyone who wants to use it will have bought and installed Windows. Figure 1-3 illustrates Windows 3.

Windows 3 will not be of any use on computers with processors predating the 80286 and, for practical purposes, requires 2Mb of memory. Even using the current Windows software development kit—a decided improvement over its predecessors—Windows application development is a long and tedious process.

Other lesser-used packages resembling Windows are available, each with reduced power and consequently requiring less computer to run. One turning up

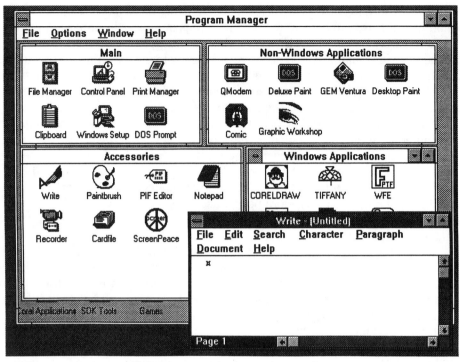

1-3 Microsoft's Windows 3 environment.

occasionally is the Digital Research GEM package. Aside from being shipped as a stand-alone graphical user interface with GEM's own applications, a modified version of it forms the basis of one of the versions of the popular Ventura desktop publishing package. Figure 1-4 is a screen from a GEM-based application.

As with Windows, programs written to run under GEM presuppose that all their users will have GEM. Software development for GEM applications is perhaps a bit less restrictive than for Windows programs—you can use one of several language implementations, rather than being tied to Microsoft's C compiler (as is the case with Windows)—but you still must boot up GEM every time you want to run the program you're working on.

The next step down in complexity from these two large working environments are linkable graphical user interface libraries, of which there are quite a few. These are simply function libraries that give you all the tools you need to create and maintain the metaphor of a mouse-driven user interface. They behave just like any other libraries, such as the ones normally coming with a compiler. You can link in the functions to draw and manage menus, open windows, and so on. Examples of these include Zinc, TEGL, and the packages from Island Systems.

The advantage of using an interface library over a complete graphical environment like Windows is that the resulting programs will run independently of any additional third-party code—your users won't have to buy anything extra in order to use your applications. Secondly, developing such applications is much easier; you can usually work within an integrated development environment, such as

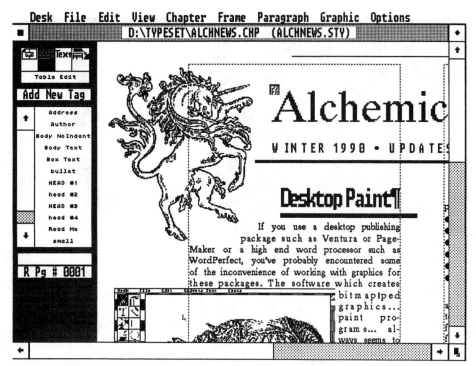

1-4 A GEM application, Ventura Publisher.

Turbo C. Finally, programs written with a dedicated graphical user interface library typically require far fewer hardware resources. Of course, such programs won't have all the multitasking and other features of Windows.

The least intensive approach to a graphical user interface is to create one yourself, which of course is what this book describes. Commercial user interface libraries are handy and frequently very powerful, but they're likely to produce some pretty immense programs. They also restrict you to running the interface the way the library's author designed it, which might not be compatible with the way you want your applications to work.

Figure 1-5 illustrates some screens from the graphical user interface in this book. These are taken from a working application called Desktop Paint, which was developed along with the user interface code. You can find a rudimentary version of Desktop Paint called *Tiny Paint* in Chapter 11, and a complete version of its executable form is included with the companion source code disk. Desktop Paint is handy for creating icons and bitmaps to include in your own programs.

If you write a user interface yourself, you can make it as complex as necessary without having to carry around elements of it that your applications don't need.

Hardware and software requirements

This book will discuss the details of writing your own graphical user interface in a PC environment. The code in this book is all written in Borland's Turbo C 2.0 lan-

1-5 Examples of the graphical user interface.

guage. It will also run—with a few modifications, as noted—under Turbo C++.
Running it under other C compilers will require some moderately serious modifications. For reasons that will become clearer later in the discussion of the code, a workable graphical user interface requires pretty intimate contact with the innards of the language it's written in. The bit of assembly language also involved can be handled with either Microsoft's MASM assembler or the Borland TASM package.

There's nothing really tricky about the code in this book, but you should be familiar with the basics of C programming before you try to understand it.

All of the programs in this book should be compiled using the large memory model. You should disable the case-sensitive link option and the ANSI C extensions of Turbo C before you begin compiling things.

You can run the programs on nearly any type of PC, even the really slow 8088-based machines. No expanded memory is required. You should keep in mind, however, that a graphical user interface is by nature highly processor intensive; thus, running one on a slow computer won't be very much fun.

For reasons to be discussed a little later, the user interface in this book will be entirely monochrome. For this reason, it will look essentially the same on all the popular PC display cards, save for differing screen dimensions.

If you're experienced in programming for EGA and VGA displays, you'll probably be aware that these cards don't have monochrome modes per se. However, if you ignore the plane switching logic of EGA and VGA cards in their 16-color modes, writing to the graphics buffer effectively writes to all four planes at once and makes the card behave like a monochrome display. This is how the custom graphics code for the user interface works. See Chapter 3 for a more detailed discussion.

For reasons to be explained a bit later in conjunction with mouse drivers, you will need an EGA, VGA, or Hercules card to use the code shown in this book.

Drawing an interface

There are a number of important considerations in creating a graphical user interface. If you buy the Windows software development kit, you'll find a whole book by IBM on such considerations; however, this interface can probably get by with only a few paragraphs on the subject.

The first popular application of the graphical user interface concept was, of course, the Macintosh. You actually can learn a great deal from the Mac, even if you might never want to own one. Perhaps more to the point, people think of user interfaces in Macintosh terms—they look for menus at the top of the screen, expect dialogs to have boxes to click in, and so on. Rather than forcing your users to acquaint themselves with a wholly new interface metaphor to use your software, you might want to borrow some of the more global Mac elements for your own user interface.

The same concepts turn up in almost all applications supporting a graphical user interface in the PC environment, including Windows, GEM, and PC Paintbrush. In fact, Apple didn't invent the concepts upon which the Macintosh is founded: they were developed by Xerox for their Star minicomputers several years before the Mac first appeared.

Having said this, you should probably also be aware of the question of "look and feel" as it applies to this sort of software. Apple, for example, has instigated legal action against Microsoft for allegedly making Windows look and feel like a Macintosh. You can use the concepts embodied in the Macintosh in your own user interface—there can be a menu bar at the top of the screen, for example—but it would be unwise to create software that deliberately set out to duplicate the cosmetics of a Macintosh. Resist having a smiling PC appear when your program boots up, create original icons whenever possible, and—at all costs—avoid the appearance of anything even resembling a trash can on your screen.

If you've used a Mac or a PC running Windows or GEM, you probably already have an idea of the potential complexity in making a graphical user interface work. Ignoring the low level mechanics of driving the mouse—which, as it turns out, you can—the problems of responding to mouse clicks in various areas of a complex screen might begin to look a bit daunting. In fact, the strategy of drawing, maintaining, and responding to all the screen objects in a graphical user interface is really what this book is about. The graphics, by comparison, are pretty tame.

In addition to this, writing a user interface for the PC involves a number of pragmatic problems. The Borland BGI graphics library is pretty tight, but it's not as fast as you might like it to be for the things people do a lot in a graphical environment (such as pulling down menus). It lacks a few important tools as well, and Turbo C's memory management facilities are rudimentary. You might do better writing a whole graphics package from scratch, along the lines of the *QuickDraw* package forming the basis of the Macintosh; doing this, however, is beyond the scope of this book.

To get a feel for the problems involved in making a graphical user interface work on the PC, let's start with a few of the concepts involved in one. Figure 1-6 illustrates the dialog box used by the interface if a program wants to open a file.

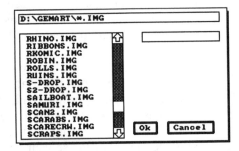

1-6 The Choose File dialog box.

For the program's point of view, all that's involved is this:

```
chooseFile(path,name,48,48,drivemap);
```

The argument path is a string holding the path to the directory possibly containing the file to be opened. The argument name will contain the selected file name if the chooseFile function returns a true value. The next two arguments are integers representing the upper left corner of the dialog invoked by this call. The final argument, drivemap, is a string containing all the legal drive letters. (The necessity for some of this may become clearer a bit later on.)

In order to create this dialog, the user interface must do a number of things, including opening a window on the screen, drawing the window frame, filling in the interior with white, and drawing the drop shadow. As will be discussed in a minute, it also must preserve the area overwritten by the window so that it can be replaced when the window closes.

Everything inside the window is an *object*. In an ideal user interface, one might stipulate that nothing but objects can be placed within a window—but it's not always practical to do so. Objects are not drawn per se but are added to the window.

The objects in this window are the text field object at the top (containing the file path), the edit field object below it and to the right (containing the selected file name), the list object to the left (containing the available names), the scroll bar object just to the right of the list, and the two button objects in the lower right corner of the window (containing the text "Ok" and "Cancel," respectively).

For reasons that will become clearer shortly, keeping the management of all the clickable things in this window down to a manageable level of chaos requires that they be handled not as graphics but as objects, much in the same way that a drawing program like Corel Draw or AutoCAD manipulates the drawing of objects. The actual nature of what objects are will be discussed momentarily.

In order to open a window, you would create an object of the type WINDOW and tell the user interface to add it to the screen. Subsequently, you would create an object of the type TEXTFIELD and add that to the window. There would also be objects of the type EDITFIELD, LIST, SCROLLBAR, and BUTTON.

As will be discussed later, the difference between a TEXTFIELD object and an EDITFIELD object is that the latter allows a user to edit the text in the box.

The process of adding an object to a window involves both drawing it on the screen and telling the window how to find it should the mouse be clicked and some question arise as to the location of its clicking.

Among the things that make up a WINDOW object is an *object pointer*. When the window first opens, this is assigned the value NULL (i.e., it doesn't point to an object). If you then add a TEXTFIELD object to the WINDOW object, the object pointer in the WINDOW object will point to the TEXTFIELD. The object pointer in the TEXTFIELD object will point to NULL.

If you subsequently add a BUTTON object to the WINDOW object, the WINDOW will point to the TEXTFIELD, the TEXTFIELD to the BUTTON, and the BUTTON to NULL. Adding yet another object to the WINDOW will cause the BUTTON to point to it, and so on.

This is a fundamental concept in managing windows and is called a *linked list*. If you know where a window is, you can locate any object within it by "walking" up the linked list until you find the desired object.

In addition to an object pointer, each object has a *type*, such as WINDOW, BUTTON, and so on. Having found an object by walking up the linked list, you can read its type.

Finally, each object is defined by its location on the screen, called its *frame*. By definition, no circumstance exists wherein two objects in the same window can overlap. As such, if the mouse is clicked in a window, you can locate the object it was clicked in, find out what type of object it was, and (in the case of a window with more than one of the same type of object—such as two buttons) which of the objects of the type in question was in fact clicked.

Having been clicked in and identified, an object must first be *tracked* and then responded to. Tracking an object involves doing whatever is necessary to make the object appear to have been clicked in, so that the user of your program knows that something is happening. A BUTTON object is tracked by inverting it until the mouse is released. An EDITFIELD object is tracked by allowing someone to type in new text or modify what's there. A TEXTFIELD object is tracked by doing nothing (because you can do nothing but look at a TEXTFIELD).

Finally, your program must do whatever is involved when a particular object is clicked.

I'll explain this shortly in considerably greater detail.

The nature of objects

Graphical user interfaces employ more specialized struct definitions than almost any other type of program. All objects are handled as structs, or, in this case, as typedefed structs.

These are the two simplest objects involved in making the interface work:

```
typedef struct {
    int x,y;
    } POINT;

typedef struct {
    int left,top,right,bottom;
    } RECT;
```

The POINT object defines a point on the screen, where point (0,0) is the upper left corner of the screen. It's usual to associate a POINT object with the location of the mouse. As you'll see in the next chapter, if p is an object of the type POINT, this will return the location of the mouse in it.

```
MouseLoc(&p);
```

The function MouseLoc is part of the user interface library.

The RECT structure—for rectangle—defines a rectangular area on the screen. The frame of an object, for example, is defined as a RECT.

Here's a WINDOW object. Notice the RECT object within it defining its frame. Also, the back element points to a buffer defining the image behind the window before it was drawn.

```
typedef struct {
        OBJECTHEAD head;
        RECT frame;
        char *back;
        } WINDOW;
```

The OBJECTHEAD element of the window is obviously another struct, but one that hasn't been seen yet:

```
typedef struct {
        unsigned int type;
        void *next;
        } OBJECTHEAD;
```

This is, in fact, the object pointer mentioned earlier. Every object type that relates to windows starts with an OBJECTHEAD element. If p points to an object of an unknown type, you can find out what the object is like this:

```
n = (OBJECTHEAD *)p->type;
```

There are a number of predefined constants that might appear in the type element of an OBJECTHEAD.

The next element of an OBJECTHEAD points to the next object in the linked list, or to NULL if this is the last object in the chain.

Memory management

One of the biggest concerns in creating windows is what to do about closing them when they're no longer needed. In order to create the impression that a window has vanished from the screen, all the details originally in the occupied area must be redrawn. You can follow one of two approaches.

The simplest approach to closing a window—and, incidentally, the one the user interface in this book will adopt—involves copying an image of the screen area the window will occupy to memory before the window is drawn and then replacing it when the window closes. This is very easy to do under Turbo C using the getimage and putimage functions. The back pointer in a WINDOW object points to a buffer where the area behind the window in question is stored.

This approach has several drawbacks, mostly involving memory. Each time you open a window this way, you must allocate a fairly substantial block of memory to accommodate the background image. If you open multiple windows one atop another, each will require a background buffer.

If your program is running on a 16-color display, such as an EGA or VGA card, you can easily run into the problem of a window too large to open. Turbo C's getimage can only deal with image fragments less than one segment in size—they must occupy less than 64K. Thus, you can only open windows about half the area of a full EGA screen.

The putimage function is not blindingly fast in the 16-color modes, and it's responsible for making the window appear to vanish. One could argue that you shouldn't create really large windows in any case. However, Chapter 3 will show you how to cheat on this rule.

The other way to close a window is to regenerate all the screen objects beneath it (which, coincidentally, is how the Mac handles closing windows). Because it's possible to have windows popping up on the Mac not under the control of the principal program that's running, the Mac uses a system of signals—or *events*—that allow a closing window to signal all the other windows below it that might need updating. The windows themselves know what their own contents should be and how to update them.

In fact, it's pretty easy to understand how this might work based on the window structures discussed earlier. In the case of the file chooser window, you could redraw the contents of the window by "walking" the linked list of objects, beginning with the window itself. Starting with the OBJECTHEAD in the window, you would work out the object type and draw it. You would then move on to the next object in the list and repeat the procedure until an object pointer was NULL.

This relieves windows of the responsibility of preserving the area behind themselves when they open, as they can tell the objects they obscure to redraw themselves when necessary. However, this approach also has some drawbacks. In dealing with the speed of the BGI graphics library, closing a window this way can be time consuming if many windows exist beneath it. Secondly, this approach requires that only recognizable objects be drawn in windows, as the windows would not know how to regenerate anything else.

Many of the things that make this approach to handling windows practical on the Mac don't really exist in this user interface. For example, you needn't concern yourself with windows appearing unexpectedly in the midst of your program.

Another important difference between this graphical user interface and that of some of the more elaborate packages, such as Windows and the Macintosh, is the way memory is managed. Turbo C comes with memory management facilities constituting little more than a convenient interface to the DOS memory allocation functions. Thus, if you ask for some memory (by using *malloc* or one of its descendants), DOS will find the first available block that will suit your needs and return a pointer to it.

For reasons probably obvious by now, a graphical user interface allocates and releases memory blocks almost constantly. For the most part, these will be handled in a manner consistent with the structure of a memory "heap"—the most recently allocated blocks will be the first to be released. As such, circumstances shouldn't occur in which you wind up with a fragmented heap—a scattering of small allocated blocks with unallocated areas trapped between them.

The problem with pointer-based memory allocation is that the heap can be easily fragmented under some circumstances. More sophisticated memory management systems overcome this danger by using memory *handles* rather than pointers. A handle is a pointer to a pointer (or, in some cases, an index into a table of pointers).

Under a handle-based memory management system, blocks of allocated memory are referenced by a pointer you get that points to a second pointer owned by the memory management software. Your pointer to a pointer is a memory handle. Having allocated a block of memory, you can't know its location directly—you can only know the location of the pointer pointing to it. If you want to write something to it, you must read the contents of this pointer pointing to it. This procedure is called *de-referencing*.

The advantage in this somewhat convoluted system of nested pointers is that the memory manager is free to move your block of memory around whenever it feels like it. As long as its pointers all stay put, you needn't know that your memory is moving. As such, the memory manager is empowered to do whatever "garbage collection" is required to deal with trapped blocks on the heap. It can fuse many little free areas into one big free area if you call for more memory.

Several drawbacks exist, however, with handle-based memory allocation. First, it's much slower than using simple pointers. The memory manager must tie up some processor time to juggle memory blocks, and your programs must de-reference a handle every time they want to access a block of allocated memory. In fact, they must also lock and unlock blocks being de-referenced—they must tell the memory manager not to move anything while a de-referenced block is being accessed.

The largest drawback to handle-based memory management for this user interface, however, is that Turbo C doesn't contain it. A rather involved piece of code, a handle-based memory manager is well beyond the scope of this book to create. Thus, this user interface will have to limit itself to only what can be intelligently handled with pointer-driven memory.

The only situations in which a handle-based memory management system really becomes necessary in managing windows is when you want to resize them or change the order of stacked windows (i.e., to bring an inactive window forward). Turbo C's graphics don't lend themselves to the graphic manipulations involved in either of these operations any more than its memory management does, and they'll be dealt with here by excluding them from the interface.

You might want to see if you can devise a way to add them once you understand how the basic interface code works.

As mentioned previously, the graphical user interface in this book is effectively monochrome. If you run it on a machine with a 16-color display, you can easily add color to it. I haven't included color in the sample code in order to keep it simple and to minimize the memory requirements.

An introduction to mice

While mice will be discussed in exhaustive detail in the next chapter, I'll mention a few generalities of rodents here because the mouse is an integral part of the user interface.

The Microsoft mouse—and all clones thereof—come with mouse "drivers." A mouse driver will usually be called MOUSE.COM or MOUSE.SYS, with the latter form being a device driver intended to be loaded through your CONFIG.SYS file. The operation of the mouse driver is identical for both the .COM and .SYS implementation.

A Microsoft compatible mouse driver provides both a standardized interface to the mouse and some very clever code to simplify the implementation of a mouse cursor. For one thing, the mouse driver will create and maintain a graphic cursor on your screen—assuming, of course, that your screen is in a graphic mode recognizable by the mouse driver.

Figure 1-7 illustrates the two mouse cursors used in this book.

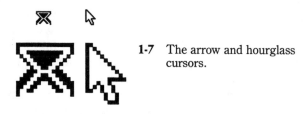

1-7   The arrow and hourglass cursors.

As discussed in the next chapter, you can change the mouse cursor to any shape you like.

One unfortunate aspect of the Microsoft mouse driver is that it doesn't support the super VGA modes available on most VGA cards. Thus, while you might well be able to create graphics in the 800 by 600 pixel 16-color mode of your system, you can't make the graphical user interface in this book work with it because the Microsoft mouse won't display a cursor in it.

The Microsoft mouse driver will work under the graphics modes of CGA, EGA, VGA, and Hercules cards. The user interface in this book assumes that it will have one of the latter three cards to run with.

Most PC mice come with two or three buttons. In this book, "clicking the mouse" will refer to clicking the left button. As you'll see in the next chapter, however, you're free to assign things to the right button. Note that, as the number of mouse buttons isn't standardized among compatible mice, using all the buttons on a three-button mouse is a bit questionable. Many mice only have two buttons.

Aside from the popular Microsoft and Logitech mice, there are countless ostensibly Microsoft-compatible mice—many of which aren't. The graphics-related functions of economical mice are usually the areas wherein their compatibility most readily falls apart. If you plan to develop commercial programs using the code in this book, you should probably acquire a mouse of known compatibility, preferably a genuine Microsoft one.

An introduction to fonts

As with mice, fonts will be dealt with in greater detail in Chapter 9. However, you might want to remember the following considerations until you get there. The font issue is particularly tricky for several reasons, not the least of which is that screen fonts for PC applications aren't easily available in any convenient form.

Screen fonts in the graphical user interface have two distinct uses. The first—and most obvious—involves the font used by the interface to display menus, dialogs, and so on. The second involves fancy proportionally spaced fonts in which you might want to display text if you're writing a word processor based on the user interface. It's convenient to treat these two sorts of fonts in very different ways.

The PC screen in monochrome or 16-color graphics mode is highly byte-oriented, even though it's intended to be thought of as a bitmap. Copying a bit image of an arbitrary size and byte orientation to the screen—such as a Turbo C *getimage* fragment—is very much slower than would be copying an image existing within even byte boundaries and will appear on the screen in even byte boundaries. For example, you can draw text in graphics mode very quickly if all the characters in the text font are constrained to be eight bits wide and appear starting on even eight-bit boundaries.

Menus and dialogs should appear quickly in the graphical user interface; we will handle this by using a special screen font consisting of monospaced eight-by-eight pixel characters and printing them to the screen on byte boundaries. While Turbo C could do this using its default bitmapped font, it's much quicker to write a bit of assembly language code to drive the screen font.

Figure 1-8 illustrates some examples of the screen font.

```
            Desktop Paint version 1.3
            Copyright (c) 1990 Alchemy
                  Mindworks Inc.
```

1-8 The screen font.

```
               FONT NAME: meath24
             FONT NUMBER: 47
              POINT SIZE: 24
              FONT DEPTH: 24
         WIDEST CHARACTER: 31
```

The biggest problem in all this isn't displaying the font (which is actually pretty simple) but rather in first finding the font data. In fact, every computer containing an EGA or VGA card has a very attractive eight-by-eight serif screen font in its extension ROM and even provides a way to locate it easily. The process of appropriating the font from your display adapter will be dealt with in Chapter 4.

The biggest problem with proportionally spaced bitmap display fonts is finding a source of them. Admittedly, the code working with them is slightly more complex as well.

As of this writing, no readily available source of screen fonts exists that you can simply buy and attach to your program. By comparison, the Macintosh—being a graphics-based machine—has dozens of third-party font suppliers. Certain PC applications, such as Ventura and Windows, come with screen fonts. Their structures and how to appropriate them will turn up in Chapter 8.

Figure 1-9 illustrates some proportionally spaced bitmap fonts from several sources.

If you own a copy of Ventura Publisher, for example, you'll find that Ventura uses a pretty complete set of screen fonts. Third-party PostScript fonts for Ventura also come with matching screen fonts. Likewise, Microsoft Windows includes lots of equally attractive screen fonts, which turn up in Windows Write among other places. Finally, countless FONT resources for the Macintosh are in the public domain.

This is 24 point dutch from a GEM VDI font.

Cḣıs ıs 24 pòınc Eıre fròm a Macıncòsḣ Fònc.

This is 24 point Helv from Windows 3.

1-9 Proportionally spaced bitmapped screen fonts drawn from Microsoft Windows 3, Ventura Publisher, and numerous Macintosh files.

While the legal status of using these fonts in commercial applications may be a bit murky (see Chapter 9), the techniques for getting them into a common format and using them as part of your programs are fairly easy to handle.

An introduction to resources

Resources are a concept native to the Macintosh, but one that ports over into the PC environment fairly cleanly. It's particularly applicable to larger applications using a graphical user interface because such programs tend to have many little data structures that must be made available to the software without necessarily being linked into the program itself. Linking things will be discussed shortly.

Figure 1-10 illustrates the About box of Desktop Paint. For those who haven't used software running under some form of graphical user interface, all graphical programs traditionally have About boxes that tell you the version number and the author or owner of the program in question.

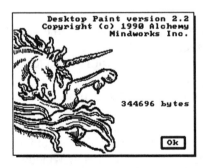

1-10 The About box of Desktop Paint.

This About box consists of a number of easily identifiable objects: the window itself, the Ok button that will close the window, several lines of text, and the bitmap of the unicorn.

The only object in this window occupying any meaningful amount of memory is the bitmap of the unicorn, which requires several kilobytes. It must be available whenever anyone opens the About box.

As you'll see later on, under the graphical user interface in this book, the data for bitmap objects is stored in a standard form corresponding to the structure of monochrome Turbo C *getimage* fragments.

The unicorn can be dealt with in several ways, with the simplest being to save it as a disk file and load it into a buffer whenever someone opens the About box. This advantageously leaves the unicorn out of memory so that it doesn't use any space when it's not actually doing something helpful. Unfortunately, this method also demands that you keep track of an additional file. In a large application with many little data structures like this, the number of small files can get pretty substantial. More than merely being inconvenient, such files can eat more than their share of hard drive space. A typical hard drive allocates space in 4K chunks. A 300-byte file occupies 4K, but a 4097-byte file—only 4K plus 1 byte long—occupies 8K.

As a second approach, you could turn the unicorn into a linkable object file and link it permanently into Desktop Paint. This removes it from the disk but also means that it will remain permanently in memory. Some data structures are best handled this way—the screen font, for example, is permanently linked because it's always needed. Linking the unicorn might well be regarded as a flagrant waste of space.

Thirdly, you could make the unicorn into a *resource* and add it to the common resource file for Desktop Paint. A resource file is simply a file with many individual data structures in it, such that the program owning it can easily locate and access whatever bits of data it wants.

On the Macintosh, every file consists of two chunks, or *forks*—the data fork and the resource fork. A data file, such as a MacPaint picture, would consist of a data fork with much data and an empty resource fork. A program, such as Mac-Paint itself, would consist of many resources and little or no data in the data fork.

The Macintosh's operating system has very sophisticated tools for managing resources; in applications, the working parts of the program are handled as resources such that the program will constantly fetch parts of itself from the disk as they're needed, use them, and then throw them away. This enables the Macintosh to run large programs in small amounts of memory—sometimes—but also makes many programs relatively slow because their resources are repeatedly fetched from the disk.

It's not practical to use resources in a PC program to quite the extent that the Macintosh does. Turbo C doesn't lend itself to parceling out its code into little loadable chunks, and the two-forked file structure of the Macintosh isn't really available on a PC. However, one can emulate some of the useful aspects of resources with little difficulty.

In this book, a resource will be any chunk of data that a program might want to use for a while and then discard. When your program wants such a resource, it will go to the resource file, find the resource, ascertain the size of the resource, allocate a buffer to contain it, load the resource data, and then use it. When the data is no longer needed, your program can simply free the buffer.

Because a resource file can contain as many resources as your program needs, you only need one of them, which you can open when your program boots up and access it as necessary.

In order to make the operation of a resource file reasonably efficient, the resources contained therein must be organized in a logical, flexible way. Once again, the interface in this book will borrow a bit of resource lore from the Macintosh in this regard.

Every resource consists of a type, a number, a size, and then the data constituting the resource itself. The data structure will be determined by the type of the resource. If you call for a particular type of resource, it can be assumed that you'll know how to handle it once it arrives.

A resource type is a string of four chars. A few resource types that will turn up in this book are as follows:

BTMP   A bitmap resource, such as the unicorn.
MENU   A menu definition.
FONT   A proportionally spaced screen font.
PDRV   A printer driver.

You're free to create resource types as you see fit (see Chapter 8 for more details).

A resource file consists of a header defining the nature of the file and tells your program how many resources it contains. Each resource in the file is a data structure that includes, among other things, the size of the resource. The file is structured a bit like a linked list. Having located the first resource—it begins immediately after the resource file header—you can work your way from one resource to the next by finding the size of each resource and searching forward by that amount.

Resources are constrained to be no larger than 64K each, although the resource file itself can be any size that you like.

The PDRV resource, a printer driver, illustrates a useful point. Resources can contain executable code. However, because Turbo C can't easily generate modular code like this, such code resources are typically written in assembly language. I'll give you the details for creating one later in this book.

The MENU resource illustrates another useful aspect of resources. As you'll see, a MENU data structure consists both of the text that will appear in the menus and pointers to the functions corresponding to each item. If you create a MENU object as a resource and load it from a resource file, all the pointers will be wrong and your program will almost certainly crash. If you load resources containing pointers, you must "swab" those aspects of the resource definitions that are location-dependent.

A resource file allows you to let your users customize your program without having to provide a lengthy configuration file. Many aspects of Desktop Paint illustrate this—its DTP.RES resource file can contain all sorts of custom data. The largest part usually consists of FONT resources, and users can add whatever fonts they have to the program by putting them in the resource file. If Desktop Paint finds a BTMP resource in the file when it first boots up, it displays it in the screen's center while it takes stock of the other resources. This allows users of the program to add a custom "startup screen" to the software—another idea borrowed from the Macintosh.

As will be discussed in Chapter 4, any menu item can be given an alternate key equivalent by including ASCII character 4 (◆—a diamond) followed by the alternate key in the text string of the menu. As such, selected menu functions can also be accessed from the keyboard. Figure 1-11 illustrates a menu with alternate key combinations.

1-11   Alternate key
        combinations.

The graphical user interface menu manager handles these keys by actually reading the menu definitions for your program. If you hit Alt-O, for example, it would find the string "◆O" in the menu shown in Fig. 1-11 and execute the function corresponding to the string in which it located this combination.

No memory is saved by loading menus as resources because they'll always be needed. Still, you might want to allow your program to read MENU resources from its resource file if they're found, replacing the ones in your program. This will allow your users to assign their own alternate keys to menu items if they want, assuming that you provide them with a way to create menu resources.

Desktop Paint maintains a current block of fill patterns whenever it's working on a picture and also has a default set of patterns. It loads and saves pattern blocks to disk as resource files. Users who don't like the default fill patterns can create their own and add them to Desktop Paint's resource file, which will write them over the standard default palette set.

Having resource files associated with your programs will let you keep infrequently used data out of memory until it's needed. However, you'll find that, as you begin to think more in terms of using data resources rather than linked data, resources can be used in many ways to make your programs more flexible without resorting to involved installation routines.

An introduction to libraries and linking

When you compile a program under Turbo C's integrated development library, a number of things happen behind your back. To begin with, your C language source code is compiled. The resulting file, an OBJ file, is then linked with any other OBJ files specified in the PRJ file for your program.

Under C, if you call a function in your program not explicitly defined in your code—printf, for example—the compiler assumes that the function lives somewhere else. It doesn't know where "somewhere else" actually is but simply assumes that smarter programs than itself will figure it out.

When Turbo C encounters a call to a function not existing in your program, it adds the name of the function to its list of *unresolved externals*. An unresolved external is a function outside your program beyond Turbo C's ability to find.

The object file that Turbo C eventually generates will include its final list of unresolved externals. Having finished compiling your source file, it passes control over to the linker, which is in fact the program supposedly smarter than Turbo C and hence able to deal with the unresolved externals.

The linker first looks at your PRJ file and then attaches all the other OBJ files it finds there to the one handed it by Turbo C. If you put the name of a C language file in your PRJ file, the linker will assume that Turbo C has previously compiled it and hence that an OBJ file for it will be available. As it adds object files, it resolves as many of the unresolved externals as it can by finding the functions it's after in the object files.

When the linker runs out of object modules, it looks at its list of remaining unresolved externals. If any remain—and some invariably will—it starts looking through the available libraries (the LIB files). It will begin with any libraries included in the PRJ file and wind up with Turbo C's libraries. The latter libraries are where the standard C functions, such as printf, live.

Having resolved all its unresolved externals, the linker creates a finished EXE file. If you've used the Run command from within the Turbo C integrated environment, Turbo C will run the EXE file for you so you can see what your program does.

A fundamental difference exists between object modules and libraries, aside from the order in which the linker deals with them. Object modules are added to your program in their entirety, even if some of the functions in the modules are never actually called. However, when the linker searches a library to resolve external functions, it will only extract those portions of the library that it requires to complete your program.

Libraries are created by a utility called TLIB, which comes with Turbo C. TLIB is an object module librarian allowing you to create libraries, add object modules to them, extract object modules from an existing library, and delete object modules from a library.

The code in this book will result in a library called GUI.LIB. When it's included in your PRJ files, your programs will have a complete graphical user interface at their disposal.

It's frequently convenient to include binary data in an object module so it ultimately can be added to a library. Turbo C doesn't provide an elegant way to do this. Examples of such binary data are the graphical user interface screen font and the toolbox icons in Desktop Paint, which are things not created as C language data and not appropriate for loading as resources. In the case of the screen font, a program that sought to load it as a resource would certainly find itself in trouble if the resource file containing it was missing. It wouldn't be able to display any text to complain about the missing file.

There's a discussion in Chapter 4 of a utility that creates linkable Microsoft-compatible—and Turbo C-compatible—object modules from small bits of binary data.

An introduction to controls

Controls have been discussed informally as window-dependent objects without being really defined. Controls are essentially anything defined as an object to appear with a window. Figure 1-12 illustrates the controls in this graphical user interface.

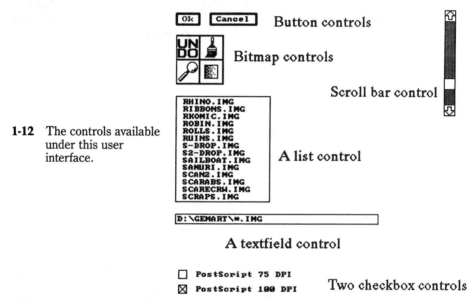

1-12 The controls available under this user interface.

Button controls

Bitmap controls

Scroll bar control

A list control

A textfield control

Two checkbox controls

Controls may be thought of as being data structures or screen phenomena. If you define a control by its data structure and pass the data structure to the function drawing the control, the graphic representation of the control will appear as you've defined it.

Controls in general have two variable states: they can be either active or inactive, and they can be either selected or unselected. An active control will respond to being clicked on, while an inactive one will not. In the case of controls having text, inactive controls will have their text dimmed out. Figure 1-13 illustrates active and inactive button controls.

1-13 Active and inactive controls. [Cancel] [Ok]

The nature of a selected control varies with the individual controls.

Each of the control types to be discussed here has a corresponding object type in the graphical user interface. Thus, if you wanted a button control to appear in a window you were defining, you would in fact add a BUTTON object to the window.

The simplest type of control—and the most commonly used—is a *button*. A button is a box with a word or two of text in it. In fact, buttons can be of any length you like, although a button containing a whole sentence will probably confuse your users.

Buttons are used to select major options in a window. The most commonly used button is one that says "Ok," usually indicating that you're finished with the window in question. The next most common button is "Cancel," which indicates that you're finished with the window but you'd like the program you're running to ignore whatever you did while it was open.

A distant relative of button controls, *checkboxes* consist of squares with text beside them. A checkbox is used in a window in which the users of your software might want to select among several options. For example, in the window in Fig. 1-14, users of Desktop Paint can choose to output a picture to various types of printers.

| ☐ LaserJet 75 DPI |
| ☐ LaserJet 100 DPI |
| ☐ LaserJet 150 DPI |
| ☐ LaserJet 300 DPI |
| ☐ PostScript 75 DPI | **1-14** A list of checkboxes.
| ☒ PostScript 100 DPI |
| ☐ PostScript 150 DPI |
| ☐ PostScript 300 DPI |
| ☐ Epson FX-80 |

A selected checkbox has a cross through it.

Checkboxes can behave in either an exclusive or aggregate manner, depending on what you have in mind for them. In the case of the printer list, printing to more than one printer at the same time would probably constitute a system crash at best. As such, this list of controls would be exclusive—selecting one would disable the previously selected one. In some cases, however, you might want to enable one or more options with a list of checkboxes.

There are three types of controls relating to text, with the simplest being a *text* control. This isn't really a control at all, as users of your program can't actually interact with it. It can't be selected, only stared at until it's no longer interesting. However, it's convenient to treat it as a control because the user interface can add it to windows as such.

Text controls are used when you plan to have the same text in an area of a window for the duration of the window's existence, because changing the text may not erase the previous text. In Desktop Paint, all the various windows that pop up use text objects for their titles, such as the one in Fig. 1-15.

A *textfield* control is also a nonselectable control. It differs from a text control in that it has a predefined maximum length and a box around its text. If the text in the control changes, the box is cleared and the new text drawn into it.

1-15 The Grid Select box of Desktop Paint. The title at the top is a text control.

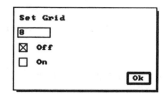

An *editfield* control looks like a textfield control; but if you click in one, a cursor will appear and you'll be able to edit the text. The editing behaves pretty much like the line editor in BASIC.

The *list* controls are very large. They consist (as you might expect) of lists of things, such as file names. If you click on a line of text in a list, the contents of the line will be returned to the window to which the list control is attached. The most common example of a list control is the file name selector in the file chooser box.

The most complex controls are *scroll bars*, of which there are two types—vertical scroll bars and horizontal scroll bars. Scroll bars can also be either active or inactive. Inactive scroll bars are drawn with white backgrounds, while active ones have grey backgrounds.

Scroll bars are typically used in conjunction with some other sort of display to indicate the relative position of one part of the display to the whole. Hence, you can use scroll bars in conjunction with a list control to decide which part of a long list will be visible in the control. You can also use them to set variable quantities, as an analog to a sliding volume control.

Figure 1-16 illustrates two scroll bars and the names of their parts.

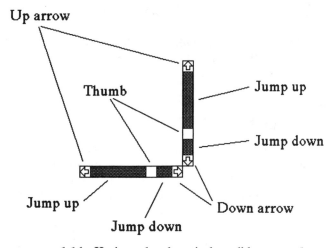

1-16 Horizontal and vertical scroll bars.

You can click inside five distinct parts of a scroll bar: the *up arrow*, the *down arrow*, the *jump up* area, the *jump down* area, and the *thumb*. The thumb will move to indicate the new setting of the scroll bar whenever one of the parts is clicked in. The arrows move the thumb by small increments, while jump areas move it by larger increments.

In the case of a horizontal scroll bar, the left end of the scroll bar is commonly referred to as being up and the right end as being down.

Bitmap controls are potentially the most decorative. A bitmap control can display any reasonable size bitmapped image. Clicking in the control will cause the bitmap to be inverted if the control is active and will have no effect if it's inactive.

Figure 1-17 illustrates two examples of bitmap controls. The upper one is a dialog window. The icon is a bitmap control. In fact, it has no function other than as an attention getter, so it's inactive and clicking on it will have no effect. The second is the toolbox from Desktop Paint, which is comprised of an array of bitmap controls. One of these is always selected, as indicated by the inverted icon.

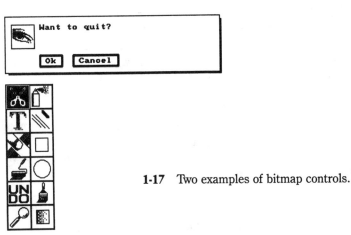

1-17   Two examples of bitmap controls.

There is nothing particularly magical about this selection of controls. Once you get used to the structure of the user interface, you can add additional control types of your own.

C language considerations

In order to make the graphical user interface work at a reasonable speed with most of its functions in C, it has been written to take advantage of specific characteristics of Borland's Turbo C and Turbo C++ compilers. While it can, of course, be ported to other implementations of C (such as Microsoft C), you should be quite familiar with both languages if you decide to try it.

You can compile programs that access the graphical user interface from either the Turbo C integrated environment or by using the command line compiler—TCC.EXE. The former is a great deal easier, of course; and, unless you ultimately write some very large applications, you should be able to run your programs from the editor directly. Desktop Paint, which resulted in almost 200K of EXE code—a fairly complex application—was developed entirely from within the integrated environment.

It's important that all the modules of your programs—including the ones that will form GUI.LIB—be compiled under the large memory model. Turn off the register variables and the case-sensitive link. If you're using Turbo C+ +, you will probably want to disable some of the ANSI warnings, especially the "obsolete declaration form" complaint. All the code in this book uses traditional C function declarations rather than the quasi-Pascal style favored by ANSI. Hence, this book might declare a function like this:

```
OpenWindow(w,r)
    WINDOW *w;
    RECT *r;
{
    /* code goes here */
}
```

When Turbo C+ + is being faithful to the ANSI standard, it wants you to declare like this:

```
OpenWindow(WINDOW *w,RECT *r)
{
    /* code goes here */
}
```

Neither style makes any difference to your final program, of course.

It's important to find a style of programming that works for you and stick to it. This is especially true when you're writing programs using the graphical user interface because the code you write can become very involved very quickly. If you write in a familiar, consistent style, you'll be more likely to spot mistakes.

This book is written in a C language style that I've found comfortable. If it differs from your own, change it.

Much of the impetus toward the ANSI extensions to C and toward object-oriented C (that is, C+ +) has been the need for a language lending itself to large projects written by teams of programmers. C+ + is robust with type checking and ways to use code over and over again. Much of this is superfluous to the code in this book, which lends itself to less-than-epic programs.

Note, however, that when you write programs that use the graphical user interface, you will be calling functions that you didn't write and might not be as familiar to you as your own code would be. For this reason, the library's header file, GUI.H, contains prototypes for the callable functions. Make sure you don't disable prototype checking under Turbo C.

Most C programmers who work on modest size programs don't bother with prototypes, usually with good cause. As long as you know what you're doing and no one else needs to, prototyping is largely unnecessary—unless you're particularly absentminded. This isn't as true when you're calling someone else's library and is especially questionable when you confront the code in this book. The graphical user interface passes around pointers to data structures and even executable functions quite routinely, and using the library functions incorrectly will almost always crash your computer in a very colorful way.

It's probably worth a quick overview of prototyping for those C programmers who usually don't bother with it.

Unless you instruct it otherwise, C thinks that everything is an integer. Hence, if you define a function this way,

```
printchar(c)
{
    /* some code goes here */
}
```

C will not complain; the code is sloppy, but still legal. The argument, c, is assumed to be of the type int, and this function is assumed to return an int because no one has told C anything to the contrary.

If you call this function in some other way, such as

```
printchar("Roast wombats and gravy");
```

the function will probably print something meaningless. However, C still won't complain because it doesn't know that printchar always gets an int argument. Perhaps printchar is very clever and knows the difference between an integer and a string pointer.

Here's an example illustrating why this can be very nasty.

```
dosomething(l,proc)
        long l;
        int (proc)( );
{
    /* some code goes here */
}
```

The two arguments to this function are a long and a pointer to a function. Presumably, dosomething will actually execute the function pointed to by proc. Here are two examples of passing the wrong arguments to this function that are certain to crash your system in ways hitherto only discussed in whispers.

```
int i,myproc( );

dosomething(i,myproc);

long l;
char *string;

dosomething(l,string);
```

In the first case, dosomething will be passed a two-byte argument, the int, and then the four-byte pointer to proc. However, it will think that it has been passed a four-byte long and then the pointer. As such, it will read the two bytes of the int and the first two bytes of the pointer to proc as the long, and then it will read the second two bytes of the pointer to proc and two bytes of whatever happened to be on the stack as the pointer. When it tries to execute proc, it will leap into the twilight zone and not be heard from again.

In the second case, it will attempt to execute a string of text, probably with no less unpredictable results.

All this could be avoided if the function dosomething had a prototype. A prototype tells C exactly what a function should return, how many arguments it should be passed, and exactly what those arguments are supposed to be. Here's a prototype for dosomething:

```
int dosomething(long l,int(*proc)( ));
```

Prototypes are usually stashed away in a header. If you attempt to pass an argument to dosomething that isn't what its prototype declares as what's expected, C will complain at compile time and give you the opportunity to fix your mistake before it causes your system to attempt the execution of a WordStar file.

You can enable a warning under Turbo C that will make it complain if it encounters any functions without prototypes. You might want to enable this if you like function names containing embedded capital letters. As far as C is concerned, these two functions are identical with the case-sensitive link switched off:

```
dosomething(l,myProc);
```

```
doSomeThing(l,myProc);
```

However, if you've written a prototype for the first one, its protection will not extend to the second one because C's symbol checking is case-sensitive no matter how you set up the linker.

Using the stack

It's important to know a bit about how C works internally in order to write effective code for the graphical user interface. Part of this involves knowing how it uses its stack.

The processor in a PC only has one stack, but it can be used for several things at once. A *stack* is an area of memory addressed by a pointer, predictably called the *stack pointer* (abbreviated as SP in machine language).

In fact, the stack pointer always relates to the stack segment—it's a 32-bit pointer and would properly be written SS:SP for large model programs. For the sake of this discussion, you can ignore the actual structure of the stack pointer.

The stack pointer begins at the top of its memory segment and progresses downward. Thus, as things are added to the stack, the stack pointer points lower in the absolute memory address space.

When something is added to the stack, it is said to be *pushed* onto the stack. In other words, it's written to the address that the stack pointer points to and then the pointer is decremented. When something is removed from the stack, it's said to be *popped* off, which means that the stack pointer is incremented and the contents of where it points are read from the stack.

On a PC, each position on the stack is one word wide. Thus, the stack pointer will always be incremented or decremented in units of two bytes.

When you call a function under C, the processor executes a subroutine call. It figures out where it is, pushes this address onto the stack, executes the function, and then pops the return address off the stack so it can return to what it was doing before it encountered the function call. If the function contains other functions, this process occurs again, nesting the calls and returns.

C also uses the stack for other things. If you pass an argument to a function, the contents of the argument are pushed onto the stack, the function is called, and then the argument is popped off the stack and thrown away. The function finds its argument by figuring out where the stack pointer is and peeking back up the stack.

If you pass many arguments to a function, many things are pushed up onto the stack and then popped off afterwards. In fact, it's faster just to increment the stack pointer rather than to execute actual pops after the function call because the data on the stack will be discarded.

Using the stack like this is a very powerful system for passing objects around in a program because no permanent storage is necessary. The objects take up some stack space for as long as necessary and are then abandoned, the stack subsequently being used for other things.

Stacks are also used for local variables. If you declare a function like this,

```
dosomething( )
{
    int i;

    /* some code goes here */
}
```

C will create a place to put i by subtracting 2 from the stack pointer when the function starts and adding 2 to the stack pointer when it's finished. In the meantime, the stack will have a two-byte gap in which the function can store i.

As an aside, this illustrates why there's little point in declaring local single char variables under Turbo C. Even though a char only needs one byte to hold it, the stack works in jumps of two bytes and so Turbo C effectively allocates an int.

In this version of the function, i will not wind up on the stack:

```
dosomething()
{
    static int i;

    /* some code goes here */
}
```

The static declaration causes C to put i in permanent memory in the data segment of your program. If you assign a value to it the first time you call this function, the value will remain unchanged upon later executions of the function until it's explicitly changed.

This allows you to initialize static variables, as in

```
static char myString[ ] = "Let's hear it for big pixels!";
```

while you can't initialize local ones:

```
char myString[ ] = "Let's hear it for big pixels!";
/* this is illegal */
```

If you allocate lots of local variable space on the stack for a complex function, there's a moderately good chance that your program will experience a stack overflow and either crash back to DOS with a nasty message or simply hang. This can happen if you allocate big buffer on the stack,

```
char bigbuffer[8192];
```

or if you just have a lot of data objects hanging around. You could avoid it if you define a bigger stack. However, it's rare that you would create enough local variables to overflow the stack. In the above example, bigbuffer should really be dynamically allocated with malloc. Functions that just squeak by under the limits of the stack when you write them have a way of coming back and chewing your feet after you've forgotten how fast and loose you played with the stack.

Bear in mind that multiple nested function calls in which each of the functions uses a lot of local variables can eat a great deal of stack space. There is a certain amount of stack space required for things like interrupt handlers and DOS calls as well, which you will never actually see being used.

In the graphical user interface, you'll find that many functions have a lot of fairly sinister-looking objects allocated as local variables. It's probably worth mentioning that none of them are particularly large. For example, this is the local variable list for the choose file dialog box.

```
SCROLLBAR sb,*sp;
LIST ls,*lp;
TEXT errt;
TEXTFIELD fspec;
EDITFIELD fname,*ep;
RECT r,errr;
WINDOW w,errw;
POINT p;
BUTTON ok,can,errok,*bp;
char *thespec,drive[MAXDRIVE];
char dir[MAXDIR],file[MAXFILE],ext[MAXEXT];
unsigned int rt;
int loc=0,a_inner,a_outer=0xff,erra,i,isname( );
```

In fact, this whole list only works out to a few hundred bytes worth of stack space.

Memory and memory models

The graphical user interface is a memory pig. Every time you open a window, it chews up a pretty substantial bit of memory (the exact magnitude depending on the window's size). Desktop Paint is more of a memory pig than others because it must allocate a lot of memory buffers in which to manipulate image elements. However, by very nature, a graphical user interface lends itself to graphic manipulations. Even if you don't plan to write a paint program, don't assume you'll sail by without having to consider memory.

For reasons to be discussed in greater detail in Chapter 3, the graphical user interface may require four times the memory running on a system with an EGA or VGA card than it does on a machine equipped with a lowly Hercules card.

The memory situation on a PC is a bit unusual—perhaps highly unusual if you haven't had to deal with it before. While some elements of it will have to wait for later in this book, let's review a few of the more fundamental ones now.

If you were designing a microprocessor, you would probably arrange the memory so it started at address zero and carried along until no more room existed or there was no more budget for memory. If a program wanted to address the 105036th byte of memory, it would load the number 105036 into the appropriate register and think no more of it.

The original Intel chips, the precursors of the ones upon which PCs are based, worked this way. However, by the time the boys at Intel got around to designing the 8088, the chip that drove first generation PCs, they had loftier ideas—one idea being *segmented memory*.

In segmented memory, memory addresses are made up of two 16-bit numbers called the *segment* and the *offset*. If you want to address the first 64K memory, you would set the segment to zero and the offset to something between zero and 65535, depending upon the actual byte in the first 64K you were interested in. If you wanted to address the next 64K, you would set the segment to 4096.

One might well ask how 4096 got into the discussion. The segment value moves in increments of 16 bytes as things relate to absolute memory addresses. Each 16-byte boundary is called a *paragraph*. Thus, if the offset is zero and the segment is one, the absolute address involved is 16.

The usual notation for memory pointers having segment and offset components is SEGMENT:OFFSET, with the numbers in hexadecimal.

There are a number of consequences to segmented memory. The first is that for small programs—those occupying less than 64K—you can forget about the segment registers entirely and merely deal with the offsets. Thus, small programs can have the size and speed advantages inherent in 16-bit pointers, even though the computer is really using 32-bit pointers.

One source of confusion and potential system crashes is that every byte in memory can be addressed by numerous different 32-bit pointer values. For example, you could address the sixteenth byte in memory as 0000:0010H—segment zero, offset 16. You could also address the same byte as 0001:0000H—segment one, offset zero. This makes comparing 32-bit pointers questionable at best.

Programs fitting in one segment are called *small model* programs. Programs requiring multiple segments—more than 64K—are called *large model* programs. Turbo C also offers something called the *huge* model. The huge model is like the large model except that all pointers are converted to absolute addresses when you use them, rather than segment and offset values, and then back to the 8088's internal notation when they actually go to point at something. The huge model is a bit more convenient for handling large data objects, but it's also very much slower.

The Turbo C BGI graphics library is written using the large model, as should be programs calling it. All the functions in this book assume that your compiler will be set to work with the large model. The assembly language functions are especially sensitive to this and will crash your system if you try to compile programs using them under a different model.

The Turbo C bitmapped graphics functions can't actually deal with graphic objects occupying more than one segment. While this may impose a limit on the maximum size of the windows you can open (see Chapter 3), it also obviates the need for a way to handle multiple segment memory buffers.

Creating the library

Three files you'll want to add things to as you work through this book are GUI.C, GUIASM.ASM, and GUI.H. If you buy the companion disk for the book, you'll have these files already typed in. Alternately, you'll find the complete listings for all three files in the appendices at the back of this book.

The GUI.H file should be included in any program that will use the graphical user interface.

You will probably want to set up a batch file to make GUI.LIB each time you add something to it. Here's a typical one:

```
del gui.lib
tlib gui.lib + gui.obj + guiasm.obj
tlib gui.lib + thefont.obj + herc.obj + egavga.obj
```

Specifically, this creates GUI.LIB by adding the compiled object file from GUI.C, the assembled object file from GUIASM.ASM, the binary image of the screen font, and the object versions of the two pertinent BGI drivers (see Chapter 2 for more details).

This book also contains numerous example programs that you might want to key in if you haven't bought them on disk. In fact, the structure of all the programs using the graphical interface is pretty constant—having typed in one, you'll be able to derive the subsequent ones from it in most cases.

Finally, one problem encountered by a book describing graphics programs is providing examples of the graphics in a useful form. While it's possible to list source code in a way to make it easily reproducible—printed function listings can be keyed in—the same isn't really true of pictures. In a few cases, example programs will need small bitmapped images for things like icons. These don't have to look like anything in particular—they simply must be around to make the code work. Be prepared to create some small pictures.

Graphical interface application

Depending upon your intended applications for the graphical user interface to be discussed over the next few chapters, you might want to work through all the details of this book in the order they appear. However, once it's complete, the graphical user interface library doesn't really require that you know how it works unless you want to change some aspect of its operation. In the great majority of applications that use the library, you won't have to make changes.

It's quite acceptable to treat the graphical user interface library as a "black box." For example, if you want to open a window or get a file name with the file chooser, all you really have to know is how to call the appropriate function. The actual working of the functions in GUI.LIB can usually be ignored.

If you want to start writing applications using the graphical user interface immediately, you might want to skip ahead. Type in the listings in the appendices or get them on a disk, generate GUI.LIB, and only refer to the rest of the book as you need to in learning how to use the GUI.LIB function calls.

The most powerful aspect of GUI.LIB is that it relieves you of the responsibility for knowing how a window is opened or how a string of 24-point Courier text is printed to the screen. It allows you to get on with the original part of your program without having to deal with the details of creating a brand new user interface.

The time has come, the Walrus said, to speak of many things.
from Lewis Carroll

2

Of graphic modes and mice

THE BORLAND BGI INTERFACE SHOULD, AT LEAST IN THEORY, SHELTER programmers from the details of working with the hardware specifics of graphic display cards—in much the same way that the PC's BIOS was intended to shelter programmers from having to deal with the text mode hardware directly. Both are a bit optimistic in this respect for pretty much the same reason. In order to do things quickly, one usually must bypass the hardware-independent elements of the system software and get right down to the bytes and registers.

Making graphics happen quickly is a complicated process, made more so by the actual nature of a PC's display adapter. While a graphic screen is usually described as being bitmapped, it turns out to be no such thing in the modes the graphical user interface will be using. It's byte-mapped; and, in some cases, it's byte-mapped and drunk.

Fortunately, for reasons that will become clearer when I cover mice, the graphical user interface can only be used with a small number of graphic display modes. Specifically, the screen must be in one of the modes recognized by the Microsoft mouse driver lest it refuse to display a cursor. The four applicable modes in this case are the CGA, EGA, VGA, and Hercules graphics modes (with the VGA mode being the 640 × 480 pixel, 16-color mode).

The CGA graphics mode, at 640 × 200 pixels, is sufficiently ugly to make it largely unsuitable for serious applications. No further mention of it will be made here.

Figure 2-1 illustrates the relative sizes of the three cards in the modes to be discussed in this book.

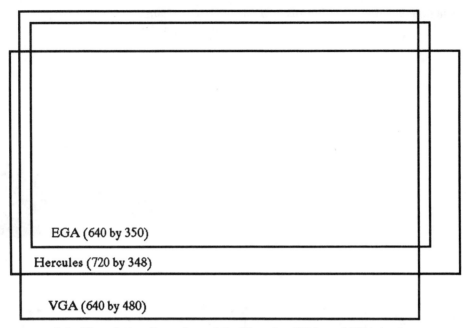

EGA (640 by 350)

Hercules (720 by 348)

VGA (640 by 480)

2-1 The relative dimensions of the Hercules, EGA, and VGA cards.

The EGA and VGA graphics modes are the easiest to understand and work with. To begin with, they both behave identically except that the EGA mode, mode 10H, has a vertical dimension of 350 lines, while the VGA mode, mode 12H, has a vertical dimension of 480 lines. Both support 16 colors from a palette of 64, although the code in this book won't be using their color facilities.

Note that the VGA card also has what is called MCGA mode, mode 13H, which has screen dimensions of 320×200 pixels and supports 256 colors. This mode won't be discussed herein.

The mode numbers represent arguments passed to the BIOS to change modes—something that you won't actually have to do because Turbo C will handle it.

The VGA mode is nicer to look at because it has a more natural aspect ratio.

When an EGA or VGA card is in its graphics mode, its graphics memory lives at A000:0000H. Thus, if you write something to this area in memory, the display on your screen will change.

Each line of the screen occupies 640 pixels, which corresponds to 640 bits. Thus, each line has 80 bytes. If the screen is in an appropriate graphics mode and initially all black, this code will turn on the very first pixel:

```
char *p;

p = MK_FP(0xa000,0);
*p = 0x01;
```

This bit of code creates a pointer to location A000:0000H and sets the first bit of the byte there.

In the EGA and VGA cards, the memory conveniently is laid out linearly. The second line on the screen is represented by the second 80 bytes, and so on. This isn't so in a Hercules card.

The EGA and VGA cards have a rather involved way of handling colors in their 16-color modes. There are four actual pages of memory that live in the screen buffer location (or "page frame") when the card is in a 16-color graphics mode. Any one of them can be made to appear in the page frame by tickling the appropriate registers. In order to select a particular color, you would write to each page in turn to set the bits needed to turn on the color.

Alternately, you can have all the pages in the page frame at once, such that writing to the page frame writes to them all. As the EGA and VGA cards are set up immediately after a mode change, this is how things look to a program that wants to deal with them. Thus, unless you deliberately page some of the memory out of the page frame, the card behaves as a monochrome display. In fact, what really happens is that areas of the screen in which the bits in all four pages are off display color zero—which defaults to black—and areas of the screen where the bits in all four pages are on display color fifteen—which defaults to white. Because writing to the page frame without selecting specific pages deals with all four pages at once, the only two colors that can possibly be displayed are black and white.

There's a much more detailed discussion of this process in Chapter 3.

Regrettably, Turbo C is a bit inflexible in how it wants to treat EGA and VGA displays. While much of the code in the graphical user interface manages to cheat and use EGA and VGA cards as monochrome displays, Turbo C insists on dealing with them in 16 colors. A certain amount of cunning will be required to circumvent this.

The Hercules card

The original Hercules monochrome graphics card predates the EGA card by several years, and represented the first really usable popular graphics card for PCs. The Hercules company has since gone on to produce many more sophisticated graphics cards, and the Hercules card has gone on to be cloned by everyone with a wave soldering machine and a few spare transistors. Hercules compatible display cards are often called *monochrome graphics cards*.

The graphics buffer of the Hercules card begins at B000:0000H. The card displays its graphics on a screen of 720×348 pixels, so each line requires 90 bytes. As with the EGA and VGA cards, putting a Hercules card in its graphics mode and writing 0x01 to B000:0000H will turn on the first pixel. The bitmapped structure of the lines is the same as it was on the EGA and VGA cards.

Because the design of Hercules cards predates the availability of custom large scale integrated circuits, its memory appears to the screen display in a way convenient for the hardware but less so for programmers. The order of the lines in memory doesn't correspond to the order of the lines on the screen.

A Hercules card divides its screen memory into four "leaves" of 8192 bytes each. The first line on the screen is the first line of the first leaf, the second line is the first line of the second leaf, and so on. The fifth line is the second line of the first leaf.

Figure 2-2 illustrates the effect of writing an image to a Hercules card one line at a time, beginning with the first. This procedure would have caused an EGA or VGA card to display the picture from the first line to the last in the order you'd expect.

Aside from this peculiarity and its differing screen dimensions—neither of which will turn out to be a problem—Hercules cards can be treated just like EGA or VGA cards, allowing that you want them all to be monochrome displays.

I should mention that many things pertinent to Hercules cards have been left out of this discussion. They're quite complex if you want to use all their facilities—something that the graphical user interface needn't do.

The EGA and VGA cards
High speed screen drivers

In a sense, the graphical user interface has two isolated screen drivers that both access the same screen. The first and most obvious of these is the Borland BGI library, which does all the drawing. The second is a set of custom routines in GUI.LIB that handles moving byte-aligned bitmap data to and from the screen. For the most part, this will be the text used by the interface itself.

You don't need to understand how the Borland BGI code works—just know how to call it.

The following is a skeletal application for the graphical user interface. It will start the interface, clear the screen to grey, display the mouse cursor, and then wait for a keypress, at which point it will return to DOS. Not all these function calls will make sense just yet.

```
#include "stdio.h"
#include "alloc.h"
#include "dos.h"
#include "dir.h"
#include "graphics.h"
#include "gui.h"

main( )
{
    POINT thePoint;
    int rt;

    if(initMouse( )) {
        if(initGraphics( )) {
            MouseOn( );
            ClearScreen( );
            getch( );
            MouseOff( );
```

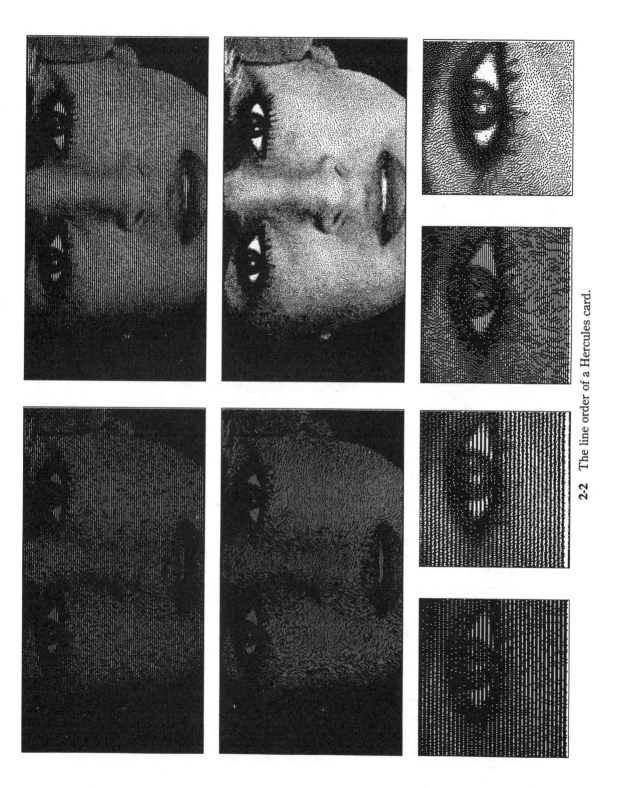

2-2 The line order of a Hercules card.

```
                deinitGraphics( );
           } else puts("Cannot establish graphics mode");
       } else puts("Cannot locate mouse driver");

   }
```

The two functions important to this discussion are initGraphics and deinit-Graphics. Later in this chapter, I'll discuss ClearScreen, MouseOn, and MouseOff.

The initGraphics function is the first bit of code to add to GUI.C, eventually to become GUI.LIB. It puts your screen into graphics mode using the BGI initgraph function, but it also sets up the second screen driver just discussed.

```
   initGraphics( )
   {
       int d,m;

       detectgraph(&d,&m);

       if(d<0) return(0);
       initgraph(&d,&m,"");
       if(graphresult( ) < 0) return(0);
       setcolor(getmaxcolor( ));
       graphicmode=d;
       if(graphicmode= =VGA) graphicmode=MCGA;
       DoTable(graphicmode);
       SetupMouse(2,2,SCREENWIDE-8,SCREENDEEP-8,graphicmode);

   }
```

If you've used the BGI graphics functions, you should easily understand the first part of this function. InitGraphics uses detectgraph to determine which sort of card it will be asked to run and then starts graphics mode using initgraph. It then calls DoTable (which I haven't yet explained).

The DoTable function is the initialization code for the second graphics handler. It establishes the dimensions of the screen (from a choice of three sets) and creates a "line start table."

A line start table is the mechanism by which the widely varying characteristics of the various display cards to be supported can be dealt with painlessly, while at the same time allowing for exceedingly fast screen updates.

You can easily figure out how to address a particular line of an EGA or VGA card. If n is the line number, MK__FP(0 × a000,n*80) will return a pointer to the line. Also, a formula exists for deriving a pointer to the lines of a Hercules card: MK__FP(0 × b000,(0 × 2000*(n%4)) + (90*(n/4))).

One way to update the lines of a card would be to just work out pointers to each of the lines in question and write to them as needed. However, this is fairly slow, even for EGA and VGA cards, because it entails the use of a machine language MUL instruction for each line.

You can update card lines more elegantly by creating a table of pointers and indexing it with the number of the line you're interested in. Because the largest vertical dimension involved is 480, you can know the maximum size of a table; and all the possible pointers for a particular card can be calculated and loaded into the table when the program starts.

In fact, because the part of the code using the table will be written in assembly language, the table will consist of a list of integer or word offsets into the appropriate screen buffer. The segment part of each resulting pointer will be constant, as none of the display cards requires more than 64K for one page of its screen buffer.

There will, in fact, be five global elements set up by DoTable:

SCREENWIDE The width of the screen in pixels.
SCREENDEEP The depth of the screen in pixels.
SCREENBYTES The width of the screen in bytes.
SCREENSEG The segment at which the screen buffer resides.
SCREENTBL An indexed table of offsets into the buffer.

These values are useful in the C language part of the user interface code. You should include these lines in GUI.H to make them accessible:

```
extern unsigned int SCREENTBL[ ];
extern unsigned int SCREENSEG,SCREENBYTES;
extern unsigned int SCREENWIDE,SCREENDEEP;
```

The GUIASM.ASM module includes a number of low-level functions and will include a few more as the library develops. Figure 2-3 is the assembly language source code for those functions of GUIASM.ASM pertaining to this chapter. Appendix D contains the complete GUIASM.ASM file, including a few functions that will be added in subsequent chapters.

You should recognize a number of things about this code if you've done any assembly language programming for use with C. If you haven't, you can still get by quite comfortably without knowing how this module works, as you probably won't ever have cause to modify it. If you want to work entirely in the elegance and comfort of C, assemble the code and skip the next section.

When you have the source code for GUIASM.ASM typed in, assemble it to produce the GUIASM.OBJ file.

The screen driver

Assembly language modules intended to be linked to C code essentially serve to duplicate what might have been generated by your compiler but do so with rather more tightly coded results. Assembly language functions behave very much like C functions would, except that they allow you to fine tune them to a greater degree and, in some cases, do things that simply aren't available to someone programming exclusively in C.

For the most part, the assembly language module for the graphical user interface exists to ensure that certain functions work quickly. You could replace what it does with C code, but the performance of the library would suffer.

One peculiarity of Turbo C's linking system is worth mentioning here because it affects how you name things in assembly language modules and other external objects. Under Turbo C, when you call for a library function or a function you've defined within a C program, the compiler will add an underbar to the beginning of the name. Hence, when you call printf, the compiler will actually add _printf to its list of unresolved externals.

If you write an assembly language module that has things to be called from within C, you must be careful to add the underbars. Hence, the external variable SCREENSEG, as seen from within a C program, must really be called _SCREEN-SEG in the assembly language module.

You should also note the difference between the way both C and the assembler handle external functions. Under C, if you define a function in the current module of your program, it's automatically declared as being public. A public function may be called from within any other module that will ultimately be linked to your program. In the same way, any function called but not defined in your program is assumed by the compiler to reside in another module.

Assemblers aren't quite as accommodating. If you want a function or a variable to be accessible by something outside the assembly language module in question, you must explicitly declare it as being public. It you want to call a function in your assembly language module external to the module, you must declare it as being external.

The GUIASM.ASM file presents several examples of the syntax for declaring public functions and variables.

The most fundamental part of the assembly language module is DoTable, which generates the line start table discussed earlier in this chapter. This function sets the values of the four screen dimension variables _SCREENWIDE, _SCREEN-DEEP, _SCREENBYTES, and _SCREENSEG, and fills in as much of _SCREENTBL as is required for the screen mode in question. It bases its decision on the graphic mode constant passed to it by InitGraphics, described earlier.

If you haven't done any assembly language programming for use with C before, the way assembly language functions deal with passed and returned arguments might seem a bit strange to you. As was discussed briefly in Chapter 1, arguments are passed between C language functions by pushing them onto the stack. Inasmuch as assembly language functions are constrained to behave like C functions when linked to C programs, they must deal with arguments in the same way. They differ only in that, in an assembly language function, you must write code to handle the actual mechanism of the arguments.

When DoTable is called, the stack pointer register, SP, will point to the next available word on the stack. There will be two words above it in relation to where it was after the argument to the function was pushed, these being the segment and offset values of the return address for the subroutine call. For reasons that will become apparent, the first thing any assembly language function must do is to push the BP register onto the stack, which means that there will be three words, or six bytes, up there.

Just prior to calling DoTable, the C program will have pushed the graphic mode constant onto the stack. As such, if the assembly language code were to look at location SP+6, it would find the value passed to it as an argument.

You can't actually do this, however. The stack pointer cannot be indexed, and hence an instruction such as MOV AX,[SP+6] is illegal.

The base pointer (or BP) register was designed to enable you to accomplish this task. It has the peculiar characteristic of always wanting to refer implicitly to things in the stack segment, just as the SI register always wants to refer to things in the data segment. If the function starts by doing

```
MOV BP,SP
```

it will be able to access the arguments on the stack as numbers added to the BP register. To make this process a bit less obtuse, the GUIASM.ASM assembly language module defines a constant called __AOFF representing the number of bytes on the stack before the first argument (which will be six in the case of the graphical user interface). If you were writing code in the small memory model, however, it would be four because no segment value would be pushed onto the stack.

The first argument would be accessed like this:

```
MOV AX,[BP + __AOFF + 0]
```

The second argument would be

```
MOV AX,[BP + __AOFF + 2]
```

and so on.

If an argument is in fact two words, as would be the case if you passed a far pointer to an assembly language function, the first word would be the offset and the second the segment. If the argument was a pointer to a string, you could get the location of the string into DS:SI like this:

```
MOV SI,[BP + __AOFF + 0]
MOV DS,[BP + __AOFF + 2]
```

There are a number of registers that you must take care to preserve through an assembly language function, such that the C language function calling it can still operate when it gets control of things again. The most important of these is BP because the calling function will use it to access its stack arguments as well.

You should also preserve the DS register. Under the large model of Turbo C, the actual program data segment is limited to 64K shared by all the functions in a program. As such, the data segment of an assembly language module will be the same as that of the C function calling it. While you can preserve the DS register by pushing it onto the stack, it's equally acceptable to simply return it to the common data segment value when your assembly language function is finished. Contained in GUIASM.ASM is a macro that does this. Simply put the line

```
DATASEG
```

at the end of your function.

This macro actually loads the DS register with the constant __DATA, which is defined as being the segment value of the common data segment. When you run an EXE file containing functions from GUIASM.ASM, the program will begin by replacing all the instances of __DATA with whatever the actual data segment turns out to be.

If you have register variables enabled under Turbo C, you must also preserve the SI and DI registers by pushing them onto the stack before you do anything else in your function and by popping them off when you're done. In fact, register variables don't improve the performance of code such as is found in the graphical user interface. It's preferable to disable them, which you must do to use the code in GUIASM.ASM.

When an assembly language function wants to return something to its calling C language function, it should load the value into the AX register. The AX register is 16 bits wide and can be thought of as being an int or unsigned int. If a function wants to return something larger than an int—such as a long integer or a pointer—it should put the low order part in AX and the high order part in DX. In the case of a pointer, the segment would go in DX and the offset in AX.

Using the line start table

Once DoTable has loaded all the values required by the rest of the code into their respective buffers, addressing the screen buffer is pretty simple. It's also extremely fast.

If BX holds the number of the line to address, you would get a pointer to the line in ES:DI like this:

```
DATASEG
MOV ES,[__SCREENSEG]
SHL BX,1
MOV DI,[__SCREENTBL + BX]
```

This little bit of code works by multiplying BX by two—shifting it left by one—so it represents an offset in words rather than bytes. The __SCREENTBL array is, after all, an array of words. The BX register serves as an index into the table. The value at the appropriate offset from the base of __SCREENTBL is the offset into the screen buffer for the line in question.

Note that it no longer matters whether the actual values in __SCREENTBL progress in orderly increments of 80 bytes, as would be the case for an EGA or VGA card or with the peculiar interleave of a Hercules card. The screen interface is effectively device independent after DoTable has been called.

The ClearScreen function is a simple example of how to use the line start table and can be found back in Fig. 2-3.

```
          COMMENT +

          The assembly language module for the
          graphical user interface version 1.0

               +

__AOFF         EQU     6          ;STACK OFFSET TO FIRST ARG

CGA            EQU     1          ;THESE EQUATES ARE EQUIVALENT TO
```

2-3 The assembly language source code for GUIASM.ASM.

```
MCGA              EQU     2          ;THE VALUES RETURNED BY THE
EGA               EQU     3          ;TURBO C DetectGraph FUNCTION
HERCMONO          EQU     7


_AOFF             EQU     6          ;FAR STACK OFFSET

;THIS MACRO FETCHES THE DATA SEGEMENT
DATASEG           MACRO
                  PUSH    AX
                  MOV     AX,_DATA
                  MOV     DS,AX
                  POP     AX
                  ENDM


MOUSEON           MACRO
                  MOV     AX,0001H
                  INT     33H
                  ENDM


MOUSEOFF          MACRO
                  MOV     AX,0002H
                  INT     33H
                  ENDM


GUIASM_TEXT       SEGMENT BYTE PUBLIC 'CODE'
                  ASSUME  CS:GUIASM_TEXT,DS:_DATA

;                 ARG1 = DEPTH
;                 ARG2 = TOPLINE
                  PUBLIC  _WhiteRule
_WhiteRule        PROC    FAR
                  PUSH    BP
                  MOV     BP,SP

                  DATASEG
                  MOUSEOFF
                  MOV     AX,DS:[_SCREENSEG]
                  MOV     ES,AX

                  MOV     CX,[BP + _AOFF + 0]
                  MOV     BX,[BP + _AOFF + 2]
                  SHL     BX,1
                  MOV     DX,DS:[_SCREENBYTES]
WR1:              PUSH    CX
                  MOV     DI,DS:[_SCREENTBL+BX]
                  ADD     BX,2
                  MOV     CX,DX
                  CLD
                  MOV     AL,0FFH
                  REPNE   STOSB
                          POP     CX
                          LOOP    WR1
                          MOUSEON
                          POP     BP
                          RET
```

```
_WhiteRule        ENDP

;                 ARG1 = DEPTH
;                 ARG2 = TOPLINE
                  PUBLIC    _BlackRule
_BlackRule        PROC      FAR
                  PUSH      BP
                  MOV       BP,SP

                  DATASEG
                  MOUSEOFF
                  MOV       AX,DS:[_SCREENSEG]
                  MOV       ES,AX

                  MOV       CX,[BP + _AOFF + 0]
                  MOV       BX,[BP + _AOFF + 2]
                  SHL       BX,1
                  MOV       DX,DS:[_SCREENBYTES]
BR1:              PUSH      CX
                  MOV       DI,DS:[_SCREENTBL+BX]
                  ADD       BX,2
                  MOV       CX,DX
                  CLD
                  MOV       AL,00H
         REPNE    STOSB
                  POP       CX
                  LOOP      BR1
                  MOUSEON
                  POP       BP
                  RET
_BlackRule        ENDP

                  PUBLIC    _ClearScreen
_ClearScreen      PROC      FAR

                  MOV       AX,_DATA
                  MOV       DS,AX

                  MOV       AX,_SCREENSEG
                  MOV       ES,AX

                  FOURPLANES
                  MOUSEOFF

                  MOV       CX,_SCREENDEEP
                  SUB       CX,MENULINEDEPTH
                  MOV       BX,(MENULINEDEPTH*2)

CLS1:             PUSH      CX
                  TEST      CX,1
                  MOV       AL,0AAH
                  JZ        CLS2
                  MOV       AL,055H
```

```
CLS2:           MOV     DI,[_SCREENTBL+BX]
                MOV     CX,_SCREENBYTES
                CLD
        REPNE   STOSB
                POP     CX
                ADD     BX,2
                LOOP    CLS1

                MOUSEON

                RET
_ClearScreen    ENDP

;               ARG1 = GRAPHIC CONSTANT
                PUBLIC  _DoTable
_DoTable        PROC    FAR
                PUSH    BP
                MOV     BP,SP

                DATASEG

                CMP     WORD PTR [BP + _AOFF + 0],CGA
                JNE     NOT_CGA         ;CHECK CARD TYPE

                ;IT'S A CGA CARD - BETTER HAVE THIS JUST IN CASE
                MOV     _SCREENSEG,0B800H
                MOV     _SCREENBYTES,80
                MOV     _SCREENWIDE,640
                MOV     _SCREENDEEP,200

                MOV     CX,_SCREENDEEP
                SUB     DX,DX
                MOV     SI,OFFSET _SCREENTBL

CTB0:           PUSH    CX
                PUSH    DX
                MOV     AX,_SCREENBYTES ;AX = WIDTH OF TUBE
                MOV     BX,DX           ;BX =
                MOV     CL,1            ;
                SHR     BX,CL           ; ... LINE NUMBER DIV 4
                PUSH    DX
                MUL     BX              ;MUL WIDTH OF SCREEN
                MOV     DI,AX           ;DI IS NOW THE PARTIAL OFFSET
                POP     DX

                SUB     DH,DH           ;
                MOV     AX,2000H        ;MULTIPLY DX MOD 4 BY 2000H
                AND     DX,1
                MUL     DX
                ADD     DI,AX           ;ADD TO THE OFFSET
                POP     DX
                POP     CX

                MOV     BX,DX           ;AND PUT IT IN THE TABLE
                SHL     BX,1
```

```
                MOV     [SI+BX],DI
                INC     DX
                LOOP    CTB0
                SUB     AX,AX              ;EVERYTHING'S FINE
                JMP     TABLE_OK

NOT_CGA:        CMP     WORD PTR [BP + _AOFF + 0],EGA
                JNE     NOT_EGA

                ;IT'S AN EGA CARD
                MOV     _SCREENSEG,0A000H
                MOV     _SCREENBYTES,80
                MOV     _SCREENWIDE,640
                MOV     _SCREENDEEP,350

                MOV     CX,_SCREENDEEP
                SUB     DX,DX
                MOV     SI,OFFSET _SCREENTBL

ETB0:           PUSH    DX
                MOV     AX,_SCREENBYTES
                MUL     DX
                MOV     [SI],AX
                ADD     SI,2
                POP     DX
                INC     DX
                LOOP    ETB0
                SUB     AX,AX              ;EVERYTHING'S FINE
                JMP     TABLE_OK

NOT_EGA:        CMP     WORD PTR [BP + _AOFF + 0],MCGA
                JNE     NOT_MCGA

                ;IT'S AN MCGA CARD
                MOV     _SCREENSEG,0A000H
                MOV     _SCREENBYTES,80
                MOV     _SCREENWIDE,640
                MOV     _SCREENDEEP,480

                MOV     CX,_SCREENDEEP
                SUB     DX,DX
                MOV     SI,OFFSET _SCREENTBL

MTB0:           PUSH    DX
                MOV     AX,_SCREENBYTES
                MUL     DX
                MOV     [SI],AX
                ADD     SI,2
                POP     DX
                INC     DX
                LOOP    MTB0
                SUB     AX,AX              ;EVERYTHING'S FINE
                JMP     TABLE_OK
```

```
NOT_MCGA:        CMP      WORD PTR [BP + _AOFF + 0],HERCMONO
                 JNE      NOT_HERCMONO

                 ;IT'S A HERCULES CARD
                 MOV      _SCREENSEG,0B000H
                 MOV      _SCREENBYTES,90
                 MOV      _SCREENWIDE,720
                 MOV      _SCREENDEEP,348
                 MOV      CX,_SCREENDEEP
                 SUB      DX,DX
                 MOV      SI,OFFSET _SCREENTBL

HTB0:            PUSH     CX
                 PUSH     DX
                 MOV      AX,_SCREENBYTES ;AX = WIDTH OF TUBE
                 MOV      BX,DX           ;BX =
                 MOV      CL,2            ;
                 SHR      BX,CL           ; ... LINE NUMBER DIV 4
                 PUSH     DX
                 MUL      BX              ;MUL WIDTH OF SCREEN
                 MOV      DI,AX           ;DI IS NOW THE PARTIAL OFFSET
                 POP      DX

                 SUB      DH,DH           ;
                 MOV      AX,2000H        ;MULTIPLY DX MOD 4 BY 2000H
                 AND      DX,3
                 MUL      DX
                 ADD      DI,AX           ;ADD TO THE OFFSET
                 POP      DX
                 POP      CX

                 MOV      SI,OFFSET _SCREENTBL
                 MOV      BX,DX
                 SHL      BX,1
                 MOV      [SI+BX],DI
                 INC      DX
                 LOOP     HTB0
                 SUB      AX,AX           ;EVERYTHING'S FINE
                 JMP      TABLE_OK

NOT_HERCMONO:    MOV      AX,-1

TABLE_OK:        POP      BP
                 RET
_DoTable         ENDP

GUIASM_TEXT      ENDS

DGROUP           GROUP    _DATA,_BSS
_DATA            SEGMENT WORD PUBLIC 'DATA'

                 PUBLIC   _SCREENTBL
                 PUBLIC   _SCREENSEG,_SCREENBYTES
                 PUBLIC   _SCREENWIDE,_SCREENDEEP
```

```
_SCREENTBL       DW      480 DUP(0)      ;MAXIMUM LINE COUNT
_SCREENSEG       DW      ?               ;POINTER TO SCREEN
_SCREENBYTES     DW      ?               ;WIDTH OF SCREEN IN BYTES
_SCREENWIDE      DW      ?               ;WIDTH OF SCREEN IN PIXELS
_SCREENDEEP      DW      ?               ;DEPTH OF SCREEN IN PIXELS

_DATA            ENDS

_BSS             SEGMENT WORD PUBLIC 'BSS'

_BSS             ENDS
                 END
```

The ClearScreen function clears the screen from the bottom of the menu bar to the bottom of the screen, filling it with an even grey field. It does so by stepping through the lines of the screen as pointed to by the line start table and filling alternate rows with 55H and AAH. These are very useful values, consisting of bytes with every alternating bit set, one being the complement of the other. Filling an area with them produces the effect of 50 percent grey.

Two other functions do similar things: WhiteRule and BlackRule. They are used to complete the initial setup of the screen by drawing the space in which the menu bar will reside once the menu system has been initialized. While they're part of the GUIASM.ASM file, their application won't come up until Chapter 4 and the discussion of menus.

These functions work identically to ClearScreen except that the area they cover can be defined by the arguments passed to them and they fill the lines in question with white and black, rather than with grey.

You'll also note the use of two macros in these functions: MOUSEON and MOUSEOFF. I will discuss them shortly.

BGI driver considerations

There's very little to concern yourself with when you use the BGI graphics functions to set the screen mode—a few rather more subtle ones will crop up in the next chapter. However, you can make your program a lot more seamless by taking a bit of care over what happens to the BGI drivers.

In order to make the the BGI graphics library device-independent, Borland set it up with loadable drivers. The drivers handle all the code specific to a particular display card. In theory, a program working with one sort of display card through a BGI driver will work with any display card if there's a driver for it.

The portability afforded by the BGI drivers is not really an issue in the graphical user interface. Quite a lot of the code violates all sorts of device independence precepts in the interest of greater speed or memory efficiency, and the limitations of the Microsoft mouse driver effectively restricts the choice of display adapters in any case. Hence, providing users of your programs with the opportunity to use specialized BGI drivers won't really benefit them.

There are only two BGI driver files applicable to the user interface code, these being EGAVGA.BGI and HERC.BGI. If you leave the InitGraphics function discussed at the beginning of this chapter as it is, the Turbo C graphics library will attempt to load the appropriate BGI driver from the disk.

Using loadable drivers in this case isn't really very desirable. They take a finite time to load and your users must keep track of them—they represent one more file to get lost. Instead, you should link both drivers into your programs.

Turbo C provides a very simple way to do this, although one not terribly well documented. First off, you must create linkable versions of EGAVGA.BGI and HERC.BGI, which can be done using a program provided with Turbo C called BGIOBJ.EXE.

With BGIOBJ.EXE, EGAVGA.BGI, and HERC.BGI all in your Turbo C subdirectory, type

```
BGIOBJ EGAVGA
BGIOBJ HERC
```

This will create two object files that should be included in GUI.LIB. The batch file for invoking TLIB, discussed in the previous chapter, includes references to these two files.

In order to tell the Turbo C initgraph function that these drivers are linked into your program and needn't be loaded from the disk, you must include these two lines somewhere in your code before calling initgraph:

```
registerbgidriver(EGAVGA__driver);
registerbgidriver(Herc__driver);
```

The arguments to these functions are constants defined in graphics.h.

The InitGraphics function in GUI.LIB does not include the calls to registerbgidriver. You should add them to the main function of your program before it calls InitGraphics. You can omit them if you prefer to have the graphics drivers loaded from the disk, which might come up in situations where memory was really tight.

A compatibility issue

If you look at the complete source code for GUI.C and GUIASM.ASM in Appendices C and D respectively, you'll note that there are calls to the function fourplanes in the first and instances of a macro called FOURPLANES in the second. The following is the C language function fourplanes:

```
fourplanes( )
{
    if(ismonomode( )) return(0);

    outportb(0 × 3c4,0 × 02);
    outportb(0 × 3c5,0 × 0f);
}
```

The macro for GUIASM.ASM doing the same thing as the C language function is as follows:

```
FOURPLANES    MACRO
              LOCAL    FPEXIT
              CMP      DS:[_SCREENSEG],0A000H
              JNE      FPEXIT
              MOV      AL,2
              MOV      DX,03C4H
              OUT      DX,AL
              INC      DX
              MOV      AL,0FH
              OUT      DX,AL
FPEXIT:
              ENDM
```

These bits of code haven't been included in the example library functions discussed in this chapter because they shouldn't be needed at all. They're a compatibility patch, one that you might or might not want to include in your version of the graphical user interface. In both cases, they select all four planes of an EGA or VGA display such that data written to the graphic screen buffer will indeed be written to all the planes.

In theory, this should not be necessary (at least on properly designed display adapters). However, some low-end cards might behave erratically when confronted with the code in this chapter. The foregoing two patches deal with these low-end cards.

Patches like this one will make your software more widely useful, but you must keep track of what they are and why you've included them. It's easy to forget about them until they produce some side effects later on. For example, if you decide to add color to the graphical user interface, these bits of code will selectively defeat it.

The complete source listings in the aforementioned appendices include both these functions and their appropriate calls.

Using the mouse

There are actually several incompatible standards for mouse interfacing, but the Microsoft and Microsoft-compatible mice represent the most common implementation of a mouse driver and are thus used here as the basis of the graphical user interface. Microsoft mice are exceedingly easy to handle; and many other rodents, such as Logitech mice, support this standard.

A mouse consists of the mechanical thing you hold in your hand and a *mouse driver*, a bit of resident code that handles the data from the mouse and provides it to software designed to accept mouse input in a standardized and useful form. In this way, the graphical user interface needn't know whether you have a real Microsoft mouse or a compatible, whether it's a serial mouse or a bus mouse, and so on; it simply reads the driver.

The driver is typically called either MOUSE.COM or MOUSE.SYS, the latter version to be loaded as a device driver through your CONFIG.SYS file rather than being run directly as a resident program. Again, the details of loading your mouse driver can remain an issue between you and your mouse.

A Microsoft compatible mouse driver presents your programs with information about the mouse in a useful and easily dealt-with form. It also maintains a graphic cursor if it finds that the screen is in one of the graphics modes it recognizes (which, for a standard Microsoft mouse driver, are CGA, EGA, VGA, and Hercules). The Hercules mode requires a bit more meddling with your computer's mind than do the first three (which I will discuss presently).

Having the driver manage the cursor enormously reduces the task of making the user interface work.

When you first load the driver for your mouse, the driver captures a software interrupt for itself—INT 33H. Having done so, you can communicate with the driver by issuing INT 33H calls with the appropriate values in the AX, BX, CX, and DX registers.

The mouse driver has quite an array of mouse-related functions, some of which won't really be of interest in this discussion. The basic ones include returning the mouse position and the state of its buttons, moving the mouse cursor under program control, changing the appearance of the cursor, and hiding and unhiding the cursor.

The two mouse-related macros discussed earlier this chapter in the discussion of the screen functions are, in fact, examples of the latter two functions. For reasons to be discussed in a moment, the mouse cursor must always be hidden if you write something to the screen or capture an image fragment.

You can deal with the mouse from within a C language program by using the int86 function to generate INT 33H calls. You must include the dos.h header file in any programs that will do this.

In any program expecting to deal with a mouse, you first must initialize the driver. The following function illustrates the form of most mouse calls:

```
int InitMouse(void)
{
    union REGS r;

    r.x.ax = 0;
    int86(0 x 33,&r,&r);
    return(r.x.ax);
}
```

The union REGS contains elements representing the processor registers AX, BX, CX, and so on. If the AX register is loaded with zero, the driver will be initialized. This call will return with a non-zero value in the AX register if everything works as expected.

The two most used functions in dealing with a mouse in the graphical user interface are MouseOn and MouseOff, which respectively display and hide the cursor:

```
void MouseOff(void)
{
    union REGS r;

    r.x.ax = 2;
    int86(0 × 33,&r,&r);
}

void MouseOn(void)
    union REGS r;

    r.x.ax = 1;
    int86(0 × 33,&r,&r);
}
```

Whenever you draw something to the screen, you must turn off the mouse cursor first and turn it back on immediately afterwards. The actual process of animating the cursor involves having the driver alternately print and erase a square area containing the cursor. If you happen to draw over it, a block will vanish from the area you've drawn in the next time the mouse moves.

This is also true if your program goes to capture an area of the screen with the getimage function from the BGI graphics library. You must turn off the mouse cursor while you're copying data from the screen, lest your copied image contain the image of the cursor as well.

The MouseDown function does returns both the current location of the mouse and the status of its buttons. The argument to the MouseDown function is a pointer to a POINT variable.

When you call function three of the mouse driver—that is, when you issue an INT 33H with the AX register set to three—the driver will return the horizontal position of the mouse in the CX register, the vertical position in the DX register, and an integer in the BX register in which each bit corresponds to the status of one mouse button. On a two-button mouse, only the first two bits will mean anything. As the graphical user interface only uses the left button as written, the value in the BX register AND 0001H will be true if the left button of the mouse is down. The value of BX is what gets returned by MouseDown.

```
int MouseDown(p)
    POINT *p;
{
    union REGS r;

    r.x.ax = 3;
    int86(0 × 33,&r,&r);

    p->x = r.x.cx;
```

```
            p->y = r.x.dx;

        return(r.x.bx & 0×01);
    }
```

In fact, the graphical user interface works with a slightly more elaborate version of MouseDown to facilitate a bit of keyboard input:

```
int MouseDown(p)
    POINT *p;
{
    union REGS r;

    if(fakeMouseDown.x != -1 && fakeMouseDown.y != -1) {
        memcpy((char *)p,
            (char *)&fakeMouseDown,sizeof(POINT));
        fakeMouseDown.x = -1;
        fakeMouseDown.y = -1;
        return(1);
    }

    r.x.ax = 3;
    int86(0×33,&r,&r);

    p->x = r.x.cx;
    p->y = r.x.dx;
    return(r.x.bx & 0x01);
}
```

The additional code in this version of MouseDown assumes the existence of a global POINT variable called fakeMouseDown. In most cases, this is set to the point (-1,-1), which is illegal and will be ignored by MouseDown. However, if some other part of the user interface wants to simulate a mouse click in a particular part of the screen, it can do so by filling in real values for fakeMouseDown. If Mouse-Down is called and sees legal values in fakeMouseDown, it will copy these into the POINT passed to it and return a true value, indicating that a mouse click has happened even though one probably hasn't.

This facility is used by the as-yet-undiscussed code dealing with BUTTON objects. The graphical user interface equates hitting the Enter key with clicking the mouse in an Ok button if one is visible. Rather than force every function with an Ok button to deal with the keyboard, the function that tracks buttons watches the keyboard surreptitiously. If it detects an Enter key in the keyboard buffer buttons are visible, it issues a synthetic mouse click in the Ok button to fool the function managing the buttons into thinking that the Ok button has been clicked. (See Chapter 5 for more details.)

The MoveMouse function will allow your program to change the position of the mouse cursor without anyone actually moving the mouse itself. This is rarely used, as having the mouse cursor suddenly go somewhere under its own steam is likely to confuse the users of your programs.

```
void MoveMouse(p)
    POINT *p;
{
    union REGS r;

    r.x.ax = 4;
    r.x.cx = p->x;
    r.x.dx = p->y;
    int86(0x33,&r,&r);
}
```

The MouseButton function returns the status of the mouse buttons without returning the location of the mouse—i.e., you needn't provide a POINT for it to store things in:

```
int MouseButton(void)
{
    union REGS r;

    r.x.ax = 3;
    int86(0x33,&r,&r);

    return(r.x.bx & 0x03);
}
```

Likewise, the MouseLoc function provides the location of the mouse without dealing with the button status:

```
void MouseLoc(p)
    POINT *p;
{
    union REGS r;

    r.x.ax = 3;
    int86(0x33,&r,&r);

    p->x = r.x.cx;
    p->y = r.x.dx;
}
```

The mouse driver provides a function for changing the appearance of the mouse cursor. The shape of the cursor as it first appears—the arrow—is stored in the driver. You can modify it by passing the driver a new cursor using function nine.

A cursor is defined by three elements—the mask, the image, and the *hotspot*. The mask is a bitmapped image defining the area to be masked out of the background image before the cursor can be drawn (typically one pixel larger than the cursor itself). Using a mask will place a white line around the cursor, so that a black cursor won't be lost against a black background. On a white background, of course, the outline becomes invisible; but the cursor itself will contrast with the screen.

The cursor image is the actual bitmapped picture defining what the cursor will look like. The hotspot is the displacement from the upper left corner of the square enclosing the cursor and defining where the cursor is considered to be.

Figure 2-4 illustrates the mask, the image, and the hotspot of the standard arrow cursor.

2-4 The mask and image of a cursor.

The mask   The image   The cursor

A cursor is always 16×16 pixels. If the hotspot is (0,0), calling MouseLoc or MouseDown will return the coordinates of the upper left corner of the cursor rectangle. If the hotspot is (8,8), MouseDown will return the coordinates of the middle of the cursor rectangle. If the hotspot is (−1,−1), MouseDown will return the coordinates of a point one pixel to the left and one pixel above the upper left corner of the cursor.

Figure 2-5 illustrates the relationship between the cursor and the hotspot.

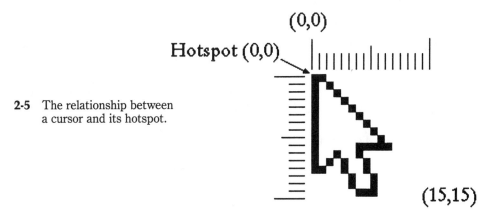

2-5 The relationship between a cursor and its hotspot.

The graphical user interface displays two kinds of cursors; you can easily add others if your application demands it. The first cursor is the standard arrow cursor, with a hotspot directly beneath the arrow's point. The other cursor is the hourglass, displayed if the computer is waiting for a task to be completed. The hotspot exists in middle of the cursor; but, because this cursor will only be visible if the machine is busy and can't deal with input, the location of the hotspot really doesn't matter.

The actual design of the arrow cursor comes directly from the Microsoft mouse driver. The hourglass cursor comes from the Microsoft *Mouse Programmer's Reference Guide*. It's a bit stylized—you might want to design a more traditional hourglass.

This function sets the arrow cursor:

```
void arrowCursor(void)
{
    union REGS r;
    struct SREGS sr;
    static char cursor[ ] = {
        0×FF,0×3F,0×FF,0×1F,0×FF,0×0F,0×FF,0×07,
        0×FF,0×03,0×FF,0×01,0×FF,0×00,0×7F,0×00,
        0×3F,0×00,0×1F,0×00,0×FF,0×01,0×FF,0×10,
        0×FF,0×30,0×7F,0×F8,0×7F,0×F8,0×7F,0×FC,
        0×00,0×00,0×00,0×40,0×00,0×60,0×00,0×70,
        0×00,0×78,0×00,0×7C,0×00,0×7E,0×00,0×7F,
        0×80,0×7F,0×00,0×7C,0×00,0×6C,0×00,0×46,
        0×00,0×06,0×00,0×03,0×00,0×03,0×00,0×00  };

    r.x.ax = 0x0009;
    r.x.bx = 0;
    r.x.cx = 0;
    r.x.dx = FP_OFF(cursor);
    sr.es = FP_SEG(cursor);
    int86×(0×33,&r,&r,&sr);
}
```

Note that, in function nine, the mouse driver departs from its usual structure for arguments and wants a pointer to the bitmapped data in ES:DX. The int86x function allows for passing segment registers.

The bitmapped data at cursor defines both the mask and the cursor. The first 32 bytes define the mask. The hotspot coordinates are passed in the BX and CX registers.

This function displays the hourglass cursor:

```
void waitCursor(void)
{
    union REGS r;
    struct SREGS sr;

    static char cursor[ ] = {
        0×00,0×00,0×00,0×00,0×00,0×00,0×01,0×80,
        0×03,0×C0,0×07,0×E0,0×0F,0×F0,0×07,0×E0,
        0×03,0×C0,0×01,0×80,0×00,0×00,0×00,0×00,
        0×00,0×00,0×00,0×00,0×FF,0×FF,0×FF,0×FF,
        0×00,0×00,0×FE,0×7F,0×06,0×60,0×0C,0×30,
        0×18,0×18,0×30,0×0C,0×60,0×06,0×C0,0×03,
        0×60,0×06,0×30,0×0C,0×98,0×19,0×CC,0×33,
        0×E6,0×67,0×FE,0×7F,0×00,0×00,0×00,0×00  };
```

```
        r.x.ax = 0 × 0009;
        r.x.bx = 7;
        r.x.cx = 7;
        r.x.dx = FP__OFF(cursor);
        sr.es = FP__SEG(cursor);
        int86 × (0 × 33,&r,&r,&sr);
}
```

These functions only are used by the interface library itself in one instance, this being the call made by the Choose File box to get the file names to choose from. However, your programs should display the hourglass cursor whenever it's likely that the system will be unresponsive for a meaningful amount of time. You should take into account that, in some cases, your users might be running on very old, slow machines or running exclusively with floppy disks.

Because the graphical user interface is handled as a library rather than as link-able object modules, you're free to write your own waitCursor and arrowCursor functions and ignore the ones in the library. In a program displaying multiple types of cursors to indicate which mode is active, you probably would want an arrowCursor function that selects among several possible cursors. In this case, the arrowCursor function in GUI.LIB would be ignored by the linker, its unresolved external having been resolved by your arrowCursor function prior to the linker getting to GUI.LIB. Thus, the Choose File box would also call your arrowCursor function rather than the one in GUI.LIB.

SetupMouse, the final mouse-related function to be discussed, is something of a catch-all, handling a number of things related to using the mouse in real-world applications.

The most arcane aspect of this function deals with Hercules cards. Remarkably, the Microsoft mouse driver standard does allow the mouse to work with Hercules cards even though they aren't supported by the PC's BIOS and historically have been pointedly ignored by IBM. However, because Hercules cards use the low memory of a PC in rather unconventional ways, you must adjust a few things for the mouse driver if it must dealing with Hercules.

Hercules cards have two pages of display memory in their graphics mode, which means that you can have two distinct pictures in the graphics buffer and instantly switch between them with little more than a bit of register tickling. Unfortunately, an external bit of software—such as a mouse driver—has no way to know which page is visible at the moment. The driver must be told which page to display its cursor on by the software that has put the screen into graphics mode in the first place.

The graphical user interface always uses page zero of a Hercules card.

The flag to tell the mouse driver which page of a Hercules card to use is located at 0040:0049H. Load six into this location for page zero and five for page one.

Unfortunately, this location is also used in text mode. If its contents are changed, your computer may misbehave when you exit from a program using the graphical user interface. As such, before you set up to use the mouse, you must copy the contents of this byte (stored in the global integer hercdivet) to a safe place and then restore it before exiting. Also for this reason, it's important that any program using the graphical user interface include a call to ctrlbrk to keep someone from exiting before you can restore this byte.

SetupMouse also defines the area in which the mouse may move, which defaults (rather undesirably) to the entire screen. Allowing the mouse to move over the entire screen actually means that it can move fifteen pixels beyond the right and bottom edges, something that will certainly confuse many of your software users. As the mouse gets batted around on one's desk between phone calls and quests for paper clips to bend out of shape, it will vengefully tend to place its cursor in the invisible world just beyond the range of real pixels. Thus, the user interface works much more comfortably if the mouse is constrained to remain visible.

A second problem confronted by setting the mouse limits is a bug in some versions of the Logitech mouse driver. Left to its default settings, it will limit the mouse to a vertical travel of no more than 200 pixels. By setting the mouse dimensions explicitly, your software will override these settings and circumvent the bug:

```
SetupMouse(mx,my,x,y,n)
     int mx,my,x,y,n;
{
     char *p;
     union REGS r;

     if(n = = HERCMONO) {
          p = MK_FP(0 × 0040,0 × 0049);
          hercdivet = *p;
          *p = 6;
          r.x.ax = 0;
          int86(0 × 33,&r,&r);
     }

     r.x.ax = 0 × 0007;
     r.x.cx = mx;
     r.x.dx = x;
     int86(0 × 33,&r,&r);

     r.x.ax = 0 × 0008;
     r.x.cx = my;          r.x.dx = y;
     int86(0 × 33,&r,&r);
}
```

The mx and my arguments are the upper left coordinates of the mouse's range. The x and y arguments are the lower right coordinates. The n argument is the graphic mode constant returned by the BGI detectgraph function.

Finally, after using a Hercules card, your software should clean up after itself by calling RestoreHercDivet before quitting to DOS.

```
RestoreHercDivet( )
{
    char *p;

    p = MK__FP(0 × 0040,0 × 0049);
    *p = hercdivet;
}
```

All other things being equal, it works better if you plug it in.
Murphy's Laws of Computers

3

Windows

THE MOST FUNDAMENTAL GRAPHICAL ELEMENT OF THE USER INTERFACE is a window. In its simplest sense, a window is a rectangular area drawn on the screen in which things can happen and that can subsequently vanish when no longer required.

A window may be thought of as being analogous to the current piece of paper you're writing on or reading, should you want to hang onto the desktop metaphor for a while longer.

In fact, a window is really a rectangular box on your screen and an object in memory allowing its contents to be dealt with conveniently. Part of the object in memory (as discussed in Chapter 1) is a bitmap of the area behind the window, such that when it's time for the window to go away—or "close"—it can be erased by replacing the area it formerly occupied with whatever used to be there.

Managing windows involves several primary considerations. Windows must appear and disappear quickly and also must occupy as little memory as possible. They must lend themselves to the convenient management of objects that will later be associated with them. Finally, they should be simple enough to occupy a minimum amount of screen real estate with cosmetics.

To "open" a window, (i.e., to create the various screen and memory elements that actually constitute a window), the window functions of the graphical user interface must do the following things:

1. Define the area that the window will occupy.
2. Allocate a buffer big enough to contain an image of it.

3. Copy the current contents of the area to the buffer.
4. Draw a white area the size of the window.
5. Draw a black box around it.

Having used the window for a while, you would close it by doing the following:

1. Copy the image from the buffer back to the screen.
2. Free the buffer.

Most of these steps will immediately suggest some C language code to you if you've been using the BGI graphics library for a while. There's nothing particularly tricky about handling windows—at least, not yet.

You can conveniently define a rectangular area on the screen with a RECT variable (see Chapter 1) rather than as four separate integers. If you wanted to open a window on your screen with its upper left corner at location (10,20) and its lower right corner at (100,200), you would load its coordinates into a RECT variable r like this:

```
SetRect(&r,10,20,100,200);
```

The SetRect function sets up a RECT variable to a predetermined state with one line of code. You also could type this:

```
r.left = 10;
r.top = 20;
r.right = 100;
r.bottom = 200;
```

In fact, this is really what SetRect does for you.

Here's the actual function, to be added to GUI.C if you're typing it in as you go:

```
SetRect(r,left,top,right,bottom)
    RECT *r;
    int left,top,right,bottom;
{
    r->left = left;
    r->top = top;
    r->right = right;
    r->bottom = bottom;
}
```

You should also add a prototype for this function to GUI.H (which is a good practice to get into if you plan to build up GUI.C as you work through this book):

```
SetRect(RECT *r,int left,int top,int right,int bottom);
```

Finally, add the struct definition for a RECT variable to GUI.H as well:

```
typedef struct {
    int left,top,right,bottom;
```

} RECT;

You'll also need a variable of the type WINDOW, which keeps track of whatever a window must know about itself. Here's the struct for that. As discussed in Chapter 1, a window almost always consists of the window itself plus an associated linked list of objects. The first element in a WINDOW variable is a pointer to the first object in the list, an OBJECTHEAD.

```
typedef struct {
    unsigned int type;
    void *next;
    } OBJECTHEAD;

typedef struct {
    OBJECTHEAD head;
    RECT frame;
    char *back;
    } WINDOW;
```

The internal structure of a WINDOW variable isn't particularly complex. The frame element contains the actual coordinates of the window and is useful for determining if a mouse click has occurred within a particular window's area. The back element will point to the bitmapped image fragment overwritten by the window when it opens. Note that a WINDOW object and its background image are dealt with as two separate objects.

In practice, a program using the graphical user interface need not know about the internal structure of a WINDOW variable—there's never any need for code outside GUI.LIB to actually manipulate its elements. As such, you can add things to the definition of a WINDOW object—and, for that matter, to any other object—without having to do more than recompile the programs using GUI.LIB.

You might want to do this, for example, if you expand the graphical user interface to include different styles of windows. All the windows currently have the same style—a box with a line around it and a drop shadow to the lower right.

Figure 3-1 shows the code to open a window.

```
OpenWindow(w,r)
        WINDOW *w;
        RECT *r;
{
        int size;

        w->frame.left   = r->left-1;
        w->frame.top    = r->top-1;
        w->frame.right  = r->right+DROPSHADOW+1;
        w->frame.bottom = r->bottom+DROPSHADOW+1;

        if((size=buffersize(&w->frame))== -1) return(0);

        w->head.next=NULL;
        w->head.type=inWindow;
```

3-1 The OpenWindow function.

```
    if((w->back=malloc(size)) != NULL) {
            MouseOff();
            getimage(w->frame.left,w->frame.top,
                    w->frame.right,w->frame.bottom,
                    w->back);
            setwritemode(COPY_PUT);
            setfillstyle(SOLID_FILL,getmaxcolor());
            setlinestyle(SOLID_LINE,0,NORM_WIDTH);
            setcolor(BLACK);
            bar(r->left-1,r->top-1,r->right+1,r->bottom+1);
            rectangle(r->left-1,r->top-1,r->right+1,r->bottom+1);
            setlinestyle(SOLID_LINE,0,THICK_WIDTH);
            line(r->right+2,r->top+DROPSHADOW,r->right+2,r->bottom+3);
            line(r->left+DROPSHADOW,r->bottom+2,r->right,r->bottom+2);
            MouseOn();
            return(1);
    } else return(0);
```

Let's look at OpenWindow in detail.

The actual value of frame differs somewhat from the coordinates of the window as defined by the RECT passed to it because the window has a drop shadow that must be taken into account. You must preserve not only the area behind the window but behind the drop shadow as well. The drop shadow size is defined in GUI.H:

#define DROPSHADOW 4

The OBJECTHEAD pointer to the next object to be added to the window is set initially to NULL, indicating that there aren't any associated objects yet. As will be discussed in the next chapter, menus are actually windows with no objects in them, so it's important to fill in this field even though it will be immediately overwritten in most other cases.

The OBJECTHEAD type element is set to the constant inWindow, which will tell any code trying to "walk" the linked list what sort of object this one is. While the subject doesn't come up in this book, there's no reason why you couldn't create a linked list having child windows associated with a parent window (in which case knowing the type of a WINDOW object would be important).

The size of the window background buffer varies with the display card type, an issue to surface later in this chapter. If the user interface is running on a 16-color display, this value will be about four times bigger than the actual dimensions of the window would lead you to suspect. The buffersize function is simply a call to the BGI imagesize function that uses a RECT for its argument:

```
buffersize(r)
    RECT *r;
{
    return(imagesize(r->left,r->top,r->right,r->bottom));
}
```

Note the calls to MouseOff and MouseOn (discussed in Chapter 2). The rest of the code just deals with drawing the window and its drop shadow. When drawing things under the graphical user interface, it's very important that all the relevant parameters be set up before you use any of the drawing functions. The user interface can't know if the line characteristics or drawing colors have been changed since the last time it drew something.

You also should note that, when the user interface wants to draw a black area, it can do so by using the predefined constant BLACK (which is zero). A white area would be color one on a Hercules card but color fifteen on an EGA or VGA card, so you should fetch the true white value with a call to getmaxcolor. This is largely to maintain compatibility with future BGI drivers—at the moment, using the defined constant WHITE seems to work well enough with all three cards.

The OpenWindow function returns a true value if it's successful in opening a window. It might fail for two reasons. For one, the function might not be able to allocate enough memory to store the background image. A more subtle reason for failure could appear when using EGA and VGA cards. As has been discussed, the BGI getimage and putimage functions can only deal with image fragments requiring less than 64K to store. On a two-color display, such as a Hercules card, this isn't a problem because the whole screen only occupies about 30K. The EGA and VGA cards, however, have four image planes. On an EGA card, an image fragment encompassing the entire screen would require a buffer of over 100K. The imagesize function returns a value of −1 if you try to work out the buffer size for an image area resulting in more than 64K of data. I'll tell you how to avoid this problem later in this chapter.

Here's a typical call to OpenWindow.

```
RECT r;
WINDOW w;

SetRect(&r,48,48,348,228);
if(openWindow(&w,&r)) {
    /* some code goes here */
    CloseWindow(&w);
}
```

Figure 3-2 illustrates the resulting window.

The CloseWindow function is a great deal less involved than OpenWindow was, and does pretty much what you'd expect:

```
CloseWindow(w)
    WINDOW *w;
{
    MouseOff( );
    if(w->back != NULL) {
        putimage(w->frame.left,w->frame.top,w->back,COPY_PUT);
        free(w->back);
    }
    MouseOn( );
}
```

3-2 The result of a call to OpenWindow.

All that's involved in closing a window is replacing the area overwritten by the window itself and then freeing the buffer containing the background image.

Faster windows

The window functions just discussed have three drawbacks. First, the windows that they work with occupy a great deal of memory on 16-color displays, three quarters of which is redundant. The graphical user interface is, after all, monochrome. Preserving 16 colors is hardly necessary, but the BGI interface offers no practical way to drive EGA and VGA cards as monochrome devices.

Second, because a window background can be no larger than 64K, the size of opened windows is effectively limited.

Third, the getimage and putimage functions are not too fast. Because there's no way of telling how the byte boundaries of the lines being put and gotten will fall, every line captured from the screen must be shifted left to fall on an even byte boundary when getimage acquires it and then shifted right again to fit into the designated area on the screen when putimage replaces it. On a 16-color display, this happens four times for each line, with the result that closing a reasonably large window on a slow computer seems to take forever.

All of these problems can be gotten around by cheating. The resulting variations on the OpenWindow and CloseWindow functions appear to operate just like the foregoing ones did, but they're blindingly fast and much more reasonable in their memory requirements. In working out how these function, you should keep in mind the discussion of line start tables from Chapter 2.

Actually fetching lines of image data from the screen and subsequently stuffing them back is not too time consuming. Getimage and putimage tie up your processor when they're shifting the bits of those lines around to form them into proper image fragment buffers. This part would be convenient to circumvent.

It wouldn't be difficult to write versions of getimage and putimage that worked without doing any bit shifting if all the windows to be opened could be constrained to have their left edges on even byte boundaries. Then all that would be required would be a function to copy the right number of bytes out of each line and put them in a buffer. The lines could be found by using the SCREENTBL array from the last chapter. Unfortunately, this isn't the case.

Even though your windows might not open on even byte boundaries, they are constrained not to move, which turns out to be just about as helpful. If one were to create a pseudo getimage function that copied an image from the nearest byte boundaries—rounded down for the left edge and up for the right edge—the result would be image fragments containing the window area and probably some of the surrounding countryside as well. However, because the background will always go back exactly where it was found, this won't matter. No bit shifting is required in this case, and such a function would be much faster than the image fragment functions coming with BGI toolkit. You can't really use these functions for most of the things getimage and putimage are used for, but they work admirably in this one situation.

Figure 3-3 illustrates the relationship between the image and the byte boundaries for a typical window.

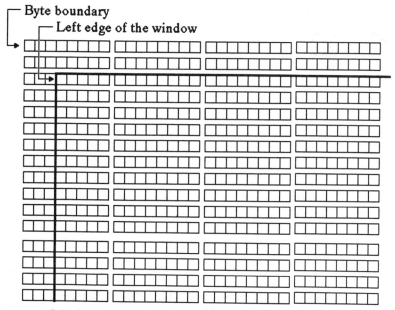

3-3 The window and byte boundaries for a fast window.

Understanding display planes

It might not be apparent how working with image fragments in the way just described serves to use less memory on a 16-color display. In fact, the display buffer of an EGA or VGA card is structured in a peculiar way—it contains four planes of memory. If you write to the first one, color number one will be displayed. If you write to the second, color number two will be displayed. If you write to the first and second, color number three will be displayed, and so on.

The four planes occupy the same area of memory, beginning at A000:0000H. There's a register, called the *barrel register*, that selects which of them will be written to when data is written to this address space. If you wanted to write to the first page, you'd put 01H in the barrel register, 02H for the second, 04H for the third, and 08H for the fourth.

If you wanted to write to the four planes at once, you'd put 0FH in the barrel register (i.e., set all four significant bits).

Using the default 16-color palette of an EGA or VGA card, any area with its bits set in all four planes will display as white, and any area without them set will display as black. As such, with the barrel register set to select all four planes, the display behaves as a monochrome card. While Turbo C doesn't allow you to regard it as such through the BGI interface, custom code can do so.

This getimage replacement for OpenWindow uses the fast, byte-aligned image fragment technique:

```
fastgetimage(left,top,right,bottom,p)
    int left,top,right,bottom;
    char *p;
{
    int i,width,depth,bleft,bytes;

    left &= 0xfff8;
    if(right & 0x0007) right = (right | 0x0007) + 1;
    width = right-left;      depth = bottom-top;
    bleft = left > >3;
    bytes = pixels2bytes(width);

    *p+ + = (width – 1);
    *p+ + = ((width – 1)> >8);
    *p+ + = (depth – 1);
    *p+ + = ((depth – 1)> >8);

    for(i = 0;i < depth; + +i) {
        memcpy(p,MK_FP(SCREENSEG,
            SCREENTBL[top + i] + bleft),bytes);
        p+ =bytes;
    }
}
```

There's nothing particularly clever in the fastgetimage function. The line width is calculated by working out the bit positions of the window's limits rounded down on the left and up on the right. The image fragment is stored as a standard monochrome BGI image fragment. The structure of this has not really been discussed as yet but is fairly simple. The first two bytes of the fragment represent an integer one less than the width of the picture in pixels, while the next two bytes represent an integer one less than the depth.

While the fragments created by fastgetimage won't actually be used with the standard BGI putimage, there's no good reason not to be consistent in how the fragments are created.

You'll also notice the use of another hitherto unmentioned function, pixels2 bytes. In fact, this is a macro defined in GUI.H that returns the number of bytes a line of pixels will need to contain it. This will be the number of pixels divided by eight—plus one if the number isn't evenly divisible by eight. The macro looks like this:

```
#define    pixels2bytes(n)    ((n + 7)/8)
```

This is the first situation in which the line start table SCREENTBL, from the GUIASM module, is used from within a C language function. Notice that it behaves just like a normal array of integers.

The working part of fastgetimage is the for loop at the bottom, which copies the appropriate parts of the screen lines into the buffer passed to the function.

The corresponding fastputimage is equally easy to fathom:

```
fastputimage(left,top,p)
    int left,top;
    char *p; {
    int i,width,depth,bleft,bytes;

    width = ImageWidth(p);
    depth = ImageDepth(p);
    bleft = left > >3;
    bytes = pixels2bytes(width);
    p+ =4;

    for(i = 0;i < depth; + +i) {
        memcpy(MK_FP(SCREENSEG,
            SCREENTBL[top + i] + bleft),p,bytes);
        p+ =bytes;
    }
}
```

The fastputimage function merely does what fastgetimage did but in reverse. Note that the horizontal dimension passed to it is rounded down to the nearest byte boundary.

You'll also probably spot two more unfamiliar functions—ImageWidth and ImageDepth. These, too, are actually macros that return the dimensions of a BGI image fragment based on the two integers at the beginning of the fragment discussed a moment ago. In fact, GUI.H contains three macros for this purpose:

```
#define    ImageWidth(p)    (1 + p[0] + (p[1] < < 8))
#define    ImageDepth(p)    (1 + p[2] + (p[3] < < 8))
#define    ImageBytes(p)    (pixels2bytes((1 + p[0] + (p[1] < < 8))))
```

The last of the three, ImageBytes, returns the number of bytes in a line of an image fragment.

Finally, the standard Borland imagesize function is not applicable to the fast image fragment functions. It will return a value way too big on a 16-color display and a bit small on a two color one—usually crashing your computer in the latter case. If you use fastgetimage, make sure you use fastbuffersize to determine the memory needs for the image it will get.

```
fastbuffersize(r)
    RECT *r;
{
    int left,right;

    left = r->left & 0xfff8;
    right = r->right;
    if(right & 0x0007) right = (right | 0x0007) + 1;
    return(4 + (pixels2bytes(right-left) * ((r->bottom-r->top) + 1)));
}
```

You should keep in mind that these fast image fragment functions aren't a replacement for the getimage and putimage functions except in the one special case of opening and closing windows.

Figure 3-4, then, is the OpenWindow function rewritten to use the fast functions. There is no real difference in the way it operates, only in what functions it calls to work.

```
OpenWindow(w,r)
        WINDOW *w;
        RECT *r;
{
        int size;

        w->frame.left   = r->left-1;
        w->frame.top    = r->top-1;
        w->frame.right  = r->right+DROPSHADOW+1;
        w->frame.bottom = r->bottom+DROPSHADOW+1;

        if((size=fastbuffersize(&w->frame)) == -1) return(0);

        w->head.next=NULL;
        w->head.type=inWindow;
        if((w->back=malloc(size)) != NULL) {
                MouseOff();
                fastgetimage(w->frame.left,w->frame.top,
                    w->frame.right,w->frame.bottom,w->back);
                setwritemode(COPY_PUT);
```

3-4   The OpenWindow function rewritten to use fast image fragment calls.

```
                setfillstyle(SOLID_FILL,getmaxcolor());
                setlinestyle(SOLID_LINE,0,NORM_WIDTH);
                setcolor(BLACK);
                bar(r->left-1,r->top-1,r->right+1,r->bottom+1);
                rectangle(r->left-1,r->top-1,r->right+1,r->bottom+1);
                setlinestyle(SOLID_LINE,0,THICK_WIDTH);
                line(r->right+2,r->top+DROPSHADOW,r->right+2,r->bottom+3);
                line(r->left+DROPSHADOW,r->bottom+2,r->right,r->bottom+2);
                MouseOn();
                return(1);
        } else return(0);
}
```

This is the corresponding CloseWindow function:

```
closeWindow(w)
    WINDOW *w;
{
    MouseOff( );
    if(w->back != NULL) {
        fastputimage(w->frame.left,w->frame.top,w->back);
        free(w->back);
    }
    MouseOn( );
}
```

If you plan to use the graphical user interface as presented in this book, you'll probably want to use the fast version of the window functions because there's no disadvantage in doing so. You may find that you want to switch back to the earlier functions, using the true BGI getimage and putimage functions, if you want to modify the library to support colors or if you want to add code to allow windows to be resized or moved.

The complete source code for the library has a define in GUI.H called FASTWINDOW. If you set FASTWINDOW to a non-zero value, the library will compile with the the fast functions in the OpenWindow and CloseWindow functions. All the other functions using image fragment handling will still use the Borland getimage and putimage calls.

Demonstration program

At this point, you're ready to write a program that does something with the graphical user interface library. Compile GUI.C and use the procedure discussed in Chapter 1 to invoke TLIB and make GUI.LIB.

The test program in Fig. 3-5 is a simple routine to test the OpenWindow and CloseWindow functions. It will open up to 64 nested windows—assuming there's enough memory available—and then close them one at a time, with the most recently opened one closing first. The location and size of each window will be random and should vary between executions of the program.

The program in Fig. 3-5 is an example of recursion—the principal function, goForIt, will repeatedly call itself (opening a new window each time) until something stops it. In this case, it will cease its recursion if it runs out of memory or if

```
#include "stdio.h"
#include "graphics.h"
#include "dos.h"
#include "stdlib.h"
#include "time.h"
#include "gui.h"

#define MAXWINDOW        64

main()
{
        /* this will need a big stack */
        _stklen=0x8000;

        randomize();
        if(initMouse()) {
                /* register the drivers */
                registerbgidriver(EGAVGA_driver);
                registerbgidriver(Herc_driver);
                if(initGraphics()) {
                        MouseOn();
                        ClearScreen();
                        InitWindowManager();
                        /* start recursing */
                        goForIt(0);
                        MouseOff();
                        deinitGraphics();
                } else puts("Cannot establish graphics mode");
        } else puts("Cannot locate mouse driver");
}

goForIt(n)
        int n;
{

        RECT r;
        WINDOW w;
        int left,top,width,depth;

        delay(50);
        left=random(getmaxx()-100)+10;
        top=random(getmaxy()-100)+10;
        width=random((getmaxx()-left)-50)+40;
        depth=random((getmaxy()-top)-50)+40;
        SetRect(&r,left,top,left+width,top+depth);

        if(n < MAXWINDOW && OpenWindow(&w,&r)) goForIt(n+1);
        delay(50);
        CloseWindow(&w);

}
```

3-5   A program to test the window functions.

the number passed to it by a former iteration of itself exceeds the value of the constant MAXWINDOW (defined here as 64).

   When goForIt finally decides that it has opened enough windows, there will be
64 sets of WINDOW objects scattered back along the stack, along with 64 return
addresses of various iterations of the function. The most recent iteration will call
CloseWindow and return. The one behind it will do the same, and so on until the

3-6 Running the window demonstration program.

first iteration returns to main. The effect on the screen will be to have the windows unstack themselves.

Figure 3-6 illustrates the progress of one execution of this program.

To compile this program, type the source code in Fig. 3-5 into a file called WINDEMO.C. Create a project file called WINDEMO.PRJ having the following lines:

```
WINDEMO.C
GUI.LIB
```

Set the project in Turbo C to WINDEMO.PRJ and compile the program.

As elegant as the recursive approach to generating random windows might be, recursion is almost never used in real world applications. Very few practical problems lend themselves to a recursive solution. Most programmers would deem this exceedingly sad, as recursion is one of the more interesting things to use, as well as something that a stack-oriented language like C can manage well.

Microsoft Windows: faster than a dead sea turtle crawling up the beach with a boxcar on its back, but only just.

graffiti

4

Menus

THE WONDERFUL THING ABOUT A GRAPHICAL USER INTERFACE—ONCE you get the initial code working—is that much of what the complicated-looking parts consist of can be swiped from the simple parts. You might observe that a menu is, in fact, merely a window that opens at the top of the screen. Half of the graphics are already written.

The mechanics of making menus appear and function on your screen is fairly trivial, as will be discussed shortly. A number of other issues make implementing menus more complex, really requiring a bit of forethought and analysis before you warm up your C compiler and start writing code.

The ways in which these issues have been dealt with in this book don't represent the last word on them, and you can change some or all of them if you think you have a good enough reason. The modular nature of the graphical user interface library will make this particularly painless to accomplish. For example, if you decide you don't like the cosmetics of the menus as they're handled in the code in this book, you can change them without having to actually change any of the programs that call the library. The calling programs want to call up menus, but they needn't know what the menus will look like.

This chapter will deal with the creation of a collection of menu-related functions that together will form the "menu manager" of the graphical user interface. The exact nature of the menu manager will become clearer as you work through this chapter. There will also be a discussion of several related issues, such as obtaining a screen font.

Menu and menu item objects

I'll begin with a few terms specific to a discussion of menus, most of which are probably already familiar to you.

First, Fig. 4-1 illustrates the geography of a menu.

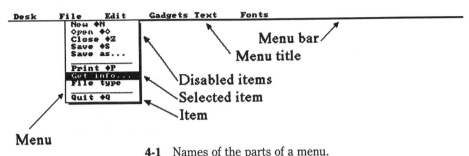

4-1   Names of the parts of a menu.

The white area at the top of the screen is called the *menu bar*. It contains the menu *titles*, which should divide the menu functions into logical groups. Clicking on a title will pull down a menu, (i.e., make it appear below the menu bar).

Each line in a menu is called an *item*. Menu items can be active—drawn in black type—or inactive, in which case they're drawn in grey type. Astute readers will note that grey type is actually black type with every other pixel missing.

Menu items may also be *checked*—i.e., have checkmarks drawn beside them. Checkmarked menu items are usually used to indicate that one of many menu items has been selected or that a menu item has been toggled by selecting it when no other obvious result of doing so will be apparent.

Figure 4-2 illustrates an example of a menu with a checkmark. This is the font menu from Desktop Paint, and the checkmark indicates which font is currently selected.

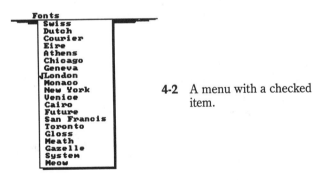

4-2   A menu with a checked item.

A menu will stay visible for as long as you keep your finger on the mouse button. During this time, if you drag the mouse cursor through the menu items, a black selector bar will follow it. Releasing the mouse button will select the item under the selector bar, causing whatever it represents to happen. The exact mechanism of its happening will be dealt with in a moment.

If the mouse cursor is dragged outside the menu area and released, nothing will happen—no item will be selected.

As soon as the mouse button is released, the menu vanishes—in reality, its window closes. If an item has been selected, its function is executed and control is returned to the program where it was when the menu was initially clicked on.

The issues behind the implementation of menus fall into two groups—how best to make the menus work in a user-friendly, efficient manner, and how to make them easy to work with when you're writing programs that will call the graphical user interface library. The first question is probably a lot more subjective than the second.

Menus form the basis of the control structure of most programs that will use the graphical user interface. They are, in effect, a combination of a set of selectable options or subfunctions and a very short help file. People who have become used to working with a graphical user interface naturally gravitate to the menu bar when they aren't sure what to do next.

Because just about everything ancillary to the principal function of a program using the graphical user interface happens through menu selections, you should give considerable thought to making the menus fast and easy to use—particularly leaning towards the fast part. Having to wait while a menu unwinds itself every time you want to do something will probably quickly turn you off from using an otherwise workable program.

Menus should support keyboard alternatives for their more commonly used commands; several of these have fallen into common use. Ctrl-S or Alt-S is usually used to save a file, for example, no matter which graphical user interface you find yourself using.

This graphical user interface uses alternate key combinations for keyboard menu item selections. While you can change these to suit your own needs, the following represents a list of keyboard alternatives that most people will find comfortable. Not all of them will apply to all applications.

Alt-O Open
Alt-Z Close
Alt-S Save
Alt-P Print
Alt-Q Quit
Alt-C Copy
Alt-X Cut
Alt-V Paste

As will be discussed, the keyboard alternatives are displayed in the menu items, so the menus will serve to prompt new users of the keyboard alternatives until they're committed to memory.

By comparison, Windows uses two-key combinations to run its menus. For example, to open a file you would hit Alt-F for the File menu and then O for the Open item. This allows the menus to be opened and operated without any recourse to the mouse, but it requires more keystrokes.

In this graphical user interface, the alternate key is represented in menu items by a diamond, which is character four. When the menu manager code is passed an alternate key, it actually looks through all the menu items in all the menus at its disposal to find one with character four followed by the alternate key in question to determine which menu item is to be selected by the key.

As with most elements of the graphical user interface, the menu handler should look as much like a black box to the rest of the program as possible. The menus shouldn't entail the program running under the interface having to actually do any of the graphic manipulation involved in working with the menus—this should be handled by the menu functions in GUILIB—nor should it tie up any meaningful amount of processor overhead to keep track of any potential menu activity.

The ideal sort of menu manager would be one wholly interrupt-driven—i.e., one called directly by the mouse if it finds itself clicked in a menu. This is elegant but still tricky to write and debug. The Macintosh arrives at it not by having the menu manager interrupt-driven but by placing notes in a queue of "events" indicating menu activity. The queue itself is polled by the foreground program whenever time permits.

Once again, you should bear in mind the asynchronous nature of life on the Macintosh. Menu selections frequently must be interpreted by any of several different windows, depending upon which one is foremost on the screen. As this graphical user interface doesn't have the windowing complexity of the Macintosh, it doesn't need the event handling of it either. Simply polling and dispatching menu item selections is considerably easier.

On the Macintosh, menu "events" must be decoded through a complex nest of switch statements. It would be much more elegant if the menu items themselves knew what they were to do directly and could just go ahead and do it when selected. The C language provides elegant, if somewhat exotic, notation for doing this.

Thus far, menu items have been discussed as screen graphics. Here's what one looks like as the data object that actually represents it:

```
typedef struct {
    char name[MENULINESIZE + 1];
    int (*proc)( );
    } MENUITEM;
```

The first element of this struct is a string holding the actual text that defines the menu item. The constant MENULINESIZE is defined in GUI.H.

The second element in this struct is a function pointer—a pointer that will point to some executable code. It's very likely that you won't have encountered these things before if you're fairly new to C, as there's little cause to use them in most sorts of programming. They make doing things like menus very powerful, however.

If this is a function,

```
int doSomething( )
{
    /* some code goes here */
}
```

then you can define a pointer to the function like this:

```
int (*somethingPtr)( );
```

```
somethingPtr = doSomething;
```

Having done this, you can execute the function doSomething by executing the place where the function pointer points. The syntax for this is a bit convoluted under C:

```
int n;
```

```
n = (somethingPtr)( );
```

This assumes that there aren't any arguments to be passed to the function pointed to by somethingPtr. If you wanted to pass it arguments, they'd go in the currently empty set of parentheses after the function name.

Function pointers are powerful because they let you call functions without necessarily hard-wiring them into your code. In the case of the menu items, each item can be assigned a function that it's to execute directly if selected.

There will be cases in which you'll want to define menu items that don't call anything, such as menu items that are rules to separate logical groups of real items, or items for which you haven't figured out actual functions yet. For this reason, GUI.LIB includes a function called idle:

```
idle( )
{

}
```

The idle function does nothing and does it very well. Menu items that don't do anything yet can call it until something better comes along, and menu items that are never to be selected—such as separator lines—can use idle as a filler.

This is what a complete MENU object looks like:

```
typedef struct {
    int count;
    char title[MENUTITLESIZE + 1];
    MENUITEM item[MAXMENUITEM];
    } MENU;
```

This definition includes the item count, which tells the menu manager how many valid items there are in the menu. It also includes title, which is the text that will appear in the menu bar. Finally, it adds an array of MENUITEM objects to serve as the actual items in the menu.

You can initialize one of these MENU objects at compile time under C. This is the File menu of Desktop Paint. Note that, in order to create function pointers to the various functions that the menu will call, you must declare prototypes for them even if you would not otherwise do so.

```
int idle( );          /* in GUI.H */
int doNew(void);
int doSetFiletype(void);
int doOpen(void);
int doClose(void);
int doSaveAs(void);
int doSave(void);
int doPrint(void);
int doGetInfo(void);
int doQuit(void);
```

The menu itself is initialized like this:

```
MENU file = {11," File",
             " New \004N ",doNew,
             " Open \004O ",doOpen,
             ".Close \004Z ",doClose,
             ".Save \004S ",doSave,
             ".Save as... ",doSaveAs,
             "._____ ",idle,
             ".Print \004P ",doPrint,
             " Get info... ",doGetInfo,
             " File type ",doSetFiletype,
             "._____ ",idle,
             " Quit \004Q ",doQuit,
             };
```

Figure 4-3 illustrates what this menu actually looks like in its initial state—the various inactive items can be made active by the program owning the menu.

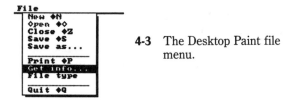

4-3   The Desktop Paint file menu.

There are a number of important conventions illustrated in the initialization for the File menu. Note that the title and each of the items has a blank space in front. In the case of the title, this is merely cosmetic—having the leftmost menu title right up against the left side of the screen looks unattractive. However, in the case of the item strings, the first character serves as a flag to tell the menu manager how to draw the text.

If the first character is a blank space, the menu item will be drawn normally and will be active. If it's a period, the item will be drawn active but with a check-mark before it.

The keyboard alternate entries are included in the menu item strings—they serve the dual function of reminding anyone who pulls down a menu what the keyboard alternatives are and also telling the menu manager which keyboard equivalents relate to which menu items. I'll discuss the actual code to scan the menu items for keyboard equivalents shortly.

Defining menus as fixed data structures in this way makes them fairly inflexible. Under more complex graphical user interfaces, menus are typically defined in a way allowing the menu manager to determine the size of the window that a menu pops up in on the fly, based on the longest menu item name string. This is arguably more elegant but also means that the menu manager must undertake a considerable amount of calculation each time a menu is called for, something that the design of this interface seeks to avoid. The fixed size data structure enables much faster menus.

There are a number of important constants that are used in this chapter but haven't been explained yet. Here they are, as they should appear in GUI.H:

```
#define CHECKMARK      251

#define ACTIVE         0xffff
#define INACTIVE       0xaa55

#define KEYMENUCHAR    4      /* the symbol for an alternate key */
#define MAXMENUITEM    16     /* maximum number of menu items */
#define MENULINESIZE   13     /* maximum length of menu item */
#define MENULINEDEEP   10     /* depth of menu line */
#define MENUCOUNT      9      /* maximum number of menus */
#define MENUTITLESIZE  8      /* maximum length of menu title */
#define MENUBARDEEP    10     /* depth of menu bar */
```

The CHECKMARK constant is the PC ASCII symbol that looks most like a checkmark. It is, in fact, a square root sign. The KEYMENUCHAR is the symbol used for keyboard alternatives in the menu item names. Character four is a diamond. The ACTIVE and INACTIVE constants might seem like rather odd choices, but they aren't arbitrary at all. Their true meaning will become apparent shortly.

Using the menu manager

Having defined some individual menus, a program using the graphical user interface must add them to the screen. This works in a way analogous to adding controls to a window, although because menus behave in a much more predictable way, they can be handled with less juggling of objects and pointers.

There are two initial calls into the menu manager portion of the graphical user interface. The first call sets it up and prepares it to accept some menus:

```
InitMenuManager( )     /* call this before using any menus */ {
    int i;
```

```
        for(i = 0;i < MENUCOUNT; + + i)
            menuarray[i] = NULL;
        SetRect(&menubarRect,0,0,SCREENWIDE,MENUBARDEEP);
    }
```

This function actually initializes two things: the global RECT variable menu-barRect (used by the graphical user interface to decide if the mouse is in the menu bar), and a table of MENU pointers, menuarray (used to point to the menus ultimately to be added to the screen). Initially, all the entries are set to NULL, indicating that no menus are currently available.

This is how the two data objects should be defined:

```
MENU *menuarray[MENUCOUNT];
RECT menubarRect;
```

There is also an int to serve as an index into menuarray:

```
int menuindex = 0;
```

Having initialized the menu manager, a program setting up the graphical user interface would add individual menus to the screen by calling addMenu. To add the File menu defined above, it would do this:

```
addMenu(&file);
```

The addMenu function adds menus to the menu bar in order of their appearance. Thus, if you wanted to have a menu bar with a menu called Desk first and one called File next, you would define the two menus in memory and then call add-Menu twice, like this:

```
addMenu(&desk);
addMenu(&file);
```

The actual code for the addMenu isn't a great deal more complex than the menu manager initialization function. It simply finds the first free entry in the menuarray table and sets it to point to the menu passed to the function.

```
addMenu(m)
    MENU *m;
{
    if(menuindex < MENUCOUNT) {
        menuarray[menuindex + +] = m;        return(1);
    } else return(0);
}
```

Remember that addMenu doesn't copy the data pointed to by the MENU pointer passed to it: it only keeps track of pointers. It assumes that the menu will stay put for the duration of the program. For this reason, there's no point in dynamically allocating menu definitions in most cases or in loading them from a resource file. All menus must be available all the time, and as such might as well be handled as fixed data objects.

There are certainly exceptions to this, and they usually crop up in situations wherein the program calling the menu manager can't know how many items will be in a menu at compile time; the Font menu of Desktop Paint is a good example. The fonts are stored as resources in Desktop Paint's resource file, and users are free to add fonts to the resource file as they see fit. As such, Desktop Paint builds the Font menu each time it boots up, storing it in an allocated buffer.

Once all the menus have been added to the screen, the menu bar must be drawn to make them visible. This function does this:

```
DrawMenuBar(void)
{
    int i;

    WhiteRule(MENUBARDEEP,0);
    BlackRule(2,10);
    for(i = 0;i < menuindex; + + i)
        DrawString(i*(8*MENUTITLESIZE),1,
        menuarray[i]- > title,ACTIVE);

}
```

The DrawMenuBar function uses two of the hitherto unspoken-for assembly language functions discussed in Chapter 2 that simply clear out some space at the top of the screen. This could have been handled using the Turbo C graphics library, but the code to draw the menu bar is exceedingly trivial, even in assembly language, and very much faster.

The DrawString function is used to place the menu titles in the menu bar. The exact nature of this function will be discussed next. It's a machine-language function, because it's called often and should be as fast as possible. It involves the first awkward bit of problem solving in designing the graphical user interface—finding a screen font.

Drawing screen text

Drawing screen text under the graphical user interface could be relatively easy if one used the Turbo C outtextxy function to handle it. The default bitmapped font that's part of this function is of the right size, and this approach is a great deal easier to use than what will be discussed in this section.

The outtextxy function suffers from two drawbacks. To begin with, it's slow. Because it can draw text in any color you like and isn't limited to fitting it into byte boundaries, it carries around a lot of baggage not really necessary for the simple screen text of the graphical user interface. Menus drawn with outtextxy are decidedly languid in being pulled down, especially on slower 8088-based PCs.

Secondly, the character set provided for use with outtextxy lacks many of the PC's familiar special characters, which are handy to have for things like the diamond and checkmark symbols already encountered.

The ideal situation would be to use the same character set as the PC does when it prints through the BIOS. On EGA and VGA cards, attempting to print to the screen through the BIOS will cause the text in question to be drawn as graphics. As such, it might be surmised that a graphic character set exists somewhere for the BIOS to draw on.

The BIOS on an EGA or VGA card will, conveniently, tell you how to find this character set. In fact, it could be used this way—by having the graphical user interface locate it in the BIOS and read it as needs be. However, this presents the DrawString code with rather more segment juggling than is desirable. It also means that the graphical user interface would cease to be useful on Hercules cards, which lack built-in graphics characters.

For this reason, it's better to swipe the character set from an EGA or VGA card and subsequently link the character set data into programs that use the graphical user interface library.

There are, in fact, a variety of character sets available in every EGA and VGA card. While all of them have more or less the same appearance—they all look like the traditional PC serif screen font—they vary in the size of their characters.

For the purposes of the DrawString function, the screen font characters must be eight pixels—one byte—wide and some number of pixels deep. Each pixel of depth represents one byte. In theory, the depth of the screen font can be whatever you want it to be. The screen fonts available in an EGA or VGA card BIOS are available in depths of eight, fourteen, and sixteen bytes.

Figure 4-4 illustrates the relationship between a character's bitmap and the bytes containing it.

Eight bytes {
Eight bytes {
Eight bytes {
Eight bytes {
Eight bytes {
Eight bytes {
Eight bytes {
Eight bytes {
Eight bytes {
Eight bytes {
Eight bytes {

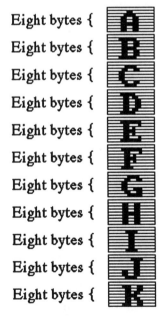

4-4 The geography of a system font character.

The graphical user interface in this book works with an eight-byte deep font. This is a questionable choice—especially on a VGA card in its 640×480 pixel mode, 8×8 pixel characters look a bit small. 8×16 pixel characters would be a lot easier to read, but they're so tall as to unduly limit things like the number of menu items that will fit on the screen.

The 8×14 pixel font would seem like a good compromise in this respect. However, in order to actually draw characters on the screen, the DrawString function must locate the appropriate character patterns in the screen font bitmap. The first byte of any character in the bitmap can be defined as

(characterDepth * asciiNumber)

For an eight- or sixteen-byte deep font, this will involve multiplying asciiNumber by an even power of two. For an eight-byte deep font, then, the expression could be simplified to

(asciiNumber << 3)

Shifting a number left by three is equivalent to multiplying it by eight.

There is no convenient way to multiply by fourteen. Each character would entail the use of at least one MUL instruction, which is quite slow. Because one of the goals of the interface was to have menus and other screen phenomena pop up quickly, the eight-byte deep screen font seems like the best choice. It also involves writing the least amount of actual graphic data to the screen, another factor in its improved speed.

If you've bought the companion source code disk for this book, the process of wresting the screen font from your system BIOS can be done away with because the screen font is provided with the disk in both binary and object module forms. You might want to skip this next section unless you're particularly interested in this bit of code.

All that's required to generate a binary file containing the screen font is a very simple C language program and a PC with either an EGA or a VGA card. If you have a Hercules card, you'll have to convince someone with an EGA or VGA card to let you copy their screen font.

Figure 4-5 illustrates the program. If you run this on a machine with a suitable card, it will ensconce the font in EGAFONT.BIN, which should be 2048 bytes long.

The structure of the binary font image is exceedingly simple. The first eight bytes represent the pattern for the first character, the next eight bytes the next character, and so on. There are 256 characters, and the first eight bytes will always be zero.

In order to use this font, it must be stored in memory somewhere so Draw-String—when it's eventually written—can locate it. While it could be loaded into a buffer each time it's needed, it's a good deal more elegant to compile it into the code. In fact, it will be added to the GUI.LIB library file, as touched on previously. This will require another slight digression.

```
#include "stdio.h"
#include "dos.h"

main()
{
        struct REGPACK r;
        FILE *fp;

        puts("Swipe the EGA 8 x 8 screen font");

        /* open the binary file */
        if((fp=fopen("EGAFONT.BIN","wb")) != NULL) {

                /* get a pointer to the first 128 characters */
                r.r_ax=0x1130;
                r.r_bx=0x0300;
                intr(0x10,&r);

                /* write them to the file */
                fwrite(MK_FP(r.r_es,r.r_bp),1,1024,fp);

                /* get a pointer to the next 128 characters */
                r.r_ax=0x1130;
                r.r_bx=0x0400;
                intr(0x10,&r);

                /* write them to the file */
                fwrite(MK_FP(r.r_es,r.r_bp),1,1024,fp);

                /* that's all, folks */
                puts("Done");
                fclose(fp);
        } else puts("Can't create the font file");
}
```

4-5   A program to capture the eight-point screen font of an EGA or VGA card.

Creating object modules

Any sort of data can be made suitable for linking into a complex C language program's EXE file by turning said data into a Microsoft-compatible OBJ file. The Microsoft OBJ format is the same one used by Turbo C's built-in linker and the Borland TLINK and TLIB programs. It's as inscrutable as any data format devised for use on a PC.

The complete implementation of the OBJ format is quite complex—it allows for all sorts of records, depending upon the nature of the data you want to stash away in an object file. An object file can consist of many different sorts of data, and the format allows for all this data to be accessed with a minimum of head scratching on the part of the program working with the file.

Almost all of this is irrelevant to the task of translating little bits of binary data such as the font file just created into little OBJ files. Such OBJ files will have one data object per file and a very simple one at that. A program doing this is actually pretty simple and consists of little more than code to write some cryptic-looking record specifiers to a file.

Figure 4-6 is the code for the program Prelink, a utility to create small OBJ files.

```
/*
        PRELINK - binary data to Microsoft OBJ module
        converter copyright (c) 1990 Alchemy Mindworks Inc.
*/

#include "stdio.h"
#include "alloc.h"

#define buffersize      0xfff0

FILE *infile,*outfile;
char *buffer;
unsigned int buffsize=0;

main(argc,argv)
        int argc;
        char *argv[];
{
        puts("Prelink V1.0 copyright (c) 1990 Alchemy Mindworks Inc.");
        if(argc > 3) {
                if((buffer=malloc(buffersize))!=NULL) {
                        if((infile=fopen(argv[1],"rb")) != NULL) {
                                if((outfile=fopen(argv[2],"wb")) != NULL) {
                                        /* get the binary data */
                                        fillbuffer();
                                        /* write a T record */
                                        trecord();
                                        /* write the segment names */
                                        lnames("\004DATA\006DGROUP\005_DATA");
                                        segmentdef();
                                        /* write the group deffinition */
                                        groupdef();
                                        /* write the actual data - at last */
                                        drecord();
                                        /* write the symbol for the data */
                                        pnames(argv[3]);
                                        /* write the end module record */
                                        endmodule();
                                        fclose(outfile);
                                }
                                fclose(infile);
                        } else printf("%s not found.\n",argv[1]);
                        free(buffer);
                } else puts("Memory allocation error");
        }
        else {
                puts("SYNTAX:");
                puts("    PRELINK <source file> <destination file> <symbol>");
        }
}

/* load the data into a buffer with the appropriate record header */
fillbuffer()
{
        static char b[16]="\xa0\x04\x00\x01\x00\x00";
        char *p;
        int c;

        p=buffer+6;
        memcpy(buffer,b,6);
        do {
                c=fgetc(infile);
```

4-6 The Prelink program.

4-6 Continued

```
                if(c != EOF) {
                        *p++=c;
                        ++buffsize;
                        ++buffer[1];
                        if(!buffer[1])++buffer[2];
                }
        } while(c !=EOF && p < buffer+buffersize);
}

/* write a module end record */
endmodule()
{
        static char b[16]="\x8a\x02\x00\x00";

        checksum(b);
        wrecord(b);
}

/* write a segment deffinition record */
segmentdef()
{
        static char b[16]="\x98\x07\x00\x48\x00\x00\x04\x02\x01";

        b[4]=buffsize & 0xff;
        b[5]=buffsize >> 8;
        checksum(b);
        wrecord(b);
}

/* write a group deffinition record */
groupdef()
{
        static char b[16]="\x9a\x04\x00\x03\xff\x01";

        checksum(b);
        wrecord(b);
}

/* write a public names record */
pnames(s)
        char *s;
{
        static char b[128]="\x90\x00\x00\x00\x01\x00";
        int i=6;

        while(*s) {
                b[i++]=*s++;
                ++b[5];
        }
        b[1]=i+1;
        checksum(b);
        wrecord(b);
}

/* write a data record */
drecord()

{
        checksum(buffer);
        wrecord(buffer);
}

/* write a t record */
```

```
trecord()
{
        static char b[16]="\x80\x03\x00\x01\x41\x3b";

        wrecord(b);
}

/* write a list of names record */
lnames(s)
        char *s;
{
        static char b[128]="\x96\x00\x00\x00";
        int i=4;

        while(*s) b[i++]=*s++;
        b[1]=i-2;
        checksum(b);
        wrecord(b);
}

/* write a record */
wrecord(s)
        char *s;
{
        int i;

        for(i=0;i<3;++i) fputc(s[i],outfile);
        for(i=0;i<(s[1] + (s[2] <<8));++i) fputc(s[i+3],outfile);
}

/* set the checksum for record p */
checksum(p)
        char *p;
{
        int l,i,c = 0;

        l=(p[1]+(p[2]<<8))+2;

        for(i=0;i<l;++i) c = c + *p++;
        c = (c ^ 0xff)+1;
        *p=c;
        return(c);
}
```

It's not necessary to understand the structure of OBJ files to use them—or to use Prelink, for that matter. There's a fairly complete discussion of them in *MS-DOS Technical Reference Encyclopedia* (published by Microsoft Press) should you want to really get inside Prelink and see what it's up to.

You should keep several important things in mind about Prelink as it stands. To begin with, it's hard wired to generate object modules for use in large model Turbo C programs—other C compilers or programs compiled for other memory models will probably entail different segment naming conventions. Also, the simple structure of the data records in the object modules Prelink generates limit the amount of data that can be put in one to about 16K per OBJ file.

The syntax for Prelink is fairly obvious and requires three arguments: the binary file to be converted, the name of the OBJ file to be created, and the symbol that will be used to refer to the file within your program. You should make the symbol name uppercase and include a leading underbar.

This is how to create THEFONT.OBJ for EGAFONT.BIN:

PRELINK EGAFONT.BIN THEFONT.OBJ __THEFONT

Having created THEFONT.OBJ, you should run the batch file discussed in Chapter 1 to rebuild GUI.LIB with the font included.

The Prelink program will turn up again later in this book. It's useful, for example, in creating linkable bitmap fragments for use as icons in your graphical user interface programs.

Drawing text

In practice only the GUIASM.ASM file will ever need to get at the __THEFONT object, because all the system font text drawing is handled by assembly language. It might be a bit easier to see how the system font is used, however, if the discussion begins with a hypothetical C language DrawString function.

This code assumes that THEFONT has an extern declaration and that SCREENTBL and SCREENSEG have been properly set up.

```
DrawString(x,y,string)
    int x,y;
    char *string;
{
    char *d,*f;
    int i,n;

    while((n = *string + +) ! = 0) {
        f = THEFONT + (n < <3);
        for(i = 0;i < 8; + +i) {
            d = MK__FP(SCREENSEG,SCREENTBL[y + i]);
            d[x > >3] = f[i];
            x + = 8;
        }
    }
}
```

To begin with, note that this DrawString function is extremely sloppy—in practice, it's possible to write it, even in C, with far fewer calculations to perform. However, this function illustrates the basic process of drawing system font text characters to a graphics mode monochrome screen. As has been discussed, the EGA and VGA 16-color screens behave as monochrome screens for this sort of code.

Because each character of the system font is eight pixels deep and eight pixels wide, each character occupies eight bytes. The ASCII value of a character multiplied by eight represents the offset from the beginning of THEFONT where start of the bitmap for the character in question resides. The expression f = THEFONT + (n < <3) performs this calculation, using bit shifts to handle the multiplication.

The screen lines to have text written to them are located by creating pointers into the screen buffer based on the entries in SCREENTBL. The pointers point to the start of each line—the offset into the line is represented by the x argument to DrawString. Because the actual offset is required in bytes, rather than in pixels, the x value must be shifted right by three (i.e., divided by eight). For this reason, the x position will automatically be rounded down to the next lowest eight pixel boundary.

This function has a number of drawbacks. It writes the string to the screen one character at a time, which means that it must scan through SCREENTBL and create the appropriate pointers eight times for each character to be drawn. A much better way to handle it—if a bit more involved to code—is to write the entire first row of the string, calculate the next pointer, write the entire second row, and so on.

You will note that earlier calls to DrawString actually had four arguments, the last being a flag called active. The active flag determines whether the text should be drawn in solid black on white or in grey. You will recall that GUI.H has two constants defined for ACTIVE and INACTIVE—0xffff and 0xaa55 (respectively).

This rewritten version of the C language DrawString function allows for an active flag:

```
DrawString(x,y,string,active)
     int x,y;
     char *string;
     unsigned int active;
{
     char *d,*f;
     int i,n;

     while((n = *string + +) != 0) {
         f = THEFONT + (n < < 3);
         for(i = 0;i < 8; + + i) {
             d = MK__FP(SCREENSEG,SCREENTBL[y + i];
             d[x > > 3] = f[i] & active;
             x + = 8;
             active = ((active & 0xff00) > > 8) |
                      ((active & 0x00ff) < < 8);
         }
     }
}
```

The active argument is just a mask that gets ANDed with the font bitmap data written to the screen. Odd numbered lines get ANDed with the low order byte and even numbered lines get ANDed with the high order byte, both by virtue of the two bytes in the active variable being swapped with each pass through the loop.

If the active argument is set to the constant ACTIVE—0xffff—it has no effect on the font data. If it's set to INACTIVE—0xaa55—the alternate bits get ANDed off, resulting in the text looking grey.

Once again, this has been simplified and written in a less than optimum way to make it easier to understand. Figure 4-7 illustrates the assembly language version

```
;                      ARG1 = X
;                      ARG2 = Y
;                      ARG3 = STRING
;                      ARG4 = MASK
                       PUBLIC  _DrawString
_DrawString    PROC    FAR
               PUSH    BP
               MOV     BP,SP

               DATASEG
               FOURPLANES
               MOUSEOFF
               MOV     AX,DS:[_SCREENSEG]
               MOV     ES,AX

               MOV     CL,3
               SHR     WORD PTR [BP + _AOFF + 0],CL

               MOV     CX,FONTDEPTH
DS1:           PUSH    CX
               DEC     CX

               MOV     AX,[BP + _AOFF + 8]
               XCHG    AH,AL
               MOV     [BP + _AOFF + 8],AX

               MOV     BX,[BP + _AOFF + 2]
               ADD     BX,CX
               SHL     BX,1

               DATASEG
               MOV     DI,DS:[_SCREENTBL+BX]
               ADD     DI,[BP + _AOFF + 0]

               MOV     SI,[BP + _AOFF + 4]
               MOV     DS,[BP + _AOFF + 6]

DS2:           MOV     BH,00H
               MOV     BL,DS:[SI]
               CMP     BL,0
               JE      DS3

               PUSH    DS
               SHL     BX,1
               SHL     BX,1
               SHL     BX,1

               ADD     BX,CX

               DATASEG
               MOV     AL,DS:[_THEFONT+BX]
               AND     AX,[BP + _AOFF + 8]
               NOT     AL
               STOSB

               POP     DS
               INC     SI
               JMP     DS2
DS3:           POP     CX
               LOOP    DS1

DSX:           DATASEG
```

4-7 The assembly language DrawString function.

```
                MOUSEON
                POP        BP
                RET
_DrawString     ENDP


;PUT THIS LINE IN THE _DATA SEGEMENT

EXTRN           _THEFONT:BYTE
```

that will actually be used by the graphical user interface. You should add it to
GUIASM.ASM, reassemble it, and rebuild GUI.LIB.

As you write code that uses the DrawString function of the graphical user interface, you should remember that you can specify the y argument in individual pixels
but that the x argument is only accurate to the nearest eight-pixel boundary. Thus,
for example, this call,

    DrawString(10,10,"Electric frog", ACTIVE);

and this call,

    DrawString(14,10,"Electric frog", ACTIVE);

will print exactly the same thing in exactly the same place as this one:

    DrawString(8,10,"Electric frog", ACTIVE);

There's one more function you'll want to look at before the actual menu-han-
dling code will be completely understandable. The function, called InvertRect, is
essential to the display and operation of menus: it flips all the pixels in a rectangular area of the screen from black to white, and it's responsible for making the menu
item selector bar appear. Like the DrawString function, it uses the SCREENTBL
array to address the screen. However, in this case, the graphical user interface
code can get away with using a C language version of it.

Despite its fairly reasonable selection of graphics primitives, the Turbo C
graphics library doesn't offer an easy way to invert screen data. You could use getimage and putimage, passing the NOT_PUT verb to putimage so that it will invert
the image fragment it's putting to the screen. Such a function would be written like
this:

```
InvertRect(r)
    RECT *r;
{
    char *p;
    int size;

        if((size = imagesize(r->left,r->top,r->right,r->bottom)) != -1) {
        if((p = malloc(size)) != NULL) {
            MouseOff( );
            getimage(r->left,r->top,r->right,r->bottom,p);
            putimage(r->left,r->top,p,NOT_PUT);
            MouseOn( );
```

```
        free(p);
      }
    }
  }
```

This approach has two problems. First, it's slow; second, it involves allocating memory and thus might fail in conditions of restricted memory, which would confuse someone using the menus in a program.

Inverting a rectangular area can be handled much more intelligently and more rapidly if one observes that the longest possible screen line can't exceed 80 bytes and that all the lines of the area to be inverted are the same.

Figure 4-8 is the code for the InvertRect function that will actually be used in the graphical user interface. It's a bit more complex than the one using image fragments, but it's considerably faster. First, it works out the byte width of the area to be inverted and creates a mask with a pixel set in every bit position within the area. It then XORs the mask with the appropriate part of each screen line in the area in question, as located by SCREENTBL.

```
InvertRect(r)
        RECT *r;
{
        char *p,b[81];
        int i,j,width,depth,bleft,bytes;
        int left,right,pleft,pright;

        left=r->left & 0xfff8;
        right=r->right;
        if(right & 0x0007) right=(right | 0x0007)+1;
        width=right-left;
        depth=r->bottom-r->top;
        bleft=left>>3;
        pleft=r->left-left;
        pright=pleft+(r->right-r->left);
        bytes=pixels2bytes(width)+1;

        memset(b,0,bytes);

        for(i=pleft;i<=pright;++i) b[i>>3] |= masktable[i & 0x0007];

        fourplanes();
        MouseOff();
        for(i=0;i<=depth;++i) {
                p=MK_FP(SCREENSEG,SCREENTBL[r->top+i]+bleft);
                for(j=0;j<bytes;++j) p[j] ^= b[j];
        }
        MouseOn();
}
```

4-8   The InvertRect function.

Figure 4-8 is the first instance of another useful bit of bitmapped trickery that will appear in many places throughout this book. You will notice the use of an undefined array of some sort called masktable. This is, in fact, a global array of chars in the graphical user interface and is defined as

```
char masktable[8] = {0x80,0x40,0x20,0x10,0x08,0x04,0x02,0x01};
```

The use of masktable may not be wholly clear as yet, and it will entail another slight digression to explain.

Bits and bitmasks

A monochrome bitmap, such as the screen of a PC in one of the graphics modes of interest in this book, consists of lines of byte-oriented data. Getting at a single pixel in such a line involves some bit fiddling. Figure 4-9 illustrates the relationship between an image fragment and its bits and bytes.

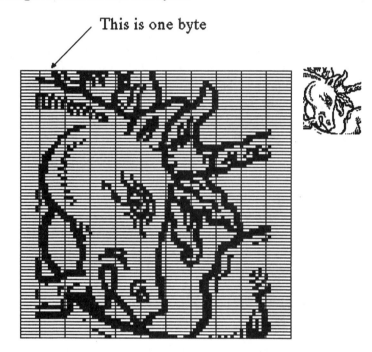

This is one byte

4-9 The bit structure of a bitmapped image.

The procedure for dealing with individual bits, based on masks, is very simple. In the following discussion, the pixel to be dealt with will be specified by its coordinates on a screen, but the same procedure would work for an image fragment where all the data was in a buffer.

Let's begin by returning the status of a pixel at (x,y). The line containing the pixel would be found like this:

```
char *line;

line = MK_FP(SCREENSEG,SCREENTBL[y]);
```

The byte with the pixel in it would then be line[x / 8]. As division by eight is the same as shifting right by three places, this can be simplified to line[x > >3], which means that one of the eight bits in this byte represents the pixel in question.

Note that in shifting x right by three places, the three least significant bits of information in the horizontal location of the pixel have been discarded. These bits are, in fact, the specification of the location of the appropriate bit in the byte in question.

The position of the bit in question can be expressed as (0x80 > > (x & 0x0007)), which means to begin with 0x80 (a byte having its high order bit set) and rotate it right by the value that's in the first three bits of x.

To find out whether or not the pixel at (x,y) is set, then, you would do this:

```
char *line;
line = MK__FP(SCREENSEG,SCREENTBL[y]);
if(line[x > >3] & (0x80 > >(x & 0x0007))) /*it's white */
else /* it's black */
```

The only drawback to this procedure—especially when applied to a great deal of data—is that calculating (0x80 > > (x & 0x0007)) is somewhat time-consuming and could be speeded up somewhat. Observing that this bit of code can only produce eight unique results, the time it takes to execute can be reduced by about half by simply storing the eight results in a table and thereafter accessing the table (with the table in question being masktable, as described previously).

The code fragment determining the value of a pixel at (x,y) would be rewritten like this to use masktable:

```
char *line;

line = MK__FP(SCREENSEG,SCREENTBL[y]);
if(line[x > >3] & masktable[x & 0x0007]) /*it's white */
else /* it's black */
```

You would set a pixel at (x,y) to white like this:

```
line[x > >3]¦ = masktable[x & 0x0007];
```

This line will set it to black by ANDing off the bit in question:

```
line[x > >3] &= masktable[x & 0x0007];
```

Finally, this will toggle it by XORing the appropriate entry in masktable with the byte in question:

```
line[x > >3] ^= masktable[x & 0x0007];
```

In the InvertRect function, rather than invert every bit one at a time, the code creates a big mask the width of the area to be inverted and then XORs it bytewise with the screen data. However, the mask itself is built up from masktable.

The menu manager

As has been discussed in earlier chapters, the main functional part of a program under the graphical user interface is a pretty simple bit of code. With the introduction of menus, it will get a little more complicated as it will acquire the primary loop that actually does all the work.

Figure 4-10 illustrates the main function of a simple graphical user interface program. A number of functions in it will be unfamiliar, with the first of them being whereMouse. While this function doesn't pertain specifically to menus, it will be discussed here because the menu manager is the first thing in this book to require it.

```
main()
{
        POINT thePoint;
        int rt;

        if(initMouse()) {
                registerbgidriver(EGAVGA_driver);
                registerbgidriver(Herc_driver);
                if(initGraphics()) {
                        MouseOn();
                        ClearScreen();
                        InitWindowManager();
                        InitMenuManager();
                        AddMenu(&file);
                        DrawMenuBar();

                        do {
                                dispatchMenuItem();
                                if(MouseDown(&thePoint)) {
                                        rt=whereMouse(&thePoint,&screenwindow);
                                        if(rt & inMenuBar) doMenu(&thePoint);
                                        else errorbeep();
                                }
                        } while(alive);
                        MouseOff();
                        deinitGraphics();
                } else puts("Cannot establish graphics mode");
        } else puts("Cannot locate mouse driver");
```

4-10 The main function of a simple application.

When the mouse is clicked, the graphical user interface doesn't really care where its absolute location on the screen is. Rather, it wants to know what general area it's in so it will know what to do with the click. The owner of the area may subsequently want to know exactly where it was clicked.

The menu manager owns the menu bar.

The whereMouse function returns a constant based on the location of the mouse when it's clicked. These are the possible locations:

#define inNothing	0x0000
#define inWindow	0x0001
#define inMenuBar	0x0002
#define inButton	0x0004
#define inBitmap	0x0008
#define inText	0x0010
#define inTextfield	0x0020
#define inList	0x0040
#define inVertScroll	0x0080
#define inHorScroll	0x0100
#define inUpArrow	0x0200

```
#define inDownArrow   0x0400
#define inJumpUp      0x0800
#define inJumpDown    0x1000
#define inThumb       0x2000
#define inCheckBox    0x4000
#define inEditField   0x8000
```

These constants actually have several uses in the graphical user interface. They specify where the mouse has been clicked and also serve as the type values for the OBJECTHEAD pointers in every object type so that something walking up the linked list of a window can know what sort of object it's found. Some of them are never actually used as object types. The inUpArrow value, for example, is actually a modifier of the inVertScroll and inHorScroll constants; it's never found on its own.

Figure 4-11 is the code for the complete whereMouse function. Some of this will be exceedingly unfathomable at this point, as many of the things that the mouse can be clicked in haven't been discussed in detail.

```
whereMouse(p,w)
     POINT *p;
     WINDOW *w;
{
     EDITFIELD *f;
     CHECKBOX *cb;
     SCROLLBAR *sb;
     TEXTFIELD *tf;
     LIST *ls;
     BITMAP *bmp;
     BUTTON *b;
     OBJECTHEAD *oh;
     int r=inNothing,i;

     if(PointInRect(p,&menubarRect)) return(inMenuBar);
     else {
          oh=(OBJECTHEAD *)w;
          if(!PointInRect(p,&w->frame)) return(inNothing);
          else {
               while(oh != NULL) {
                    switch(oh->type) {
                         case inButton:
                              b=(BUTTON *)oh;
                              if(PointInRect(p,&b->frame))
                                   r |= inButton;
                              break;
                         case inWindow:
                              r &= inWindow;
                              break;
                         case inBitmap:
                              bmp=(BITMAP *)oh;
                              if(PointInRect(p,&bmp->frame))
                                   r |= inBitmap;
                              break;
                         case inList:
                              ls=(LIST *)oh;
                              if(PointInRect(p,&ls->frame))
                                   r |= inList;
                              break;
```

4-11 The whereMouse function.

```
            case inTextfield:
                tf=(TEXTFIELD *)oh;
                if(PointInRect(p,&tf->frame))
                    r |= inTextfield;
                break;
            case inVertScroll:
                sb=(SCROLLBAR *)oh;
                if(PointInRect(p,&sb->frame)) {
                    r |= inVertScroll;
                    if(PointInRect(p,&sb->uparr))
                        r |= inUpArrow;
                    else if(PointInRect(p,&sb->dnarr))
                        r |= inDownArrow;
                    else if(PointInRect(p,&sb->thumb))
                        r |= inThumb;
                    else {
                        /* it's in a jump zone */
                        if(p->y < sb->thumb.top) r |= inJumpUp;
                        else r |= inJumpDown;
                    }

                }
                break;
            case inHorScroll:
                sb=(SCROLLBAR *)oh;
                if(PointInRect(p,&sb->frame)) {
                    r |= inHorScroll;
                    if(PointInRect(p,&sb->uparr))
                        r |= inUpArrow;
                    else if(PointInRect(p,&sb->dnarr))
                        r |= inDownArrow;
                    else if(PointInRect(p,&sb->thumb))
                        r |= inThumb;
                    else {
                        /* it's in a jump zone */
                        if(p->x < sb->thumb.left) r |= inJumpUp;
                        else r |= inJumpDown;
                    }
                }
                break;
            case inCheckBox:
                cb=(CHECKBOX *)oh;
                if(PointInRect(p,&cb->frame))
                    r |= inCheckBox;
                break;
            case inEditField:
                f=(EDITFIELD *)oh;
                if(f->select) {
                    f->select=0x00;
                    drawEditfield(f);
                }
                if(PointInRect(p,&f->frame)) {
                    r |= inEditField;
                    f->curpos=(p->x-f->frame.left)/8;
                    if(f->curpos > (i=strlen(f->text)))
                        f->curpos=i;
                }
                break;
        }
        oh=oh->next;
    }
    return(r);
}
```

The whereMouse function is, in fact, the first example of code that actually walks up the linked list of a window and peeks at all the objects therein. You'll note that the first thing it does is check the menu bar, as this isn't actually linked to anything, being in effect independent of any individual window. This allows windows that you open to ignore the menu bar—you wouldn't want users to be able to get at the tasks called by menu items while one was already in progress.

In calling whereMouse, the calling code passes it a pointer to a POINT variable with the location of the mouse click to be identified—presumably the same point used in a call to MouseLoc or MouseDown—and a pointer to the window the click is to be associated with. In the main loop, the window argument should be &screenwindow, although at this point the window involved doesn't matter because the program in Fig. 4-10 only cares about the menu bar.

Assuming that the mouse click doesn't occur in the menu bar, whereMouse will retrieve the object pointer from the OBJECTHEAD of the window passed to it and peek up it. What it will see at the location pointed to by the pointer will, in fact, be another OBJECTHEAD (because all objects start with one). It will find out what type of object it is, cast a pointer to it, and see if the mouse click is within its frame element. If it isn't, it will carry on up the list until it finds a NULL pointer.

In some cases, locating the object the click belongs to involves a bit more work. In the case of a scroll bar, for example, it must decide which part of the scroll bar is involved. In this case, it might return inVertScroll | inUpArrow.

Because the value returned by whereMouse might have more than one flag set, you can't simply test it against the list of constants as with a switch statement. Rather, you must test the appropriate bits. For example, to see if a mouse click was in the menu bar, you would load rt with the value returned by whereMouse and test (rt & inMenuBar) rather than (rt == inMenuBar). In this version of the graphical user interface, the inMenuBar constant can't have any modifiers in the way that inVertScroll can, but you can save yourself a great deal of later frustration by handling the mouse click constants consistently.

The other function called by Fig. 4-10 and not discussed yet is the visible part of the menu manager—doMenu. The doMenu function is passed a pointer to a POINT holding the mouse click. It will figure out which menu title the mouse has been clicked in, unroll the appropriate menu, handle the animation for the menu cursor, and dispatch a function to handle a menu item if one is selected. Despite all this, it's not actually all that complicated. The complete doMenu function is illustrated in Fig. 4-12.

```
doMenu(p)          /* handle a menu */
     POINT *p;
{
     WINDOW w;
     RECT r,lr;
     POINT pn;
     int m,n,i;

     m=p->x / (MENUTITLESIZE<<3);
     if(m >= menuindex) return(0);
```

4-12 The doMenu function.

```
r.left=(m*(MENUTITLESIZE<<3))+16;
r.top=menubarRect.bottom+1;
r.right=r.left+(MENULINESIZE<<3);
r.bottom=r.top+(menuarray[m]->count*MENULINEDEEP);

if(openWindow(&w,&r)) {
    for(i=0;i<menuarray[m]->count;++i) {
        if(menuarray[m]->item[i].name[0]==' ')
            DrawString(r.left+8,r.top+(i*MENULINEDEEP)+1,
                menuarray[m]->item[i].name+1,ACTIVE);
        else if(menuarray[m]->item[i].name[0]==CHECKMARK)
            DrawString(r.left,r.top+(i*MENULINEDEEP)+1,
                menuarray[m]->item[i].name,ACTIVE);
        else
            DrawString(r.left+8,r.top+(i*MENULINEDEEP)+1,
                menuarray[m]->item[i].name+1,INACTIVE);
    }
    i=-1;
    while(MouseDown(&pn)) {
        if(PointInRect(&pn,&r)) {
            n=(pn.y-r.top)/MENULINEDEEP;
            if(n != i) {
                if(i != -1) {
                    SetRect(&lr,r.left,r.top+(i*MENULINEDEEP),
                        r.right,r.top+(i*MENULINEDEEP)+MENULINEDEEP);
                    if(menuarray[m]->item[i].name[0]==' ')
                        InvertRect(&lr);
                }
                SetRect(&lr,r.left,r.top+(n*MENULINEDEEP),
                    r.right,r.top+(n*MENULINEDEEP)+MENULINEDEEP);
                if(menuarray[m]->item[n].name[0]==' ')
                    InvertRect(&lr);
                i=n;
            }
        }
    }
    closeWindow(&w);
    if(PointInRect(&pn,&r) && menuarray[m]->item[n].name[0]==' ') {
        n=(pn.y-r.top)/MENULINEDEEP;
        (menuarray[m]->item[n].proc)(n);
    }
    return(1);
} else return(0);
}
```

Figuring out which menu is to be opened is fairly simple. The number of characters between menu titles is defined as MENUTITLESIZE. Because each character is known to be eight bits wide, this code will set m to the appropriate menu number:

m = p->x / (MENUTITLESIZE < <3);

Once again, note that multiplication by eight has been handled by bit shifting.

The menu in question is menuarray[m], the menuarray having been loaded by addMenu. The amount of area the menu will require on the screen can be worked out from the maximum width of a menu item in bytes—MENULINESIZE, as defined previously— multiplied by eight and by the number of items in the menu multiplied by MENULINEDEEP. The code can then open a window just below the menu bar.

The rest of the function is pretty basic. Each of the menu items is drawn in the window. This is a bit illegal, actually—by rights, they should be added as TEXT objects, but this takes longer and serves no real purpose in this particular case.

Note that the menu window is closed before the menu item (if one has been selected) is dispatched. There's no pressing need to do this, save that it frees up whatever memory the window might have occupied before the function is called.

The syntax for actually calling the function is admittedly an example of C at its most convoluted:

```
(menuarray[m]->item[n].proc)(n);
```

This code executes the procedure pointed to by item n of the menu pointed to by item m of the array of menu pointers at menuarray. The function will be passed the item number of the menu itself as an argument. It might be argued that a menu item should know what it's intended to do without this—and most functions can ignore this argument—but in cases where menus are generated by an application on the fly (such as with the Font menu of Desktop Paint), it's often handy to have a single function for multiple items that will base its actions on which item was selected.

The doMenu function is one of the few bits of code in the graphical user interface that uses function pointers. You might take comfort in this if the idea of calling code not really there based on a pointer that moves around and points to something that might or might not exist troubles you in some way.

Keyboard alternatives to menu items

Pulling down menus is a very easy way to work a program—if you can remember where the menu bar is, you're most of the way there—but it's not very fast. After a while, most people find they'd like to be able to run things from the keyboard. To this end, you should include keyboard alternatives for at least the most commonly used menu items. The way these are expressed in a menu item was discussed earlier in this chapter.

Handling keyboard alternatives for menu items involves modifying the main loop of the program in Fig. 4-10 by adding a new function, dispatchMenuItem, like this:

```
do {
    dispatchMenuItem( );
    if(MouseDown(&thePoint)) {
        rt = whereMouse(&thePoint,&screenwindow);
        if(rt & inMenuBar) doMenu(&thePoint);
        else errorbeep( );
    }
} while(alive);
```

The dispatchMenuItem function watches the keyboard buffer. If it finds an alternate key combination therein, it attempts to find a menu item corresponding to it and dispatch it, using much the same process as doMenu did.

This is complicated somewhat by the nature of the alternate keys on a PC keyboard. While it's frequently convenient to treat key presses as bytes, the PC stores them in its keyboard buffer as words (i.e., two-byte objects). If you hit the letter A on your keyboard, the value that will appear in the keyboard buffer will be the ASCII code for A—65—in the lower byte of the key code and nothing of any importance in the upper byte. If you hit A with the Alt key held down, the lower byte will be zero, indicating that this word represents an alternate key. The upper byte will be 30.

This would make perfect sense if you'd been working for IBM in the early eighties.

When you hit an alternate key combination, the keyboard doesn't return a value that has any relationship to the ASCII code of what would have been if the Alt key had not been held down. Instead, it returns a *scan code*. Scan codes represent the physical position of the key in question on the keyboard. To make matters a bit more confusing, they represent the key positions on the keyboard of an old style IBM-PC. Many of them may be a bit meaningless in this respect if you have a newer keyboard with the keys arranged differently. Fortunately, they are consistent.

Figure 4-13 is a list of the alphabetic alternate key codes.

```
#define ALT_Q          0x1000
#define ALT_W          0x1100
#define ALT_E          0x1200
#define ALT_R          0x1300
#define ALT_T          0x1400
#define ALT_Y          0x1500
#define ALT_U          0x1600
#define ALT_I          0x1700
#define ALT_O          0x1800
#define ALT_P          0x1900

#define ALT_A          0x1E00
#define ALT_S          0x1F00
#define ALT_D          0x2000
#define ALT_F          0x2100
#define ALT_G          0x2200
#define ALT_H          0x2300
#define ALT_J          0x2400
#define ALT_K          0x2500
#define ALT_L          0x2600

#define ALT_Z          0x2C00
#define ALT_X          0x2D00
#define ALT_C          0x2E00
#define ALT_V          0x2F00
#define ALT_B          0x3000
#define ALT_N          0x3100
#define ALT_M          0x3200

#define ALT_1          0x7800
#define ALT_2          0x7900
#define ALT_3          0x7a00
#define ALT_4          0x7b00
#define ALT_5          0x7c00
#define ALT_6          0x7d00
#define ALT_7          0x7e00
#define ALT_8          0x7f00
#define ALT_9          0x8000
#define ALT_0          0x8100
```

4-13   The alternate key codes.

The modern typewriter—an oxymoron if there ever was one—was invented by Christopher Latham Sholes in 1867. It was initially built by the Remington Manufacturing Company, which at the time was heavily into sewing machines. The combination of these two technologies appears to have resulted in the QWERTY keyboard. The keys were laid out in a format easy to design the typewriter mechanism around, as opposed to a logical order for typists.

The keyboard alternatives in the menu strings are indicated by real alphabetic characters, not obscure scan codes. As such, the menu manager will need a way to derive the ASCII value corresponding to the scan code of an alternate key combination. As no logical relationship exists between the layout of a keyboard and the ASCII codes representing the alphabetic characters, the menu manager will need a lookup table to associate the alternate key scan codes with the alphabetic characters found in the menu item strings. This is what it looks like, based on the alternate key definitions from Fig. 4-13:

```
unsigned int altkeytable[ ] = {
    ALT_Q,'Q',ALT_W,'W',ALT_E,'E',ALT_R,'R',
    ALT_T,'T',ALT_Y,'Y',ALT_U,'U',ALT_I,'I',
    ALT_O,'O',ALT_P,'P',ALT_A,'A',ALT_S,'S',
    ALT_D,'D',ALT_F,'F',ALT_G,'G',ALT_H,'H',
    ALT_J,'J',ALT_K,'K',ALT_L,'L',ALT_Z,'Z',
    ALT_X,'X',ALT_C,'C',ALT_V,'V',ALT_B,'B',
    ALT_N,'N',ALT_M,'M',ALT_1,'1',ALT_2,'2',
    ALT_3,'3',ALT_4,'4',ALT_5,'5',ALT_6,'6',
    ALT_7,'7',ALT_8,'8',ALT_9,'9',ALT_0,'0',
    0xffff
        };
```

At this point, the general function of the dispatchMenuItem function will probably be pretty evident. Each time it's called in the main loop of your program, it checks to see if there's a key waiting in the keyboard buffer. If there is, it peeks at the key to see if it's an extended key scan code of some sort. This is fairly easy to do—the Turbo C bioskey function provides a way to look at the next keypress without actually fetching it from the buffer; and if the value returned by bioskey(1) has zero in its low order byte, the pending key is an extended key of some sort.

Having found an extended scan code, the dispatchMenuFunction can find its corresponding ASCII character by comparing it to each odd numbered entry in the altkeytable array until it either finds one that matches or finds 0xffff in the table, indicating that no match can be found. This latter case would happen if the key was, for example, a function key.

Once it knows what alphabetic character it's looking for, the dispatchMenuItem will look through each name element of every MENUITEM object in every MENU object in the menuarray until it finds character four followed by the character code in question or until it runs out of menu items. Assuming it does find a corresponding menu item, it will call the appropriate proc element function pointer, just as doMenu does when a menu item is selected.

Figure 4-14 is the complete dispatchMenuItem function.

```
dispatchMenuItem()
{
    char *p;
    unsigned int c,ca=0,i=0,menu,item,rt=0;

    if(kbhit()) {
        if(!(bioskey(1) & 0x00ff)) {
            c=GetKey();
            while(altkeytable[i] != 0xffff) {
                if(altkeytable[i]==c) {
                    ca=altkeytable[i+1];
                    break;
                }
                i+=2;
            }
            if(!ca) return(0);

            for(menu=0;menu<menuindex;++menu) {
                if(rt) break;
                for(item=0;item<menuarray[menu]->count;++item) {
                    if(rt) break;
                    if((p=strchr(menuarray[menu]->item[item].name,
                        KEYMENUCHAR)) != NULL) {
                        if(ca==(unsigned int)p[1]) {
                            (menuarray[menu]->item[item].proc)(item);
                            rt=1;
                        }
                    }
                }
            }
        }
    }
}
```

4-14 The dispatchMenuItem function.

Some menu enhancements

One of the design objectives of the graphical user interface in this book was to keep it reasonably simple. The menus, for example, simply appear and vanish, dispatch their functions, and rarely participate in any collective bargaining or deep philosophical thought.

One of the many corollaries to Murphy's laws of computers reads "If it isn't broken, don't fix it." This is in direct contradiction to an important law of software marketing, which reads "If it isn't broken, no one will buy the fix." To this end, the people who market software are forever leaning on the people writing it to discover broken things—or, in the absence of genuine breaks, just to discover something that could have been fixed had it been broken, if only the authors of the original version of the software had possessed sufficient forethought to do so.

Menu architecture is a good example of fixing something that isn't broken in the interest of making it more "feature rich" (i.e., more likely to be regarded as a new package and reviewed in a computer magazine). Simple pull-down menus have been enhanced considerably. For example, the pull-down menus discussed in this chapter have been implemented as drop-down menus in some applications. In a program with drop-down menus, once it appears, a menu stays visible without the need for one's mouse button to be continually depressed.

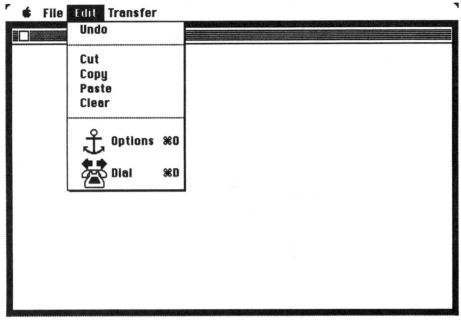

4-15A Macintosh Edit menu with icon items.

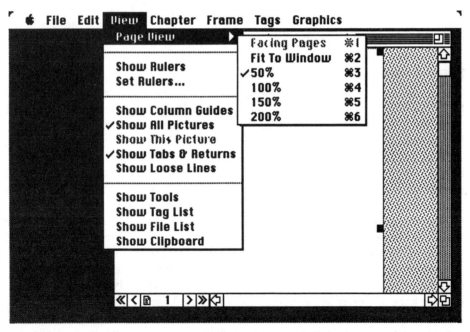

4-15B Macintosh View menu with subsidiary menus.

Several applications, such as Ventura Publisher for GEM, have appeared offering both sorts of menus.

The Macintosh has more and weirder menu enhancements than do most PC applications. Two of the most visible are subsidiary menus and menu items with icons, illustrated in Figs. 4-15A and B.

Subsidiary menus are menus appearing to the right of some conventional menu items, such that secondary options relevant to that item can be selected without the use of a dialog box. Subsidiary menus can have sub-subsidiary menus of their own, and so on, until the menus fall off the right edge of your screen and tumble into oblivion. Figure 4-16 illustrates how the Print item of Desktop Paint works now and how it could have been handled with subsidiary menus if this graphical user interface had offered them—which it doesn't.

4-16 A hypothetical subsidiary menu.

Subsidiary menus increase the demand for mouse dexterity considerably.

Menu items with icons are almost wholly decorative unless you envision a large body of users who are either illiterate or don't speak any English. In the latter case, a foreign language version of your program might be more appropriate, as icons rarely seem to work very well as interlinguistic symbols.

Once you have the graphical user interface working in its present form, you might want to consider implementing some of these enhancements to the menu manager. They're all within the capabilities of the interface as it stands with only nominal tinkering.

The first rule of Ventura Publisher: you will always have to install Ventura Publisher at least one time more than you anticipated even if you take into account the first rule of Ventura Publisher.

5

Adding controls

SO FAR IN THE EVOLUTION OF THE GRAPHICAL USER INTERFACE, THE code has been fairly simple because the graphical elements have all behaved in a predictable manner. There was little need for functions that would respond to mouse clicks in random places about the screen, as all the phenomena that might get clicked in—the menu bar and its menus—could be expected to remain *in situ* without any tendency to walk about.

With the addition of true controls to the library, this will change. Controls can appear anywhere you see fit to put them, and the ability to deal with them in an organized and sensible manner is really what makes a graphical user interface work— or fail to.

It's fairly simple, for example, to draw one button on the screen and wait for it to be clicked in. The graphics are pedestrian and the code to see if a mouse has been clicked in a rectangle—the PointInRect function previously discussed—is hardy worth discussing.

Consider the code to deal with an array of twenty-eight buttons. If this doesn't seem daunting enough, add a few of the other controls mentioned in Chapter 1. If you write custom code to handle each of these controls, the function to manage them all will be huge.

Clearly, controls can't merely be approached as screen graphics. Just as windows and menus have been treated as objects, so must controls be handled, lest the user interface of your program swell to dimensions excluding many functional parts of it from memory.

The advantage of handling controls as objects is that you must only write the handling code once—it can live in the GUI.LIB library—and thereafter the external code required to manage any particular type of control will be simple (a half-dozen lines in C will usually be sufficient).

Adding buttons

Buttons are the simplest sort of controls under the graphical user interface, both in appearance and in construction. A button consists of a rectangular area and has two sets of states. First, a button can be active or inactive. Then, if it's active, it can either be clicked or not clicked. The clicked state is exceedingly temporary—it only lasts for as long as the mouse is held down in the button in question.

Figure 5-1 illustrates a button in its various states.

5-1 The states of a button control.

A button is defined as a data structure, not surprisingly called BUTTON. Here it is:

```
typedef struct {
    OBJECTHEAD head;
    RECT frame;
    char *text;
    unsigned int active;
    } BUTTON;
```

This simplest of controls also has a fairly simple data structure defining it. The OBJECTHEAD element has been discussed at length previously. The frame element defines the area that the button will occupy. This has several uses, not the least of which is in knowing where a mouse click has taken place. You can check to see if it's in a particular button by using the Point In Rect function with the POINT returned by MouseDown and the RECT that defines the button's frame.

The text element is a pointer to the text that will appear in the button. Note that this is a pointer, not an actual buffer. Controls never contain any substantial amount of storage, although many include pointers to other storage areas. This could be a bit cumbersome in theory—in practice, as you'll see, the various static storage options of C make it pretty painless.

The active element is a flag defining the state of the button. This could, of course, have been defined as a char, saving a byte. In fact, the value loaded into it will be one of the ACTIVE or INACTIVE constants defined previously, which must be integers; making the active element of a control hold the actual constant, rather than just a flag, simplifies the code that will actually draw the control.

A set of routines handles the management of buttons. You'll find that these functions are reflected in each of the other types of controls that will be used in the graphical user interface. This is the list for a button:

addButton	Adds a new button to a window.
drawButton	Draws a previously added button.
findButton	Finds a particular selected button.
trackButton	Handles the selection of a button.

The scroll bar controls, which are a bit more complex, have slight variations on this pattern. The rest of the controls have equivalent sets of functions. Hence, for dealing with check boxes, you would use addCheckbox, drawCheckbox, and so on.

If you've worked with other graphical user interfaces at the programming level—and particularly if you've done any programming for the Macintosh—you might wonder why there's no function for disposing buttons. As you'll see throughout this chapter, no provision is made for dispensing with controls under this graphical user interface because none is required. None of the controls allocate any dynamic storage for themselves—their data structures live on the stack. As such, once a function is done with its window and controls, it can simply close the window and throw the controls away. Closing the window will erase all the control graphics, and the control data structures will simply cease to exist. In any case, only the window will have known where they were.

You should also note that there's a distinction between adding a control to a window and making it visible (i.e., drawing it). The first procedure really only involves loading the appropriate fields of the control's data object—a BUTTON struct in this case—with the appropriate values and then adding it to the linked list of the window in question. Adding an object to a window's linked list involves walking up the list until a NULL pointer in one of the OBJECTHEAD elements is found, changing this pointer to point to the OBJECTHEAD of the new control being added, and changing its OBJECTHEAD next pointer, in turn, to point to NULL, indicating the end of the list.

Figure 5-2 illustrates a simple dialog. At the moment, it only consists of a window with a button in the lower left corner that says "Ok." When you click in the button, the window will close.

5-2   A simple dialog.

The code creating the window in Fig. 5-2 is pretty simple—at least, the part of it existing outside the GUI.LIB library is (see Fig. 5-3). This is a pretty standard skeletal template for a dialog.

The first function in Fig. 5-3 not yet discussed in detail is addButton. While you might not know exactly what happens in addButton, you can probably make a

```
simpleDialog(s)
        char *s;
{
        BUTTON ok,*bp;
        WINDOW w;
        RECT r;
        POINT p;
        unsigned int rt,a=0xff;

        SetRect(&r,48,48,348,348);

        arrowCursor();
        if(OpenWindow(&w,&r)) {

                SetRect(&ok.frame,r.right-40,r.bottom-23,r.right-8,r.bottom-8);
                AddButton(&w,&ok,"Ok",ACTIVE);

                while(a) {
                        Keyboard(&w);
                        if(MouseDown(&p)) {
                                rt=whereMouse(&p,&w);
                                if(rt & inButton) {
                                        bp=findButton(&w,&p);
                                        trackButton(bp);
                                        if(bp==&ok)  a=0;
                                } else errorbeep();
                        }
                }
                CloseWindow(&w);
        } else errorbeep();
}
```

5-3 The code for the dialog in Fig. 5-2.

pretty reasonable guess based on its parameters. The calling syntax for addButton
is as follows:

    addButton(w,b,tx,active);

The w argument is a pointer to the window to which the button is to be added.
The b argument is a pointer to the BUTTON struct that will define this button.
The tx argument is a pointer to the text to be installed in the button. The active
argument is the state flag.

You should note how C stores things like the text "Ok" in the call to addButton
in Fig. 5-3. You could handle this explicitly by declaring it as static and then passing a pointer to it:

    static char ok[ ] = "Ok";

    addButton(&w,&b,ok,ACTIVE);

However, the following line also works, and with somewhat less typing. In this
case, C stores the string "Ok" as a static buffer as well (after all, the data has to go
somewhere):

    addButton(&w,&b, "Ok",ACTIVE);

In a complex program, this can result in having multiple copies of the same
string in static storage, as things like the string "Ok" will be used in many dialog

boxes. This doesn't actually result in all that many redundant bytes, but you might want to define global strings for any text that will be used in multiple places. Alternately, you can instruct Turbo C to merge the duplicate strings, although this can cause some side effects if you're not careful.

The addButton function assumes that the BUTTON argument passed to it will have its frame element properly initialized before the call to addButton is made. As such, a call to addButton will usually be preceded by a call to SetRect.

Figure 5-4 is the complete code for addButton.

```
addButton(w,b,tx,active)
        WINDOW *w;
        BUTTON *b;
        char *tx;
        int active;
{
        OBJECTHEAD *oh;
        /* start by finding end of chain */
        oh=(OBJECTHEAD *)w;
        while(oh->next != NULL) oh=oh->next;

        oh->next=(OBJECTHEAD *)b;
        b->text=tx;
        b->active=active;
        b->head.type=inButton;
        b->head.next=NULL;
        b->frame.left &= 0xfff8;
        b->frame.right &= 0xfff8;
        drawButton(b);
}
```

5-4 The addButton function.

A number of things happening in addButton might be a bit mysterious. The first might be the juggling with the OBJECTHEAD next pointer at the top of the function. This is a very compact way of finding the end of the linked list of a window. It casts the window pointer to an OBJECTHEAD pointer (this is safe, as the definition for a WINDOW object starts with an OBJECTHEAD element). It then walks its way up the list by repeatedly assigning the OBJECTHEAD pointer the value of its own next element until the pointer finds itself pointing to NULL.

Both the BUTTON object passed to addButton and the WINDOW object to which it will be added consist of some fixed storage somewhere, in most cases on the stack. Subsequent controls will be allocated similarly, and walking the linked list will usually involve moving around exclusively in the stack segment. There's no reason why you can't dynamically allocate controls, of course—you might want to do this if you create a dialog with a large or variable number of controls.

The syntax for allocating a BUTTON with malloc is as follows:

```
BUTTON *b;

if(((char *)b = malloc(sizeof(BUTTON)) = = NULL)
/* there's a problem */
else {
    SetRect(b,10,10,74,33);
    addButton(w,b, "Cancel",ACTIVE);
    ...
}
```

If you do this, make sure you remember to free all your dynamically allocated controls when you're done with them.

The values loaded into the frame element of a button bear a bit of consideration, both in how you derive them and what they actually turn out to be. This can both save you much retyping (if you later want to modify the sizes of dialogs you create) and also give your programs a consistent feel. None of the following is essential, however, and you can ignore it as you see fit.

As you develop a complex application with the graphical user interface, you'll probably find that you modify the sizes and locations of your dialog boxes—and hence, reposition their controls—quite frequently. As such, when you specify the location of a control, it's much more practical to do so relative to the window it will be added to, rather than in absolute screen coordinates. Back in Fig. 5-3, the button control's frame was specified as offsets from the bottom right corner of the window. If you change the location of the window, the location of the button will also change without your having to alter the code around it.

In most simple dialogs, buttons will be near the bottom of the window—they're tied to the lower right corner, while other controls are defined relative to the upper left. If you must make a dialog deeper to accommodate more elements, the buttons at the bottom will automatically move down too.

A button should be eight pixels wide for each character of text it will contain plus sixteen pixels—eight on either side of the text—to keep the text from looking too cramped within it. Because text can only be printed on even eight pixel boundaries, the horizontal coordinates of a button will be adjusted to eight pixel boundaries as well. The lines of addButton in Fig. 5-4 that handle this are as follows.

```
b->frame.left &= 0xfff8;
b->frame.right &= 0xfff8;
```

You can establish any offset from the lower right corner of your dialogs you like for button controls, although it's a good idea to choose one and stick with it. I place the lower right corner of the rightmost button eight pixels above and eight pixels to the left of the window corner and have the buttons twenty-three pixels high. I leave sixteen pixels between buttons. I'd set up two buttons in the dialog, with the BUTTON objects being called ok and can, and the WINDOW object named w:

```
SetRect(&ok.frame,r.right-40,r.bottom-23,r.right-8,r.bottom-8);
AddButton(&w,&ok, "Ok",ACTIVE);

SetRect(&can.frame,r.right-120,r.bottom-23,r.right-56,r.bottom-8);
AddButton(&w,&can, "Cancel",ACTIVE);
```

The addButton sets up the BUTTON object passed to it and then calls drawButton, which actually makes the button visible. In some of the more complex controls, you might have cause to call the draw functions explicitly—this would probably only happen with drawButton if you wanted to change the text of a button while it was visible.

The drawButton function draws a button by filling its frame area with white—usually unnecessary—and then outlining it with a thick black line. The rectangle function of the Turbo C graphics library is inconsistent when confronted with thick lines in that it leaves one pixel off at each of the corners. This serves to give the corners of buttons the appearance of being rounded, which is quite attractive.

Note that the mouse cursor must be shut off while the button is drawn.

Figure 5-5 shows the code for drawButton.

```
drawButton(b)
        BUTTON *b;
{
        MouseOff();
        setwritemode(COPY_PUT);
        setfillstyle(SOLID_FILL,getmaxcolor());
        setlinestyle(SOLID_LINE,0,THICK_WIDTH);
        setcolor(BLACK);
        bar(b->frame.left,b->frame.top,b->frame.right,b->frame.bottom);
        rectangle(b->frame.left,b->frame.top,b->frame.right,b->frame.bottom);

        DrawString(b->frame.left+8,b->frame.top+4,b->text,b->active);
        MouseOn();
}
```

5-5 The drawButton function.

Once you have the complete graphical user interface working, you might want to return and customize the draw functions of the various controls—drawButton being one of the most obvious potential victims. If you change the way buttons are drawn, all the buttons in all your applications will change the next time you compile them. Figure 5-6 illustrates an alternate style of buttons reminiscent of the three-dimensional buttons popular in Windows at the moment.

5-6 Some alternate buttons.

Aside from requiring more code to draw, three-dimensional buttons aren't really as effective in monochrome as they are when you have several shades of grey to work with (as in the Windows 3 button implementation).

The principal loop of a dialog such as the one in Fig. 5-3 calls whereMouse each time a mouse click is encountered. The whereMouse function (as mentioned previously) returns a constant based on the type of control or other area the mouse click occurred in. As such, in the simple single button dialog discussed thus far, having whereMouse return the inButton constant would really be enough to figure out what has been clicked. This wouldn't be the case in a dialog containing two buttons.

To deal properly with an instance in which whereMouse returns the inButton constant, you can call findButton. The findButton function will return a pointer to the actual BUTTON structure defining the button that has been clicked in.

In a complex dialog, then, the constant returned by whereMouse is used to define which class of dialogs is involved, and hence which of the find functions to call to further narrow things down to a specific dialog.

If the pointer returned by findButton is bp, you would use this piece of code to see if it indicates the BUTTON control ok:

```
if(bp = = &ok) {
    /* handle the click in ok */
}
```

This is an example of one of the less obvious sorts of syntax the C language's dogmatic pointer and address notation imposes on programmers.

Figure 5-7 illustrates the code for findButton.

```
BUTTON *findButton(w,p)
        WINDOW *w;
        POINT *p;
{
        OBJECTHEAD *oh;
        BUTTON *b;

        oh=(OBJECTHEAD *)w;
        while(oh != NULL) {
                if(oh->type == inButton) {
                        b=(BUTTON *)oh;
                        if(PointInRect(p,&b->frame) && b->active==ACTIVE)
                                return(b);
                }
                oh=oh->next;
        }
        return(NULL);
}
```

5-7   The findButton function.

The findButton function has elements that you'll probably find at least slightly familiar. It works by walking up the linked list of the window that owns the controls in question and looking for objects of the type BUTTON. When it finds one, it checks to see if the mouse click in its POINT argument is located within the frame element of the button it has found. If the click is within the frame element, findButton shouts "eureka" and returns a pointer to the button. If the click isn't, findButton carries on up the linked list.

FindButton should never fail to find a button, thus returning NULL—unless you call it improperly.

After findButton finds a control that has been clicked in, the control must be tracked. Tracking a control can mean different things to different controls. In the case of a button control, it simply indicates to whoever owns the hand clicking the mouse in question that the software has, in fact, recognized the click. A button control is tracked by inverting the area defined by its frame element.

Figure 5-8 is the code for trackButton.

If you elect to implement a more interesting button design—such as the three-dimensional buttons discussed earlier—you will probably also want to change how buttons are tracked. Three-dimensional buttons are usually tracked by redrawing them to look as if they have been pressed.

As an aside, when I created a 256-color version of the graphical user interface to handle a full color implementation of Desktop Paint, I decided to give it three-

```
trackButton(b)
        BUTTON *b;
{
        POINT p;

        if(b != NULL && b->head.type==inButton && b->active==ACTIVE) {
                InvertRect(&b->frame);
                while(MouseDown(&p));
                InvertRect(&b->frame);
        } else errorbeep();
}
```

5-8 The trackButton function.

dimensional buttons—all the colors were handy, and the effect looked very contemporary. Users of the software frequently comment on this—at least, most of them do. A few of them curse over it. Because 256-color graphics are fairly processor-intensive to begin with, running the software on a really low-end AT or an old XT system means that every button is laboriously drawn each time a dialog appeared. The appeal of the three-dimensional buttons is lost on anyone who must wait for them to appear.

In fact, the full-color paint program itself is so processor-intensive as to make it impractical to run on low-end equipment, the nature of its buttons notwithstanding. The buttons quickly ceased to be an issue. However, you should probably consider this even if you're only concerned with a monochrome graphical user interface, and especially if you write code on a fast, high-end 386 system. If you'll be creating dialogs with many controls, having them fast and simple might not look quite as slick as having them graced with all the affectations that, for example, Windows 3 exhibits. It will probably make them much more usable, however, especially for users owning slower computers.

One infrequently used feature of most high-end systems is the speed compatibility switch. If you have a fast 386 system, you can probably slow it down to the effective speed of a slow AT by hitting an alternate key combination—it's Ctrl-Alt-Backslash on mine. If you embellish the controls in the graphical user interface, you might want to run your program either on a slower machine or with your system in its slower mode to get a good feel for what your application will be like to use.

Figure 5-9 illustrates some of the contentious three-dimensional buttons from the full color version of Desktop Paint.

5-9 Some contentious three-dimensional buttons.

Adding checkboxes

Checkboxes are similar in operation to buttons except that their selected state isn't quite as transitory. A checkbox can be thought of as a toggle; it changes state from being select or unselected each time it's clicked in. Figure 5-10 illustrates some checkboxes in use.

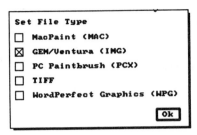

5-10 A dialog with some checkboxes.

Note that a checkbox always has text associated with it. The text to the left of the actual box is part of the checkbox object.

Checkboxes can appear singularly or in exclusive groups. A single checkbox can be clicked to select or unselect its option. An exclusive group of checkboxes is set up such that only one item in the group can be selected, and selecting a previously unselected item in the group will automatically unselect the currently selected one.

As an aside, the Macintosh differentiates between individual check boxes and exclusive groups of them by calling the latter objects *radio buttons* and drawing them differently. The term "radio buttons" is drawn from the operation of the station selector buttons on a car radio. Figure 5-11 illustrates check boxes and radio buttons on a Macintosh.

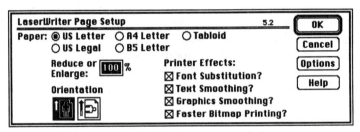

5-11 Macintosh checkboxes and radio buttons.

The rationale for this distinction on the Mac is that individual checkboxes behave slightly differently than do exclusive groups of boxes and thus there should be some visual distinction between them. You might find that you agree with this and want to modify the graphical user interface to include a radio button class of controls as well. On the other hand, one could argue that for most applications, a user can discern the operation of checkboxes from their context.

The CHECKBOX data structure looks like this:

```
typedef struct {
    OBJECTHEAD head;
    int x,y;
    RECT frame;
    unsigned int active;
```

```
        char *text;
        char select;
      } CHECKBOX;
```

Most of the fields in a CHECKBOX object will be pretty easy to understand. The x and y fields specify the actual location of the checkbox in question for this type of control. The frame element is filled in the the addCheckbox function, as are all checkboxes of the same size. The frame element encloses only the checkbox itself, not the text associated with it.

The addCheckbox function is shown in Figure 5-12. You can specify the initial state of a checkbox as being either selected or unselected. You would pass 0x00 as the select argument if it was to be drawn initially unselected and 0xff to have it drawn selected.

```
addCheckbox(w,cb,x,y,text,select,active)   /* add a checkbox object to the window */
        WINDOW *w;                /* the window */
        CHECKBOX *cb;             /* the checkbox */
        int x,y;                  /* the upper left corner */
        char *text;               /* the items */
        int select;              /* true if selected */
        int active;              /* active */
{
        OBJECTHEAD *oh;
        /* start by finding end of chain */

        oh=(OBJECTHEAD *)w;
        while(oh->next != NULL) oh=oh->next;

        oh->next=(OBJECTHEAD *)cb;

        cb->x=x;
        cb->y=y;
        cb->text=text;
        cb->select=select;
        cb->active=active;
        cb->frame.left=x-1;
        cb->frame.top=y-1;
        cb->frame.right=x+10;
        cb->frame.bottom=y+10;
        cb->head.type=inCheckBox;
        cb->head.next=NULL;
        drawCheckbox(cb);
}
```

5-12   The addCheckbox function.

Unlike as in the case of button controls, you will probably have cause to directly call drawCheckbox yourself. While it's called by addCheckbox initially, it must be called by you any time you subsequently want to change the state of a checkbox. Specifically, if a mouse click appears in a checkbox—as deduced by whereMouse—you must find out which checkbox has been clicked, toggle its state, and then redraw it.

Figure 5-13 is the code for drawCheckbox. The graphics are fairly pedestrian. A check box consists of a rectangle with a cross drawn through it if the checkbox is selected (i.e., if the select field of the checkbox pointer passed to drawCheckbox is true).

Just as with button controls, when whereMouse returns a value indicating that a checkbox has been clicked in, you must first find the control in question and then track it. The findCheckbox function (see Fig. 5-14) works exactly like findButton, except that it deals with CHECKBOX pointers.

The trackCheckbox function, shown in Fig. 5-15, behaves much like trackButton did except that it again wants to work with CHECKBOX objects. It inverts the

```
drawCheckbox(cb)
      CHECKBOX *cb;
{
      MouseOff();
      setwritemode(COPY_PUT);
      setfillstyle(SOLID_FILL,getmaxcolor());
      setlinestyle(SOLID_LINE,0,NORM_WIDTH);
      setcolor(BLACK);
      bar(cb->frame.left,cb->frame.top,cb->frame.right,cb->frame.bottom);
      rectangle(cb->frame.left,cb->frame.top,cb->frame.right,cb->frame.bottom);
      DrawString(cb->frame.right+16,cb->frame.top+2,cb->text,cb->active);
      if(cb->select) {
             line(cb->frame.left,cb->frame.top,cb->frame.right,cb->frame.bottom);
             line(cb->frame.left,cb->frame.bottom,cb->frame.right,cb->frame.top);
      }
      MouseOn();
}
```

5-13 The drawCheckbox function.

```
CHECKBOX *findCheckbox(w,p)          /* return a pointer to the selected checkbox */
      WINDOW *w;
      POINT *p;
{
      OBJECTHEAD *oh;
      CHECKBOX *cb;

      oh=(OBJECTHEAD *)w;
      while(oh != NULL) {
             if(oh->type == inCheckBox) {
                    cb=(CHECKBOX *)oh;
                    if(PointInRect(p,&cb->frame) && cb->active==ACTIVE) return(cb);
             }
             oh=oh->next;
      }
      return(NULL);
}
```

5-14 The findCheckbox function.

```
trackCheckbox(cb)
      CHECKBOX *cb;
{
      POINT p;

      MouseLoc(&p);
      if(PointInRect(&p,&cb->frame)) {
             InvertRect(&cb->frame);
             while(MouseDown(&p));
             InvertRect(&cb->frame);
      }
}
```

5-15 The trackCheckbox function.

checkbox being tracked for as long as the mouse is held down, providing whoever clicked it with a visual indication that something has happened. Note that track

120 *Adding controls*

Checkbox doesn't toggle the state of a checkbox—the code supporting it must do this explicitly.

You should note that, while several checkboxes might appear as an exclusive group to the users of an application, the graphical user interface regards all checkboxes as being single, unrelated objects. Thus, if you want to manage several checkboxes as an exclusive group, you must write code to track them as such.

The simplest application of a checkbox can be seen in Fig. 5-16. It's a dialog with one checkbox and one button (you need the button to exit from the dialog).

5-16 A simple dialog with a checkbox.

Figure 5-17 is the code for the function that generated Fig. 5-16. It resembles the code in Fig. 5-3 except that it has acquired a call to addCheckbox and some code in its main loop to deal with the possibility of whereMouse returning a value with the inCheckBox flag set.

```
simpleDialog(s)
        char *s;
{
        BUTTON ok,*bp;
        CHECKBOX cb,*cp;
        WINDOW w;
        RECT r;
        POINT p;
        unsigned int rt,a=0xff;

        SetRect(&r,48,48,348,348);

        arrowCursor();
        if(OpenWindow(&w,&r)) {

                SetRect(&ok.frame,r.right-40,r.bottom-23,r.right-8,r.bottom-8);
                AddButton(&w,&ok,"Ok",ACTIVE);

                AddCheckbox(&w,&cb,r.left+8,r.top+20,"Click me!",0x00,ACTIVE);

                while(a) {
                        Keyboard(&w);
                        if(MouseDown(&p)) {
                                rt=whereMouse(&p,&w);
                                if(rt & inButton) {
                                        bp=findButton(&w,&p);
                                        trackButton(bp);
                                        if(bp==&ok)  a=0;
                                }
                                else if(rt & inCheckBox) {
                                        cp=findCheckbox(&w,&p);
                                        trackCheckbox(cp);
                                        if(cp==&cb) {
                                                if(cp->select) cp->select=0x00;
```

5-17 The code that produced Fig. 5-16.

```
                                        else cp->select=0xff;
                                        drawCheckbox(cp);
                                }
                        } else errorbeep();
                }
        }
        CloseWindow(&w);
} else errorbeep();
}
```

As with the simple one-button dialog, a dialog containing only one checkbox can arguably do without a call to findCheckbox. If whereMouse returns a value indicating that a checkbox has been clicked in and there's only one checkbox in your dialog, the odds are pretty good that you can identify the checkbox in question with no further deliberations. However, the code in Fig. 5-17 includes a call to findCheckbox both because it serves as an example for dialogs having multiple checkboxes and because it's a good idea to do this even when you don't really think it's needed. Doing this will help you catch bugs in complex dialogs—if findCheckbox returns a pointer to something other than the one checkbox in your dialog, you'll know that something's amiss.

Figure 5-18 illustrates a dialog having multiple checkboxes arranged as an exclusive group. The code to handle this dialog is shown in Fig. 5-19.

5-18   A dialog with multiple checkboxes.

```
simpleDialog(s)
        char *s;
{
        BUTTON ok,*bp;
        CHECKBOX cb[2],*cp;
        WINDOW w;
        RECT r;
        POINT p;
        unsigned int rt,a=0xff;

        SetRect(&r,48,48,348,348);

        arrowCursor();
        if(OpenWindow(&w,&r)) {

                SetRect(&ok.frame,r.right-40,r.bottom-23,r.right-8,r.bottom-8);
                AddButton(&w,&ok,"Ok",ACTIVE);

                AddCheckbox(&w,&cb[0],r.left+8,r.top+20,
                    "Click me!",0x00,ACTIVE);
                AddCheckbox(&w,&cb[1],r.left+8,r.top+40,
                    "Click me too",0xff,ACTIVE);
```

5-19   The code to generate Fig. 5-18.

```
                    while(a) {
                            Keyboard(&w);
                            if(MouseDown(&p)) {
                                    rt=whereMouse(&p,&w);
                                    if(rt & inButton) {
                                            bp=findButton(&w,&p);
                                            trackButton(bp);
                                            if(bp==&ok) a=0;
                                    }
                                    else if(rt & inCheckBox) {
                                            cp=findCheckbox(&w,&p);
                                            trackCheckbox(cp);
                                            if(cp==&cb[0]) {
                                                    cb[0].select=0xff;
                                                    sb[1].select=0x00;
                                                    drawCheckbox(cb[0]);
                                                    drawCheckbox(cb[1]);
                                            }
                                            else if(cp==&cb[1]) {
                                                    cb[0].select=0x00;
                                                    sb[1].select=0xff;
                                                    drawCheckbox(cb[0]);
                                                    drawCheckbox(cb[1]);
                                            }
                                    } else errorbeep();
                            }
                    }
                    CloseWindow(&w);
            } else errorbeep();
    }
```

The dialog code in Fig. 5-19 and the earlier Fig. 5-17 differs in the addition of more calls to addCheckbox and of quite a bit more activity in the part of the big if statement sorting out the value returned by whereMouse. In this example, you must look through each of the checkboxes in the exclusive group to find the previously selected one and the one just clicked in, unselect the former and select the latter—in that order, just in case someone clicks in the currently selected checkbox—and then redraw both of them.

You could argue that this is an awful lot of code to support a few rather unexciting checkboxes and (more to the point) that a dialog having several groups of exclusive checkboxes would get positively elephantine. I can't argue with this. However, you could also claim that a dialog box having so many checkboxes as to demand unwieldy code probably has too many checkboxes to be easily understood by the users looking at it. By their nature, dialog boxes should be simple, small, and have single purposes.

Apparently, arguments about the zen of interface design are far more difficult to resolve than are things like how to locate one checkbox among many.

Adding scroll bars

Scroll bars are the nastiest and most temperamental of controls. They have more parts than all the other control types to be discussed in this book and require much more code to animate them. Scroll bars are also subject to what is probably the greatest degree of variation in the circles inhabited by designers of graphical user interfaces. Everyone seems to have a different idea as to exactly how a scroll bar should operate—derived in part by the environment in which they find themselves. Some things that are practical to do with monochrome scroll bars don't really work well with multiple color modes.

Figures 5-20A, B, and C illustrate some examples of scroll bars. The first two—image positioning scroll bars and the scroll on a file dialog—are fairly common ones. The third is a bit more esoteric and is in fact the palette override control drawn from the 256-color version of Desktop Paint. It's included here because it illustrates scroll bars used as a fairly comfortable desktop analogy: they simulate the slider controls used by some stereo equipment.

5-20A Applications of scroll bars—image positioning.

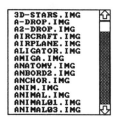

5-20B Applications of scroll bars—file listing.

124 *Adding controls*

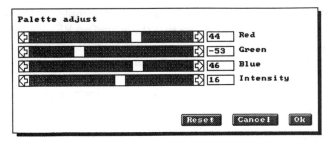

5-20C Applications of scroll bars—slider bars.

As was touched on in Chapter 1, scroll bars consist of five elements or "parts." Using the vertical scroll bar as the base example, there is an *up* arrow and a *down* arrow. The box in the center is called the *thumb*. The grey bit above the thumb is called the *jump up* zone, and the grey bit below the thumb is the *jump down* zone. If the thumb is at one of its extremes, one of the jump zones may be absent.

Inexperienced users of graphical user interfaces frequently refer to scroll bars as elevators, or (to make the analogy work in the case of horizontal scroll bars) as turbo-lifts.

In dealing with horizontal scroll bars, the left arrow will be referred to as the up arrow and the right arrow as the down arrow. However, to keep the code tracking scroll bars down to a manageable level of complexity, the graphical user interface differentiates between vertical and horizontal scroll bars as unique objects.

The dual function of the thumb makes handling scroll bars tricky. The thumb serves both as an indicator of the current setting of the scroll bar, and it also allows someone using your software to change the setting by dragging the thumb to a new location. If you like the analogy of a scroll bar being like the slider control on a stereo, you might want to expand it a bit and think of a scroll bar as being one of the servo-controlled sliders that are used in high-end computer-controlled audio mixing consoles. You can adjust the level of such a control either by physically moving the knob or by having the computer actuate its servo, in which case the knob will move by itself.

Having noted the generally finicky nature of the code to track scroll bars, I'll mention that none of it will be visible to code outside GUI.LIB. In fact, tracking a scroll bar control is pretty much the same as tracking a button or a checkbox as far as a dialog is concerned.

The data structure defining a scroll bar looks like this:

```
typedef struct {
    OBJECTHEAD head;
    int x,y;
    int size;
    RECT frame,uparr,dnarr,thumb,jump;
    unsigned int active;
    int min,max,cur;
    } SCROLLBAR;
```

The scroll bar structure resembles those of the simpler controls discussed in this chapter. However, you should note that there are five RECT elements, locating the various parts of a scroll bar. Note also that a scroll bar maintains three state values: min, max, and cur. The cur value contains a value between min and max representing the thumb position.

The function for adding a scroll bar to a window isn't much more complex than the earlier functions adding controls. However, you should remember that two functions exist—one for adding vertical scroll bars and one for horizontal scroll bars. Figure 5-21 illustrates the both sets of code.

```
addVertScroll(w,sb,x,y,len,min,max,cur,active)
        WINDOW *w;
        SCROLLBAR *sb;
        int x,y;
        int len;
        int min,max;
        int cur;
        int active;
{
        OBJECTHEAD *oh;
        /* start by finding end of chain */

        oh=(OBJECTHEAD *)w;
        while(oh->next != NULL) oh=oh->next;

        oh->next=(OBJECTHEAD *)sb;

        sb->x=x;
        sb->y=y;
        sb->size=len;
        sb->min=min;
        sb->max=max;
        sb->cur=cur;
        sb->active=active;
        sb->frame.left=x;
        sb->frame.top=y;
        sb->frame.right=x+15;
        sb->frame.bottom=y+len;
        SetRect(&sb->uparr,sb->frame.left,sb->frame.top,
            sb->frame.right,sb->frame.top+15);
        SetRect(&sb->dnarr,sb->frame.left,sb->frame.bottom-15,
            sb->frame.right,sb->frame.bottom);
        SetRect(&sb->thumb,sb->frame.left,sb->frame.top+16,
            sb->frame.right,sb->frame.top+32);
        SetRect(&sb->jump, sb->frame.left,sb->uparr.bottom,
            sb->frame.right,sb->dnarr.top);
        sb->head.type=inVertScroll;
        sb->head.next=NULL;
        drawVertScroll(sb);
}

addHorScroll(w,sb,x,y,len,min,max,cur,active)
        WINDOW *w;
        SCROLLBAR *sb;
        int x,y;
        int len;
        int min,max;
        int cur;
```

5-21 The functions to add scroll bars to a window.

```
            int active;
{
        OBJECTHEAD *oh;
        /* start by finding end of chain */

        oh=(OBJECTHEAD *)w;
        while(oh->next != NULL) oh=oh->next;

        oh->next=(OBJECTHEAD *)sb;
        sb->x=x;
        sb->y=y;
        sb->size=len;
        sb->min=min;
        sb->max=max;
        sb->cur=cur;
        sb->active=active;
        sb->frame.left=x;
        sb->frame.top=y;
        sb->frame.right=x+len;
        sb->frame.bottom=y+15;
        SetRect(&sb->uparr,sb->frame.left,sb->frame.top,
            sb->frame.left+15,sb->frame.bottom);
        SetRect(&sb->dnarr,sb->frame.right-15,sb->frame.top,
            sb->frame.right,sb->frame.bottom);
        SetRect(&sb->thumb,sb->frame.left+16,sb->frame.top,
            sb->frame.left+32,sb->frame.bottom);
        SetRect(&sb->jump, sb->uparr.right,sb->frame.top,
            sb->dnarr.left,sb->frame.bottom);
        sb->head.type=inHorScroll;
        sb->head.next=NULL;
        drawHorScroll(sb);
}
```

The arguments to the add functions for scroll bars should be pretty easy to follow if you keep in mind what a scroll bar looks like. As with check boxes, you need only specify the upper left corner of a scroll bar (because they're a fixed width). You must also specify the length of the scroll bar. The min argument should be the value you want the cur element of the corresponding SCROLLBAR object to be at when the thumb is at the top of the scroll bar (zero, in most cases). The max argument should be the value you want the cur element to be at when the thumb is at the bottom. Note that the difference between max and min need have nothing to do with the length of the scroll bar itself.

The active argument determines whether the scroll bar (when drawn) will be adjustable. Applications exist for inactive scroll bars (see Fig. 5-22 for an obvious one). If the file dialog contains enough file names to require the ability to scroll through them, the scroll bar will be active. If only a few file names are present, the scroll bar will be inactive.

Note that the appropriate add functions also set the RECT elements corresponding to the scroll bar parts being added.

Drawing a scroll bar is somewhat more involved than drawing the previous controls. The arrows (as well as the thumb) are actually handled as bitmaps rather than as line drawings, resulting in their being drawn considerably quicker. Figure 5-23 illustrates the drawing functions for vertical and horizontal scroll bars.

Bitmaps have not been discussed yet—they won't turn up until Chapter 7. You will probably recognize the Turbo C putimage function, but a complete explanation

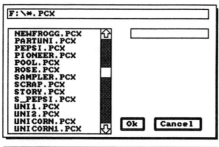

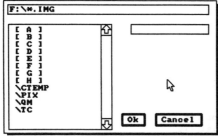

5-22 The Choose File dialog box with active and inactive scroll bars.

```
drawVertScroll(sb)
      SCROLLBAR *sb;
{
      static char uparrow[]={ 0x0f,0x00,0x0f,0x00,
              0x00,0x00,0x7E,0x7E,0x7D,0xBE,0x7B,0xDE,
              0x77,0xEE,0x6F,0xF6,0x5F,0xFA,0x03,0xC0,
              0x7B,0xDE,0x7B,0xDE,0x7B,0xDE,0x7B,0xDE,
              0x78,0x1E,0x7F,0xFE,0x7F,0xFE,0x00,0x00 };

      static char downarrow[]={ 0x0f,0x00,0x0f,0x00,
              0x00,0x00,0x7F,0xFE,0x7F,0xFE,0x78,0x1E,
              0x7B,0xDE,0x7B,0xDE,0x7B,0xDE,0x7B,0xDE,
              0x03,0xC0,0x5F,0xFA,0x6F,0xF6,0x77,0xEE,
              0x7B,0xDE,0x7D,0xBE,0x7E,0x7E,0x00,0x00 };

      char *p;

      MouseOff();
      if(sb->active==ACTIVE) setfillpattern(scrollbarfill,getmaxcolor());
      else setfillstyle(SOLID_FILL,getmaxcolor());

      setwritemode(COPY_PUT);
      setlinestyle(SOLID_LINE,0,NORM_WIDTH);
      setcolor(BLACK);
      bar(sb->frame.left,sb->frame.top,sb->frame.right,sb->frame.bottom);
      rectangle(sb->frame.left,sb->frame.top,sb->frame.right,sb->frame.bottom);

      if(ismonomode())
        putimage(sb->uparr.left,sb->uparr.top,uparrow,COPY_PUT);
      else {
              if((p=mono2ega(uparrow)) != NULL) {
                      putimage(sb->uparr.left,sb->uparr.top,p,COPY_PUT);
                      free(p);
              } else errorbeep();
      }
```

5-23 The scroll bar drawing functions.

```
        if(ismonomode())
          putimage(sb->dnarr.left,sb->dnarr.bottom-15,downarrow,COPY_PUT);
        else {
                if((p=mono2ega(downarrow)) != NULL) {
                        putimage(sb->dnarr.left,sb->dnarr.bottom-15,p,COPY_PUT);
                        free(p);
                } else errorbeep();
        }

        drawThumb(sb);

        MouseOn();
}

drawHorScroll(sb)
        SCROLLBAR *sb;
{
        static char leftarrow[]={ 0x0f,0x00,0x0f,0x00,
                0x00,0x00,0x7E,0x7E,0x7D,0x7E,0x7B,0x7E,
                0x77,0x7E,0x6F,0x06,0x5F,0xF6,0x3F,0xF6,
                0x3F,0xF6,0x5F,0xF6,0x6F,0x06,0x77,0x7E,
                0x7B,0x7E,0x7D,0x7E,0x7E,0x7E,0x00,0x00 };
        static char rightarrow[]={ 0x0f,0x00,0x0f,0x00,
                0x00,0x00,0x7E,0x7E,0x7E,0xBE,0x7E,0xDE,
                0x7E,0xEE,0x60,0xF6,0x6F,0xFA,0x6F,0xFC,
                0x6F,0xFC,0x6F,0xFA,0x60,0xF6,0x7E,0xEE,
                0x7E,0xDE,0x7E,0xBE,0x7E,0x7E,0x00,0x00 };

        char *p;


        MouseOff();
        if(sb->active==ACTIVE) setfillpattern(scrollbarfill,getmaxcolor());
        else setfillstyle(SOLID_FILL,getmaxcolor());

        setwritemode(COPY_PUT);
        setlinestyle(SOLID_LINE,0,NORM_WIDTH);
        setcolor(BLACK);
        bar(sb->frame.left,sb->frame.top,sb->frame.right,sb->frame.bottom);
        rectangle(sb->frame.left,sb->frame.top,sb->frame.right,sb->frame.bottom);

        if(ismonomode())
          putimage(sb->uparr.left,sb->uparr.top,leftarrow,COPY_PUT);
        else {
                if((p=mono2ega(leftarrow)) != NULL) {
                        putimage(sb->uparr.left,sb->uparr.top,p,COPY_PUT);
                        free(p);
                } else errorbeep();
        }

        if(ismonomode())
          putimage(sb->dnarr.left,sb->dnarr.bottom-15,rightarrow,COPY_PUT);
        else {
                if((p=mono2ega(rightarrow)) != NULL) {
                        putimage(sb->dnarr.left,sb->dnarr.bottom-15,p,COPY_PUT);
                        free(p);
                } else errorbeep();
        }

        drawThumb(sb);

        MouseOn();
}
```

of mono2ega's nature must wait for a while. Suffice it to say that putimage fragments bound for an EGA screen are structured differently than those for use with a monochrome screen. The static data at the top of each function is, in fact, the bitmaps for the two arrows in each scroll bar.

Each scroll bar draw function calls a common function—drawThumb—that, predictably, draws the thumb. There is also eraseThumb, which is called by the tracking functions to animate the thumb as it's dragged around. Drawing the thumb is handled, once again, with a bitmap.

It's very important that the thumb be drawn quickly, lest the time it takes to draw it makes the mouse appear unresponsive while a scroll bar thumb is selected. There really isn't time to use the mono2ega function that provides EGA style bitmaps of the arrow heads forming the ends of a scroll bar. As such, the drawThumb function contains static images of the thumb in both forms.

As an aside, you can change these to produce more interesting looking thumbs if you're very determined.

Erasing a thumb is a lot easier than drawing one. Because the background is always grey, the eraseThumb function must only paint a grey rectangle over the area occupied by the thumb.

Figure 5-24 illustrates the code to draw and erase scroll bar thumbs.

```
eraseThumb(sb)
        SCROLLBAR *sb;
{
        MouseOff();
        setcolor(BLACK);
        setfillpattern(scrollbarfill,getmaxcolor());
        if(sb->head.type==inVertScroll) bar(sb->thumb.left+1,
          sb->thumb.top,sb->thumb.right-1,sb->thumb.bottom-1);
        else bar(sb->thumb.left,sb->thumb.top+1,sb->thumb.right-1,
          sb->thumb.bottom-1);
        MouseOn();
}

/* internal routine - draw the scroll bar thumb */
drawThumb(sb)
        SCROLLBAR *sb;
{
        static char thumb2[]={ 0x0f,0x00,0x0f,0x00,
                0x00,0x00,0x7F,0xFE,0x7F,0xFE,0x7F,0xFE,
                0x7F,0xFE,0x7F,0xFE,0x7F,0xFE,0x7F,0xFE,
                0x7F,0xFE,0x7F,0xFE,0x7F,0xFE,0x7F,0xFE,
                0x7F,0xFE,0x7F,0xFE,0x7F,0xFE,0x00,0x00 };

        static char thumb16[]={ 0x0f,0x00,0x0f,0x00,
                0x00,0x00,0x00,0x00,0x00,0x00,0x00,0x00,
                0x7F,0xFE,0x7F,0xFE,0x7F,0xFE,0x7F,0xFE,
                0x7F,0xFE,0x7F,0xFE,0x7F,0xFE,0x7F,0xFE,
                0x7F,0xFE,0x7F,0xFE,0x7F,0xFE,0x7F,0xFE,
                0x7F,0xFE,0x7F,0xFE,0x7F,0xFE,0x7F,0xFE,
                0x7F,0xFE,0x7F,0xFE,0x7F,0xFE,0x7F,0xFE,
                0x7F,0xFE,0x7F,0xFE,0x7F,0xFE,0x7F,0xFE,
                0x7F,0xFE,0x7F,0xFE,0x7F,0xFE,0x7F,0xFE,
                0x7F,0xFE,0x7F,0xFE,0x7F,0xFE,0x7F,0xFE,
                0x7F,0xFE,0x7F,0xFE,0x7F,0xFE,0x7F,0xFE,
```

5-24 The scroll bar thumb functions.

```
                0x7F,0xFE,0x7F,0xFE,0x7F,0xFE,0x7F,0xFE,
                0x7F,0xFE,0x7F,0xFE,0x7F,0xFE,0x7F,0xFE,
                0x7F,0xFE,0x7F,0xFE,0x7F,0xFE,0x7F,0xFE,
                0x7F,0xFE,0x7F,0xFE,0x7F,0xFE,0x7F,0xFE,
                0x7F,0xFE,0x7F,0xFE,0x7F,0xFE,0x7F,0xFE,
                0x00,0x00,0x00,0x00,0x00,0x00,0x00,0x00  };

    if(sb->active==ACTIVE) {
        MouseOff();
        if(ismonomode()) putimage(sb->thumb.left,sb->thumb.top,
          thumb2,COPY_PUT);
        else putimage(sb->thumb.left,sb->thumb.top,thumb16,COPY_PUT);
        MouseOn();
    }
}
```

Finding a scroll bar is no more involved than would be finding any other sort of control (see Fig. 5-25 for the code). Its operation should be familiar by now—when it's called, it walks up the linked list of a window until it finds a scroll bar with a frame element enclosing the point passed to it and returns a pointer of the type SCROLLBAR.

```
SCROLLBAR *findScrollbar(w,p)
        WINDOW *w;
        POINT *p;
{
        OBJECTHEAD *oh;
        SCROLLBAR *b;

        oh=(OBJECTHEAD *)w;
        while(oh != NULL) {
                if(oh->type == inVertScroll || oh->type == inHorScroll) {
                        b=(SCROLLBAR *)oh;
                        if(PointInRect(p,&b->frame) && b->active==ACTIVE)
                            return(b);
                }
                oh=oh->next;
        }
        return(NULL);
}
```

5-25 The findScrollbar function.

The real complexity, however, lies with the code to track scroll bars. The track-Scrollbar function is responsible for doing the actual animation of the scroll bar parts. When whereMouse returns a value with either inVertScroll or inHorScroll set, it will also set a flag for the appropriate part of the scroll bar, telling trackScrollbar whether the click in question occurred in an arrow, a jump zone, or in the thumb. The part flags are inUpArrow, inDownArrow, inJumpUp, inJumpDown, and inThumb.

Most of trackScrollbar is fairly easy to follow. If a click occurs in an up arrow, for example, the cur value of the scroll bar in question is decremented if it isn't less than the min value, and then the thumb is redrawn. Clicking in a jump zone causes a jump of eight, assuming that this wouldn't cause cur to exceed the min or max limits.

Handling a moving thumb is where trackScrollbar really gets involved in some difficulties. The numerical value of cur has no direct relationship to the physical position of the thumb as it's dragged along the scroll bar. There's a mathematical relationship based on the ratio of the difference between the scroll bar's max-min range and the length of the travel of the thumb. However, in order to make the scroll bar's thumb appear to track the movement over the mouse naturally, the thumb must move in relation to the mouse with the value of cur falling where it will.

This is further complicated by the potentially unfriendly nature of integer math, which tends to round things like ratios down to frequently awkward numbers. The trackScrollbar function must ensure that the thumb doesn't actually exceed its allowed range due to rounding errors. While all this sounds simple in theory, the code doing it is a bit involved (see Fig. 5-26).

```
trackScrollbar(sb,rt)
        SCROLLBAR *sb;
        int rt;
{
        POINT p,oldp;
        int i,n;

        if(sb != NULL && (sb->head.type==inVertScroll ||
          sb->head.type==inHorScroll) && sb->active==ACTIVE) {
                if(rt & inUpArrow) {
                        InvertRect(&sb->uparr);
                        n=250;
                        while(sb->cur > sb->min && MouseDown(&p) &&
                          PointInRect(&p,&sb->uparr)) {
                                eraseThumb(sb);
                                adjustThumb(sb,-1);
                                drawThumb(sb);
                                delay(n);
                                n=25;
                        }
                        InvertRect(&sb->uparr);
                }
                else if(rt & inDownArrow) {
                        InvertRect(&sb->dnarr);
                        n=250;
                        while(sb->cur < (sb->max-1) &&
                          MouseDown(&p) && PointInRect(&p,&sb->dnarr)) {
                                eraseThumb(sb);
                                adjustThumb(sb,1);
                                drawThumb(sb);
                                delay(n);
                                n=25;
                        }
                        InvertRect(&sb->dnarr);

                        if(sb->head.type==inVertScroll) {
                                eraseThumb(sb);
                                if(sb->thumb.top==sb->jump.top)
                                  sb->cur=sb->min;
                                else if(sb->thumb.bottom==sb->jump.bottom)
                                  sb->cur=sb->max;
                                else sb->cur=(int)((float)(sb->max-sb->min)/
                                  ((float)(sb->size-48)/
                                  (sb->thumb.top-sb->jump.top)));
                                drawThumb(sb);
```

5-26 The trackScrollbar function.

```
                }
                else {
                        eraseThumb(sb);
                        if(sb->thumb.left==sb->jump.left)
                          sb->cur=sb->min;
                        else if(sb->thumb.right==sb->jump.right)
                          sb->cur=sb->max;
                        else sb->cur=(int)((float)(sb->max-sb->min)/
                          ((float)(sb->size-48)/
                          (sb->thumb.left-sb->jump.left)));
                        drawThumb(sb);
                }
        }
        else if(rt & inJumpUp) {
                eraseThumb(sb);
                adjustThumb(sb,-8);
                drawThumb(sb);
        }
        else if(rt & inJumpDown) {
                eraseThumb(sb);
                adjustThumb(sb,8);
                drawThumb(sb);
                if(sb->head.type==inVertScroll) {
                        eraseThumb(sb);
                        if(sb->thumb.top==sb->jump.top)
                          sb->cur=sb->min;
                        else if(sb->thumb.bottom==sb->jump.bottom)
                          sb->cur=sb->max;
                        else sb->cur=(int)((float)(sb->max-sb->min)/
                          ((float)(sb->size-48)/
                          (sb->thumb.top-sb->jump.top)));
                        drawThumb(sb);
                }
                else {
                        eraseThumb(sb);
                        if(sb->thumb.left==sb->jump.left)
                          sb->cur=sb->min;
                        else if(sb->thumb.right==sb->jump.right)
                          sb->cur=sb->max;
                        else sb->cur=(int)((float)(sb->max-sb->min)/
                          ((float)(sb->size-48)/
                          (sb->thumb.left-sb->jump.left)));
                        drawThumb(sb);
                }
        }
        else if(rt & inThumb) {
                if(sb->head.type==inVertScroll) {
                        MouseDown(&oldp);
                        while(MouseDown(&p)) {
                                if(oldp.y != p.y &&
                                  PointInRect(&p,&sb->jump)) {
                                        eraseThumb(sb);
                                        i=p.y-oldp.y;
                                        if((sb->thumb.top+i) <=
                                          sb->jump.top ||
                                          (sb->thumb.bottom+i) >
                                          sb->jump.bottom) i=0;
                                        sb->thumb.top+=i;
                                        sb->thumb.bottom+=i;
                                        drawThumb(sb);
                                        memcpy((char *)&oldp,
                                                (char *)&p,
                                                sizeof(POINT));
                                }
```

```
                        }
                        eraseThumb(sb);
                        if(sb->thumb.top==sb->jump.top)
                          sb->cur=sb->min;
                        else if(sb->thumb.bottom==sb->jump.bottom)
                          sb->cur=sb->max;
                        else sb->cur=(int)((float)(sb->max-sb->min)/
                          ((float)(sb->size-48)/
                          (sb->thumb.top-sb->jump.top)));
                                drawThumb(sb);
                        }
                        else if(sb->head.type==inHorScroll) {
                                MouseDown(&oldp);
                                while(MouseDown(&p)) {
                                        if(oldp.x != p.x &&
                                          PointInRect(&p,&sb->jump)) {
                                                eraseThumb(sb);
                                                i=p.x-oldp.x;
                                                if((sb->thumb.left+i) <=
                                                  sb->jump.left ||
                                                  (sb->thumb.right+i) >
                                                  sb->jump.right) i=0;
                                                sb->thumb.left+=i;
                                                sb->thumb.right+=i;
                                                drawThumb(sb);
                                                memcpy((char *)&oldp,
                                                       (char *)&p,
                                                       sizeof(POINT));
                                        }
                                }
                                eraseThumb(sb);
                                if(sb->thumb.left==sb->jump.left)
                                  sb->cur=sb->min;
                                else if(sb->thumb.right==sb->jump.right)
                                  sb->cur=sb->max;
                                else sb->cur=(int)((float)(sb->max-sb->min)/
                                  ((float)(sb->size-48)/
                                  (sb->thumb.left-sb->jump.left)));
                                drawThumb(sb);
                        }
                }
        }
        while(MouseDown(&p));
    }
}

/* internal routine - adjust the scroll bar thumb */
adjustThumb(sb,n)
        SCROLLBAR *sb;
        int n;
{
        int i,rn,f;

        i=sb->cur+n;
        if(i < sb->min) i=sb->min;
        else if(i >= sb->max) i=sb->max-1;
        sb->cur=i;
        rn=sb->size-48;
        if(sb->cur==sb->min) f=0;
        else if(sb->cur==(sb->max-1)) f=rn;
        else f=(int)((float)rn/((float)(sb->max-sb->min)/(float)sb->cur));

        if(sb->head.type==inVertScroll) {
```

```
          if(f==rn) sb->thumb.top=sb->dnarr.top-16;
          else sb->thumb.top=sb->uparr.bottom+f+1;
          sb->thumb.bottom=sb->thumb.top+16;
     }
   else if(sb->head.type==inHorScroll) {
          if(f==rn) sb->thumb.left=sb->dnarr.left-16;
          else sb->thumb.left=sb->uparr.right+f+1;
          sb->thumb.right=sb->thumb.left+16;
     }
}
```

You will note the existence of an ancillary function to trackScrollbar called adjustThumb. This function is responsible for doing some floating-point cheating to resolve the ratio between the range of the SCROLLBAR object and the area over which the thumb may legally travel.

Figure 5-27 illustrates a dialog containing a scroll bar.

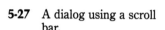 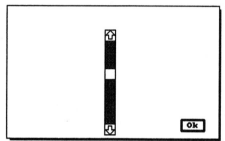

5-27 A dialog using a scroll bar.

Having looked at the pretty complex code to maintain scroll bars, you should note that the code generating the dialog in Fig. 5-27 is little more complicated than that used to support the simpler controls. All the tricky bits take place in the library; and, once you have them working, you can largely forget about them. Figure 5-28 shows the code generating the dialog.

```
simpleDialog()
{
        SCROLLBAR sb,*sp;
        BUTTON ok,*bp;
        POINT p;
        RECT r;
        WINDOW w;
        unsigned int rt,a=0xff;

        SetRect(&r,48,48,438,228);

        if(openWindow(&w,&r)) {
                SetRect(&ok.frame,r.left+168,r.bottom-25,
                    r.left+200,r.bottom-10);
                AddButton(&w,&ok,"Ok",ACTIVE);

                AddVertScroll(&w,&sb,ls.frame.right,ls.frame.top,
                    ls.frame.bottom-ls.frame.top,0,0,0,INACTIVE);

                do {
                        if(MouseDown(&p)) {
```

5-28 The code that generated Fig. 5-27.

```
                                 rt=whereMouse(&p,&w);
                                 if(rt & inButton) {
                                         bp=findButton(&w,&p);
                                         trackButton(bp);
                                         else if(bp==&ok) a=0;
                                 }
                                 else if(rt & inVertScroll) {
                                         sp=findScrollbar(&w,&p);
                                         trackScrollbar(sp,rt);
                                 }
                                 else errorbeep();
                         }
                 } while(a);
                 closeWindow(&w);
         } else errorbeep();
}
```

The dialog in Fig. 5-28 is unique in that it doesn't actually do anything except allow its users to play with a scroll bar until they get bored. In most cases, you'll want to do something when trackScrollbar returns; that something will probably involve setting a value elsewhere in your program based on the value of the scroll bar's cur function. Right now, all that happens is that the value is displayed in the dialog using a TEXTFIELD control, something not dealt with here in detail yet.

One area over which designers of graphical user interfaces frequently come to blows—at least, to virtual blows—is that of scroll bar *callback* procedures. A callback procedure for a scroll bar is a function that can be called by trackScrollbar to update the thing being scrolled as the thumb is dragged around. In this book's graphical user interface, nothing happens to the thing being scrolled until the thumb is released, for the obvious reason that the scroll bar functions don't support callback procedures.

If callback procedures were supported, dragging the thumb of the scroll bar in a file dialog would cause the list of names to move with the thumb, rather than simply having them reposition themselves after the thumb is released.

Callback procedures for scroll bars are an issue because very often they result in more elegant applications that are also maddeningly frustrating to use. Having a list of file names track the movement of a scroll bar's thumb as it's dragged (the case under Windows 3, for example) is fairly elegant. However, having a large amount of screen area redrawing itself every time the thumb of a scroll bar so much as wiggles—as would be the case in Desktop Paint if its main window scroll bars supported this feature—is infuriating. Perhaps the best example of this in commercial software can be found in the Xerox Grey F/X package, which insists on laboriously redrawing its image work space for every pixel that a scroll bar thumb moves.

Bear in mind that Windows requires a minimum of an 80286 processor to run. Windows applications can be assured that they won't be asked to run on very slow computers.

Because the graphical user interface in this book is based on the none-too-fast Turbo C graphics library, and because it's intended to produce applications that will run on low-end systems at an acceptable speed, its scroll bars don't support callback procedures. You might want to include callbacks, however, if you feel that it's important to the applications you'll write with the user interface library.

Adding lists

List controls are probably the most specialized controls in the graphical user interface. The only example of their implementation in the Desktop Paint program is as part of the file dialog box. You'll probably be able to find other applications for them.

A list control displays a list of text lines from which you can select one line by clicking on it. In the case of a file dialog, a list control and a scroll bar control can allow you to select from a list of strings longer than the list allows for by itself.

Figure 5-29 illustrates a list control.

5-29 An example of a list control.

While lists occupy a lot of real estate as controls go, they're actually pretty simple to create and manage. As with all the other controls in this chapter, a list can be reduced to a fairly simple data structure.

```
typedef struct {
    OBJECTHEAD head;
    int x,y;
    int length,depth;
    int count;
    int top;
    RECT frame;
    char *base;
    } LIST;
```

Some elements of the LIST object will probably be familiar. The unique ones—length, depth, count, top, and base—all pertain to managing the contents of the list in question.

A list control expects to list the contents of a buffer containing an array of fixed-length, C-style text strings. The length of each string is set by the length element, and the buffer is pointed to by base. Thus, the first string will be at base, and the second string will be at base + length + 1. The extra byte allows for the null at the end of the first string. You can locate any string in the buffer using the following expression, where ls is a LIST object and n is the number of the string you want to locate:

ls.base + (n*(ls.length + 1))

The length element also tells the function that draws list controls how wide the list control in question should be. Inasmuch as each character in the system font is eight pixels wide, the width of the box enclosing a list control will be eight times the length value—plus a bit for the graphics.

The depth element of a LIST object defined the number of lines of text that can be visible in the list at one time. It also defines the depth of the list control being drawn, as characters are also all eight pixels deep.

The top element tells the drawList function which of the strings in the buffer pointed to by the base element constitutes the uppermost visible string in the list. If this is zero, the first visible string will be the first one in the buffer. If this is ten, it will be the tenth string. Figure 5-30 illustrates the relationship between a complete buffer of strings and the visible area of the buffer as set by the top value.

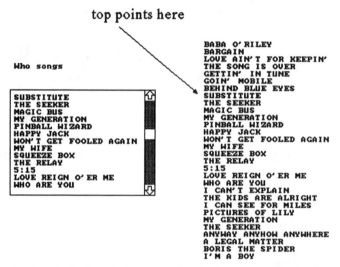

5-30   The buffer of a list control and what's actually visible.

Changing the top value allows the list to scroll through a buffer containing more names than room exists for in the list control's visible area at one time.

The count element specifies the number of actual strings in the buffer pointed to by the base element.

You can list anything you like in a list control, and the dimensions of a list needn't be confined to the ones associated with choosing file names. Implementing a list control as part of a file dialog will be discussed in greater detail in Chapter 10.

As with the other controls in this chapter, four primary functions pertain to lists. The first is addList (see Fig. 5-31).

```
addList(w,l,x,y,width,depth,count,top,base)
        WINDOW *w;
        LIST *l;
        int x,y;
        int width,depth;
        int count;
```

5-31   The addList function.

```
         int top;
         char *base;
{
         OBJECTHEAD *oh;
         /* start by finding end of chain */

         oh=(OBJECTHEAD *)w;
         while(oh->next != NULL) oh=oh->next;

         oh->next=(OBJECTHEAD *)l;

         x &= 0xfff8;

         l->x=x;
         l->y=y;
         l->length=width;
         l->depth=depth;
         l->count=count;
         l->top=top;
         l->base=base;
         l->frame.left=x-2;
         l->frame.top=y-2;
         l->frame.right=x+((width+2)*8)+2;
         l->frame.bottom=y+(depth*MENULINEDEEP)+2;
         l->head.type=inList;
         l->head.next=NULL;
         drawList(l);
}
```

Note that, as with all the controls that contain system font text, the horizontal position of a list control will always be rounded down to the nearest eight-pixel boundary. For this reason, if you'll be associating a scroll bar with a list, make sure you position it relative to the frame element of the list rather than to the value you pass to addList as the x argument.

The function to draw list controls—drawList—is quite simple, as it simply draws a box and fills it with text (see Fig. 5-32).

```
drawList(l)
        LIST *l;
{
        int i;
        MouseOff();
        setwritemode(COPY_PUT);
        setfillstyle(SOLID_FILL,getmaxcolor());
        setlinestyle(SOLID_LINE,0,NORM_WIDTH);
        setcolor(BLACK);
        bar(l->frame.left,l->frame.top,l->frame.right,l->frame.bottom);
        rectangle(l->frame.left,l->frame.top,l->frame.right,l->frame.bottom);

        if(l->base != NULL) {
                for(i=0;i<l->depth;++i) {
                        if((l->top+i) >= l->count) break;
                        DrawString(l->x+8,l->y+(i*MENULINEDEEP)+2,
                          l->base+((l->top+i)*(l->length+1)),ACTIVE);
                }
        }
        MouseOn();
}
```

5-32   The drawList function.

The findList function works like all the other functions that find controls, save that it returns a pointer of the type LIST (see Fig. 5-33).

```
LIST *findList(w,p)
        WINDOW *w;
        POINT *p;
{
        OBJECTHEAD *oh;
        LIST *b;

        oh=(OBJECTHEAD *)w;
        while(oh != NULL) {
                if(oh->type == inList) {
                        b=(LIST *)oh;
                        if(PointInRect(p,&b->frame)) return(b);
                }
                oh=oh->next;
        }
        return(NULL);
}
```

5-33 The findList function.

Finally, the trackList function is also pretty easy to deal with. It differs from the other tracking functions discussed in this chapter, however, in that it actually returns something. It determines where the mouse click occurring within the list in question actually resides, and decides which of the visible list elements has been selected, taking into account the value of the top element of the list control. It then copies the string in question to the s argument passed to it—hopefully a pointer to a buffer that will be large enough to contain the string. As you will have set up the array that the list will operate with, the maximum length of the string will be known (because it can't exceed one plus the value in the length element of the LIST object).

Figure 5-34 illustrates the trackList function.

```
trackList(lp,s)
        LIST *lp;
        char *s;
{
        RECT r;
        POINT p;
        int n;

        MouseLoc(&p);
        if(PointInRect(&p,&lp->frame)) {
                if((n=((p.y-lp->frame.top)/MENULINEDEEP)) <
                        lp->depth && n < lp->count) {
                        SetRect(&r,lp->frame.left+1,
                                lp->frame.top+(n*MENULINEDEEP)+1,
                                lp->frame.right-1,
                                lp->frame.top+((n+1)*MENULINEDEEP)+3);
                        InvertRect(&r);
                        while(MouseDown(&p));
                        InvertRect(&r);
                        strcpy(s,lp->base+((n+lp->top)*(lp->length+1)));
                }
        }
}
```

5-34 The trackList function.

Using controls intelligently

Once you've completed GUI.LIB, you'll find that creating dialogs is less like programming and more like virtual bricklaying. You can add controls to a window with a line or two of code, which makes it pretty easy for you to add many of them.

Several very good reasons exist for avoiding dialogs containing a lot of controls. For one thing, they're usually pretty confusing to work with. By nature, a dialog should serve a single purpose. If you want to perform multiple functions, you really should generate multiple single purpose dialogs.

In addition, very immense dialogs will take a noticeable period of time to open and set themselves up on slower hardware.

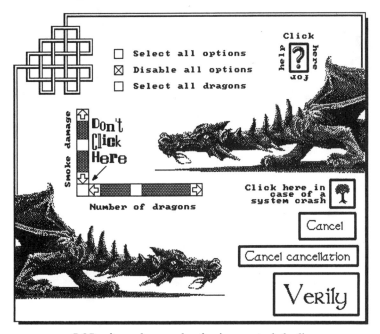

5-35   A good example of using controls badly.

You might want to consider the hypothetical dialog in Fig. 5-35 as an example of how not to design dialogs. While challenging, engaging to the eye, and certainly removed from any potential accusation of being dull, this particular screen makes finding any particular function difficult. In addition, it could be accused of using too many of the graphical user interface features in non-intuitive ways.

For example, you might not have immediately discerned that clicking on the lower dragon would bring up yet another dialog with list of spells to turn lizards into carburetors. Clicking on the upper dragon returns you immediately to DOS. This vagueness is clearly a failing of this dialog design, although it's one of so many as to be almost trivial in itself.

As an aside, the dragons in Fig. 5-35 are legitimate, clickable controls in this graphical user interface—they're just of a type not yet discussed.

A man without a god is like a fish without a bicycle.
Anon

6

Adding text controls

THE IDEAL GRAPHICAL USER INTERFACE WOULD USE NO TEXT AT ALL (and hence, no text controls). Everything would be handled with icons, making all applications written under it portable between all potential users, even if some of the users couldn't read English or couldn't actually read at all.

Several potential problems arise when creating a workable implementation of such a graphical user interface. To begin with, the idea is impossible—far too many of the concepts involved in anything beyond trivial computer operations simply don't translate adequately into universal pictographs or icons. While you could, of course, create a wholly icon-based user interface, you'd probably need to write an accompanying manual explaining what all the icons meant, largely defeating the purpose of the undertaking.

In addition, such a graphical user interface would be one more reason to avoid learning how to read in a world already containing far too many illiterates. No author would be willing to write a book about an operating system designed to do away with authors; likewise, no publishing company would publish such a book. Very few people are willing to buy software so obscure or difficult to understand that even the people who write software books for a living have decided to leave it alone.

The graphical user interface in this book supports three distinct types of text controls (or four, if you regard the list controls discussed in Chapter 5 as being text controls). The three dealt with in this chapter are TEXT objects, TEXTFIELD objects, and EDITFIELD objects. All consist of single lines of text, but each one behaves differently and is used for a distinct function (see Fig. 6-1).

```
Observe this text

Read this text

Edit this| text
```

6-1 Text, textfield, and editfield controls.

Adding text and textfield controls

The simplest sort of text control is simply a TEXT object. Once could easily argue about whether this is really a control at all, as TEXT objects are prohibited from changing once added to a window and also don't respond to mouse clicks. It's convenient to regard them as controls, however, because they can be added to windows in the same way as other controls are.

A TEXT object is simply a line of text that can be placed in a window, (e.g., a title). It can't be clicked in, nor can the window subsequently alter the text. It can only be read by users of your software, and perhaps admired if it says something unusually profound.

The data structure for a TEXT object is as follows:

```
typedef struct {
    OBJECTHEAD head;
    int x,y;
    char *text;
    unsigned int active;
    } TEXT;
```

Objects of the type TEXT represent the simplest type of controls. Besides the obligatory OBJECTHEAD, all this data structure contains are fields to specify the location of the text on your screen, a pointer to the text itself, and a flag indicating whether it should be active or inactive (i.e., drawn in black or grey).

The addText and drawText functions are equally simple and probably require no explanation (see Fig. 6-2).

```
addText(w,t,x,y,p,a)
        WINDOW *w;
        TEXT *t;
        int x,y;
        char *p;
        int a;
{
        OBJECTHEAD *oh;
        /* start by finding end of chain */

        oh=(OBJECTHEAD *)w;
        while(oh->next != NULL) oh=oh->next;

        oh->next=(OBJECTHEAD *)t;
        t->x=x;
        t->y=y;
        t->text=p;
        t->active=a;
        t->head.type=inText;
        t->head.next=NULL;
```

6-2 The AddText and drawText functions.

```
        drawText(t);
}

drawText(t)
        TEXT *t;
    {
        MouseOff();
        DrawString(t->x,t->y,t->text,t->active);
        MouseOn();
    }
```

You might well ask why one would go to the trouble of adding text to a window when it's so much easier to simply call DrawString to draw there. Well, for one thing, you can't just call DrawString—you must remember to turn the mouse off before you do and then on again afterwards. This isn't an easy bug to catch if you forget to do it because it'll only manifest itself if your mouse cursor happens to be right where the text is supposed to appear as it's drawn.

In addition, after you've got your graphical user interface working and have dreamt up some applications to write with it, you'll find expanding it more difficult if you've used DrawString to write text. You'll probably find situations where you'll want to be able to regenerate a window and its contents by walking up the linked list and redrawing each object you encounter. Having text added as objects, rather than just drawn in place, makes this possible.

Textfield controls are very much like text controls except that they embody the possibility of the text within them changing after a textfield control has been added to its window. You can't do this with a straight text control—or, at least, you shouldn't—because a text control doesn't know how long its existing text string is and hence no way of clearing the space it occupies so that new text can be written. If the old text was longer than the new text, some of the old characters would remain.

You would use a text control for text that won't change throughout the life of a window (e.g., the title of a dialog) and a textfield control for text that might change (such as the selected file name in a file selector box).

A textfield control defines the maximum area that text associated with the control may occupy and draws a frame around it. If you add a textfield control to a window and subsequently redraw it, the area in the frame will be erased before new text is drawn in it. As such, a textfield control can have its contents altered.

The data structure for a textfield control is as follows:

```
typedef struct {
    OBJECTHEAD head;
    int x,y;
    int length;
    RECT frame;
    char *text;
    unsigned int active;
    } TEXTFIELD;
```

The TEXTFIELD object looks just like a TEXT object, with the addition of two elements—frame and length. The former defines the area that would enclose the text in question if the text was as long as allowed. The latter defines how long it's allowed to be.

Figure 6-3 illustrates the addTextfield and drawTextfield functions. As you might expect, these behave just like the addText and drawText functions, save for the addition of a frame around the area the control occupies.

```
addTextField(w,t,x,y,l,p,a)
        WINDOW *w;
        TEXTFIELD *t;
        int x,y;
        int l;
        char *p;
        int a;
{
        OBJECTHEAD *oh;
        /* start by finding end of chain */

        oh=(OBJECTHEAD *)w;
        while(oh->next != NULL) oh=oh->next;

        oh->next=(OBJECTHEAD *)t;
        t->x=x;
        t->y=y;
        t->text=p;
        t->active=a;
        t->length=l;
        t->frame.left=x-3;
        t->frame.top=y-3;
        t->frame.right=x+(8*l)+2;
        t->frame.bottom=y+FONTDEEP+2;
        t->head.type=inTextfield;
        t->head.next=NULL;
        drawTextfield(t);
}

drawTextfield(t)
        TEXTFIELD *t;
{
        MouseOff();
        setwritemode(COPY_PUT);
        setfillstyle(SOLID_FILL,getmaxcolor());
        setlinestyle(SOLID_LINE,0,NORM_WIDTH);
        setcolor(BLACK);
        bar(t->frame.left,t->frame.top,t->frame.right,t->frame.bottom);
        rectangle(t->frame.left,t->frame.top,t->frame.right,t->frame.bottom);
        DrawString(t->x,t->y,t->text,t->active);
        MouseOn();
}
```

6-3 The addTextfield and drawTextfield controls.

Adding editfield controls

The third type of control to be discussed in this chapter, editfield controls, represents one of the most complex sorts of controls in the graphical user interface. An editfield control looks like a textfield control, but users of your software will be able to edit the contents of it by clicking in it.

As an aside, the people who think about graphical user interfaces in philosophical terms would say that it's philosophically wrong to have textfield and editfield controls look the same, that there should be some obvious visual indication as to what can be clicked in and what can't. The people who just write programs and believe that philosophy has no place in the same room as constructive thought would say that the context in which textfield and editfield controls find themselves makes it obvious what to click in and what not to. Besides, if you click in the wrong sort of control, it beeps. The philosophers would probably shake their heads ruefully at this point and leave, muttering to themselves about the sorry state that human intellect has come to.

While the current implementation of these two types of controls is visually identical, you might want to think about the foregoing argument. You might decide to modify one control or the other so there's some way of immediately spotting the editfield controls in a dialog having controls of both types.

An editfield control can be selected, unlike the other two text controls discussed in this chapter. If it's clicked in, a vertical text edit cursor will appear between those two characters of the text in the control closest to where the control was clicked in, or at the end of the text if the mouse was clicked to the right of the last character in the string. Once selected, an editfield control allows its text to be edited using fairly intuitive editing controls. The right and left cursor mover keys move the cursor around, the backspace key deletes the character to the left of the cursor, the delete key deletes the character to the right of the cursor, and printable characters typed while the control is selected will appear at the cursor point (assuming the string isn't currently full).

If you consider the general structure of a dialog as it's been evolving over the previous few chapters, you'll probably realize that handling editfield controls is a bit tricky. Until now, all controls were clicked in, tracked, and then ignored when the mouse button was released. Editfield controls are unique in that, once selected, they must continue to respond to input—and hence input must be directed to them—even after the mouse has long since scurried away.

Under Windows and in the Macintosh environment, everything that flows into a window is handled by a common message stream. Every mouse click and keyboard character, among other things, is handled as a separate message with a type and destination window attached to it. Windows are responsible for watching the stream of messages and dealing with those messages addressed to them.

This represents a flexible system for dealing with complex environments but probably qualifies as severe overkill for the graphical user interface in this book. Because there can only be one foremost window at a time, and as the structure of this environment precludes multitasking, asynchronous events such as mouse clicks and keyboard data can be handled by whatever window is open at the moment.

Mouse clicks are handled by calling MouseDown and whereMouse. In order to deal with the keyboard information that would have to be directed to a selected editfield control, a dialog would need a keyboard equivalent of this combination. This function is called Keyboard and can be found in Fig. 6-4.

```
Keyboard(w)
    WINDOW *w;
{

    OBJECTHEAD *oh;
    BUTTON *bp;
    EDITFIELD *f;
    int c,len,i,bcount=0;

    /* if there's a key waiting */

    if(kbhit()) {
        c=GetKey();
        oh=(OBJECTHEAD *)w;
        while(oh != NULL) {
            if(oh->type==inButton) {
                bp=(BUTTON *)oh;
                ++bcount;
                if(bcount==1 && c==13) {
                    fakeMouseDown.x=bp->frame.left+1;
                    fakeMouseDown.y=bp->frame.top+1;
                }
                else if(bcount==2 && c==27) {
                    fakeMouseDown.x=bp->frame.left+1;
                    fakeMouseDown.y=bp->frame.top+1;
                }
            }
            if(oh->type==inEditField) {
                f=(EDITFIELD *)oh;
                if(f->select) {
                    len=strlen(f->text);
                    switch(c) {
                        case DEL:
                            if(f->curpos < len) {
                                for(i=f->curpos;i<=len;++i)
                                    f->text[i]=f->text[i+1];
                            }
                            break;
                        case HOME:
                            f->curpos=0;
                            break;
                        case END:
                            f->curpos=len;
                            break;
                        case CURSOR_LEFT:
                            if(f->curpos) --f->curpos;
                            break;
                        case CURSOR_RIGHT:
                            if(f->curpos < len) ++f->curpos;
                            break;
                        case 'X'-0x40:
                            f->curpos=0;
                            f->text[0]=0;
                            break;
                        case 8:
                            if(f->curpos && len) {
                                if(f->curpos < len) {
                                    for(i=f->curpos;i<=len;++i)
                                        f->text[i-1]=f->text[i];
                                    --f->curpos;
                                }
                                else {
                                    --f->curpos;
```

6-4 The Keyboard function.

148 *Adding text controls*

```
                                    f->text[len-1]=0;
                            }
                    }
                    break;
            default:
                    if(f->proc != NULL) c=(f->proc)(c);
                    else {
                            if(!isprint(c)) c=0;
                    }
                    if(c && (len+1) < f->length) {
                            for(i=(len+1);i>f->curpos;--i)
                                    f->text[i]=f->text[i-1];
                            f->text[f->curpos]=c;
                            ++f->curpos;
                    }
                    break;
            }
            drawEditfield(f);
        }
    }
    oh=oh->next;
    }
}
}
```

The Keyboard function should be called as often as possible in the main loop of a dialog. It looks for keyboard activity and, if it finds a character waiting, it attempts to find an editfield control to pass it along to.

In fact, this function does a few other things. You may recall that, in Chapter 2, I briefly mentioned an object called fakeMouseDown in conjunction with the MouseDown function. Its purpose will become clear with the advent of Keyboard.

If Keyboard finds a character waiting when it's called, it begins to walk up the linked list of the window object passed to it. It will be particularly interested in two types of objects. If a window contains button controls, hitting the Enter key should cause the window to respond as if the first button control had been clicked in, and hitting the Esc key should be equivalent to clicking in the second button. The first and second buttons refer to the order in which the buttons are added to a window, as this will determine their location in the linked list.

By convention, an Ok button will be the first button added to any window, and hence hitting Enter will make the window behave as if the Ok button has been clicked. The Cancel button, if there is one, will be the second button added and will respond to the Esc key.

If the key waiting when Keyboard is called is either a carriage return or an escape—characters 13 and 27 respectively—the Keyboard function will stop at the first or second object of the type BUTTON it finds in the linked list of the window in question and make the graphical user interface believe that a mouse click has occurred in the appropriate button. It does this by setting the global POINT object fakeMouseDown to a location within the frame element of the appropriate button. You may recall from Chapter 2 that, when the MouseDown function is called, it checks fakeMouseDown before actually checking the status of the mouse buttons. If fakeMouseDown contains a set of legal point values, the MouseDown indicates that a mouse click has occurred at that point although one hasn't.

The other type of objects of interest to Keyboard are editfield controls. If the waiting character isn't a carriage return or an escape, Keyboard wanders up the linked list passed to it until it encounters an editfield. If the editfield is selected, it passes the character to it and returns. If the editfield is not selected, it carries on looking for one that is.

Passing a character to a selected editfield control involves modifying the buffer at the control's text element according to the nature of the character in question. Cursor control codes, such as the left and right arrow keys, Backspace and Delete, Home and End, and Ctrl-X are used to position the cursor in the editfield. Printable characters are added to the text buffer and the contents of the control are redrawn.

The Ctrl-X code erases the contents of an editfield control. This function is usually performed by the Esc key in similar situations, but it's already in use as the keyboard equivalent of the Cancel button. Ctrl-X is historically used for this function and dates back to a time before keyboards had Esc keys. You might want to select another key for this function.

Using text-related controls

Dialogs using the controls discussed in this chapter will follow the same basic form as the previous examples of dialogs in this book but with a few added features. One of these will be a call to the Keyboard function.

Both the example dialogs to be discussed here have been drawn from the 256-color version of Desktop Paint. However, they're equally applicable to the monochrome graphical user interface, as all the calls are the same.

Figure 6-5 illustrates an example of a dialog using multiple textfield controls.

```
adjustPaletteColour(colour)
    int colour;
{
    WINDOW w;
    POINT p;
    BUTTON ok,can,*bp;
    SCROLLBAR rsc,gsc,bsc,*sp;
    TEXTFIELD ref,gef,bef;
    TEXT tx,rtx,gtx,btx,cnt;
    char rbf[8],gbf[8],bbf[8],cbf[64],*pl;
    RECT r;
    unsigned int rt,rc,gc,bc;
    int a=0xff;

    SetRect(&r,32,32,400,230);

    if(OpenWindow(&w,&r)) {
        rc=thePalette[(colour*3)+0];
        gc=thePalette[(colour*3)+1];
        bc=thePalette[(colour*3)+2];

        sprintf(rbf,"%u",rc);
        sprintf(gbf,"%u",gc);
        sprintf(bbf,"%u",bc);

        AddText(&w,&tx,r.left+8,r.top+10,"Colour adjust",ACTIVE);
```

6-5 Code for a dialog using multiple textfield controls.

```
SetRect(&ok.frame,r.right-40,r.bottom-23,r.right-8,r.bottom-8);
AddButton(&w,&ok,"Ok",ACTIVE);

SetRect(&can.frame,r.right-120,r.bottom-23,r.right-56,r.bottom-8);
AddButton(&w,&can,"Cancel",ACTIVE);

AddHorScroll(&w,&rsc,r.left+8,r.top+30,(r.right-100)-(r.left+8),
    0,255,rc,ACTIVE);
AddHorScroll(&w,&gsc,r.left+8,r.top+50,(r.right-100)-(r.left+8),
    0,255,gc,ACTIVE);
AddHorScroll(&w,&bsc,r.left+8,r.top+70,(r.right-100)-(r.left+8),
    0,255,bc,ACTIVE);

AddTextField(&w,&ref,rsc.frame.right+8,rsc.frame.top+4,3,rbf,ACTIVE);
AddTextField(&w,&gef,gsc.frame.right+8,gsc.frame.top+4,3,gbf,ACTIVE);
AddTextField(&w,&bef,bsc.frame.right+8,bsc.frame.top+4,3,bbf,ACTIVE);

AddText(&w,&rtx,ref.frame.right+8,ref.frame.top+1,"Red",ACTIVE);
AddText(&w,&gtx,gef.frame.right+8,gef.frame.top+1,"Green",ACTIVE);
AddText(&w,&btx,bef.frame.right+8,bef.frame.top+1,"Blue",ACTIVE);

do {
    keyboard(&w);
    if(MouseDown(&p)) {
        rt=whereMouse(&p,&w);
        if(rt & inButton) {
            bp=findButton(&w,&p);
            trackButton(bp);
            if(bp==&ok) {
              a=0;
              thePalette[(colour*3)+0]=rc;
              thePalette[(colour*3)+1]=gc;
              thePalette[(colour*3)+2]=bc;
            }
            else if(bp==&can)  a=0;
        }
        else if(rt & inHorScroll) {
            sp=findScrollbar(&w,&p);
            trackScrollbar(sp,rt);
            if(sp==&rsc) {
                rc=sp->cur;
                SetColour(colour,rc,gc,bc);
                sprintf(rbf,"%u",rc);
                drawTextfield(&ref);
            }
            else if(sp==&gsc) {
                gc=sp->cur;
                SetColour(colour,rc,gc,bc);
                sprintf(gbf,"%u",gc);
                drawTextfield(&gef);
            }
            else if(sp==&bsc) {
                bc=sp->cur;
                SetColour(colour,rc,gc,bc);
                sprintf(bbf,"%u",bc);
                drawTextfield(&bef);
            }
        }
        else errorbeep();
    }
} while(a);

SetColour(colour,(int)thePalette[(colour*3)+0],
```

```
                    (int)thePalette[(colour*3)+1],
                    (int)thePalette[(colour*3)+2]);

        CloseWindow(&w);
    } else errorbeep();
}
```

There are, to begin with, a number of things in Fig. 6-5 irrelevant to the discussion of controls at all; because this is a real function from a real program, it also actually does something aside from being illustrative. In this case, it adjusts the red, green, and blue values of a color. Thus, you can ignore the calls to SetColour.

Figure 6-6 is what the dialog created by this code actually looks like.

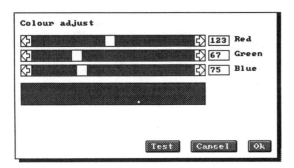

6-6 The dialog created by the code in Fig. 6-5.

The adjustPaletteColour function sets up three scroll bars—one for each color—and three textfield objects to display the numerical values represented by the sliders. Each time a mouse click occurs within a scroll bar, the appropriate scroll bar must be tracked and then the corresponding textfield control updated with a new value.

Note that none of the text controls know what to do with a number. If you want to display numerical data in a text control, you must convert it to a string with sprintf.

This function is a good example of a dialog in which the results of findScrollbar really do matter. In situations encompassing a single control of any given type, the find functions will invariably return pointers to the one extant control. Here, though, findScrollbar does sort out which of the three scroll bars actually has been selected.

Despite the increased complexity of tracking editfield controls, using them is fairly simple—the graphical user interface library does most of the work. Figure 6-7 is a dialog containing several editfield controls.

```
doOverrides()
{
    static char ttl[MAXOVERRIDE][16]= {
        "Default Width:",
        "Default Depth:",
        "      Smudge:"
    };
```

6-7 A dialog using multiple editfield controls.

```
static int min[MAXOVERRIDE]={32,32,1};
static int max[MAXOVERRIDE]={9999,9999,6};

WINDOW w;
POINT p;
BUTTON ok,can,*bp;
TEXT tx,etx[MAXOVERRIDE];
EDITFIELD ef[MAXOVERRIDE],*ep;
char buffer[MAXOVERRIDE][8];
RECT r;
CONFIG cnf;
unsigned int i,j,rt,a=0xff;

SetRect(&r,48,48,250,272);
if(OpenWindow(&w,&r)) {
    memcpy((char *)&cnf,(char *)&theConfig,sizeof(CONFIG));

    AddText(&w,&tx,r.left+8,r.top+10,"Overrides",ACTIVE);

    sprintf(buffer[0],"%u",cnf.defwidth);
    sprintf(buffer[1],"%u",cnf.defdepth);
    sprintf(buffer[2],"%u",cnf.smudgevalue);

    for(i=0;i<MAXOVERRIDE;++i) {
        AddText(&w,&etx[i],r.left+8,r.top+30+(i*16),
            ttl[i],ACTIVE);
        AddEditField(&w,&ef[i],r.left+136,r.top+30+(i*16),
            5,buffer[i],numbertrap,ACTIVE);
    }

    SetRect(&ok.frame,r.right-40,r.bottom-23,r.right-8,r.bottom-8);
    AddButton(&w,&ok,"Ok",ACTIVE);

    SetRect(&can.frame,r.right-120,r.bottom-23,r.right-56,r.bottom-8);
    AddButton(&w,&can,"Cancel",ACTIVE);

    while(a) {
        Keyboard(&w);
        if(MouseDown(&p)) {
            rt=whereMouse(&p,&w);
            if(rt & inButton) {
                bp=findButton(&w,&p);
                trackButton(bp);
                if(bp==&ok) {
                    a=0;
                    for(i=0;i<MAXOVERRIDE;++i) {
                        j=atoi(buffer[i]);
                        if(j < min[i]) j=min[i];
                        if(j > max[i]) j=max[i];
                        sprintf(buffer[i],"%u",j);
                    }
                        cnf.defwidth=atoi(buffer[0]);
                        cnf.defdepth=atoi(buffer[1]);
                        cnf.smudgevalue=atoi(buffer[2]);
                        memcpy((char *)&theConfig,(char *)&cnf,
                            sizeof(CONFIG));
                    }
                    else if(bp==&can) a=0;
                }
                else if(rt & inEditField) {
                    ep=findEditfield(&w,&p);
                    trackEditfield(ep);
                    for(i=0;i<MAXOVERRIDE;++i) {
                        if(ep==&ef[i]) {
```

```
                        j=atoi(buffer[i]);
                        if(j < min[i]) j=min[i];
                        if(j > max[i]) j=max[i];
                        sprintf(buffer[i],"%u",j);
                }
        }
        drawEditfield(ep);
}
        else errorbeep();
}
}
CloseWindow(&w);
} else errorbeep();
}
```

You might want to consider that most applications of any size that will use the graphical user interface will probably require a catch-all dialog for adjusting various parameters. Figure 6-8 illustrates what the one in the color version of Desktop Paint looks like, as generated by the code in Fig. 6-7. This has been simplified a bit here, as the real version contains quite a few other controls extraneous to this discussion.

6-8   The dialog created by the code in Fig. 6-7.

The doOverrides function sets up various user configurable parameters in Desktop Paint. All the parameters are constrained in a data structure of the type CONFIG. In reality, the CONFIG structure is quite large; but for the sake of this example, you might consider that it looks like this:

```
typedef struct {
        int defwidth;
        int defdepth;
        int smudgevalue;
        } CONFIG;
```

There is a global variable of type CONFIG called theConfig. The value of MAXOVERRIDE is three. The three parameters to be dealt with here set both the default width and depth values for pictures when New item is selected from the Desktop Paint File menu and also set the *smudge* value (the amount of image disintegration caused by the Smudge item of the Edit menu).

The relevant aspect of this function involves its use of editfield controls (of which there are again three). When one is selected, the findEditfield function will return a pointer to it. The combination of Keyboard and trackEditfield function will handle all the actual text editing in the selected editfield. From the point of view of this function, the three text buffers associated with the three editfield controls will change by themselves. The function must only concern itself with reading the contents and replacing them in the CONFIG struct when the Ok button is finally clicked.

Text control applications

All sorts of applications involving little more than text are suitable for use with the graphical user interface. Such applications might seem more applicable to handling in the PC's text mode. Figure 6-9 is an example of such a program—a mailing list manager.

6-9   A mailing list manager.

The advantage of writing this program under the graphical user interface is that it appears considerably more user friendly—if only in the very corporate, commercial sense—by virtue of its mouse and menus. People have been conditioned to think of applications resembling this as being easy to learn.

If your use of the library in this book leans toward extensively text-oriented applications, you might want to enhance the Keyboard function a bit. For example, on a screen with many editfields (such as that of a mailing list manager), things might go a bit quicker if the up and down arrow keys could be used to move between fields. Bear in mind that people using this program will usually have their hands on the keyboard rather than on the mouse.

The real world is a special case.
Murphy's Laws of Computers

7

Adding bitmaps

ONE OF THE NICEST THINGS ABOUT WORKING WITH A GRAPHICAL USER
interface is that it can support graphics. Text-based programs are limited to only
the crudest forms of block and line graphics—while it's always impressive to see
what someone has done with the IBM-PC line graphic characters when they turn
up in an innovative design, the results rarely look all that sophisticated.

By comparison, real graphics are limited only by your imagination and how
well you can draw.

As with several other areas of the graphical user interface being discussed in
this book—most notably fonts—the problems of working with bitmapped images in
your programs may be decidedly secondary to those of getting images into a form
in which your program can deal with them. There are no standard image file formats lending themselves to the inclusion of images in a program, and no dedicated
tools for handling image manipulations.

This chapter will deal with these sorts of issues presently.

The problems involved in adding bitmapped graphics to a graphical user interface application break down into several areas. To begin with, you will need a way
to create the images; a paint program, such as Desktop Paint, will serve to handle
this. Secondly, you will need some way to convert a paint file into something that
can be dealt with by the graphical user interface library code. There are several
approaches to this, depending upon the ultimate use to which the graphics in question will be put. Finally, you'll need code to actually display bitmapped graphic
fragments in your program screens.

Unlike the sorts of objects discussed thus far, bitmapped graphics are big. A two-color graphic the size of a VGA screen requires about 38K of memory to contain it. On slower machines, transferring this much graphic information between a buffer and the screen can take a noticeable amount of time. In addition, the structure of the graphic will vary depending upon which of the three display cards supported by the graphical user interface is being used.

Dealing with all these imponderables in a sensible, orderly way takes a fair bit of forethought—and a not inconsequential amount of C code.

Bit planes and bitmaps

Figure 7-1 illustrates a bitmapped graphic fragment excised from a larger file. It could be used as a bitmapped graphic object in a program.

7-1 Part of a bitmapped image.

To begin with, this picture is a monochrome graphic, as will be all the bitmaps dealt with in this chapter. It can be displayed on any of the display cards discussed in this book and will look pretty much as it does here—except that on a VGA card enough of the picture would be visible to cause some people to label it sexist or, at the least, in questionable taste.

Potentially questionable taste is one of the drawbacks to having graphics available in a program.

Monochrome bitmaps are structured as a single "bit plane." Essentially, the picture is stored as an array of bytes in which each byte represents one pixel in the picture. The picture in Fig. 7-1 has the dimensions 576×720 pixels—actually with much of the lower half of the image invisible, as it's deeper than the screen it's being displayed on. This means that the first line is represented by 72 bytes—576 divided by 8.

Figure 7-2 illustrates the bitmapped nature of part of the image.

The screen buffer of a display card in one of its graphics modes is also a bitmap, as was discussed in Chapter 2. Copying the lines of bitmapped data from the

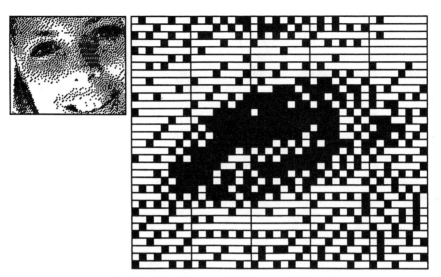

7-2 The bit structure of a bitmapped image.

image in Fig. 7-1 into the appropriate lines of a display card will make the image appear on your screen.

Actually, it will make the image appear on your screen inverted black for white, as bitmaps are stored the wrong way around in most monochrome bitmapped file formats. However, inverting the data corrects this situation.

Assuming that p points to the above picture, and that your screen is in a monochrome graphics mode (as discussed in Chapter 2), you can use the line start table to copy the picture into the upper left corner of your screen like this:

```
int i;
for(i = 0;i < 720; + + i) {
    if(i > = SCREENDEEP) break;
    memcpy(MK__FP(SCREENSEG,SCREENTBL[i]),p + (i*72),72);
}
```

This bit of code will only work with a picture having the dimensions 576×720 pixels. It works by creating pointers into the screen buffer based on the contents of the SCREENTBL array set up by the code in Chapter 2. It locates each line of the image and copies it into the corresponding line of the screen. It assumes that the picture at p has been inverted if necessary.

As an aside, the dimensions 576×720 are quite common in monochrome bitmaps. They're the fixed dimensions of all MacPaint image files. Legions of MacPaint files have found their way over to PC systems in recent years.

This is a very fast way to display an image in the upper left corner of your screen. However, it insists on the left edge of the image being aligned to an even eight bit boundary, in the same way that the display font used by the menus and controls of the graphical user interface must be. It would be desirable to be able to place an image fragment anywhere in a program's screen, regardless of where the byte boundaries fall.

Turbo C provides a function to this. The putimage function will shift the lines of bitmapped data right by enough places to have them align with any arbitrary coordinates you like; it was discussed in some detail earlier in this book in conjunction with opening and closing windows.

The putimage function expects to be passed a buffer consisting of two integers followed by a lot of bitmapped data of the sort in Fig. 7-1. The first of the two integers should be one less than the image's horizontal dimension, and the second should be one less than the image's vertical dimension. Because image lines are always rounded up to the next highest byte if the width isn't an even multiple of eight, there may be some unused bits at the end of each line.

Assuming that the picture in Fig. 7-1 is formatted with the appropriate two integers before the actual picture data, it could be placed anywhere on your screen like this:

```
putimage(10,10,p,COPY_PUT);
```

This would place the upper left corner of the image at the coordinates (10,10).

The drawback to this example is that it's only true if your computer has a Hercules card in it, or, more specifically, if it's running with something that Turbo C regards as a truly monochrome display. Turbo C insists on regarding EGA and VGA cards as being 16-color displays, even though in reality they can be treated as purely monochrome displays.

The structure of a 16-color display was discussed in Chapter 3. The structure of a putimage buffer for a 16-color display corresponds roughly to the card it's intended to be put to. It begins with two integers, as with the monochrome version. There are, however, four lines of image data for each line of the displayed picture. When putimage displays a bitmap on a 16-color display, it selects the first of the four display planes and writes the first line to the screen. It then selects the second display plane and writes the second line. When it has run through all four lines of data, it proceeds to the next line on the screen.

Clearly, storing two versions of every bitmapped object to be used in a program (one for Hercules cards and the other for EGA and VGA cards) is awkward. Fortunately, you don't need to do this. It's pretty easy to turn a monochrome putimage fragment into a 16-color putimage fragment—assuming, of course, that you want them both to look identical on their respective types of displays.

To generate a 16-color putimage fragment from a monochrome one, you would simply duplicate each line in the original four times. When it's passed to putimage, such a fragment will cause identical data to be written to each of the four planes of the screen, and thus will produce the appearance of a monochrome bitmap. Although this is rather inefficient, it allows you to use the convenient facilities of the putimage function—that of position independent bitmaps—which is arguably worth it.

Figure 7-3 is a function called mono2ega that will return a pointer to a 16-color bitmap fragment based on the monochrome fragment passed to it. Note that mono2ega returns a char pointer—it will require a prototype—and that it actually

```
char *mono2ega(source)
        char *source;
{
        char *p;
        int x,y,j,ls,sz;

        x=1+source[0]+(source[1] << 8);
        y=1+source[2]+(source[3] << 8);
        if((sz=imagesize(0,0,x,y)) != -1) {
                if((p=malloc(sz)) != NULL) {
                        memcpy(p,source,4);
                        ls=pixels2bytes(x);
                        for(j=0;j<y;++j) {
                                memcpy(p+4+((j*4)*ls),source+4+(j*ls),ls);
                                memcpy(p+4+ls+((j*4)*ls),source+4+(j*ls),ls);
                                memcpy(p+4+(ls*2)+((j*4)*ls),source+4+(j*ls),ls);
                                memcpy(p+4+(ls*3)+((j*4)*ls),source+4+(j*ls),ls);
                        }
                        return(p);
                }
        } else return(NULL);
}
```

7-3   The mono2ega function.

allocates memory for the new image fragment it creates. You must free this pointer
when you no longer need the new fragment.

   With this function available, you can write a bit of code that will display monochrome image fragments properly on all the cards supported by the graphical user
interface. This next listing will display the picture fragment pointed to by bitmap at
location (x,y) on the screen:

```
if(ismonomode( )) putimage(x,y,bitmap,COPY_PUT);
else {
    if((p = mono2ega(bitmap)) ! = NULL) {
        putimage(x,y,p,n);
        free(p);
    } else putchar(7); /* memory error */
}
```

   This code uses the function ismonomode to determine whether it's running on
a machine with a Hercules card or an EGA or VGA card. The ismonomode function looks like this:

```
ismonomode( )
{
    if(getmaxcolor( ) = = 1) return(1);
    else return(0);
}
```

   If the card is a Hercules display, the image will be displayed directly by putimage. If it's not (i.e., if it's a 16-color display instead), it will be displayed by calling mono2ega to create a new 16-color image fragment and then by passing the

new fragment to putimage. Once it's displayed, the new fragment can be thrown away by passing it to free.

The only potential drawback to this arrangement is that putimage cannot deal with 16-color fragments requiring more than 64K to store, as has been discussed. As such, mono2ega won't generate them. It's possible, if the monochrome image fragment to be displayed is fairly large, that it will display on a Hercules card but not on an EGA or VGA card for this reason.

In practice, this shouldn't happen. You shouldn't use bitmapped objects anywhere close to this size in a program, both because of the memory they tie up and because they take a considerable amount of time to display on slow, first-generation PCs.

Working with bitmaps

Figure 7-4 illustrates the odd migration of the lass in Fig. 7-1 from the beach she seems to have been standing on when originally photographed into a dialog box. She passed through a great deal of software along the way.

To begin with, note that Fig. 7-1 was cropped to produce Fig 7-4. The image dimensions are now 244 × 261 pixels.

The bitmap in Fig. 7-4 is, in fact, a control of the type BITMAP. It could be set up to actually do something were someone to click in the area occupied by the bitmap. More to the point, however, a BITMAP control can be added to a window just as can all other sorts of controls.

7-4   Girl in dialog box—a still life.

As with the less exotic sorts of controls discussed thus far, a BITMAP control is based on a BITMAP object (which looks like this):

```
typedef struct {
    OBJECTHEAD head;
```

```
    int x,y;
    RECT frame;
    char select;
    unsigned int active;
    char *bitmap;
    int (*proc)( );
  } BITMAP;
```

As with simpler controls, a BITMAP object contains an OBJECTHEAD element to make it part of the linked list of a window it's added to. It has a frame enclosing it. The bitmap element points to a monochrome putimage fragment that will actually be displayed. The proc element might be a bit mysterious, as it hasn't turned up in previous controls.

In fact, the proc element of a BITMAP object is a pointer to an optional function to be called when the bitmap is clicked in. Figure 7-5 illustrates one use of this.

Figure 7-5 actually illustrates an arguably trivial use of the proc element of a BITMAP. In a more practical sense, it's often useful to be able to associate a function with an icon. You could do this by simply checking which of several BITMAP objects had been clicked in and executing the appropriate function. However, as BITMAP controls—in the form of icons—frequently turn up in large numbers, having each one know what it's supposed to do avoids what is essentially, a duplicate decision tree.

7-5   Using the proc element of a bitmap. Clicking on the bitmap called forth a second bitmap—the speech bubble.

You should note that the Macintosh distinguishes between bitmaps and icons, with icons being a special case of bitmaps. A bitmap can be of any size, while an icon will always be 32 × 32 pixels. The graphical user interface in this book doesn't make this distinction—icons can be any size. However, you might want to set some size restrictions for yourself because huge icons look clumsy and slow things down.

Objects of the type BITMAP are handled just as simpler controls are and with corresponding functions. To begin with, Fig 7-6 illustrates the code that actually adds one to a window.

```
addBitmap(w,b,x,y,p,select,proc,active)
        WINDOW *w;
        BITMAP *b;
        int x,y;
        char *p;
        int select;
        int (*proc)();
        int active;
{
        OBJECTHEAD *oh;
        /* start by finding end of chain */

        oh=(OBJECTHEAD *)w;
        while(oh->next != NULL) oh=oh->next;

        oh->next=(OBJECTHEAD *)b;
        b->x=x;
        b->y=y;
        b->bitmap=p;
        b->select=select;
        b->proc=proc;
        b->active=active;
        b->head.type=inBitmap;
        b->head.next=NULL;
        b->frame.left=b->x;
        b->frame.top=b->y;
        b->frame.right=b->frame.left+ImageWidth(b->bitmap);
        b->frame.bottom=b->frame.top+ImageDepth(b->bitmap);
        drawBitmap(b);
}
```

7-6 The addBitmap function.

The addBitmap function behaves pretty much like all the other add functions, with the only new concern being what to pass as the proc argument. If you don't want the BITMAP to do anything when it's clicked, or if you want to handle whatever it does externally, just pass NULL for this argument. If you want it to execute a function called doSomething, you would set up the call to addBitmap like this:

```
WINDOW w;
BITMAP b;
int doSomething( );

addBitmap(&w,&b,48,48,image,0,doSomething,ACTIVE);
```

The select argument decides whether the bitmap will be initially selected. A bitmap appears inverted if it has been selected. Under Desktop Paint, the tools in the toolbox down the left side of the screen are each BITMAP objects; and one of them is always selected. In Fig. 7-7, the eraser tool is the selected BITMAP.

Drawing a BITMAP object is pretty uninvolved because it uses a variation on

7-7 The toolbox of Desktop Paint, a series of bitmap controls.

the code discussed previously to deal with 16-color displays. However, the drawing verb passed to putimage varies with the contents of the select element of a BIT-MAP object. It will be COPY_PUT if the bitmap is selected and NOT_PUT if it isn't. Note that the natural state of a bitmap is backwards as a PC display sees it— it must be displayed with NOT_PUT (i.e., inverted) if it's to appear correctly.

Figure 7-8 is the code for drawBitmap.

```
drawBitmap(b)
        BITMAP *b;
{
        char *p;
        int n;

        if(b->select) n=COPY_PUT;
        else n=NOT_PUT;
        if(b->active==INACTIVE) n=NOT_PUT;
        MouseOff();
        if(ismonomode()) putimage(b->x,b->y,b->bitmap,n);
        else {
                if((p=mono2ega(b->bitmap)) != NULL) {
                        putimage(b->x,b->y,p,n);
                        free(p);
                } else errorbeep();
        }
        MouseOn();
}
```

7-8 The drawBitmap function.

Figure 7-9 illustrates the code for findBitmap. As with the other controls discussed thus far, it doesn't do anything more involved than walk up the linked list of the WINDOW object passed to it, look first for a BITMAP object, and then for one with a frame element enclosing the mouse click in question. It returns a pointer of the type BITMAP.

```
BITMAP *findBitmap(w,p)
        WINDOW *w;
        POINT *p;
{
        OBJECTHEAD *oh;
        BITMAP *b;
```

7-9 The findBitmap function.

```
oh=(OBJECTHEAD *)w;
while(oh != NULL) {
        if(oh->type == inBitmap) {
                b=(BITMAP *)oh;
                if(PointInRect(p,&b->frame) && b->active==ACTIVE)
                        return(b);
        }
        oh=oh->next;
}
return(NULL);
}
```

Finally, the trackBitmap function is illustrated in Fig. 7-10. It allows active BIT-MAP controls to be selected; if you click in an active control, it will be inverted for as long as the mouse is held down, just as BUTTON controls are.

```
trackBitmap(b)
        BITMAP *b;
{
        POINT p;

        MouseLoc(&p);
        if(PointInRect(&p,&b->frame) && b->active==ACTIVE) {
                InvertRect(&b->frame);
                while(MouseDown(&p));
                InvertRect(&b->frame);
                if(b->proc != NULL) (b->proc)();
        }
}
```

7-10 The trackBitmap function.

It's inadvisable to make large decorative controls active—in a sensible program, one probably wouldn't set up a dialog like the one in Fig. 7-5. A large bitmap that takes a meaningful amount of time to invert and then un-invert every time it's clicked on looks peculiar. If you add a BITMAP control to a window for purely decorative purposes (such as the unicorn in the About box of Desktop Paint or the girl in Fig. 7-4), make sure you pass the INACTIVE constant for the active argument to its addBitmap call.

The trackBitmap function is responsible for calling the function stored in the proc element of a BITMAP object, if there is one. Note that it's quite allowable for this function to open a few windows, play a complete game of chess, calculate the value of pi to a hundred places, and recite Chaucer in the original middle English, just as long as it doesn't actually leave the screen in an altered state when it's done. One potential cause of very unprofessional looking graphics is a screen that changes when an icon is selected and then winds up with an inverted block where the icon used to be, because sooner or later trackBitmap will invert the BITMAP's frame a second time.

A long digression concerning PCX files

Having dealt with how bitmaps are handled, you might still be left with a bit of uncertainty about where the bitmaps originally come from. In the normal application of getimage and putimage, things are only put to the screen after having been previously gotten from somewhere else on the same screen. In dealing with BIT-MAP objects, the getimage function is wholly ignored, and it seems that the fragments passed to putimage are coming from somewhere else entirely.

As the structure of a putimage buffer is by now pretty transparent, there is little reason why graphics cannot be transferred from some format in which they're reasonably plentiful into putimage fragments. In the case of this book's examples, all the fragments will be for the monochrome implementation of putimage for reasons previously discussed.

The format in which graphics can be assumed to be reasonably plentiful is, in fact, the PCX image file format. The PCX format is what PC Paintbrush and several other paint programs, including Desktop Paint, use to store graphics. Unlike a putimage bitmap fragment, the images stored in PCX files are compressed so that large pictures can fit in small amounts of hard drive space.

In practice, you won't be using large images in the graphical user interface. However, paint programs serve as useful tools for manipulating bitmaps so they're presentable in your programs. Because no current paint programs read and write putimage fragments directly, you'll find it convenient to work with PCX files and then translate your PCX files into putimage fragments for ultimate inclusion in a program.

Later in this chapter, there'll be a discussion of a small utility that actually performs this conversion. However, before you can understand how this works, you'll probably want to have at least a nodding acquaintance with the workings of PCX files themselves. Depending upon the programs you ultimately write, you might find other applications for PCX files.

In the following examples, all the bitmap editing will be done with Desktop Paint. Among the several very good reasons for doing this is the notable possibility of capturing the screen of Desktop Paint to an image file; I was able to use the screen to illustrate things. The PC Paintbrush package seems to have disabled this by trapping the PrtSc key. You should note, however, that all of the subsequent paint program activity can be handled with PC Paintbrush instead if you like that better.

Also, you should remember that both paint programs allow you to "crop" bitmaps and export the fragments. Thus, you can select a small portion of a large bitmap and export it to a new PCX file for ultimate conversion into a putimage fragment.

As a final note in this preamble, this section will only deal with those aspects of the PCX file format germane to the graphical user interface. You might find a lot of other aspects of image file formats useful when writing graphic-based applications. In this case, you might want to read my book *Bitmapped Graphics*, also published by TAB Windcrest (TAB book #3558).

The PCX format

The PCX file format is typical of most image file formats. It consists of a header that defines things such as the size of the image in the file, the number of colors the image contains, and the actual colors involved. All discussion of color is irrelevant here, of course.

Following the header is the image data, which is always algorithmically compressed. This will be dealt with presently.

The header of a PCX file can be expressed as a C language struct; and by a happy coincidence, it represents multiple-byte numbers in the same way that C does on a PC. This isn't true of several other image file formats, such as MacPaint and TIFF.

Figure 7-11 illustrates the header of a PCX file.

```
typedef struct {
        char manufacturer;
        char version;
        char encoding;
        char bits_per_pixel;
        int xmin,ymin;
        int xmax,ymax;
        int hres;
        int vres;
        char palette[48];
        char reserved;
        char colour_planes;
        int bytes_per_line;
        int palette_type;
        char filler[58];
        } PCXHEAD;
```

7-11 The header of a PCX file.

The first byte in a PCX file's header, the manufacturer element, is always ten. This is how a program that thinks it's been given a PCX file to read can know that it's really a PCX file and not a copy of Arkanoid renamed with a PCX extension.

The version element of a PCX header tells decoding software how to handle the palette (i.e., color scheme) of the picture. As this application of PCX files only concerns itself with monochrome PCX files, you can ignore this element.

The bits_per_pixel and the color_planes elements together form a way to figure out how many colors the picture in question contains. I'll describe this further in a moment.

The width of a PCX file's image in pixels can be worked out by subtracting the xmin element from the xmax element. In most cases, xmin will be zero, although in theory a PCX file can specify that its image is supposed to start somewhere other than in the upper left corner of the screen. The applications in this chapter don't really care where a PCX file thinks its image should start.

Likewise, the vertical dimension of a PCX file can be worked out by subtracting the ymin element from the ymax element.

The hres and vres elements can be ignored, as can the palette element, which is only used in color pictures.

The bytes_per_line value specifies how long a line of image data will be when each line of the PCX file is uncompressed. Note that this might not be the same as the value you'd get if you calculated pixels2bytes(ymax-ymin). Some applications that generate PCX files will round this value up to an even number if needs be.

A PCX file header is 128 bytes long.

When you open a PCX file with the intention of reading its image into a buffer or displaying it on the screen, you should copy the first 128 bytes into a PCXHEAD variable such that its various elements will be easy to access. You should also check to make sure that the manufacturer element actually contains ten. This example will open the file called PICTURE.PCX:

```
FILE *fp
PCXHEAD pcx.

if((fp = fopen("PICTURE.PCX","rb")) != NULL) {
    if((fread((char *)&pcx,1,sizeof(PCXHEAD),fp)
      = = sizeof(PCXHEAD) {
        if(pcx.manufacturer = = 10) {

            /* do something */

        } else puts("This isn't a PCX file");
    } else puts("Error reading the header");
    fclose(fp);
} else puts("Error opening the file");
```

Assuming that the foregoing code fragment actually reaches whatever is supposed to do something, the file pointer fp will be ready to read the first byte of the first line of compressed PCX image file data.

If you consider the image fragment back in Fig. 7-1, you'll observe that it contains relatively little detail and quite a lot of white space. It takes up a lot of space in its unpacked state when it's a putimage fragment, but one could come up with a way to compress it. For example, if a line of data is nothing but white space, it could be reduced to some sort of code that said "fill this line with white space".

In fact, all image lines can be reduced to two sorts of data, these being *repeat fields* and *string fields*. A repeat field is a line or a portion of a line wherein a single byte is repeated for a fixed number of times. A string field is a line or a portion of a line with which this isn't the case, (i.e., where two or more adjacent bytes aren't identical).

The lines in the middle of Fig. 7-1 could be described as being a repeat field of white bytes, a string field containing the details of the girl's face followed by an additional repeat field for the white space to the right of her face.

In a complex image, lines are often made up of a combination of several alternating repeat and string fields. For example, in the area of the girl's forehead back in Fig. 7-1, the grey patterns have occurred such that there are actually three or four identical bytes in several lines. These would be handled as repeat fields.

The way in which string and repeat fields are encoded to allow them to take up the least amount of space in an image file is called *compression* and varies from format to format. In most cases, the compression techniques are designed around the nature of the images the file is intended to contain.

PCX files were originally designed by ZSoft, the creator of PC Paintbrush, back when PC Paintbrush was a fairly primitive drawing program. As such, they're heavily weighted toward effectively compressing areas of large, unbroken color, such as would result from using the drawing tools of a paint package. This makes the PCX format quite inefficient at compressing semi-random data, such as that resulting when a photograph wakes up on an image scanner.

One of the redeeming features of PCX image compression is that it's very simple and (as such) very quick to uncompress. Also, very little code is needed to uncompress a PCX line. An entire PCX image file decoder can be written in a few dozen lines of C code. A GIF file decoder, by comparison, requires 20K of assembly language code; and GIF files take at least twice as long to unpack, all other things being equal. The GIF file format can compress scanned images to about half the size that the PCX format can but with an obvious considerable penalty in the complexity of the compression and uncompression process.

PCX files are always compressed one line at a time. Thus, you can unpack one by starting at the first byte after the header and reading each field in the file until you have unpacked as many bytes as specified in the bytes_per_line element of the header. If after unpacking a field the result exceeds the bytes_per_line value (i.e., if the end of the line should have occurred part way through the field in question), either the file is corrupted or the encoding software contained a bug.

Unpacking a PCX file entails calling a function to decode the lines in the image once for each line in the file, as worked out by subtracting the ymin value of the header from the ymax value. The pointer p in the following code points to a buffer big enough to hold the image (and thus is (pcx.ymax-pcx.ymin)*pcx.bytes _per_line bytes in size). You would want to add four bytes to this, and move all the data up by four bytes if you planned to use putimage to display the final picture. This procedure assumes the existence of a variable of the type PCXHEAD called pcx, which has been loaded with the contents of the header of the PCX file being decoded.

```
int i,n;

n = pcx.ymax-pcx.ymin;

for(i = 0;i < n; + + y) {
        readPcxLine(p,fp,pcx.bytes_per_line);
        p+ = pcx.bytes_per_line;
}
```

As you might infer, the readPcxLine function will somehow write the uncompressed image data to the buffer passed to it. Note that this bit of code assumes that the complete uncompressed picture will occupy no more than 64K of memory. Handling pictures that unpack into more than 64K is considerably trickier. It's not really applicable to this discussion, as putimage won't display fragments bigger than this.

In order to write readPcxLine, you must understand how the PCX encoding scheme works. Each PCX line is encoded as a series of fields. The first byte after the header is the beginning of the first field. The code unpacking a field must read the first byte of the field and check to see if the upper two bits are set. If they aren't set, this byte should be written directly to the uncompressed data buffer (the field in question is one byte long).

If the upper two bits are set, this byte is a repeat counter. The upper two bits are removed, and the resulting value is stored somewhere. The next byte is read and repeated in the output buffer for as many times as were indicated by the repeat counter.

Figure 7-12 illustrates a flow chart for uncompressing one line of a PCX file.

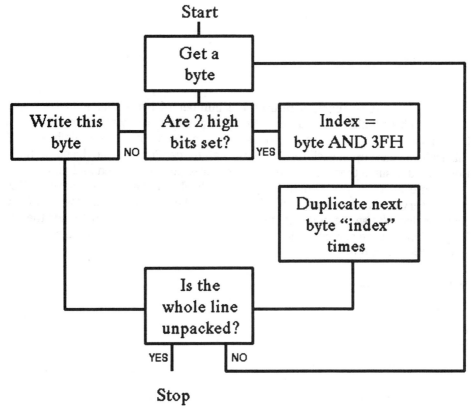

7-12 A flow chart illustrating the process of uncompressing a PCX line.

Once a field has been read, the readPcxLine function must check to see if a whole line has been unpacked. If it hasn't—if the number of bytes unpacked is less than the value in the bytes_per_line value of the header—then another field should be read.

The code for readPcxLine is as follows:

```
readPcxLine(p,fp,bytes)
    char *p;
    FILE *fp;
    int bytes;
{
    int n = 0,c,i;
```

```
        do {
                c = fgetc(fp) & 0xff;
                if((c & 0xc0) = = 0xc0) {
                        i = c & 0x3f;
                        c = fgetc(fp);
                        while(i—) p[n + +] = c;
        }
            else p[n + +] = c;
        } while(n < bytes);
        return(n);
}
```

The readPcxLine function returns the number of bytes that it has actually decoded. This should be the same as the value passed in its bytes argument, which in turn should be the value in the bytes_per_line element of the file's header. If this isn't the case upon each return from a call to readPcxLine, the decoding function should assume that the file being uncompressed is corrupted and abort.

Figure 7-13 is a very simple program for displaying small monochrome PCX files. It serves to illustrate a practical example of how PCX decoding works. Note that this doesn't use the graphical user interface library at all. It just loads the file in question into the screen buffer of your display card, and none too elegantly at that. Hit a key, and it will return to DOS.

```
/* A program to look at small monochrome PCX pictures */

#include "stdio.h"
#include "alloc.h"
#include "dos.h"
#include "graphics.h"

#define pixels2bytes(n)     ((n+7)/8)

typedef struct {
        char manufacturer;
        char version;
        char encoding;
        char bits_per_pixel;
        int xmin,ymin;
        int xmax,ymax;
        int hres;
        int vres;
        char palette[48];
        char reserved;
        char colour_planes;
        int bytes_per_line;
        int palette_type;
        char filler[58];
        } PCXHEAD;

char *mono2ega(char *p);

PCXHEAD header;                     /* where the header lives */
unsigned int width,depth;
```

7-13 A simple monochrome PCX file display.

```
        unsigned int bytes;

main(argc,argv)
        int argc;
        char *argv[];
{
        FILE *fp;
        char *p;

        if(argc > 1) {
                if((fp=fopen(argv[1],"rb")) != NULL) {
                        if(fread((char *)&header,1,sizeof(PCXHEAD),fp)
                            == sizeof(PCXHEAD)) {
                                if(header.manufacturer==0x0a) {
                                        width = (header.xmax-header.xmin)+1;
                                        depth = (header.ymax-header.ymin)+1;
                                        bytes=header.bytes_per_line;

                                        if((p=malloc(4+bytes*depth)) != NULL) {
                                                if(UnpackPcxFile(p+4,fp)==bytes)
                                                        ShowPcxPicture(p);
                                                free(p);
                                        }
                                } else printf("Not a PCX file.\n");
                        } else printf("Error reading %s.\n",argv[1]);
                        fclose(fp);
                } else printf("Error opening %s.\n",argv[1]);
        }
}
ShowPcxPicture(p)  /* display the picture */
        char *p;
{
        char *pr;

        init();

        p[0]=width-1;
        p[1]=((width-1) >> 8);
        p[2]=depth-1;
        p[3]=((depth-1) >> 8);
        if(getmaxcolor()==1) putimage(0,0,p,COPY_PUT);
        else {
                if((pr=mono2ega(p)) != NULL) {
                        putimage(0,0,pr,COPY_PUT);
                        free(pr);
                } else putchar(7);
        }

        getch();
        deinit();
}

UnpackPcxFile(p,fp)             /* open and print GEM/IMG image n */
        char *p;
        FILE *fp;
{
        int i,n;

        for(i=0;i<depth;++i) {
                n=ReadPcxLine(p,fp);
                p+=bytes;
        }
        return(n);
}
```

7-13 Continued

```
ReadPcxLine(p,fp)     /* read and decode a PCX line into p */
        char *p;
        FILE *fp;
{
        int n=0,c,i;

        memset(p,0,bytes);
        do {
                c=fgetc(fp) & 0xff;
                if((c & 0xc0) == 0xc0) {
                        i=c & 0x3f;
                        c=fgetc(fp);
                        while(i--) p[n++]=c;
                }
                else p[n++]=c;
        } while(n < bytes);
        return(n);
}

init()              /* turn on graphics mode */
{
        int d,m,e=0;
        detectgraph(&d,&m);
        if(d<0) {
                puts("No graphics card");
                exit(1);
        }
        initgraph(&d,&m,"");
        e=graphresult();
        if(e<0) {
                printf("Graphics error %d: %s",e,grapherrormsg(e));
                exit(1);
        }
        setcolor(getmaxcolor());
}

deinit()  /* turn off graphics card */
{
        closegraph();
}

char *mono2ega(source)
        char *source;
{
        char *p;
        int x,y,j,ls,sz;

        x=1+source[0]+(source[1] << 8);
        y=1+source[2]+(source[3] << 8);
        if((sz=imagesize(0,0,x,y)) != -1) {
                if((p=malloc(sz)) != NULL) {
                        memcpy(p,source,4);
                        ls=pixels2bytes(x);
                        for(j=0;j<y;++j) {
                                memcpy(p+4+((j*4)*ls),source+4+(j*ls),ls);
                                memcpy(p+4+ls+((j*4)*ls),source+4+(j*ls),ls);
                                memcpy(p+4+(ls*2)+((j*4)*ls),
                                        source+4+(j*ls),ls);
                                memcpy(p+4+(ls*3)+((j*4)*ls),source+4+(j*ls),
                                        ls);
                        }
                        return(p);
```

```
                }
        } else return(NULL);
}
```

Thus far in this discussion, I've assumed that PCX files will always contain monochrome images. Of course, this isn't always true. The number of colors in a PCX file can be found by rotating one left by the number of bits per pixel of color in the file. The number of bits per pixel can be worked out using the following formula:

```
int bits;

if(pcx.bits_per_pixel = = 1) bits = pcx.colour_planes;
else bits = pcx.bits_per_pixel;
```

If this results in bits having a value of something other than one, the file in question doesn't contain a monochrome picture and isn't suitable for use with any of the examples in this chapter. If it does equal one, the number of colors is (1 < < bits), or two—these being black and white.

Converting PCX files to image fragments

Having plumbed the tremulant mysteries of the PCX file format, you can probably work out how to convert small PCX files into small monochrome putimage fragments for use with BITMAP objects. Figure 7-14 illustrates a utility called PCX2BIN that will take care of it.

```
/*
        PCX2BIN - PC Paintbrush to binary fragment converter
*/

#include "stdio.h"
#include "alloc.h"

#define mac_ext         "PCX"
#define bin_ext         "BIN"

#define pixels2bytes(n)    ((n+7)/8)

typedef struct {
        char manufacturer;
        char version;
        char encoding;
        char bits_per_pixel;
        int xmin,ymin;
        int xmax,ymax;
        int hres;
        int vres;
        char palette[48];
        char reserved;
        char colour_planes;
        int bytes_per_line;
        int palette_type;
        char filler[58];
```

7-14 The PCX2BIN program.

```
        } PCXHEAD;

char *read_pcx();

char sourceName[128],destName[128];

int width,depth,bytes;

main(argc,argv)
        int argc;
        char *argv[];
{
        char *p;

        if(argc > 1) {
                strmfe(sourceName,argv[1],"PCX");
                strmfe(destName,argv[1],"BIN");
                if((p=read_pcx(sourceName)) != NULL) {
                        save_binary(destName,p);
                        free(p);
                } else puts("Error reading source file");
        } else puts("I need an argumnet");
}

/* write a binary fragment to a disk file */
save_binary(s,p)
        char *s,*p;
{
        FILE *fp;

        if((fp=fopen(s,"wb")) != NULL) {
                putw(width-1,fp);
                putw(depth-1,fp);
                fwrite(p,1,pixels2bytes(width)*depth,fp);
                fclose(fp);
        } else puts("Error creating distination");
}

/* return a buffer with the PCX file in it */
char *read_pcx(s)
        char *s;
{
        PCXHEAD h;
        FILE *fp;
        char *p=NULL;
        int i,size;

        if((fp=fopen(s,"rb")) != NULL) {
                if(fread((char *)&h,1,sizeof(PCXHEAD),fp) == sizeof(PCXHEAD) &&
                   h.manufacturer==0x0a) {
                        width=(h.xmax-h.xmin)+1;
                        depth=(h.ymax-h.ymin)+1;
                        bytes=h.bytes_per_line;
                        size=bytes * (depth+1);
                        if((p=malloc(size)) != NULL) {
                                for(i=0;i<depth;++i)
                                        readPcxLine(p,fp,bytes);
                        }
                }
                fclose(fp);
        }
        return(p);
```

```
}

/* read and decode a PCX line into p */
readPcxLine(p,fp,bytes)
        char *p;
        FILE *fp;
        int bytes;
{
        int n=0,c,i;

        do {
                c=fgetc(fp) & 0xff;
                if((c & 0xc0) == 0xc0) {
                        i=c & 0x3f;
                        c=fgetc(fp);
                        while(i--) p[n++]=~c;
                }
                else p[n++]=~c;
        } while(n < bytes);
        return(n);
}

/* make a new file name with a fixed extension */
strmfe(new,old,ext)
        char *new,*old,*ext;
{
        while(*old != 0 && *old != '.') *new++=*old++;
        *new++='.';
        while(*ext) *new++=*ext++;
        *new=0;
}
```

There are a few things to note about PCX2BIN. To begin with, it's a fairly trusting soul—trusting, among other things, that you will only feed it monochrome PCX files to convert. It also trusts that you won't feed it any particularly large PCX files (i.e., ones that will unpack to more than 64K).

Note that the readPcxLine function in this program has been modified slightly to invert the image being read so it will come out the way it's supposed to in the putimage fragment written to the destination file.

If you run this program with a PCX file as its argument, it will create a file with the same name and the extension BIN, containing the image from the PCX file stored as a putimage fragment. It won't change the original PCX file, of course.

The icons for Desktop Paint were created using Desktop Paint, PCX2BIN, and the PRELINK program from Chapter 4. The original developmental version of Desktop Paint had BUTTON controls for its toolbox until it was sufficiently well along to be able to create its own icons.

To create the image fragment for a BITMAP control, you would begin by drawing the image for the icon in Desktop Paint or PC Paintbrush. If you aren't all that artistic, you might consider swiping an icon from an existing image file. In this case, try to avoid using an image file that someone is likely to sue you over. Image files that have been scanned from Victorian line drawings and etchings are a safe choice, as the original art predates any copyright laws, and these will give your programs a sort of techno-Dickensian feel to them—something unlikely to be duplicated in most commercial applications.

Having drawn or swiped a suitable small image, select it and export it to a

PCX file of its own. Run PCX2BIN to create a BIN file—a putimage fragment—and then use PRELINK to transform the BIN file into an OBJ file suitable for linking into your program.

Figure 7-15 illustrates the steps involved.

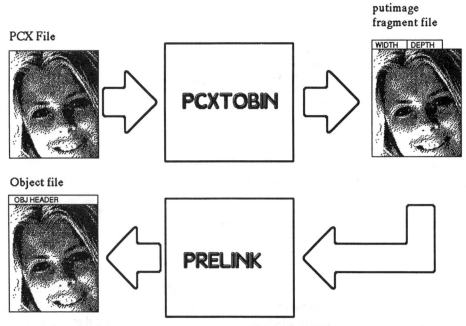

7-15 The steps involved in converting a PCX file to a linked-in object.

Note that you must declare any image fragments linked into a program this way as extern in your C language source file so the compiler won't think you're using undefined symbols.

Finally, there are a few instances in which you might find it useful to be able to convert 16-color bitmap fragments into monochrome ones (and thus reverse the process wrought by mono2ega). This can be handy if you want to create a monochrome version of a bitmap captured from a 16-color screen. The function to do this, ega2mono, is shown in Fig. 7-16.

```
char *ega2mono(source)
        char *source;
{
        char *p;
        int x,y,j,ls,sz;

        x=1+source[0]+(source[1] << 8);
        y=1+source[2]+(source[3] << 8);

        ls=pixels2bytes(x);
        sz=(ls*y)+4;
        if((p=malloc(sz)) != NULL) {
```

7-16 The ega2mono function.

```
            memcpy(p,source,4);
            for(j=0;j<y;++j) memcpy(p+4+(j*ls),source+4+((j*4)*ls),ls);
            return(p);
        } else return(NULL);
}
```

As with mono2ega, the ega2mono function allocates a buffer to put the new bitmap it creates in. Make sure you free this buffer when it's no longer needed.

Note that the ega2mono function actually works by throwing away three out of every four lines of the 16-color buffer passed to it. When you're working with a 16-color screen in the way the code in this book does (i.e., pretending it's actually monochrome), three out of every four lines are redundant, so you can get away with this. You'll lose a great deal of color information if you do it to a real 16-color fragment, however.

Using bitmap controls

The About box of Desktop Paint, shown in its final appearance in Fig. 7-16, is a fairly good example of a simple application of BITMAP objects. While it doesn't respond to a click in the unicorn's head, it illustrates how a BITMAP object should be added to a window.

The code that created the About box is illustrated in Fig. 7-17. The unicorn bitmap is stored as PARTUNI, from PARTUNI.OBJ, which is linked into the final program by including it in the project file for Desktop Paint. After all the discussion about storing bitmaps as resources earlier in this book, the unicorn is after all a permanent part of the program, as Desktop Paint is designed to be able to run without its resource file in some situations.

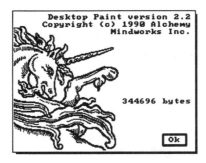

7-17 The About box of Desktop Paint.

The doAboutBox function also displays the amount of available DOS memory when it's called. In the doAboutBox function, the version number of the software is automatically set to the correct version of the program. Note that this function determines the size of its window by figuring out how deep the bitmap is. If the actual image at PARTUNI is exchanged for one of slightly differing dimensions, the doAboutBox window will compensate.

The toolbox of the small paint program in Chapter 11 is an example of using active BITMAP controls—ones that actually do something beyond just sitting about and looking decorative.

Finally, you should note that you can often use BITMAP controls to create synthetic control types without actually defining the add, draw, track, and find functions that would normally be needed to deal with a new control type. For example, Fig. 7-18 illustrates some rather exotic button controls. In fact, none of these are BUTTON objects; they're just BITMAP objects in which the bitmaps were drawn in Desktop Paint, imported into a program, and then used as if they were actually buttons.

```
doAboutBox()
{
        extern char PARTUNI[];
        static char ln[3][28] = { "Desktop Paint version 1.0",
                                   "Copyright (c) 1990 Alchemy",
                                   "Mindworks Inc."
                                 };

        TEXT tx[3],tf;
        BITMAP bmp;
        BUTTON b, *bp;
        WINDOW w;
        RECT r;
        POINT p;
        char bf[24];
        unsigned int rt,i,a=0xff;

        SetRect(&r,47,56,300,56+ImageDepth(PARTUNI));

        sprintf(bf,"%lu bytes",coreleft());

        if(OpenWindow(&w,&r)) {
                AddBitmap(&w,&bmp,r.left,r.top,PARTUNI,0x00,NULL,INACTIVE);
                SetRect(&b.frame,r.right-40,r.bottom-23,r.right-8,r.bottom-8);
                AddButton(&w,&b,"Ok",ACTIVE);

                for(i=0;i<3;++i)
                    AddText(&w,&tx[i],r.right-strlen(ln[i])*8,
                                      r.top+4+(i*MENULINEDEEP),ln[i],ACTIVE);

                AddText(&w,&tf,r.right-strlen(bf)*8,r.top+120,bf,ACTIVE);

                while(a) {
                        Keyboard(&w);
                        if(MouseDown(&p)) {
                                rt=whereMouse(&p,&w);
                                if(rt & inButton) {
                                        bp=findButton(&w,&p);
                                        trackButton(bp);
                                        a=0;
                                }
                                else errorbeep();
                        }
                }
                CloseWindow(&w);
        } else errorbeep();
}
```

7-18   The code that created the dialog in Fig. 7-17.

These are the sorts of things that look interesting when they crop up in games but perhaps inappropriate if they appear in a database manager.

7-19 Some custom controls that are really just fancy bitmaps.

No mention has been made thus far about using resources to store bitmaps. I'll deal with this in detail in Chapter 9 once I've expounded upon the true nature of resources.

Help a man when he's in trouble, and he'll remember you when he's in trouble again.
Murphy's Laws of Computers

8

Using resources

AS WILL HAVE BECOME APPARENT BY NOW, A GRAPHICAL USER INTERFACE uses data structures the way a hungry dog uses house cats. Until now, all the data structures have been fairly transitory—like the aforementioned house cats—but this isn't always the case. There are quite a few situations in which you'll want an application to be able to inhale data structures from a permanent repository in a disk file.

Disk-based data is useful for storing image fragments, such as those discussed in Chapter 7. It's all but essential for handling fonts (see Chapter 9). It can also be a handy way to deal with configuration information and other things that your users might want to modify.

If you're writing applications that will be translated into other languages, you might find it exceedingly convenient to keep all your text strings in a disk file and have them loaded into your program at run time, such that changing the text file will change the language the program uses to communicate with its users.

While you can handle disk-based data with one disk file for every discrete block of data to be made available to your program, this is clumsy and carries several meaningful penalties. In an application with numerous small blocks of data, the granulation losses in hard drive space can be pretty significant (see Chapter 1). There'll be many small files to keep track of, and your programs will spend considerable time opening and closing them.

Using a *resource* file avoids this situation. A resource file is a file containing all the little blocks of data your program might need, structured in a way that makes it easy for your program to find things and equally easy for the file contents to be manipulated.

Resources are another concept borrowed from the Macintosh. This may not be surprising—being based on a graphical user interface, the Macintosh operating system is confronted with many of the same programming problems that affect this book's user interface. The Mac arguably handles resources more elegantly than a PC can, as its disk file structure is specifically designed to maintain integral chunks of resources.

You'll have to get by with stand-alone resource files for PC-based applications that need them.

Resource management

A resource is a block of data with a header. The data in a resource can be anything you like—the only restriction inherent in the code in this chapter is that no single resource can include data requiring more than 64K to store. In most applications of resources, the size of a single resource never comes close to this. A resource file having multiple resources can be as big as you like.

Every resource has a *type*. A type is a four-byte designation, the four bytes typically being printable characters to make the type meaningful. For example, font resources are given the type FONT.

Each resource of a specific type will also have a number, such that no two resources in a single resource file can have the same type and the same number.

Finally, each resource has a size value (i.e., the number of bytes occupied by its data).

A resource header can be defined like this:

```
typedef struct {
    char type[4];
    unsigned long number;
    unsigned int size;
    } RESOURCE;
```

An unsigned integer is sufficient to define the size, as it can't be bigger than 64K.

Resources can be stored in memory—in which case they'll consist of a header like this one followed by some data—or in a resource file on disk. A resource file consists of a resource file header followed by one or more resources, like this:

```
typedef struct {
    char id[8];
    char description[65];
    unsigned int count;
    } RESHEAD;
```

The id element of a resource file is a string allowing the code that will work with resources—the resource manager, in Macintosh terms—to know that it really has a resource file when the file is first opened. This string will always be the same, and is defined like this:

```
#define resourceID "ALCHRSRC"
```

You can change this to some other string if you like, but it's handy to keep it consistent over various applications. It's interesting how often resources from one program can turn out to be useful in another.

The description field of a resource file header is an ASCII string describing what's in the file. This is optional—you can leave it blank if you like. Because this field appears right after the id string, which is also printable, using the DOS TYPE command on a resource file will tell you what's in it.

The count element defines how many resources are in a particular file.

The resources in a resource file behave as a sort of disk-based linked list, analogous to the way that objects are added to a window. If you seek past the resource file header of a resource file, the next byte to be read will be the first byte of the first resource header in the file. If you read this into a variable of the type RESOURCE, you will be able to locate the beginning of the next resource by seeking forward in the file by the number of bytes in the size element. You can walk up the whole resource file this way, one resource at a time.

There is no instance in which it will be necessary to read a resource one byte at a time—they're always handled in blocks, and the size of the blocks is always known. It will either be the size of one of the aforementioned data structures or the size of the resource data in question. As such, the facilities of the C language streamed file functions—fopen, fgetc, and so on—aren't really needed.

The streamed file functions are actually quite a bit slower than straight block-based file functions would be. The fastest way to handle files is actually to bypass the available C functions entirely and mediate directly with DOS. Because dealing with resources quickly is a desirable characteristic in any program, you should take the time to write a set of DOS file handling functions (see Fig. 8-1).

```
/* direct DOS file create */
dcreate(s)
        char *s;
{
        union REGS r;
        struct SREGS sg;

        r.x.ax=0x3c00;
        r.x.cx=0;
        r.x.dx=FP_OFF(s);
        sg.ds=FP_SEG(s);
        int86x(0x21,&r,&r,&sg);
        if(r.x.cflag) return(0);
        else return(r.x.ax);
}

/* direct DOS file open */
dopen(s)
        char *s;
{
        union REGS r;
```

8-1 Fast DOS file handling functions.

```
        struct SREGS sg;

        r.x.ax=0x3d02;
        r.x.cx=0;
        r.x.dx=FP_OFF(s);
        sg.ds=FP_SEG(s);
        int86x(0x21,&r,&r,&sg);
        if(r.x.cflag) return(0);
        else return(r.x.ax);
}

/* direct DOS file close */
void dclose(h)
        RFILE h;
{
        union REGS r;

        r.x.ax=0x3e00;
        r.x.bx=h;
        int86(0x21,&r,&r);
        if(r.x.cflag) return(r.x.ax);
        else return(0);
}

/* direct DOS file read */
dread(p,n,h)
        char *p;
        unsigned int n;
        RFILE h;
{
        union REGS r;
        struct SREGS sg;

        r.x.ax=0x3f00;
        r.x.bx=h;
        r.x.cx=n;
        r.x.dx=FP_OFF(p);
        sg.ds=FP_SEG(p);
        int86x(0x21,&r,&r,&sg);
        if(r.x.cflag) return(0);
        else return(r.x.ax);
}

/* direct DOS file write */
dwrite(p,n,h)
        char *p;
        unsigned int n;
        RFILE h;
{
        union REGS r;
        struct SREGS sg;

        r.x.ax=0x4000;
        r.x.bx=h;
        r.x.cx=n;
        r.x.dx=FP_OFF(p);
        sg.ds=FP_SEG(p);
        int86x(0x21,&r,&r,&sg);
        if(r.x.cflag) return(0);
        else return(r.x.ax);
}
```

```
/* direct DOS file read */
long dseek(h,l,m)
        int h,m;
        long l;
{
        union REGS r;
        struct SREGS sg;

        r.h.ah=0x42;
        r.h.al=m;
        r.x.bx=h;
        r.x.cx=(unsigned int)(l >> 16);
        r.x.dx=(unsigned int)l;
        int86x(0x21,&r,&r,&sg);
        if(r.x.cflag) return(-1L);
        else return(((long)r.x.dx << 16)+ (long)r.x.ax);
}

/* direct DOS file read */
long dtell(h)
        RFILE h;
{
        union REGS r;
        struct SREGS sg;

        r.h.ah=0x42;
        r.h.al=0x01;
        r.x.bx=h;
        r.x.cx=0;
        r.x.dx=0;
        int86x(0x21,&r,&r,&sg);
        if(r.x.cflag) return(-1L);
        else return(((long)r.x.dx << 16)+ (long)r.x.ax);
}
```

If you've done any machine language programming involving disk files, you'll recognize the direct DOS file functions as being the C language equivalent of calls to the INT 21H handler. This allows DOS to pass blocks of data directly between a buffer in your program and the disk. If you aren't familiar with machine language level DOS calls, don't worry. You don't really have to be in order to use these functions.

The direct DOS calls involve the use of a new data type defined like this:

```
typedef int     RFILE;
```

The RFILE data type is really just an integer, but you should define a special type for it to separate it from other integers in your programs.

A few other things should be defined in GUI.H to keep the resource manager functions happy:

```
#define BADRECNUM     0xffffffffL
#define BADRECTYPE    "\000\000\000\000"
#define RESext        "RES"
```

The BADRECNUM constant is an illegal resource number, and BADREC-

TYPE is an illegal resource type. The RESext string is the default resource file extension.

The functions to work with resources correspond in some cases to those used to deal with ordinary binary files. However, they take into account the structure of resource files specifically. This usually involves keeping track of the information in the header of a resource file and updating it as necessary.

To begin with, Fig. 8-2 illustrates the code for creating a new resource file.

```
/* create a resource file and leave it unopened */
createRF(name,description)
        char *name,*description;
{
        RESHEAD rh;
        int fh,r=0;

        if((fh=dcreate(name)) != NULL) {
                memset((char *)&rh,0,sizeof(RESHEAD));
                memcpy(rh.id,resourceID,8);
                strcpy(rh.description,description);
                if(dwrite((char *)&rh,sizeof(RESHEAD),fh) ==
                    sizeof(RESHEAD)) r=1;
                dclose(fh);
        }
        return(r);
}
```

8-2 The createRF function.

The createRF function will create a resource file with the name passed in its path argument and having whatever text is passed as its description argument as the description field of the file. The program calling this function is responsible for ensuring that the description doesn't exceed 64 characters. The createRF function will return a true value if the file was created.

Having been created, a resource file can be opened for reading and writing using openRF, as seen in Fig. 8-3. This ensures that the file in question is really a resource file by checking the id field of its header. It will return either an RFILE if the file opened successfully or zero if it didn't. Note that, unlike file functions inherent in C, openRF doesn't allow you to specify a resource file as read-only or write-only. All opened resource files can be both read from and written to.

Figure 8-3 also includes the closeRF function, which closes an opened resource file.

```
/* open a resource file and return its handle */
RFILE openRF(name)
        char *name;
{
        RESHEAD rh;
        int fh;

        if((fh=dopen(name)) != NULL) {
                if(dread((char *)&rh,sizeof(RESHEAD),fh) == sizeof(RESHEAD)) {
                        if(memcmp(rh.id,resourceID,8)) {
                                dclose(fh);
```

8-3 The openRF function.

```
                                      return(0);
                          }
                          return((RFILE )fh);
                }
                else {
                          dclose(fh);
                          return(0);
                }
        } else return(0);
}

/* close a resource file */
void closeRF(fh)
        RFILE fh;
{
        dclose(fh);
}
```

A resource is typically created in memory in two parts—as a RESOURCE object and then as the data that will go into the resource. The addRF function illustrates the code for adding these two bits of data together to form a disk based resource in a resource file (see Fig. 8-4).

```
/* add a resource to a resource file */
addRF(fh,type,number,size,res)
        RFILE fh;
        char *type;
        unsigned long number;
        unsigned int size;
        char *res;
{
        RESHEAD rh;
        RESOURCE rc;
        unsigned int i;

        if(getinfoRF(&rh,fh) && number != BADRECNUM) {
                for(i=0;i<rh.count;++i) {
                        if(dread((char *)&rc,sizeof(RESOURCE),fh) !=
                            sizeof(RESOURCE)) return(0);
                        dseek(fh,(long)rc.size,SEEK_CUR);
                }
                memset((char *)&rc,0,sizeof(RESOURCE));
                memcpy(rc.type,type,4);
                rc.number=number;
                rc.size=size;
                if(dwrite((char *)&rc,sizeof(RESOURCE),fh) != sizeof(RESOURCE))
                    return(0);
                if(dwrite(res,size,fh) != size) return(0);
                ++rh.count;
                dseek(fh,0L,SEEK_SET);
                if(dwrite((char *)&rh,sizeof(RESHEAD),fh) != sizeof(RESHEAD))
                    return(0);
                return(1);
        } else return(0);
}
```

8-4 The addRF function.

The first argument to addRF should be the RFILE variable returned by a successful call to openRF. The next argument is the type of the resource you want to add (which should be, in fact, a four-byte string). The number argument should be a long integer—you can have any number you like, as long as it isn't BADREC-NUM. The freenumberRF function, to be discussed later in this chapter, will find the first unused resource number in a resource file for any resource type.

The size argument tells addRF how many bytes of data are in the buffer pointed to by the res argument.

The addRF function actually has to juggle two disparate bits of a resource file. It always adds resources to the end of the file, so it needs the count element of the resource file header in order to locate the current end of the file. The for loop actually walks up the linked list of the file. However, because the number of elements in the list is known, the function doesn't need to ascertain where the end of the list is by looking for a disk file equivalent to a NULL pointer.

Having written the appropriate RESOURCE variable and then the data for the resource to the file, addRF must seek back to the beginning of the resource file to update the resource file header so that it reflects the updated resource count. Sadly, this can't be done before the resource is written—back when the file pointer was conveniently at the file's beginning to read the header in the first place—because the count would then be incorrect if the resource couldn't be written to the file.

The addRF function returns a true value if the resource in question has been successfully added to its resource file.

The functions thus far make it possible to create simple resource files. For example, Fig. 8-5 illustrates how you would capture a fragment from a graphic mode screen and write it to a BTMP resource. This assumes that your screen is in one of the graphic modes that the graphical user interface supports and that there's something interesting on the part being captured.

```
GrabBitmapFragment()
{
        RFILE fh;
        RESOURCE r;
        char *p,*pr;
        int size;

        if(createRF("TEST.RES","Test resource file")) {
                if((fh=openRF("TEST.RES")) != 0) {
                        size=imagesize(10,10,200,200);
                        if(size != -1) {
                                if((p=malloc(size)) != NULL) {
                                        getimage(10,10,200,200,p);
                                        if(ismonomode()) pr=p;
                                        else pr=ega2mono(p);
                                        addRF(fh,"BTMP",1L,size,pr);
                                        if(!ismonomode()) free(pr);
                                        free(p);
                                }
                        }
                        closeRF(fh);
                }
        }
}
```

8-5   Some code to capture an image fragment from the screen as a BTMP resource.

If you have Desktop Paint, you can see how this has worked out. Rename the file GALLERY.RES in the directory holding Desktop Paint to something else for a while, and rename TEST.RES to GALLERY.RES. Run Desktop Paint and open the Gallery window in the Desk menu. Your image fragment should appear in it. Figure 8-6 illustrates an example of this.

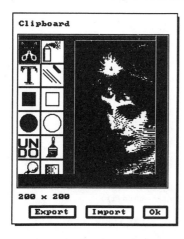

8-6 The image fragment from Fig. 8-5, as shown in the gallery window of Desktop Paint.

Retrieving data from a resource file is usually more complex than adding data. You must know the type and, optionally, the number of the resource you're interested in. You must then locate the resource header you're after in the file, which will tell you how big a buffer you'll need to contain the data, among other things. Finally, you must read the resource data itself into memory.

The getnumberedRF function will find the nth resource of a particular type in a resource file opened by openRF. You could also use getRF to find a specific resource—getRF will locate a resource when you know both the type and the number of the resource in question.

You would use getnumberedRF to find the sixth FONT resource in a file and getRF to find the FONT resource with the resource number six. The number of a resource has no relationship to its position in a resource file.

Figure 8-7 illustrates these two functions.

```
getRF(fh,type,n,rc)
        RFILE fh;
        char *type;
        long n;
        RESOURCE *rc;
{
        RESHEAD rh;
        unsigned int i;

        if(getinfoRF(&rh,fh)) {
                for(i=0;i<rh.count;++i) {
                        if(dread((char *)rc,sizeof(RESOURCE),fh) !=
                            sizeof(RESOURCE)) return(0);
                        if(!memcmp(rc->type,type,4)) {
                                if(rc->number==n) return(1);
```

8-7 The getnumberedRF and getRF functions.

```
                              }
                              dseek(fh,(long)rc->size,SEEK_CUR);
                      }
                      return(0);
              } else return(0);
}

/* get a numbered resource */
getnumberedRF(fh,type,n,rc)
        RFILE fh;
        char *type;
        int n;
        RESOURCE *rc;
{
        RESHEAD rh;
        unsigned int i,count=0;

        if(getinfoRF(&rh,fh)) {
                for(i=0;i<rh.count;++i) {
                        if(dread((char *)rc,sizeof(RESOURCE),fh) !=
                            sizeof(RESOURCE)) return(0);
                        if(!memcmp(rc->type,type,4)) {
                                if(count++==n) return(1);
                        }
                        dseek(fh,(long)rc->size,SEEK_CUR);
                }
                return(0);
        } else return(0);
}
```

In both of these functions, the code steps through the resources one at a time in the resource file being read, looking for resources of the specified type. The two functions differ only in how they break out of the for loops that do the searching. Both will return zero if their loops terminate normally, indicating that all the resources have been searched and a match wasn't found (which would happen, for example, if you asked for the sixth FONT resource in a resource file having only five).

Once you've found a resource header with getRF or getnumberedRF, you must load its data into a buffer so you can work with it. The buffer size can be found in the size element of the RESOURCE structure passed to one of the aforementioned two functions. The function that gets the data is called getdataRF (see Fig. 8-8).

```
/* get the resource data from a file */
getdataRF(p,fh,size)
        char *p;
        RFILE fh;
        unsigned int size;
{
        if(dread(p,size,fh) == size) return(1);
        else return(0);
}
```

8-8 The getdataRF functions.

There isn't much to be said about getdataRF—it's little more than a dread call.

The most complex and potentially troublesome operation with resource files is removing resources from them. You might consider how best to delete the middle of a data file without disturbing the rest of it. In theory, this involves doing one of two things—you can either copy into a new file all the old file's resources except the one to be deleted, or you can move the resources above the deleted one down so that they overwrite it.

This chapter will actually look at both approaches. The removeRF function in Fig. 8-9 uses the second approach, but it runs into some DOS specific problems that make it undesirable in some applications. Specifically, removing a resource this way doesn't actually make the resource file any smaller, although it moves the deleted space up to the file's end, where it can subsequently be reused.

```c
/* remove a resource */
removeresRF(fh,rc)
        RFILE fh;
        RESOURCE *rc;
{
        RESHEAD rh;
        RESOURCE lrc;
        long source,dest;
        char *p;
        int i,r=0;
        unsigned int size,dsize;

        if(!getinfoRF(&rh,fh)) return(0);
        for(i=0;i<rh.count;++i) {
                if(dread((char *)&lrc,sizeof(RESOURCE),fh) != sizeof(RESOURCE))
                        return(0);
                if(!memcmp(rc->type,lrc.type,4) && rc->number==lrc.number) {
                        r=1;
                        break;
                }
                dseek(fh,(long)lrc.size,SEEK_CUR);
        }
        if(!r) return(0);
        size=lrc.size+sizeof(RESOURCE);
        if((p=malloc(size)) == NULL) return(0);
        source=dtell(fh)+lrc.size;
        dest=source-(long)(lrc.size+sizeof(RESOURCE));

        do {
                dseek(fh,source,SEEK_SET);
                if((dsize=dread(p,size,fh)) > 0) {
                        dseek(fh,dest,SEEK_SET);
                        dwrite(p,dsize,fh);
                }
                source+=(long)size;
                dest+=(long)size;
        } while(dsize==size);

        free(p);

        --rh.count;
        dseek(fh,0L,SEEK_SET);
        if(dwrite((char *)&rh,sizeof(RESHEAD),fh) != sizeof(RESHEAD)) return(0)
        return(1);
}
```

8-9 The removeRF function.

Copying resources to a new file, while preferable, is very time-consuming if your resource files are of any size. It also assumes that enough free disk space exists to allow for a temporary file almost as large as the resource file being manipulated.

The difficulty in removing a resource from the middle of a resource file (as compared to doing the same thing for a file of fixed-length database records) is that the objects above the deleted record can be of any size and must be assumed to be potentially larger than the resource being deleted. Figure 8-10 illustrates the structure of a hypothetical resource file with a resource to be deleted.

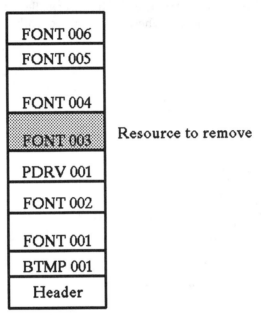

8-10   A resource file with a resource to be deleted.

To remove resources without recopying the whole file each time, you would move the remainder of the file down one chunk at a time, a chunk being the size of the deleted resource. It doesn't actually matter that this will temporarily split larger resources into multiple portions, as they'll ultimately be fused together again when the operation is complete. Likewise, you don't need to adjust the linked list of the file because each resource only knows its own size, rather than its absolute position in the file. The individual sizes of the remaining resources will not change; and after the move is complete, the location of the previously deleted resource will again contain a resource header.

Figure 8-11 illustrates the process of deleting a resource.

The actual code that handles deleting a resource, as shown in Fig. 8-12, is a bit involved. It assumes that you will have found the resource to delete by previously calling getRF or getnumberedRF, and it uses the RESOURCE variable returned by one of them to locate the resource in question. The size of the chunk of free space in the file in this case will be rc->size+sizeof(RESOURCE).

FONT 006	FONT 006	FONT 006	Empty
FONT 005	FONT 005	Empty	FONT 006
FONT 004	Empty	FONT 005	FONT 005
FONT 003	FONT 004	FONT 004	FONT 004
PDRV 001	PDRV 001	PDRV 001	PDRV 001
FONT 002	FONT 002	FONT 002	FONT 002
FONT 001	FONT 001	FONT 001	FONT 001
BTMP 001	BTMP 001	BTMP 001	BTMP 001
Header	Header	Header	Header

8-11 The process of deleting a resource with removeRF.

Having determined the location of the resource to be removed, as well as the size of the resulting gap left by its disappearance, the removal process then reads successive chunks of the remaining file into a buffer from just above the gap and writes them back into the gap. Thus, the gap works its way down the file until it reaches the end. The count element of the resource file header can then be decremented, and the next call to addRF will be able to use the space occupied by the gap.

In theory, the foregoing resource file functions should be everything you'll need to deal with resource files. In practice, a few more functions (discussed momentarily) also will prove useful.

The Gallery window of Desktop Paint, illustrated in Fig. 8-12, is actually based on a resource file called GALLERY.RES. It's a good example of a fairly controlled application of resources, one that at various times uses almost all the functions discussed thus far.

The resources in the GALLERY.RES file are of the type BTMP. A BTMP resource consists of a resource header and then a monochrome putimage fragment, as discussed in Chapter 7. If you read a BTMP resource into memory and then use the display independent bitmap display code from the last chapter, its contents will appear on your screen.

Each image-related button in Fig. 8-12 essentially calls one of the foregoing functions. The Paste button calls addRF to add a bitmap from the clipboard of Desktop Paint to the GALLERY.RES file as a BTMP resource. The Copy button calls getnumberedRF to copy the contents of a resource back to the clipboard. The Clear button calls removeRF to delete a BTMP resource from GALLERY.RES.

8-12 The Desktop Paint gallery window.

If you have a copy of Desktop Paint, you'll find that its Gallery serves as an easy way to create BTMP resources for other applications. You can extract specific resources from it using RMOVER, a program to be discussed later in this chapter. As addRF always adds resources to the end of a resource file, locating the most recently copied image in the gallery is fairly easy—it will always be the last one in the list.

Desktop Paint itself uses this facility. You can extract a BTMP resource from the GALLERY.RES file and add it to the main resource file for Desktop Paint. When Desktop Paint boots up, it will display in the screen's center any BTMP resources it finds while attending to its other housekeeping. This allows the program's users to customize the startup message.

Figure 8-13 illustrates Desktop Paint booting up. The box in the screen's center is a BTMP resource previously created in Desktop Paint, pasted into the gallery, and then extracted from GALLERY.RES.

Figure 8-14 illustrates a version of the code that drives the gallery. It's fairly complex as dialog boxes go but should illustrate the use of the foregoing functions, as well as a few others to be discussed later this chapter.

In order to understand the doGallery function, you must know about a few of the global variables and constants in Desktop Paint used by it. To begin with, clipboard is a pointer either to a putimage fragment or to NULL if nothing's on the clipboard. The CLIPWIDE and CLIPDEEP constants define the size of the gallery window's image area. For largely historical reasons, they're both set at 208.

Also note that image fragments exceeding the dimensions of the image area are cropped, and ones too small to occupy the whole area are padded out with black. This affects only the display, not the actual image fragments themselves, and should explain what the buffer pr is used for.

The theConfig object is a big struct of configuration data, of which one element—DTPpath—points to the directory where Desktop Paint's resource files live.

There's another practical example of resource files in action later in this chapter—the RMOVER utility.

8-13 Desktop Paint booting up with a BTMP resource.

```
doGallery
{
    WINDOW w;
    POINT p;
    BUTTON ok,copy,paste,clear,prev,next,*bp;
    BITMAP bmp;
    TEXT tx,tf;
    RECT r;
    RFILE fh;
    RESOURCE res;
    char *pr,*scrap=NULL,bf[30],fn[129];
    unsigned int i,cbw=0,cbd=0,rt,size,cbytes;
    int inner_a,outer_a=0xff,count,number=0;

    SetRect(&r,32,16,270,324);

    /* number of bytes across the image area */
    cbytes=pixels2bytes(CLIPWIDE);

    /* allocate a place to put a fragment of the image */
    if((pr=malloc(cbytes*CLIPDEEP+4)) == NULL) {
        errorbeep();
        return(0);
    }

    /* clear the buffer */
    memset(pr,0xff,cbytes*CLIPDEEP+4);

    /* put the dimensions in the buffer */
```

8-14 The code that produced the dialog in Fig. 8-12.

```
pr[0]=(CLIPWIDE-1);
pr[1]=(CLIPWIDE-1) >> 8;
pr[2]=(CLIPDEEP-1);
pr[3]=(CLIPDEEP-1) >> 8;

/* null the text string */
bf[0]=0;

/* open the window */
if(OpenWindow(&w,&r)) {
    /* add the title */
    AddText(&w,&tx,r.left+8,r.top+10,"Gallery",ACTIVE);

    /* add all the buttons */
    SetRect(&ok.frame,r.right-40,r.bottom-23,
        r.right-8,r.bottom-8);
    AddButton(&w,&ok,"Ok",ACTIVE);

    SetRect(&copy.frame,r.right-104,r.bottom-23,
        r.right-56,r.bottom-8);
    AddButton(&w,&copy,"Copy",ACTIVE);

    SetRect(&paste.frame,r.right-176,r.bottom-23,
        r.right-120,r.bottom-8);
    AddButton(&w,&paste,"Paste",ACTIVE);

    SetRect(&clear.frame,r.right-64,r.bottom-47,
        r.right-8,r.bottom-32);
    AddButton(&w,&clear,"Clear",ACTIVE);
    SetRect(&next.frame,r.right-128,r.bottom-47,
        r.right-80,r.bottom-32);
    AddButton(&w,&next,"Next",ACTIVE);

    SetRect(&prev.frame,r.right-224,r.bottom-47,
        r.right-144,r.bottom-32);
    AddButton(&w,&prev,"Previous",ACTIVE);

    /* add the bitmap which will show the image */
    AddBitmap(&w,&bmp,r.left+8,r.top+30,pr,0x00,NULL,ACTIVE);
    AddText(&w,&tf,bmp.frame.left,bmp.frame.bottom+10,bf,ACTIVE);

    /* draw a box around it */
    MouseOff();
    setfillstyle(SOLID_FILL,getmaxcolor());
    setlinestyle(SOLID_LINE,0,NORM_WIDTH);
    setcolor(BLACK);
    setwritemode(COPY_PUT);
    rectangle(bmp.frame.left-2,bmp.frame.top-2,
            bmp.frame.right+1,bmp.frame.bottom+1);
    MouseOn();

    /* create a path to the gallery resource file */
    waitCursor();
    strcpy(fn,theConfig.DTPpath);
    strcat(fn,"GALLERY.RES");

    /* if GALLERY.RES doesn't exist, create it */
    if(access(fn,0) != 0) {
        if(createRF(fn,"Desktop Paint Gallery") == 0) {
            arrowCursor();
            message("Can't create gallery");
            CloseWindow(&w);
            free(pr);
```

```
            return(0);
        }
    }

    /* open GALLERY.RES */
    if((fh=openRF(fn)) == 0) {
        arrowCursor();
        message("Damaged gallery");
        CloseWindow(&w);
        free(pr);
        return(0);
    }

    arrowCursor();

    do {
        waitCursor();
        /* count the BTMP resources */
        count=countRF(fh,"BTMP");
        if(scrap != NULL) {
            free(scrap);
            scrap=NULL;
        }
        if(count) {
            /* get the appropriate image */
        if(getnumberedRF(fh,"BTMP",number,&res)) {
            /* allocate some memory to put it in */
            if((scrap=malloc(res.size)) == NULL)
                errorbeep();
            else {
                if(!getdataRF(scrap,fh,res.size)) {
                    arrowCursor();
                    message("Error reading gallery");
                    free(scrap);
                    scrap=NULL;
                }
            }
        }

        else {
            arrowCursor();
            message("Error reading gallery");
            if(scrap != NULL) free(scrap);
            scrap=NULL;
        }
    }
    arrowCursor();

    /* set the image size */
    if(scrap != NULL) {
        cbw=ImageBytes(scrap);
        cbd=ImageDepth(scrap);
    } else cbw=cbd=0;

    for(i=0;i<CLIPDEEP;++i) {
        memset(pr+4+(i*cbytes),0x00,cbytes);
        if(i<cbd) {
            if(cbw < cbytes) memcpy(pr+4+(i*cbytes),
                scrap+4+(i*cbw),cbw);
            else memcpy(pr+4+(i*cbytes),
                scrap+4+(i*cbw),cbytes);
        }
        invert(pr+4+(i*cbytes),cbytes);
    }
```

```
/* show the status - this is a sort of
   illegal use of a TEXT object */
if(!count) strcpy(bf,"Empty gallery       ");
else sprintf(bf,"Item %u of %u         ",number+1,count);

/* update the image and the status */
drawBitmap(&bmp);
drawText(&tf);

/* handle mouse clicks */
inner_a=0xff;
while(inner_a) {
      Keyboard(&w);
      if(MouseDown(&p)) {
            rt=whereMouse(&p,&w);
            if(rt & inButton) {
                  bp=findButton(&w,&p);
                  trackButton(bp);
                  if(bp==&ok) inner_a=outer_a=0;
if(bp==&copy) {
      if(scrap != NULL) {
            if(isfile) {
                  if(clipboard != NULL)
                        free(clipboard);
                  size=4+ImageBytes(scrap)*
                        ImageDepth(scrap);
                  if((clipboard=malloc(size))
                      == NULL)
                        message("Can't allocate clip");
                  else {
                        memcpy(clipboard,scrap,size);
                        /* enable Paste in Edit menu */
                        if(isfile)
                             edit.item[2].name[0]=' ';
                  }
            } else message("Nothing in clipboard");
      }
}
if(bp==&paste) {
      if(clipboard==NULL)
            message("Nothing to paste");
      else {
            size=4+ImageBytes(clipboard)*
              ImageDepth(clipboard);
            if(!addRF(fh,"BTMP",
               freenumberRF(fh,"BTMP"),
               size,clipboard))
                  message("Can't add to gallery");
      }
      inner_a=0;
}
if(bp==&next) {
      if(number < (count-1)) {
            ++number;
            inner_a=0;
      }
}
if(bp==&prev) {
      if(number > 0) {
            --number;
            inner_a=0;
```

```
            }
      }
if(bp==&clear) {
      if(count) {
            if(getnumberedRF(fh,"BTMP",
                              number,&res)) {
                  waitCursor();
                  if(!removeresRF(fh,&res) {
                    message("Error removing image");
                  else {
                        if(number) --number;
                  }
                  arrowCursor();
            } else
              message("Error finding gallery");
            inner_a=0;
      }
                                    }
                              }
                        else errorbeep();
                  }
            }
      } while(outer_a);
      closeRF(fh);
      CloseWindow(&w);
} else errorbeep();
free(pr);
if(scrap != NULL) free(scrap);
}
```

Advanced resource functions

The GALLERY.RES file is actually a pretty tame example of an application for resources. All the resources are of the same type, and the file will only be accessed when a user of the Desktop Paint software specifically instructs the program to do so. This is probably a bit atypical of the way in which resource files are normally applied.

In most cases, as discussed earlier this chapter, a resource file for a complex application will be a melange of fonts, drivers, code resources, bitmaps, text strings, and most probably any number of application-specific resources that you'll dream up yourself.

An application can deal with its resource file in one or both of two ways. First, it can read through the file when the program starts up, making note of the existence of any resources that might be useful to program operation as a whole. Second, it can go to the resource file when it must retrieve specific resources that the program knows to be there.

Desktop Paint does both these things. When it first boots up, it notes all the FONT resources, adding their names to its Font menu. If someone asks it to print to a dot matrix printer, it goes to its resource file to fetch the driver for the printer in question. (Printer driver resources will be dealt with in detail toward the end of this chapter.)

None of the functions discussed thus far are suitable for trolling through a resource file and examining all the resources. It would be possible to write a modified version of getRF to handle this, but doing so would involve seeking from the beginning of the resource file through to the resource in question for each resource in the file, an unnecessarily cumbersome process.

The getallRF function in Fig. 8-15 handles the prospect of looking at all the resources in a file in a fairly peculiar way. The purpose of looking at all resources would be to do something with them (or at least with some of them), but the details of what's to be done with them will vary with the applications you write. As such, getallRF allows you to specify a function called by getallRF each time it locates a resource. You can write the function to deal with each resource in any way you like.

```
/* get each resource in the file. call proc for each.
   abort if proc returns zero. call proc with resource. */
getallRF(fh,proc)
        RFILE fh;
        int (*proc)();
{
        RESHEAD rh;
        RESOURCE rc;
        unsigned long pos;
        unsigned int i;

        if(getinfoRF(&rh,fh)) {
                for(i=0;i<rh.count;++i) {
                        if(dread((char *)&rc,sizeof(RESOURCE),fh)
                           != sizeof(RESOURCE)) return(0);
                        pos=dtell(fh);
                        if(!(proc)(&rc,fh,i)) return(0);
                        dseek(fh,pos+(long)rc.size,SEEK_SET);
                }
                return(1);
        } else return(0);
}
```

8-15 The getallRF function.

Each time getallRF searches for a new resource in the file fh, it calls the function passed to it in its proc argument. It passes the function a pointer to a RESOURCE object and the RFILE of the file being scanned, just in case the function wants to call getdataRF to see what's actually in the resource in question. It also passes the position of the resource in the file, something that you can safely ignore in most applications.

The function called by getallRF must return either a true value (if it wants getallRF to continue looking through the resource file) or zero (if it wants it to abort). Thus, getallRF can be used to either look for one of several types of resources very efficiently or to locate a finite number of resources of a particular type. After finding what it wants, the function passed to it can return a zero, informing getallRF that enough resources have been searched.

The following is a typical function that might get passed to handleRF. It's a very stripped-down version of the one used by Desktop Paint to initially read its main resource file. In the working version of handleRec, quite a few types of resources are checked for. This one only checks for a BTMP resource, displaying it on the screen if it's found.

```
handleRec(rc,fh)
    RESOURCE *rc;  RFILE fh;
{
    char *p,*pr;
    unsigned int x,y;

    if(!memcmp(rc->type,"BTMP",4)) {
        if((p=malloc(rc->size)) != NULL) {
            if(getdataRF(p,fh,rc->size)) {
                x=(getmaxx( )-ImageWidth(p))/2;
                y=(getmaxy( )-ImageDepth(p))/2;
                MouseOff( );
                if(ismonomode( )) putimage(x,y,p,COPY_PUT);
                else      {
                    if((pr=mono2ega(p)) != NULL) {
                        putimage(x,y,pr,COPY_PUT);
                        free(pr);
                    }
                }
                MouseOn( );
            }
            free(p);
        }
    }
    return(1);
}
```

You would, of course, write handleRec to deal with resources important to your particular applications. This is how it would be used in a call to getallRF:

```
RFILE fh;
int handleRec( );

if((fh=openRF("RESOURCE.RES")) != 0) {
    getallRF(fh,handleRec);
    closeRF(fh);
}
```

Some other resource functions are also useful. The countRF function will return the number of resources of a specified type in an open resource file. The getinfoRF function will fill a RESHEAD object with the data in the header of a resource file. Finally, freenumberRF will return a resource number unused for the specified resource type in an open resource file—helpful when you want to add resources to a resource file. All three functions are illustrated in Fig. 8-16.

```
/* count the resources of type in a resource file */
countRF(fh,type)
        RFILE fh;
```

8-16 The countRF, getinfoRF, and freenumberRF functions.

```
        char *type;
{

        RESOURCE rc;
        RESHEAD rh;
        unsigned int i,count=0;

        if(getinfoRF(&rh,fh)) {
                for(i=0;i<rh.count;++i) {
                        if(dread((char *)&rc,sizeof(RESOURCE),fh)
                                != sizeof(RESOURCE)) return(0);
                        if(!memcmp(rc.type,type,4)) ++count;
                        dseek(fh,(long)rc.size,SEEK_CUR);
                }
                return(count);
        } else return(0);
}

/* get the data about a resource file */
getinfoRF(rh,fh)
        RESHEAD *rh;
        RFILE fh;
{
        dseek(fh,0L,SEEK_SET);
        if(dread((char *)rh,sizeof(RESHEAD),fh)==sizeof(RESHEAD)) return(1);
        else return(0);
}

/* find a free number in a resource file */
long freenumberRF(fh,type)
        RFILE fh;
        char *type;
{

        RESOURCE rc;
        long i,rt=BADRECNUM;
        long pos;

        pos=dtell(fh);

        for(i=0;i<BADRECNUM;++i) {
                if(!getRF(fh,type,i,&rc)) {
                        rt=i;
                        break;
                }
        }
        dseek(fh,pos,SEEK_SET);
        return(rt);
}
```

In theory, you should make sure that calls to freenumberRF don't return the constant BADRECNUM whenever you use this function. This would only occur if more than 4,294,967,294 resources of the same type existed in a resource file—probably a sufficiently unlikely eventuality as to make this check superfluous.

RMOVER—a resource manager

As you work with the graphical user interface and develop programs that use its functions, you'll probably find that you also accumulate a store of resources. It's handy to be able to take resources from one application's resource file and use them in another. Thus far, the discussion of resources has dealt with the use of resource files from within a program but hasn't really done much to address the issue of managing the beasts.

The Macintosh has a powerful resource management and editing tool called ResEdit, allowing you to troll through the resources of any application as well as display and edit the common ones in formats appropriate to their nature. You might ultimately want to write such a program using the graphical user interface if you find yourself making extensive use of its resource tools.

Figure 8-17 illustrates several screens from the Macintosh ResEdit application.

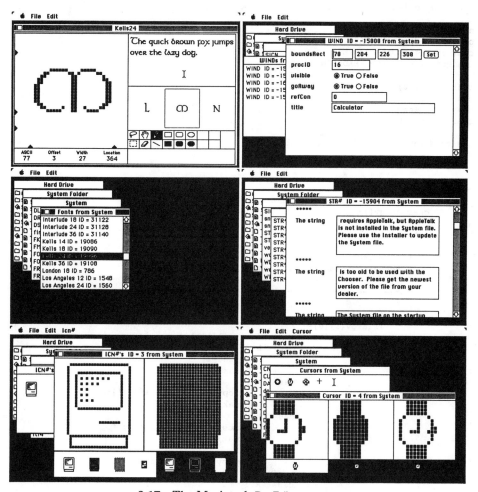

8-17 The Macintosh ResEdit program.

It would be beyond the scope of this book to deal with a PC equivalent to Res-Edit. However, this chapter will discuss RMOVER, which performs the most useful function of a resource manager—juggling resources among several resource files.

The RMOVER program is listed in its entirety in Fig. 8-18. Note that you will need a project file to link it to GUI.LIB.

```
/*
        RMOVER version 1.0
*/

#include "stdio.h"
#include "dir.h"
#include "dos.h"
#include "alloc.h"
#include "gui.h"

char filepath[MAXPATH]="";
char secondpath[MAXPATH]="";
char type[4]={BADRECTYPE};
unsigned long number=BADRECNUM;

char dolist=0;
char doadd=0;
char dodelete=0;
char doextract=0;

unsigned int deadres=0;

RFILE fh,sfh;

main(argc,argv)
        int argc;
        char *argv[];
{
        int i;

        puts("Resource mover version 1.0 - "
             "copyright (c) 1990 Alchemy Mindworks Inc.\n"
             "----------------------------"
             "---------------------------------------");

        for(i=1;i<argc;++i) {
                if(argv[i][0]=='/') {
                        switch(toupper(argv[i][1])) {
                                case 'L':
                                        dolist=1;
                                        break;
                                case 'F':
                                        strcpy(secondpath,argv[i]+2);
                                        break;
                                case 'N':
                                        number=atol(argv[i]+2);
                                        break;
                                case 'T':
                                        memcpy(type,argv[i]+2,4);
                                        break;
                                case 'A':
                                        doadd=1;
                                        break;
                                case 'D':
                                        dodelete=1;
                                        break;
```

8-18 The RMOVER utility.

```
                                case 'E':
                                        doextract=1;
                                        break;
                        }
                } else strcpy(filepath,argv[i]);
        }
        if(strlen(filepath)) {
                fixname(filepath);
                fixname(secondpath);
                if(dolist) listResources();
                else if(doadd) addResource();
                else if(doextract) extractResource();
                else if(dodelete) deleteResource();
                else puts("Nothing to do.");
        }
        else {
                puts("Arguments:      path to resource file\n"
                "               /A        - add specified resource\n"
                "               /D        - delete specified resource\n"
                "               /E        - extract specified resource\n"
                "               /F<name>  - set second file name\n"
                "               /L        - list resources in file\n"
                "               /N<long>  - set resource number\n"
                "               /T<type>  - set resource type\n"
                );

        }
}


deleteResource()
{
        RESOURCE rc;
        RESHEAD rh;
        int e=0,deleteR();

        if(number==BADRECNUM) {
                printf("Bad resource number\n");
                return(0);
        }
        if(!memcmp(type,BADRECTYPE,4)) {
                printf("Bad resource type\n");
                return(0);
        }

        strmfe(secondpath,filepath,"$$$");

        if((fh=openRF(filepath)) != 0) {
                if(getinfoRF(&rh,fh)) {
                        if(createRF(secondpath,rh.description)) {
                                if((sfh=openRF(secondpath)) != 0) {
                                        rc.number=number;
                                        memcpy(rc.type,type,4);
                                        if(removeresRF(fh,&rc)) {
                                                if(getallRF(fh,deleteR)) e=1;
                                                else printf("Error reading %s\n",
                                                        filepath);
                                                closeRF(sfh);
                                                printf("Resource type:%4.4s - "
                                                        "number %lu deleted\n",
                                                        type,number);
                                        } else printf("Resource type:%4.4s - "
                                                        number %lu not found\n",
                                                        type,number);
                                } else printf("Error opening %s\n",secondpath);
```

```
                          } else printf("Error creating %s\n",secondpath);
                  } else printf("%s is a bad resource file\n",filepath);
                  closeRF(fh);
          } else printf("Error opening %s\n",filepath);
          if(e) {
                  remove(filepath);
                  rename(secondpath,filepath);
          } else remove(secondpath);
}

#pragma warn -par
deleteR(rc,lfh,n)
          RESOURCE *rc;
          RFILE lfh;
          int n;
{
          char *p;

          if((p=malloc(rc->size)) != NULL) {
                  if(getdataRF(p,fh,rc->size)) {
                          if(!addRF(sfh,rc->type,rc->number,rc->size,p)) {
                                  puts("Error writing resource data");
                                  return(0);
                          }
                  }
                  else {
                          puts("Error reading resource data");
                          return(0);
                  }
                  free(p);
          }
          return(1);
}


extractResource()
{
          RESHEAD rh;
          int extractR();

          if((fh=openRF(filepath)) != 0) {
                  if(createRF(secondpath,"Extracted resource")) {
                          if((sfh=openRF(secondpath)) != 0) {
                                  getallRF(fh,extractR);
                                  getinfoRF(&rh,sfh);
                                  printf("%u resource(s) extracted\n",rh.count);
                                  closeRF(sfh);
                          } else printf("Error opening %s\n",secondpath);
                  } else printf("Error creating %s\n",secondpath);
                  closeRF(fh);
          } else printf("Error opening %s\n",filepath);
          exit(0);
}

#pragma warn -par
extractR(rc,lfh,n)
          RESOURCE *rc;

          RFILE lfh;
          int n;
{
          char *p;

          if(memcmp(rc->type,BADRECTYPE,4)) {
```

```
                if(memcmp(rc->type,type,4)) return(1);
        }
        if(number != BADRECNUM) {
                if(rc->number != number) return(1);
        }
        if((p=malloc(rc->size)) != NULL) {
                if(getdataRF(p,fh,rc->size)) {
                        if(!addRF(sfh,rc->type,rc->number,rc->size,p)) {
                                puts("Error writing resource data");
                                return(0);
                        } else printf("Extracting resource type:%4.4s - "
                                        "number %9.9lu - size %5.5u bytes\n",
                                        rc->type,rc->number,rc->size);
                }
                else {
                        puts("Error reading resource data");
                        return(0);
                }
                free(p);
        }
        return(1);
}


addResource()
{
        int addR();

        if(access(filepath,0))
           createRF(filepath,"Resource file created by RMOVER");

        if((fh=openRF(filepath)) != 0) {
                if((sfh=openRF(secondpath)) != 0) {
                        getallRF(sfh,addR);
                        closeRF(sfh);
                } else printf("Error opening %s\n",secondpath);
                closeRF(fh);
        } else printf("Error opening %s\n",filepath);
        exit(0);
}

#pragma warn -par
addR(rc,lfh,n)
        RESOURCE *rc;
        RFILE lfh;
        int n;
{
        RESOURCE lrc;
        char *p;

        if((p=malloc(rc->size)) != NULL) {
                if(getdataRF(p,sfh,rc->size)) {
                        if(number != BADRECNUM) rc->number=number;
                        else rc->number=freenumberRF(fh,rc->type);
                        if(!getRF(fh,rc->type,rc->number,&lrc)) {

                                if(!addRF(fh,rc->type,rc->number,rc->size,p)) {
                                        puts("Error writing resource data");
                                        return(0);
                                } else printf("Adding resource type:%4.4s - "
                                                "number %9.9lu - size %5.5u bytes\n",
                                                rc->type,rc->number,rc->size);
                        } else printf("Resource type:%4.4s - number %lu exists - "
                                        "not adding\n",rc->type,rc->number);
                }
```

```
                else {
                        puts("Error reading resource data");
                        return(0);
                }
                free(p);
        }
        return(1);
}

listResources()
{
        RESHEAD rh;
        int listR();

        if((fh=openRF(filepath)) != 0) {
                if(getinfoRF(&rh,fh)) {
                        printf("Description: %s\n",rh.description);
                        printf("%u resource(s)\n",rh.count);
                        puts("_____");
                        getallRF(fh,listR);
                } else printf("%s is a bad resource file\n",filepath);
                closeRF(fh);
        } else printf("Error opening %s\n",filepath);
        exit(0);
}

#pragma warn -par
listR(rc,lfh,n)
        RESOURCE *rc;
        RFILE lfh;
        int n;
{
        FONT f;
        char s[64];

        s[0]=0;
        if(!memcmp(rc->type,FONTid,4)) {
                if(getdataRF((char *)&f,lfh,sizeof(FONT)))
                        sprintf(s,"%s %upt #%u",f.name,f.pointsize,f.number);
                else strcpy(s,"Error reading data");
        }

        printf("Rsrc %4.4u - type:%4.4s - number %9.9lu - %5.5u bytes %s\n",
            n,rc->type,rc->number,rc->size,s);
        return(1);
}

strmfe(new,old,ext)
        char *new,*old,*ext;
{
        while(*old != 0 && *old != '.') *new++=*old++;
        *new++='.';
        while(*ext) *new++=*ext++;
        *new=0;
}

fixname(s)              /* tidy up a file name */
        char *s;
{
        char drive[MAXDRIVE],dir[MAXDIR],path[MAXPATH],ext[MAXEXT];

        fnsplit(s,drive,dir,path,ext);
```

```
        if(!strlen(ext)) strcpy(ext,".RES");
        fnmerge(s,drive,dir,path,ext);
        strupr(s);
}
```

You can do four things with RMOVER: list all the resources in a resource file, add resources to a resource file, delete resources from a resource file, and extract resources from a large resource file into a small one. A small one will be defined as a resource file with only one resource.

The syntax for using RMOVER is fairly simple and runs from the DOS command line. The simplest application of the program is in listing the contents of a resource file. In the following examples, the resource file for Desktop Paint—DTP.RES—will serve as data. To see what's in it, you would type

RMOVER DTP.RES /L

The /L option lists a resource file. Having typed this command, RMOVER would reply with the following list for the default DTP.RES file that comes with Desktop Paint:

Description: Desktop Paint resource file
22 resource(s)

Rsrc 0000 - type:BTMP - number 000000012 - 08004 bytes
Rsrc 0001 - type:PDRV - number 000000000 - 00348 bytes
Rsrc 0002 - type:FONT - number 000000000 - 02471 bytes Swiss 8pt #2
Rsrc 0003 - type:FONT - number 000000001 - 02971 bytes Swiss 9pt #2
Rsrc 0004 - type:FONT - number 000000002 - 03535 bytes Swiss 10pt #2
Rsrc 0005 - type:FONT - number 000000004 - 04559 bytes Swiss 12pt #2
Rsrc 0006 - type:FONT - number 000000006 - 07391 bytes Swiss 16pt #2
Rsrc 0007 - type:FONT - number 000000007 - 09077 bytes Swiss 18pt #2
Rsrc 0008 - type:FONT - number 000000008 - 11135 bytes Swiss 20pt #2
Rsrc 0009 - type:FONT - number 000000010 - 15575 bytes Swiss 24pt #2
Rsrc 0010 - type:FONT - number 000000011 - 20891 bytes Swiss 28pt #2
Rsrc 0011 - type:FONT - number 000000012 - 30731 bytes Swiss 36pt #2
Rsrc 0012 - type:FONT - number 000000013 - 01875 bytes Dutch 6pt #14
Rsrc 0013 - type:FONT - number 000000015 - 03215 bytes Dutch 9pt #14
Rsrc 0014 - type:FONT - number 000000016 - 03425 bytes Dutch 10pt #14
Rsrc 0015 - type:FONT - number 000000018 - 04631 bytes Dutch 12pt #14
Rsrc 0016 - type:FONT - number 000000020 - 07815 bytes Dutch 16pt #14
Rsrc 0017 - type:FONT - number 000000021 - 09293 bytes Dutch 18pt #14
Rsrc 0018 - type:FONT - number 000000022 - 11665 bytes Dutch 20pt #14
Rsrc 0019 - type:FONT - number 000000025 - 21885 bytes Dutch 28pt #14
Rsrc 0020 - type:FONT - number 000000028 - 03839 bytes Courier 12pt #102
Rsrc 0021 - type:FONT - number 000000030 - 12425 bytes Courier 24pt #102

By now, most of the information in this listing should be fairly meaningful. The first column represents the numerical position of each resource in the file.

The second column is the resource type. The third column is the actual resource number, padded out with zeros to keep the display neat. The fourth column is the size of the resource in bytes, also padded out with zeros. Finally, the last column is a bit of a cheat, and one that you might want to expand on: it lists details about some specific resource types—in this case, about FONT resources.

Font resources will be discussed in the next chapter, and the numbers in this last column will become meaningful then.

The Text menu of Desktop Paint is illustrated in Fig. 8-19. You might observe that the word "Centre" is spelled oddly in the left example. This is the British spelling and serves as an example of the second application of RMOVER.

8-19 The Desktop Paint Text menu. Although no spelling errors occur here, there is a spelling inconsistency.

In order to keep the British spellings in its menus from looking out of place to American users, Desktop Paint comes with a small resource file called AMERTEXT.RES. This is a resource of the type MENU, a menu structure of the sort discussed in Chapter 4. If Desktop Paint comes across a MENU resource in its resource file, it uses it to replace the text of one of its default menus.

This is the syntax for adding AMERTEXT.RES to DTP.RES using RMOVER:

RMOVER DTP.RES /A /FAMERTEXT.RES

The /A option tells RMOVER to add a resource to DTP.RES, and the /F option specifies the name of the resource file. The resource type and number will be obtained from the AMERTEXT.RES file.

The second resource in DTP.RES, as listed before, is of the type PDRV. This is a dot matrix printer driver, and its workings will be discussed in the next part of this chapter. However, for the moment it's sufficient to note that users of Desktop Paint with laser printers don't need it because Desktop Paint has built-in laser printer drivers. Thus, this driver can be deleted to make DTP.RES a bit smaller. The syntax for using RMOVER to delete a resource is as follows:

RMOVER DTP.RES /D /TPDRV /N0

The /D option tells RMOVER to delete a resource. The /T option specifies the type, and /N specifies the number. Note that the number in question is the resource number—the one in the third column of the /L listing—not the position number in the first column.

The RMOVER program deletes resources by copying each of the remaining resources to a new file, deleting the old file, and renaming the new file to the old file's name. As such, when it deletes a resource, the resulting resource file will actually shrink. Note that the program must have enough disk space available to allow for two copies of the resource file being manipulated (at least for a while).

Finally, you might want to extract the BTMP resource from DTP.RES if you had some reason to use it in another application. This would arguably be more likely if you'd put it there to begin with, as there are few other uses for the one that comes with Desktop Paint—it has "Desktop Paint" splashed across it. This RMOVER syntax extracts a resource:

```
RMOVER DTP.RES /E /FBITMAP.RES /TBTMP /N12
```

The /E option tells RMOVER to extract a resource from DTP.RES. The /F option specifies the name of the file that the resource will be written to. This file will always be created by RMOVER—if a file by the specified name exists, it will be deleted first (in this case, I've called the file BITMAP.RES). The /T option specifies the type of the resource to be extracted, and the /N option specifies its number.

Should you be curious, the BTMP resource in DTP.RES has the number twelve due to its origins. It was originally created in Desktop Paint and added to the gallery. At that time, there were twelve image fragments in GALLERY.RES, running from zero through eleven; thus, it became resource number twelve. It was subsequently extracted to a resource file of its own using RMOVER, and from there added it to DTP.RES.

If you want to have your applications use a BTMP resource as a startup image, similar to Desktop Paint, you should note that getallRF reads through the resource file handed to it from the first resource to the last one. As the BTMP resource is supposed to be visible while your application's tied up sorting out the remainder of its resource file, you must ensure that it's the first resource in the file.

Code resources

Thus far, all discussion of resources has dealt with data resources. There are several good reasons for stashing actual executable code in a resource. While the process is far from trivial, it's worth doing if your application calls for loadable blocks of code.

While you can get through much of this book without having to plunge into any truly monstrous assembly language, this section is decidedly an exception. You'll need a substantial understanding of assembly language programming and memory models to understand it. You might want to skip it for the moment, as it's useful but hardly crucial to applications involving the graphical user interface as a whole.

Having said this, even if you have no real interest in writing code resources, you might want to use the printer drivers in this section to print. In this case, you can apply the code to be discussed here without getting any unpleasant bytes or pseudo-ops stuck under your fingernails.

Note that this is the one area of the graphical user interface affected by the differences between Turbo C 2.0 and Turbo C + +. If you're using the latter compiler, keep in mind that you will want to modify the code being discussed in this section.

Turbo C does actually provide a way to produce loadable binary modules—it turns up, for example, if you try to write a custom BGI driver in C. It isn't particularly good for writing code resources, however, because it doesn't allow you to do a lot of things and is pretty cumbersome to implement. Thus, the discussion in this chapter will be limited to code resources written just in assembly language.

As with a data resource, code resources are simply bits of binary data loaded into memory. However, in this case, your C language program will treat them as functions and call them. A certain amount of understanding of what goes on behind your back in a C language program is required to keep an arrangement like this from crashing.

This section will deal with one of the more commonly used applications for code resources—drivers. In this case, the example will be a PDRV resource—a printer driver. The principles embodied in it, however, will apply to other sorts of code resources. Depending upon the sorts of applications you write, you might find that code resources represent a way to keep infrequently used functions out of memory until they're needed. You can load such a function as a resource, use it, and then throw it away. If your program lends itself to having a lot of its functions stored as code resources, you can free up a considerable amount of system memory.

In addition, code resources lend themselves to being loaded into expanded memory and executed there. Due to the limitations on the size of a single resource, they're small enough to fit in a single EMS page.

Drivers are the most common application of code resources because they allow the users of your programs to configure them for different printers, video cards, and so on. In the case of Desktop Paint, it can be configured to print to any of a number of dot matrix printers by adding the appropriate PDRV resource to Desktop Paint's main resource file.

This also allows Desktop Paint to drive some very peculiar output devices. There are PDRV resources around for things like film recorders, something not really envisioned when Desktop Paint was written.

A code resource is a binary file with a fixed set of *entry points*. An entry point is something that, when called by a C program, will behave like a C function. It'll cause some code to be executed and then return in an orderly manner to the C language program that called it.

In order to understand how code resources work, you should probably start by knowing about a useful, if undocumented, feature of Turbo C's malloc function. Under the large memory model, if you call malloc to allocate some memory, it will return a far pointer. A far pointer consists of a segment and an offset component. The segment will vary, depending upon where the allocated block of memory resides, while the offset will always be eight. Under Turbo C + +, the offset will be four. A bit of cheating (discussed later) will be called for if you're using Turbo C + +.

Because small model machine language programs only run in one segment at a fixed offset, this bit of esoterica makes it possible to write code resources that can be loaded into a buffer created by malloc. A small model program doesn't know about the existence of segments. It only makes near calls, near jumps, and addresses near objects. As long as it thinks that the world starts at location eight, such a program loaded into a malloc buffer and executed will function properly.

There's only one catch. While a code resource will be a small model program—or, more properly, a collection of small model functions—it'll be called by a large model program, your C language code. As such, any function in a code resource that will actually be called by something external to the resource must return with a RETF instruction rather than with a RET.

Each code resource must ORG at 0008H. One way to do this would be to use 0008H as the argument to the ORG pseudo-op. A more elegant way would be to simply leave eight bytes of blank space after an ORG 0000H or, better still, to begin the resource with an eight-byte signature string. This allows you to use the binary files created while you're writing code resources as stand-alone, loadable modules if you want to. You might want to do this while you're testing a code resource. It's also useful for checking the integrity of a code resource being loaded.

Following the signature string, a code resource requires a *dispatch table*—a list of partial pointers to the functions in the resource that allows C to use a convenient, C-like interface to your code. This concept will become clearer as you get more familiar with resources in general. The rest of the resource is the actual machine language that does the work.

Figure 8-20 is the complete code for a printer driver called EPSNFX80.ASM. Note that this doesn't assemble into a resource—the header must be added later, using yet another little program.

```
                COMMENT %

        EPSON DOT MATRIX PRINTER DRIVER
        COPYRIGHT (C) 1990 ALCHEMY MINDWORKS INC.
        VERSION 1.0


                        %

PAGEWIDE        EQU     768       ;PAGE WIDTH IN PIXELS
PAGEDEEP        EQU     1024      ;PAGE DEPTH IN PIXELS
LINEDEEP        EQU     8         ;NUMBER OF BITS (PINS) IN A LINE
COLOURS         EQU     1         ;ONLY ONE COLOUR SUPPORTED AS YET

VERSION         EQU     1         ;VERSION NUMBER
SUBVERSION      EQU     0         ;SUBVERSION NUMBER

_AOFF           EQU     6         ;STACK OFFSET

CODE            SEGMENT PARA PUBLIC 'CODE'
                ASSUME  CS:CODE

                ORG     0000H             ;ORIGIN FOR LOADABLE DRIVER

                DB      'ALCHPRDR'        ;SIGNATURE - DON'T CHANGE THIS

;THE FOLLOWING ARE THE POINTERS TO THE CALLABLE ROUTINES
;AND THE COMMON DATA. THE SEGMENTS ARE FILLED IN BY THE LOADER
DISPATCH        PROC    FAR
                DW      INIT_PRINTER      ;PRINTER INITIALIZATION
                DW      ?
                DW      PRINT_LINE        ;LINE PRINT
                DW      ?
                DW      DEINIT_PRINTER    ;TO PRINTER DEINITIALIZATION
                DW      ?
                DW      PRINT_TEXT        ;TEXT PRINT
```

8-20 A printer driver code resource.

8-20 Continued

```
                DW      ?
                DW      0,0              ;NULL ONE
                DW      0,0              ;NULL TWO
                DW      0,0              ;NULL THREE
                DW      0,0              ;NULL FOUR


V_PAGEWIDE      DW      PAGEWIDE
V_PAGEDEEP      DW      PAGEDEEP
V_LINEDEEP      DW      LINEDEEP
V_COLOURS       DW      COLOURS


                DW      VERSION
                DW      SUBVERSION


                DB      01H,'Epson FX-80        ',0
DISPATCH        ENDP
```

;THIS PROCEDURE SHOULD INITIALIZE THE PRINTER. IT SHOULD ALSO STORE THE
;FIRST THREE INTS ON THE STACK FOR FUTURE USE. THESE ARE IMAGE_WIDTH,
;IMAGE_DEPTH AND IMAGE_BYTES RESPECTIVELY.

```
INIT_PRINTER    PROC    NEAR
                PUSH    BP
                MOV     BP,SP
                MOV     AX,[BP + _AOFF + 0]
                MOV     CS:[IMAGE_WIDTH],AX

                MOV     AX,[BP + _AOFF + 2]
                MOV     CS:[IMAGE_DEPTH],AX

                MOV     AX,[BP + _AOFF + 4]
                MOV     CS:[IMAGE_BYTES],AX

                MOV     DX,OFFSET INIT_SEQ
                CALL    PRINT_STRING

                POP     BP
                RETF
INIT_PRINTER    ENDP
```

;THIS PROCEDURE SHOULD PRINT ONE LINE. A POINTER TO THE LINE IS
;ON THE STACK.

```
PRINT_LINE      PROC    NEAR
                PUSH    BP
                MOV     BP,SP
                PUSH    DS

                MOV     CX,CS:[IMAGE_WIDTH]
                CMP     CX,0
                JE      PRINT_L3
                CMP     CX,CS:[V_PAGEWIDE]
                JL      PRINT_L1
                MOV     CX,CS:[V_PAGEWIDE]

PRINT_L1:       MOV     CS:[START_LO],CL
                MOV     CS:[START_HI],CH
                MOV     DX,OFFSET START_SEQ
                CALL    PRINT_STRING

                MOV     SI,[BP + _AOFF + 0]
                MOV     DS,[BP + _AOFF + 2]

                MOV     DX,0
PRINT_L2:       PUSH    CX
```

```
                        CALL    GET_BYTE
                        CALL    PRINT_BYTE
                        INC     DX
                        POP     CX
                        LOOP    PRINT_L2

                        MOV     DX,OFFSET END_SEQ
                        CALL    PRINT_STRING

PRINT_L3:               POP     DS
                        POP     BP
                        RETF
PRINT_LINE      ENDP

;THIS SHOULD DO ANYTHING NECESSARY TO FINISH THE PICTURE.
DEINIT_PRINTER  PROC    NEAR
                        PUSH    BP
                        MOV     BP,SP
                        PUSH    DS              ˇ

                        MOV     DX,OFFSET DEINIT_SEQ
                        CALL    PRINT_STRING
                        POP     DS
                        POP     BP
                        RETF
DEINIT_PRINTER  ENDP

;THIS WILL PRINT A LINE OF TEXT TO THE PRINTER. THE STRING IS ON THE
;STACK FOLLOWED BY THE LENGTH OF THE STRING
PRINT_TEXT      PROC    NEAR
                        PUSH    BP
                        MOV     BP,SP
                        PUSH    DS

                        MOV     SI,[BP + _AOFF + 0]
                        MOV     DS,[BP + _AOFF + 2]
                        MOV     CX,[BP + _AOFF + 4]
                        CMP     CX,0
                        JE      PRINT_T2

                        CLD
PRINT_T1:               LODSB
                        CALL    PRINT_BYTE
                        LOOP    PRINT_T1

PRINT_T2:               POP     DS
                        POP     BP
                        RETF
PRINT_TEXT      ENDP

;
;       INTERNAL ROUTINES
;

;GET ONE BYTE FROM THE LINE FIELD
GET_BYTE                PROC    NEAR
                        PUSH    BX
                        PUSH    CX
                        PUSH    DX
                        PUSH    SI

                        MOV     BX,DX
                        SHR     BX,1
                        SHR     BX,1
                        SHR     BX,1
```

```
                MOV     AH,80H
                MOV     CL,DL
                AND     CL,0007H
                SHR     AH,CL

                MOV     AL,0
                MOV     CX,CS:[V_LINEDEEP]

                MOV     DH,80H
GETBYTE1:       TEST    DS:[SI + BX],AH
                JNZ     GETBYTE2
                OR      AL,DH
GETBYTE2:       ADD     SI,CS:[IMAGE_BYTES]
                SHR     DH,1
                LOOP    GETBYTE1

                POP     SI
                POP     DX
                POP     CX
                POP     BX
                RET
GET_BYTE        ENDP

;PRINT A PASCAL STYLE STRING IN CS:DX
PRINT_STRING    PROC    NEAR
                PUSH    CX
                PUSH    BX
                MOV     BX,DX
                MOV     CX,0
                MOV     CL,CS:[BX]
PRINT_S1:       INC     BX
                MOV     AL,CS:[BX]
                CALL    PRINT_BYTE
                LOOP    PRINT_S1
                POP     BX
                POP     CX
                RET
PRINT_STRING    ENDP

;PRINT ONE BYTE IN AL
PRINT_BYTE      PROC    NEAR
                PUSH    AX
                PUSH    BX
                PUSH    CX
                PUSH    DX
                PUSH    SI
                PUSH    DS
                PUSH    AX

PRINT_B1:       MOV     AH,2
                MOV     DX,0
                INT     17H
                TEST    AH,80H
                JZ      PRINT_B1

                POP     AX

                MOV     AH,0
                MOV     DX,0
                INT     17H
```

```
                    POP      DS
                    POP      SI
                    POP      DX
                    POP      CX
                    POP      BX
                    POP      AX
                    RET
PRINT_BYTE          ENDP
IMAGE_WIDTH         DW       0
IMAGE_DEPTH         DW       0
IMAGE_BYTES         DW       0

;
;        NOTE - ALL STRINGS START WITH A LENGTH BYTE
;

;THIS IS THE STRING SENT TO THE PRINTER AT THE START OF A GRAPHIC LINE
START_SEQ           DB       5,1BH,'*',06H
START_LO            DB       0
START_HI            DB       0

;THIS IS THE STRING SENT TO THE PRINTER AT THE END OF A GRAPHIC LINE
END_SEQ             DB       4,0DH,1BH,'J',18H

;THIS IS THE STRING SENT TO THE PRINTER TO INITIALIZE THE BEAST
INIT_SEQ            DB       2,1BH,'@'

;THIS IS THE STRING SENT TO THE PRINTER TO DIINITIALIZE THE BEAST
DEINIT_SEQ          DB       4,0DH,0AH,1BH,'@'

CODE                ENDS
                    END
```

A number of issues are involved in working with this driver. You'll have to know how it works, how it's called, and then how to actually print something to a PDRV resource. As they stand, PDRV resources only print graphics and rudimentary text.

A PDRV resource provides the program using it with four functions. They initialize the printer, print lines of graphic data, de-initialize the printer, and print simple ASCII text respectively. Each of these will appear as a normal C language function in time.

The first peculiar thing about this code is the dispatch table. You'll note that this contains the offsets of the functions in the rest of the program, but no segment values. Each entry in the table will look like a function pointer to C. No segment values are filled in at assembly time because the segments will vary with the segment value of the buffer the resource is loaded into. As such, the C language code loading this resource must patch the dispatch time each time it's used. This isn't as frightening as it sounds, however.

Each type of code resource used from within a C program must be understood by the code that will call its functions. Each type is represented as a C language struct defining its dispatch table and any data to be available to the calling code. If you look at the struct for a PDRV resource, you might have a better idea of what the top of Fig. 8-20 does:

```
typedef struct {
    int (*init_printer)( );
    int (*print_line)( );
    int (*deinit_printer)( );
    int (*print_text)( );
    int (*null_one);
    int (*null_two);
    int (*null_three);
    int (*null_four);
    int page_wide;
    int page_deep;
    int line_deep;
    int colours;
    int driver_version;
    int driver_subversion;
    char name[25];
    } PRINTDRIVER;
```

If printDrv is a pointer of the type PRINTDRIVER, printDrv->init_printer will be a perfectly legal, callable C function. Likewise, printDrv->page_wide will tell your C program the maximum number of horizontal dots the printer supported by the PDRV resource in question can print. You can print printDrv->name+1 to display the type of printer the PDRV resource being used is intended to support.

The four NULL entries in the dispatch table are included to make adding additional functions to future revisions of the driver possible without invalidating earlier implementations of it.

If you look at Fig. 8-20 again, you'll observe that it behaves very much like the linked-in assembly language discussed earlier in this book. It handles the stack in the same way—note that even though these are effectively near functions, they work with a far style stack when they're called by a C language function.

The actual process of printing to a dot matrix printer is a bit involved and beyond the scope of this book to describe in detail. You don't actually need to know how this driver works to use it—that's the handy thing about drivers. For a complete discussion of it, look in my book *Bitmapped Graphics*, (TAB Book #3558).

Loading a PDRV resource into a buffer works similarly to loading a data resource except that you must patch the dispatch table. The following code, as it does this, assumes that a call to getRF or getnumberedRF has previously located the PDRV resource in question and that its resource header is loaded into a RESOURCE object called rc:

```
PRINTDRIVER *printDrv;
char *p;

if((printDrv = (PRINTDRIVER *)malloc(rc->size)) != NULL) {
    p = (char *)printDrv;
    dread(p,8,fh);
    if(!memcmp(p,"ALCHPRDR",8)) {
```

```
                    if(getdataRF(p,fh,rc->size-8)) {
                        seg = FP_SEG(p);
                        p[2] = seg;
                        p[3] = (seg > > 8); /* init */
                        p[6] = seg;
                        p[7] = (seg > > 8); /* print line */
                        p[10] = seg;
                        p[11] = (seg > > 8); /* deinit */
                        p[14] = seg;
                         p[15] = (seg > > 8); /* print text */
                    }
                    else {
                        free(printDrv);
                        printDrv = NULL;
                    }
                }
                else {
                    free(printDrv);
                    printDrv = NULL;
                }
            }
```

If printDrv is NULL when all this is done, the PDRV resource didn't load properly.

Chances are that you would use this code either to set up a global
PRINTDRIVER pointer or to return a pointer of the type PRINTDRIVER, which
could be used to print with and subsequently passed to free for disposal.

If you're using Turbo C+ +, you have many ways to compensate for the different
offset value in the pointers returned by malloc. Most easily, you could simply change
the size of the signature string in any code resources you write to four bytes, such
that all the code begins at location four and is hence comfortable in a buffer with an
offset of four. In this case, make sure you change the preceding patching code to
reflect this, specifically in the calls to dread, memcmp, and getdataRF.

Alternately, you can use the existing PDRV structure by allocating a buffer
four bytes bigger than needed and then adding four to pointer returned by malloc.
This will give the buffer pointer an effective offset of eight, and all will be well.
Make sure you subtract four from it before you subsequently pass it to free; otherwise, very nasty things might happen.

Because the convenient fixed offset of Turbo C+ +'s allocated buffers is
undocumented, it isn't constrained to remain as described here. If you want to use
this code under a future release of Turbo C+ +, make sure you check what the
buffer pointer offset is (this code works):

```
char *p;

if((p = malloc(10000)) != NULL) {
    printf("The offset is %u \ n",FP_OFF(p));
```

```
        free(p);
    }
```

You might want to run this several times, perhaps with varying arguments to malloc, to confirm that the results are consistent.

Thus far, I haven't mentioned the process of assembling, linking, and subsequently translating the source code in Fig. 8-20 into a code resource. The assembly and linking is pretty painless and will be taken care of by this batch file:

```
ECHO OFF
BREAK ON
MASM %1 %1 NUL NUL
IF ERRORLEVEL 1 GOTO ERROR
TLINK %1
EXE2BIN %1 %1.DRV
DEL %1.EXE
DEL %1.OBJ
ECHO All done... :ERROR
BREAK OFF
```

This batch file, which I call DRVASM.BAT, uses MASM and TLINK—you might want to substitute the assembler and linker of your choice. If you type

```
DRVASM EPSNFX80
```

it will create a binary file called EPSNFX80.DRV from the source code in Fig. 8-20.

Converting EPSNFX80.DRV into EPSNFX80.RES requires a small program called BIN2RES.EXE (see Fig. 8-21 for the source code).

```
#include "stdio.h"
#include "dir.h"
#include "dos.h"
#include "alloc.h"
#include "gui.h"

char filepath[MAXPATH]="";
char secondpath[MAXPATH]="";
char description[65]="A binary resource";
char type[4]={BADRECTYPE};
unsigned long number=BADRECNUM;

main(argc,argv)
    int argc;
    char *argv[];
{
    int i;

    puts("Binary to resource version 1.0 - "
        "copyright (c) 1990 Alchemy Mindworks Inc.\n"
        "--------------------------------"
        "---------------------------------------");

    for(i=1;i<argc;++i) {
```

8-21 The BIN2RES utility.

```
                   if(argv[i][0]=='/') {
                        switch(toupper(argv[i][1])) {
                             case 'F':
                                  strcpy(secondpath,argv[i]+2);
                                  break;
                             case 'N':
                                  number=atol(argv[i]+2);
                                  break;
                             case 'T':
                                  memcpy(type,argv[i]+2,4);
                                  break;
                             case 'D':
                                  strncpy(description,argv[i]+2,64);
                                  description[64]=0;
                                  break;
                        }
                   } else strcpy(filepath,argv[i]);
         }
         if(strlen(filepath) && memcmp(type,BADRECTYPE,4) &&
            number != BADRECNUM) {
              strupr(filepath);
              fixname(secondpath);
              convert();
         }
         else {
              puts("Arguments:        path to binary file\n"
                   "                    /F<name> - set resource file name\n"
                   "                    /N<long> - set resource number\n"
                   "                    /T<type> - set resource type\n"
                   "                    /D<string> - description (optional)\n"
                   );
         }
}
convert()
{
    FILE *fp;
    RFILE fh;
    long size;
    char *p;

    if((fp=fopen(filepath,"rb")) != NULL) {
         fseek(fp,0L,SEEK_END);
         size=ftell(fp);
         rewind(fp);
         if(size < 0xfff1L) {
              if((p=malloc((unsigned int)size)) != NULL) {
                   if(fread(p,1,(unsigned int)size,fp) ==
                      (unsigned int) size) {
                        if(createRF(secondpath,description)) {
                             if((fh=openRF(secondpath)) != 0) {
                                  if(addRF(fh,type,number,
                                     (unsigned int)size,p))
                                       printf("Creating %s - type %4.4s - "
                                          "number %lu - %s\n",
                                          secondpath,type,number,description);
                                  else puts("Error writing resource data");

                                  closeRF(fh);
                             } else printf("Can't open %s.\n",secondpath);
                        } else printf("Can't create %s.\n",secondpath);
                   } else puts("Error reading binary data.");
                   free(p);
              } else puts("Error allocating memory");
         } else printf("%s is too large to be a resource.\n",filepath);
```

```
        fclose(fp);
    } else printf("Can't open %s.\n",filepath);
}

fixname(s)      /* tidy up a file name */
    char *s;
{
    char drive[MAXDRIVE],dir[MAXDIR],path[MAXPATH],ext[MAXEXT];

    fnsplit(s,drive,dir,path,ext);
    if(!strlen(ext)) strcpy(ext,".RES");
    fnmerge(s,drive,dir,path,ext);
    strupr(s);
}
```

The BIN2RES program simply inhales a binary file and assigns it the resource type and number you specify, writing the resulting resource out to a resource file with a suitable header. The correct syntax for converting EPSNFX80.DRV to EPSNFX80.RES is

BIN2RES EPSNFX80.DRV /FEPSNFX80.RES /N0 /TPDRV

The first argument is the binary file to be converted. The /F option specifies the name of the resource file to be created. The /N option specifies the number that the resource being written will have, while the /T option specifies the type. Using the /D option is up to you—it specifies a comment field to add to the resource file header, should you feel like including one.

An example application for code resources

In most cases, graphical user interface based applications that call for the application of code resources will be pretty sophisticated—and correspondingly large. The PRINTRES program in Fig. 8-22 is a somewhat synthetic example of a program that will actually use a PDRV resource. Given a path to a resource file having a PDRV and a BTMP resource in it, it will use the PDRV resource to print the BTMP resource to an appropriate printer.

```
/*
        PRINTRES - a PDRV example
*/

#include "stdio.h"
#include "alloc.h"
#include "dos.h"
#include "gui.h"

main(argc,argv)
        int argc;
        char *argv[];
{
        PRINTDRIVER *printDrv;
        RESOURCE rc;
        RFILE fh;
        char *p,*pr;
        int i=0,x,y,bytes,seg;
```

8-22 A program to print a BTMP resource using a PDRV resource.

```
puts("\n\nA code resource example. This program will\n"
    "look through a resource file and locate the\n"
    "first PDRV resource and te first BTMP resource.\n"
    "It will then print the BTMP resource using the\n"
    "PDRV resource as a driver\n");

if(argc > 1) {
    /* open the resource file */
    if((fh=openRF(argv[1])) == 0)
        problem("Can't open the resource file");

    /* locate a BTMP */
    if(getnumberedRF(fh,"BTMP",0,&rc) == 0)
        problem("There's no bitmap in the resource file");

    /* get a buffer */
    if((p=malloc(rc.size)) == NULL)
        problem("Can't allocate memory for the bitmap");

    if(getdataRF(p,fh,rc.size) == 0)
        problem("Error loading the bitmap");

    x=ImageWidth(p);
    y=ImageDepth(p);
    bytes=ImageBytes(p);
    printf("The dimensions of the bitmap are %u by %u.\n",x,y);

    /* locate a PDRV */
    if(getnumberedRF(fh,"PDRV",0,&rc) == 0)
        problem("There's no printer driver in the resource file");

    /* allocate a buffer for it to live in */
    if((printDrv=(PRINTDRIVER *)malloc(rc.size)) == NULL)
        problem("Can't allocate memory for the printer driver");

    /* create a dummy char pointer */
    pr=(char *)printDrv;

    /* get the header string */
    dread(pr,8,fh);

    /* check the header */
    if(memcmp(pr,"ALCHPRDR",8))
        problem("Corrupted printer driver");

    /* load the driver */
    if(!getdataRF(pr,fh,rc.size-8))
        problem("Can't load the printer driver");

    /* patch the dispatch table */
    seg=FP_SEG(pr);
    pr[2]=seg;
    pr[3]=(seg >> 8);
    pr[6]=seg;
    pr[7]=(seg >> 8);
    pr[10]=seg;
    pr[11]=(seg >> 8);
    pr[14]=seg;
    pr[15]=(seg >> 8);

    /* initialize the printer */
    (printDrv->init_printer)(x,y,bytes);

    /* print the lines */
```

```
        do {
                (printDrv->print_line)(p+4+(i*bytes));
                i+=printDrv->line_deep;
        } while(i < y);

        /* de-initialize the printer */
        (printDrv->deinit_printer)();

        /* free the buffers */
        free(printDrv);
        free(p);

        /* close the resource file */
        closeRF(fh);
    } else puts("I need the path to a resource file.");
}

/* say there's a problem and exit */
problem(s)
    char *s;
{
    puts(s);
    exit(1);
}
```

One useful place to find a resource file suitable for use with this program is Desktop Paint. Its resource file has a BTMP resource for use as a startup screen and PDRV resource that will print to an Epson FX-80 compatible printer.

The PRINTRES program will require a project file, as you must link it to GUI.LIB. While it doesn't actually need any of the graphical user interface functions, it does use the resource manager.

If you look through the code in Fig. 8-22, you'll be able to see how to drive a PDRV resource in a real world application. Most of the action takes place near the bottom of the main function. Given that pr points to a bitmapped image, the code must step through the image, calling the printDrv->print_line function once for each step. A step is defined as printDrv->line_deep times the number of bytes in a line of the image. If pr points to a monochrome putimage fragment, as is the case here, you should start printing from pr+4 to step over the two integers at the start of the image fragment.

Note that the print driver will print multiple lines in one pass of the printer's head. The number of lines varies with the number of pins available to printer. In the case of EPSNFX80.DRV, it's eight. As a PDRV resource knows the characteristics of the printer it's been written for, it's in a good position to define the number of lines in a step.

This example is a bit simple-minded. If it were designed for actual printing applications, it would check to make sure that the dimensions of the image didn't exceed the dimensions of the printer's page, as defined by printDrv->page_wide and printDrv->page_deep. It would also deal with source images not an even multiple of printDrv->line_deep lines deep. As it stands now, it might print a few lines of garbage if confronted with such an image.

If you follow this example, you should be able to make your applications print bitmaps through PDRV resources—even if you have no idea how to code up graphics for a dot matrix printer. The driver does all the work.

Resources at work

You can write pretty respectable graphical user interface applications without ever using a single resource. They're not essential, and if some of the code thus far has seemed a bit daunting, you might want to leave them alone for a while.

If you do choose to apply resources to your programs, you'll probably find that they offer you new approaches to many things. They offer great flexibility and allow your users to decide much more about how your applications will behave than is provided by simple configuration utilities.

Finally, you should remember that the resource types in this book are only a beginning—once you start thinking in terms of using resources, you will no doubt come up with plenty of custom resources of your own.

Unlike as with commercial graphical user interfaces—or with Macintosh programming, in which you're almost legally bound to follow a predefined set of guidelines—you can modify the way resources are used under the graphical user interface in any way you like. Note, however, that if you maintain a consistent format and approach to creating resources over the programs you write, you'll find numerous opportunities for booting up RMOVER and swiping resources from one project to add features to another.

We have them right where they want us.
                    Admiral J.T. Kirk

9

Using fonts

ALL THE DETAILED DISCUSSION OF FONTS SO FAR HAS CONCERNED the eight-point screen font used to form the menus and other bits of system text in the graphical user interface. While perfectly readable, this font is uninteresting and hardly suitable for display applications.

Ornate, proportionally spaced type looks interesting in graphics mode because it's so unlike the way a PC usually displays text. Desktop Paint uses proportionally spaced type in its text editing mode, allowing you to add text to a drawing. However, you can probably use it for many other things, depending upon the sorts of applications you write.

Figure 9-1 illustrates some examples of proportionally spaced type as displayed by the code to be discussed in this chapter. These fonts have been drawn from a number of sources.

Specifically, this chapter will look at using display fonts from GEM/VDI based applications, from Macintosh FONT resources, and from Windows FNT files.

The legal aspects of fonts

As mentioned in Chapter 1, one unfortunate aspect of adding display fonts to your applications written using the graphical user interface is that you can't simply buy a disk of them in a common format and plug them into a program. Unlike the Macintosh, no common format for bitmapped display fonts exists for the PC, and no one sells them as a stand-alone product. They do exist, of course, but only in conjunction with other applications.

Helvetica (A Ventura Font)
From the Ventura Publisher installation disks.

EIRE (A MACINTOSH FONT)
From Cassady & Greene, a third party font company.

Future (a Macintosh font)
From Cassady & Greene, a third party font company.

CRYPT (A MACINTOSH FONT)
Found on a bulletin board

Meath (A Ventura Font)
From Cassady & Greene, a third party font company.

San Francisco (A Macintosh font)
From the Macintosh System file.

Courier (A Ventura font)
From the Ventura Publisher installation disks.

9-1 Some proportionally spaced text.

However, quite a few fonts exist (at least ostensibly) in the public domain.

You might wonder about the relative likelihood of being sued if you take fonts from another application and place them in your own. As it turns out, this is a fairly peculiar issue worth knowing a bit about. It's also one in which a measure of conscience will serve to keep you out of trouble.

Note that none of the information in this section should be regarded as being legal council. You might want to consult an attorney regarding it.

The United States Copyright Office decided in September, 1988, that typeface designs cannot be registered and hence protected under the copyright act. The complete text of this decision can be found in the Federal Register volume 53, number 189, docket 86-4. The basis of this decision is rather interesting. The Copyright Office held that if typefaces could be copyrighted, the holders of the copyrights might be in a position to restrict the use of typefaces and hence the words printed using those typefaces. Because virtually everything printed uses one typeface or another, the holders of the typeface copyrights would be in a position to regulate all printed words.

You should understand what this decision means in regard to computer fonts. To begin with, it pertains only to the appearance of type, not to its name. As such, the typeface name "Times Roman" is a copyrighted entity owned by the International Typeface Corporation and is unaffected by the Copyright Office's decision. You couldn't create a font and call it Times Roman without the permission of the copyright owner.

You could create a font that looked exactly like Times Roman and call it something else. Most computer applications that use type resembling Times Roman call it "Dutch." In commercial typographic circles, much more obviously derivative names exist—for example, the Compugraphic version of Times Roman is called "English Times."

The letter of the Copyright Office decision also means that you can use any fonts you come across in any way you like so long as you don't use their commercial, copyrighted names without the authority of the copyright holders.

Clearly, this is a situation in which no one is likely to get upset if their interests aren't abused. Later in this chapter, I'll discuss the code that translates screen fonts used by Ventura Publisher into a form suitable for use by applications written for the graphical user interface in this book. If you write a database manager or a graphics program incorporating these fonts, you will neither violate the Copyright Office decision nor will you be doing anything unethical. Still, it would be both unethical and unwise to use these fonts to write a desktop publishing package (i.e., something performing a function similar to that of Ventura Publisher).

Some lawsuits are undertaken by large parties against small ones because the large party knows it has the financial resources to win rather than because it's certain it's right. Apple Computer has arguably done this from time to time. It would be unwise to use the Macintosh system fonts, for example, in an application duplicating a Macintosh function.

In most cases you can find many fonts on bulletin boards and from other public domain and shareware sources that either have no obvious owners or are intended for consumption as shareware. This includes fonts in all three of the commercial formats to be discussed in this chapter.

Working with display fonts

The code discussed in this chapter falls neatly into two classifications. The font manager code is part of GUI.LIB and is used by applications to manage—and particularly, draw—proportionally spaced fonts. The latter part of this chapter deals with three programs to convert commercial font formats into the format of a FONT resource.

You should note that the format of a FONT resource, as defined herein, is unique to this book. You will find that the Macintosh also uses what it calls FONT resources. The two entities aren't the same, although one of the topics of this chapter will be a discussion of translating the latter into the former.

If you haven't had cause to meddle with the structure of commercial proportionally spaced fonts yet, the structure of a FONT resource might seem unnecessarily weird. It's actually designed to be more or less like the structure of the three commercial font file types discussed here—they all behave with a similar degree of weirdness.

Under a proportionally spaced font, the maximum height of the font's characters will be a constant but the width of the characters will vary. For example, the letter "M" is usually a lot wider than the letter "i." This difference causes problems both for the function that must draw the characters and for the designer of a file format to store them in.

The most useful way to store a proportionally spaced font (at least, in the context of the graphic tools provided by Turbo C) might be as a series of monochrome putimage fragments, with one fragment per character and a table of pointers to simplify locating specific characters in a font file. If proportionally spaced fonts were stored this way, text could be "drawn" by using multiple calls to putimage.

Considering how logical and apparent this is, however, you probably won't be surprised to know that no one does it this way.

The most time-consuming, processor-intensive graphic operation in placing a bitmapped image on the screen is addressing the different lines in the screen buffer. As such, a function that draws a string of text should ideally do so once for each raster line in the text rather than multiple times per character. A system to handle drawing text strings in a proportionally spaced font should do so in such a way as to need to address only one time each line being drawn.

A FONT resource stores all the characters in a proportionally spaced font in a single extremely long bitmap. You can envision such a bitmap as being all the characters from character one through character 255 typed one after another on a single line. In order to print a character, the bits of the bitmap it occupies must be copied out of the long bitmap and placed on the screen.

Figure 9-2 illustrates how this works.

9-2 Creating a text string by copying bits from the font bitmap of a FONT resource.

Despite the fairly processor-intensive nature of this procedure, it isn't all that difficult to write a function that will handle it very quickly. Almost all the operations involved are bit shifts and addition, things at which the 8088 series of processors happens to excel.

In order to allow the function that draws text to locate characters in the big bitmap of a FONT resource, the resource also contains two tables. The first table tells the function how many bits from the left edge of the bitmap each character starts at, and the second table tells it how many bits wide each character is. There is one entry in each table for each possible character in a font (up to the maximum of 255 characters).

A FONT resource consists of a FONT data structure followed by the aforementioned long narrow bitmap. The FONT data structure looks like this:

```
typedef struct {
    char name[FONTNAMESIZE + 1];
```

```
    char number;
    char pointsize;
    char charwide[(MAXFONTCHAR-MINFONTCHAR) + 1];
    unsigned int charoff[(MAXFONTCHAR-MINFONTCHAR) + 1];
    unsigned int bitmapwidth;
    unsigned int bitmapdepth;
    unsigned int bitmapbytes;
    unsigned int widestchar;
    unsigned int padwidth;
    unsigned int spacewidth;
    } FONT;
```

A few constants are also involved:

```
#define FONTNAMESIZE   32    /* maximum size of a font name */
#define MINFONTCHAR     0    /* lowest number font character */
#define MAXFONTCHAR   255    /* highest number font character */
```

The fields in a FONT resource probably deserve some illumination. The name is, of course, what the font in question will be called. Examples of the occupants of this field are "Dutch," "Times Roman," "Symbols," and so on.

Every different font family has a number, which perhaps not surprisingly turns up in the number field of a FONT resource. All the sizes of Dutch would have the same number—by default, it's 14. No other font should have this number. Font numbers will help you manage large numbers of fonts in applications using them. You're free to assign font numbers as you like, just as long as you keep track of the numbers you've used. By virtue of the number field of a FONT resource being a char, font numbers can run from 0 through 255.

The pointsize field defines the number of points high the font in question is. This issue may make real type gurus a bit uncomfortable. A point is actually $1/72$ of an inch. As a general rule of thumb, one pixel on a typical monitor connected to a typical computer on a typical day when the power isn't browned out—shrinking the size of your monitor's raster—is about $1/75$ of an inch deep. Applications dealing with proportionally spaced type usually feel that the difference—$1/1800$ of an inch—is inconsequential enough to be ignored, and hence twelve point type is considered to be what occupies twelve screen lines.

This simplifies the managing of code dealing with drawing text. Although it's technically fallacious, it's a useful fallacy and one well worth promulgating.

Note that the point size of a particular font actually describes the height of the capital letters. Traditionally, the size measurement is made against the height of the letter "E." The descenders of lowercase letters will usually drop below the baseline of the capital letters of a font, so the number of screen lines a font occupies isn't usually the same as its point size.

The charwide array in a FONT structure contains the width of each character in the font in question in pixels. No character can be wider than 255 pixels (a situation that never occurs).

The charoff array specifies the offset from the left edge of the character bitmap for each character in the font.

The bitmapwidth element specifies the width of the character bitmap in pixels, while the bitmapbytes element specifies this value in bytes (often more useful). The bitmapdepth element defines the number of vertical lines in the bitmap and, hence, the number of vertical lines the font will occupy when drawn on your screen—descenders and all.

The widestchar element tells the font manager code the width of the font's widest character. The padwidth value is the number of pixels of blank space to leave between the characters of the font being drawn. This actually allows the font manager to deal with fonts from varying sources, some of which construct their font bitmaps with all the characters touching to save a bit of space.

Finally, spacewidth specifies the width of the space character in pixels.

Following the FONT data structure in a FONT resource will be the actual font bitmap. This bitmap will look a bit different from one source to the next. Macintosh fonts are stored with their characters touching. Windows fonts store their characters such that each character begins on an even sixteen pixel boundary—if you were to look at a Windows font bitmap, the characters would appear to have irregular gaps between them but would start at regular intervals along the bitmap.

The structure of a FONT resource allows bitmaps from all sources to be used transparently. Once they're translated into FONT resources, these diverse fonts will all behave in the same way.

You can load FONT resources into memory just as you would any other sort of resource. Specifically, you would find the size of the font to be loaded from the size element of its RESOURCE header and allocate a buffer to contain it. The pointer to the buffer should be of the type FONT.

Some examples of loading and using FONT resources will appear later in this chapter in the SEEFONT application.

The code to draw text in a font on your screen does pretty much what you'd expect it to do. It copies the bits of each character from the font being used to the appropriate area of your screen. Figure 9-3 illustrates drawstringFN, a function that draws proportionally spaced text.

```
/* draw string s int font at (x,y) */
drawstringFN(s,font,x,y)
     char *s;
     FONT *font;
     int x,y;
{
     char *pr,*bmp;
     int n,i,j,k,kl,cp,cb;

     n=strlen(s);
     bmp=((char *)font)+sizeof(FONT);

     MouseOff();
     for(i=0;i<font->bitmapdepth;++i) {
          if((y+i) >=SCREENDEEP) break;
```

9-3 The drawstringFN function.

```
                pr=(char *)MK_FP(SCREENSEG,SCREENTBL[y+i]);
                cb=x;
                for(j=0;j<n;++j) {
                        if(s[j]!=32) {
                                kl=font->charwide[s[j]];
                                cp=font->charoff[s[j]];
                                for(k=0;k<kl;++k) {
                                        if(bmp[cp>>3] & masktable[cp & 0x0007])
                                                pr[cb>>3] &= ~masktable[cb & 0x0007];
                                        ++cb;
                                        ++cp;
                                }

                                cb+=font->padwidth;
                        } else cb+=(font->spacewidth+font->padwidth);
                }
                bmp+=font->bitmapbytes;
        }
        MouseOn();
}
```

The first argument to drawstringFN is the string to be drawn. The second is a pointer of the type FONT (i.e., a pointer to a loaded FONT resource). Finally, the x and y arguments specify the upper left corner of the area that the text will occupy.

It's up to you to ensure that the text won't be drawn past the right side of the screen. Functions to help you do this will be discussed in a moment.

You might want to closely examine the code for drawstringFN as to fully understand what it does. You should note that it sacrifices clarity for speed. Also note that it writes directly to the screen using the SCREENTBL array discussed in Chapter 2. The innermost for loop actually extracts the bits from the font bitmap being drawn and places them on the screen.

Figure 9-4 illustrates an alternate function for placing text on your screen. The bitmapstringFN function will create a monochrome putimage fragment containing the text to be drawn in the font specified. It uses a few as yet undiscussed functions but works pretty well the same way that drawstringFN did.

```
char *bitmapstringFN(s,font)
        char *s;
        FONT *font;
{
        char *p,*pr,*bmp;
        int n,bytes,width,i,j,k,kl,cp,cb,bsize;

        n=strlen(s);
        width=stringwidthFN(s,font);
        bytes=pixels2bytes(width);
        bmp=((char *)font)+sizeof(FONT);
        bsize=4+(bytes*font->bitmapdepth);

        if((p=malloc(bsize)) != NULL) {
                memset(p,0xff,bsize);
                p[0]=width-1;
                p[1]=(width-1)>>8;
                p[2]=font->bitmapdepth-1;
                p[3]=(font->bitmapdepth-1)>>8;
```

9-4 The bitmapstringFN function.

```
            pr=p+4;
            for(i=0;i<font->bitmapdepth;++i) {
                cb=0;
                for(j=0;j<n;++j) {
                    if(s[j] != 32) {
                        kl=font->charwide[s[j]];
                        cp=font->charoff[s[j]];
                        for(k=0;k<kl;++k) {
                            if(bmp[cp>>3] & masktable[cp & 0x0007])
                                pr[cb>>3] &= ~masktable[cb & 0x0007];
                            ++cb;
                            ++cp;
                        }
                        cb+=font->padwidth;
                    } else cb+=(font->spacewidth+font->padwidth);
                }
                bmp+=font->bitmapbytes;
                pr+=bytes;
            }
        }
        return(p);
    } else return(NULL);
}
```

There is no obvious way to predict the width in pixels of a text string to be drawn in a proportionally spaced font. You can say that it will be no longer than the number of characters in the string times the width of the widest character in the font; but, in almost all cases, it will in fact be very much shorter. In most applications of proportionally spaced text, you'll want to fit the text to a specified area, which requires knowing how wide it will be before drawn.

You can work out the width of a proportionally spaced text string before drawing it on the screen by adding up all the character widths of the characters in the string. The character widths can be found in the charwide array of the FONT resource in question.

Figure 9-5 illustrates several functions useful in fitting text into a specific area. The charwidthFN function will return the width of any character passed to it in a specific font. The font argument to this function, as with the following two, should be a pointer to a FONT resource. Note that in measuring characters, the calculations must include whatever value is in the padwidth element of the font.

```
charwidthFN(n,font)
        int n;
        FONT *font;
{
        if(n==32) return(font->spacewidth+font->padwidth);
        else if(!font->charwide[n]) return(0);
        else return((unsigned int)font->charwide[n]+font->padwidth);
}

stringwidthFN(s,font)
        char *s;
        FONT *font;
{
        unsigned int a=0;
```

9-5 The charwidthFN, stringwidthFN, and fontdepthFN functions.

```
        while(*s) a+=(unsigned int)charwidthFN(*s++,font);
        return(a);
}

fontdepthFN(font)
        FONT *font;
{
        return(font->bitmapdepth);
}
```

The stringwidthFN function measures a whole string instead of just a single character. It simply calls charwidthFN repeatedly, once for each character in the string.

Finally, fontdepthFN returns the depth of the font in question. You could, of course, work this out for yourself—it's just the bitmap_depth value of the FONT resource being used.

In theory, any font in any size can be used with the foregoing font functions. The only restriction is that no font resource can occupy more than 64K of memory, as neither the font manager nor the resource manager can deal with objects larger than this.

Depending upon the applications you write, you might want to limit the number of distinct point sizes of proportionally spaced text available to your users. Doing this allows you to create a dialog box to select the point size for whatever font you'll be using; you can create the box much easier if you know how many items will be in it.

The islegalfontsize function in Fig. 9-6 will return a true value if the number passed to it is a legal point size; otherwise, it returns false. The legal point sizes are contained in FONTSIZEARRAY. You can add values to this if you like, although its current contents represent a pretty reasonable mix of font sizes.

```
islegalfontsize(n)
        int n;
{
        if(strchr(FONTSIZEARRAY,n)==NULL) return(0);
        else return(1);
}

char FONTSIZEARRAY[]={6,7,8,9,10,11,12,14,16,18,20,22,24,28,30,32,36,0};
```
9-6 The islegalfontsize function.

Finally, for reasons that will become a bit clearer toward the end of this chapter, it's handy to have a resource manager function that will specifically write FONT resources. The writeFontRes function is designed to write a single font resource to a resource file, adding a description field to it as was seen in the RMOVER listing in the previous chapter. This function is really only needed for font conversion programs, but making it a part of GUI.LIB means that the format and the description fields can be easily standardized.

Note that this function always destroys the existing contents (if any) of the resource file it writes to before adding the newly created FONT resource. Don't use it to add fonts to an existing resource file, such as for a font editor program.

The writeFontRes function is shown in Fig. 9-7.

```
writeFontRes(path,font,bitmap)
     char *path;
     FONT *font;
     char *bitmap;
{
     char *p,b[FONTNAMESIZE+32];
     RFILE fh;
     unsigned int size,rt=0;

     size=sizeof(FONT)+(font->bitmapbytes*font->bitmapdepth);
     if((p=malloc(size)) != NULL) {
          memcpy(p,(char *)font,sizeof(FONT));
          memcpy(p+sizeof(FONT),bitmap,font->bitmapbytes*font->bitmapdepth);
          sprintf(b,"%u point %s",font->pointsize,font->name);
          if(createRF(path,b)) {
               if((fh=openRF(path)) != 0) {
                    if(addRF(fh,FONTid,0L,size,p)) rt=1;
                    closeRF(fh);
               }
          }
          free(p);
     }
     return(rt);
}
```

9-7 The writeFontRes function.

If you have a copy of Desktop Paint, you might want to use RMOVER to extract a few of the fonts from its resource file to try out the functions just discussed. You'll also need some FONT resources to try the program to be discussed in the next section of this chapter. If you don't have any FONT resources or any font files that can be converted to FONT resources, as discussed later in this chapter, you can create a very simple FONT resource based on the system font used in the graphical user interface. While it's not very exciting to look at, it will allow you to experiment with the font manager code.

The SYS2FONT program, illustrated in Fig. 9-8, will create a file called SYSTEM.RES, a FONT resource.

```
/*
     SYS2FONT
*/

#include "stdio.h"
#include "alloc.h"
#include "gui.h"

#define CHARCOUNT     256
#define CHARWIDTH     8
#define CHARDEPTH     8
#define CHARBYTES     1

extern char THEFONT[];

main()
{
     FONT f;
     char *p;
     int i,j;
```

9-8 The SYS2FONT program.

```
strcpy(f.name,"System");
f.number=254;
f.pointsize=CHARDEPTH;
for(i=0;i<CHARCOUNT;++i) {
        f.charwide[i]=CHARWIDTH;
        f.charoff[i]=i*CHARDEPTH;
}
f.bitmapwidth=CHARCOUNT*CHARWIDTH;
f.bitmapdepth=CHARDEPTH;
f.bitmapbytes=CHARCOUNT*CHARBYTES;
f.widestchar=CHARWIDTH;
f.padwidth=0;
f.spacewidth=CHARWIDTH;
if((p=malloc(CHARCOUNT*CHARBYTES*CHARDEPTH))==NULL)
    puts("Error allocating memory");

for(i=0;i<CHARCOUNT;++i) {
        for(j=0;j<CHARDEPTH;++j) {
                p[(j*(CHARCOUNT*CHARBYTES))+i]=
                    THEFONT[(i*(CHARDEPTH*CHARBYTES))+j];
        }
}

if(!writeFontRes("SYSTEM.RES",&f,p))
    puts("Error writing font");
free(p);
}
```

You will need a project file to link SYS2FONT to GUI.LIB. You might want to work out just what SYS2FONT does to the THEFONT data when it creates its bitmap in the second of its two for loops.

Viewing FONT resources

Having created a FONT resource, you could see what it looks like by adding it to the resource file of a graphical user interface application that uses proportionally spaced text and then by causing it to appear on the screen. This is rather awkward for trying out a font, especially if you aren't sure if it will fulfill your expectations. If you write software that generates FONT resources, you will need a quick way to view them before they're actually used.

Figures 9-9A, B, C, D, E, and F illustrate several views of the SEEFONT application, which is based on GUI.LIB and will display single FONT resources. It's also the first complete application based on the library to be presented in this book. It will illustrate both how to write a graphical user interface based application in general and how to use the font manger functions discussed in this chapter.

The complete source code for SEEFONT.C is shown in Fig. 9-10. You will need a project file to link this to GUI.LIB. Note that the chooseFile call used in the doOpen function of SEEFONT hasn't been discussed yet; it'll turn up in Chapter 10.

The SEEFONT program should be pretty easy to work your way through, as almost everything in it has been dealt with in the earlier chapters of this book. Once you start writing your own applications under the graphical user interface, you'll find that SEEFONT makes a useful boilerplate to begin work with.

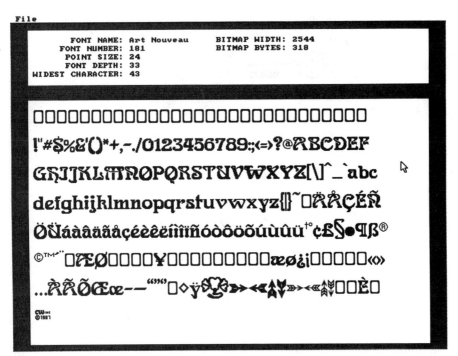

```
        FONT NAME: Art Nouveau      BITMAP WIDTH: 2544
      FONT NUMBER: 181              BITMAP BYTES: 318
       POINT SIZE: 24
       FONT DEPTH: 33
 WIDEST CHARACTER: 43
```

9-9A A screen from the SEEFONT application—Art Nouveau.

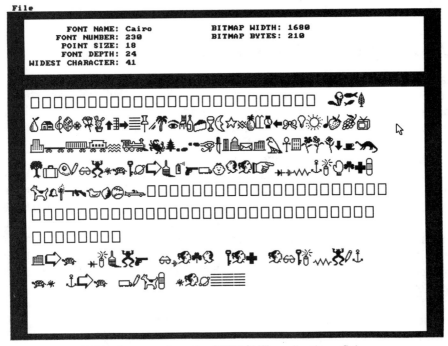

```
        FONT NAME: Cairo            BITMAP WIDTH: 1680
      FONT NUMBER: 230              BITMAP BYTES: 210
       POINT SIZE: 18
       FONT DEPTH: 24
 WIDEST CHARACTER: 41
```

9-9B A screen from the SEEFONT application—Cairo.

240 *Using fonts*

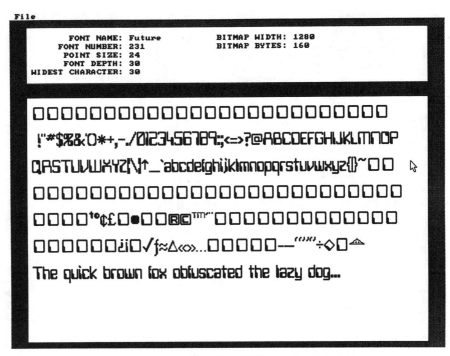

9-9C   A screen from the SEEFONT application—Future.

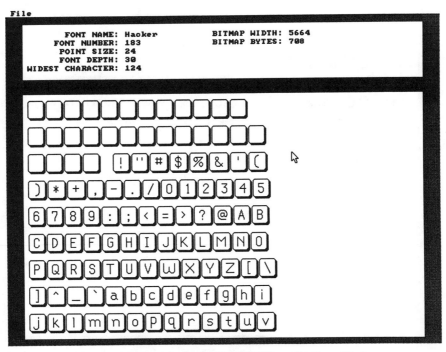

9-9D   A screen from the SEEFONT application—Hacker.

```
        FONT NAME: San Francisco     BITMAP WIDTH: 832
      FONT NUMBER: 232               BITMAP BYTES: 104
       POINT SIZE: 18
       FONT DEPTH: 20
 WIDEST CHARACTER: 22
```

□□□□□□□□□□□□□□□□□□□□□□□□□□□ !"#$%&'()*+,-./0123456789:;<=>?@ABCDEFGHIJKLMNOPQRSTUVWXYZ[\]□_abcdefghijklmnopqrstuvwxyz{}□□--‘’‘’□□□

The quick brown fox obfuscated the lazy dog...

9-9E A screen from the SEEFONT application—San Fransisco.

```
        FONT NAME: Venice            BITMAP WIDTH: 1152
      FONT NUMBER: 246               BITMAP BYTES: 144
       POINT SIZE: 14
       FONT DEPTH: 19
 WIDEST CHARACTER: 21
```

□□□□□□□□□□□□□□□□□□□□□□□□□ !"#$%&'()*+,-./0123456789:;<=>?□ABCDEFGHIJKLMNOPQRSTUVWXYZ[\]^_`abcdefghijklmnopqrstuvwxyz{}□□ÄÅÇÉÑÖÜáàâäãåçéèêëíìîïñóòôöõúùûü□□□□□□ß□□□´□□ÆØ□□□□□□□□□□□□œø¿¡□□□□«»□ÀÃÕŒœ--""''□□ÿ

The quick brown fox obfuscated the lazy dog...

9-9F A screen from the SEEFONT application—Venice.

```
/*
        SEEFONT - A FONT RESOURCE VIEWER
*/

#include "stdio.h"
#include "alloc.h"
#include "dos.h"
#include "dir.h"
#include "graphics.h"
#include "gui.h"

/* define the area the fonts will appear in */
#define BOXLEFT         24
#define BOXTOP          120

int doOpen(void);
int doClose(void);
int doQuit(void);

MENU file = {3," File",
                " Open \0040      ",doOpen,
                ".Close \004Z     ",doClose,
                " Quit \004Q      ",doQuit,
                };

FONT *myFontHeader=NULL;
char *myBitmap=NULL;
char *myFont=NULL;

char alive=1;
char filepath[129];
char drivemap[]="ABCDEFGHI";
char teststring[]="The quick brown fox obfuscated the lazy dog...";

int boxwide,boxdeep;
int isopen=0;

extern WINDOW screenwindow;
struct viewporttype theView;

main()
{
        POINT thePoint;
        int rt;

        if(initMouse()) {
                registerbgidriver(EGAVGA_driver);
                registerbgidriver(Herc_driver);
                if(initGraphics()) {
                        MouseOn();
                        ClearScreen();
                        InitWindowManager();
                        InitMenuManager();
                        AddMenu(&file);
                        DrawMenuBar();

                        getcwd(filepath,128);
                        if(filepath[strlen(filepath)-1] != '\\')
                            strcat(filepath,"\\");
                do {
                        dispatchMenuItem();
                        if(MouseDown(&thePoint)) {
```

9-10 The source code for the SEEFONT application.

```
                                      rt=whereMouse(&thePoint,
                                          &screenwindow);
                                      if(rt & inMenuBar)
                                          doMenu(&thePoint);
                                      else errorbeep();
                              }
                      } while(alive);
                      MouseOff();
                      deinitGraphics();
              } else puts("Cannot establish graphics mode");
          } else puts("Cannot locate mouse driver");
}

/* print the numerical information about the font at
   the top of the screen */
displaydata()
{
        char b[128];
        int x,y=80,py=20;

        /* clear out the data area */
        setlinestyle(SOLID_LINE,0,NORM_WIDTH);
        setcolor(BLACK);
        setwritemode(COPY_PUT);
        setfillstyle(SOLID_FILL,getmaxcolor());

        x=getmaxx()-48;

        MouseOff();
        bar(BOXLEFT,py,24+x,py+y);
        rectangle(BOXLEFT,py,24+x,py+y);
        MouseOn();

        /* print the information */
        sprintf(b,"        FONT NAME: %s",myFontHeader->name);
        DrawString(BOXLEFT+8,py+=12,b,ACTIVE);

        sprintf(b,"      FONT NUMBER: %u",myFontHeader->number);
        DrawString(BOXLEFT+8,py+=12,b,ACTIVE);

        sprintf(b,"       POINT SIZE: %u",myFontHeader->pointsize);
        DrawString(BOXLEFT+8,py+=12,b,ACTIVE);

        sprintf(b,"       FONT DEPTH: %u",myFontHeader->bitmapdepth);
        DrawString(BOXLEFT+8,py+=12,b,ACTIVE);

        sprintf(b,"WIDEST CHARACTER: %u",myFontHeader->widestchar);
        DrawString(BOXLEFT+8,py+=12,b,ACTIVE);

        py=20;

        sprintf(b,"   BITMAP WIDTH: %u",myFontHeader->bitmapwidth);
        DrawString(BOXLEFT+256,py+=12,b,ACTIVE);

        sprintf(b,"   BITMAP BYTES: %u",myFontHeader->bitmapbytes);
        DrawString(BOXLEFT+256,py+=12,b,ACTIVE);
}

/* display the actual font. this function will print as much of
   the font and then of the sample text string as will fit in the
   window.
*/
```

```
displayfont()
{
        POINT pnt;
        char *p,b[257];
        unsigned int a=0,i,j=0,n;

        /* clear out the space and draw a box */
        setlinestyle(SOLID_LINE,0,NORM_WIDTH);
        setcolor(BLACK);
        setwritemode(COPY_PUT);
        setfillstyle(SOLID_FILL,getmaxcolor());

        boxwide=getmaxx()-48;
        boxdeep=getmaxy()-128;

        MouseOff();
        bar(BOXLEFT,BOXTOP,BOXLEFT+boxwide,BOXTOP+boxdeep);
        rectangle(BOXLEFT,BOXTOP,BOXLEFT+boxwide,BOXTOP+boxdeep);
        MouseOn();

        /* draw each character, making sure that there's
           room for it first */

        pnt.x=BOXLEFT+8;
        pnt.y=BOXTOP+8;
        b[0]=0;
        for(i=0;i<=256;++i) {
                n=charwidthFN(i,myFontHeader);
                a+=n;
                if(a >= ((boxwide-myFontHeader->widestchar)-
                    myFontHeader->widestchar) || i==256) {
                        b[j]=0;
                        if((pnt.y+(fontdepthFN(myFontHeader)+8)) <
                          (BOXTOP+boxdeep))
                            drawstringFN(b,myFontHeader,pnt.x,pnt.y);
                        pnt.y+=(fontdepthFN(myFontHeader)+8);
                        a=j=0;
                }
                if(n) b[j++]=i;
        }

        /* now draw the text string the same way */
        p=teststring;
        pnt.x=BOXLEFT+8;
        do {
                n=charwidthFN(*p,myFontHeader);
                a+=n;
                if(a >= ((boxwide-myFontHeader->widestchar)-
                    myFontHeader->widestchar) || !*p) {
                        b[j]=0;
                        if((pnt.y+(fontdepthFN(myFontHeader)+8)) <
                          (BOXTOP+boxdeep))
                            drawstringFN(b,myFontHeader,pnt.x,pnt.y);
                        pnt.y+=(fontdepthFN(myFontHeader)+8);
                        a=j=0;
                }
                if(n) b[j++]=*p;
        } while(*p++);
}

/* load a font resource */
loadfile(s)
        char *s;
{
```

```
        RFILE fh;
        RESOURCE rc;
        int rt=0;

        if((fh=openRF(s)) != NULL) {
                if(getnumberedRF(fh,FONTid,0,&rc)) {
                        if((myFont=malloc(rc.size)) != NULL) {
                                if(getdataRF(myFont,fh,rc.size)) {
                                        myFontHeader=(FONT *)myFont;
                                        myBitmap=myFont+sizeof(FONT);
                                        rt=1;
                                }
                        }
                }
                closeRF(fh);
        }
        return(rt);
}

/* open a font resource with a call to the chooseFile dialog */
doOpen()
{
        char b[129],name[16],filename[16];
        char drive[MAXDRIVE],dir[MAXDIR],ext[MAXEXT];

        if(isopen) return(0);

        strcpy(b,filepath);
        strcat(b,"*.");
        strcat(b,RESext);

        if(chooseFile(b,name,48,48,drivemap)) {
                fnsplit(b,drive,dir,NULL,NULL);
                fnsplit(name,NULL,NULL,filename,ext);
                fnmerge(b,drive,dir,filename,ext);

                fnmerge(filepath,drive,dir,NULL,NULL);

                if(loadfile(b)) {
                        isopen=-1;
                        file.item[0].name[0]='.'; /* disable open */
                        file.item[1].name[0]=' '; /* enable close */
                        displaydata();
                        displayfont();
                } else errorbeep();
        }
}
/* close the current file - clear the screen, free the
   resource and do some housekeeping */
doClose()
{
        if(!isopen) return(0);

        if(myFont != NULL) {
                isopen=0;
                free(myFont);
                myFont=NULL;
                screenwindow.head.next=NULL;
                ClearScreen();
                file.item[0].name[0]=' '; /* enable open */
                file.item[1].name[0]='.'; /* disable close */
        }
```

```
}

/* get lost */
doQuit()
{
        alive=0;
}
```

Converting fonts from other sources

One reason for the early creation of SEEFONT was as a tool to help debug the three programs to be discussed in the rest of this chapter. Converting fonts from other formats to be used as FONT resources is a fairly tricky undertaking, as in all three cases to be dealt with here the font file formats documentation is a bit thin.

The programs performing the conversions—GEM2FONT for GEM/VDI font files, MAC2FONT for Macintosh FONT resources, and WIN2FONT for Windows FNT files—represent a fair bit of tinkering. The MAC2FONT program is especially obtuse for reasons that'll be obvious shortly. You might find that you want to skip the rest of this chapter entirely. Unless you're curious about these things or have some other application for these font files in their native formats, you can safely ignore the details and simply use the resulting programs.

All three programs will require project files because they use calls to GUI.LIB.

Converting GEM/VDI fonts

The discussion of font format conversion will begin with GEM/VDI files—the format used for screen fonts under Ventura Publisher as well—as these are the least monstrous of the lot.

If you have Ventura Publisher or some other GEM-based application that uses bitmapped screen fonts, you should find a number of files associated with it having the extensions EGA or VGA. This won't be the case for vector-based packages such as GEM *Artline*, which plots all its text on the screen from outline files.

Most of the EGA or VGA files included with a GEM-based application will be screen fonts—Ventura also names its screen drivers with these extensions, but it's pretty easy to tell which files these are. The default screen fonts of Ventura have the names SWISV08N.VGA through SWISV72N.VGA, DUTCV06N.VGA through DUTCV72N.VGA, COURV12N.VGA through COURV24N.VGA, and SYMBV08N.VGA through SYMBV24N.VGA. These represent respectively the Swiss, Dutch, Courier, and Symbol fonts. The numbers in each of these file names is the point size of the screen font in question.

Figure 9-11 illustrates these fonts.

One thing that makes GEM fonts easier to work with than the other two font file formats to be discussed here is that they're stored in a format not all that different from the format of a FONT resource. Each GEM font file starts with the following data structure:

```
typedef struct {
    int identifier;
    int size;
```

36 point Times Roman

28 point Times Roman

24 point Times Roman

22 point Times Roman

20 point Times Roman

18 point Times Roman

16 point Times Roman

14 point Times Roman

12 point Times Roman

11 point Times Roman

10 point Times Roman

9 point Times Roman

8 point Times Roman

6 point Helvetica
8 point Helvetica
9 point Helvetica
10 point Helvetica
11 point Helvetica
12 point Helvetica
14 point Helvetica
16 point Helvetica
18 point Helvetica

20 point Helvetica

22 point Helvetica

24 point Helvetica

28 point Helvetica

36 point Helvetica

12 point Courier

20 point Courier

24 point Courier

9-11   The screen fonts included with Ventura.

```
        char name[32];
        int firstchar;
        int lastchar;
        int topdist;
        int ascent;
        int halfline;
        int descent;
        int bottomdist;
        int widestchar;
        int widestcell;
        int leftoffset;
        int rightoffset;
        int thickening;
        int underlinesize;
        int lightmask;
        int skewmask;
        int flags;
        long h_offset_table;
        long c_offset_table;
        long font_data;
        int formwidth;
        int formdepth;
        long nextfont;
     } GEMFONTHEADER;
```

While the GEMFONTHEADER is a bit immense, it's relatively easy to understand. You can also easily ignore about half of it because it doesn't contain much information useful in the creation of a FONT resource.

The following are those fields of the GEMFONTHEADER structure important to this discussion. You might want to consult page F-5, Volume Two, of the GEM Programmer's Toolkit documentation, by Digital Research, for a complete discourse upon of all the fields of this header.

Before getting into the details of this file format, you should note that GEM font files don't contain any format specific identification data—there's no way for a program to check a file passed to it as a GEM font file and know that it hasn't been given a text file of your favorite clam sauce recipes by mistake.

The identifier field of the GEMFONTHEADER structure is actually the font number. This will be 14 for Dutch and 2 for Swiss. Other fonts will have other numbers.

The size field contains the font size in points.

The name field is the font name.

The firstchar and lastchar fields are the ASCII values of the first and last characters defined by this font. Most GEM fonts only include up to character 248.

The c_offset_table is the distance from the beginning of the file to a table of offsets into the character bitmap, this table being essentially the same as the charoff array in a FONT resource. There is no equivalent to the charwide array—

these values are calculated for a GEM font by subtracting each pair of c_offset _table values.

The font_data entry points to the start of the font bitmap. The formwidth and formdepth values specify the dimensions of the font bitmap.

The complete source code for GEM2FONT can be found in Fig. 9-12.

```
/*
    GEM2FONT
*/

#include "stdio.h"
#include "alloc.h"
#include "dos.h"
#include "gui.h"

typedef struct {
    int identifier;
    int size;
    char name[32];
    int firstchar;
    int lastchar;
    int topdist;
    int ascent;
    int halfline;
    int descent;
    int bottomdist;
    int widestchar;
    int widestcell;
    int leftoffset;
    int rightoffset;
    int thickening;
    int underlinesize;
    int lightmask;
    int skewmask;
    int flags;
    long h_offset_table;
    long c_offset_table;
    long font_data;
    int formwidth;
    int formdepth;
    long nextfont;
    } GEMFONTHEADER;

char *loadGemFont(FONT *font,char *path);

int pointsize=-1;
int fontnumber=-1;
char fontname[FONTNAMESIZE+1]="";

main(argc,argv)
    int argc;
    char *argv[];
{
    FONT fh;
    char *p;
    int i,n;

    puts("GEM VDI font converter version 1.0 - "
        "copyright (c) 1990 Alchemy Mindworks Inc.\n"
        "----------------------------------------"
        "-----------------------------------------");
```

9-12 The GEM2FONT program.

```
              if(argc > 2) {
                  for(i=3;i<argc;++i) {
                      if(argv[i][0]=='/') {
                          switch(toupper(argv[i][1])) {
                              case 'F':
                                  n=atoi(argv[i]+2);
                                  if(n>=0 && n <=255) fontnumber=n;
                                  break;
                              case 'P':
                                  n=atoi(argv[i]+2);
                                  pointsize=n;
                                  break;
                              case 'N':
                                  if(strlen(argv[i]+2))
                                      strncpy(fontname,argv[i]+2,FONTNAMESIZE);
                                  fontname[FONTNAMESIZE]=0;
                                  break;
                          }
                      }
                  }
                  if((p=loadGemFont(&fh,argv[1])) != NULL) {

                      if(fontnumber != -1) fh.number=fontnumber;
                      if(islegalfontsize(pointsize)) fh.pointsize=pointsize;
                      if(strlen(fontname)) strcpy(fh.name,fontname);

                      printf("Writing font: %s\n"
                             "        Size: %u points\n"
                             "      Number: %u\n",
                             fh.name,fh.pointsize,fh.number);

                      if(!writeFontRes(argv[2],&fh,p))
                          printf("Error creating %s\n",argv[2]);
                      free(p);
                  } else printf("Error loading %s\n",argv[1]);
              } else puts("Arguments:        path to source font\n"
                          "                  path to destination resource\n"
                          "                  /F<int>    font number\n"
                          "                  /P<int>    point size\n"
                          "                  /N<string> font name\n");

}

char *loadGemFont(font,path)
    FONT *font;
    char *path;
{

    GEMFONTHEADER *gem;
    FILE *fp;
    long size;
    char *p=NULL,*bitmap;
    unsigned int i;
    int *charoff;

    memset((char *)font,0,sizeof(FONT));

    /* open the GEM font and load it into memory */
    if((fp=fopen(path,"rb")) == NULL) return(NULL);
    fseek(fp,0L,SEEK_END);
    size=ftell(fp);
    rewind(fp);
    if(size < 0xfff0L) {
        if(((char *)gem=malloc((unsigned int)size)) != NULL) {
```

```
if(fread((char *)gem,1,(unsigned int)size,fp) ==
    (unsigned int)size) {

    /* copy the useful fields from
       the GEMFONTHEADER to the
       FONT struct */
    font->number=gem->identifier;
    font->pointsize=gem->size;
    font->padwidth=0;
    strncpy(font->name,gem->name,FONTNAMESIZE);
    font->name[FONTNAMESIZE]=0;

    font->widestchar=gem->widestchar;

    charoff=(int *)((char *)gem+
        (unsigned int)gem->c_offset_table);
    bitmap=((char *)gem)+(unsigned int)gem->font_data;

    font->bitmapwidth=charoff[1+gem->lastchar-
        gem->firstchar];
    font->bitmapdepth=gem->formdepth;

    for(i=gem->firstchar;i<=gem->lastchar;++i) {
        font->charoff[i]=charoff[i-gem->firstchar];
        font->charwide[i]=charoff[1+i-gem->firstchar]-
            font->charoff[i];
    }
    font->spacewidth=font->charwide[32];

    font->bitmapbytes=gem->formwidth;

    i=font->bitmapbytes*font->bitmapdepth;
    if((p=malloc(i)) != NULL) memcpy(p,bitmap,i);
    }
    free((char *)gem);
    }
    fclose(fp);
    }
    return(p);
}
```

All the work of GEM2FONT is done in the loadGemFont function. It begins by loading into memory the GEM font file passed to the program. The buffer being pointed to by gem (a GEMFONTHEADER pointer) can be accessed using the members of this structure. This is a bit questionable, as this buffer actually contains several objects not in the structure, such as the character offset table and the font bitmap itself. There'll be a certain amount of pointer juggling to be done later in this function.

The for loop in this function takes care of loading the charoff and charwide arrays of the FONT resource. The charoff table is simple—it's just a copy of the corresponding table in the GEMFONTHEADER structure. The charwide entry values must be derived from successive elements in the location table. This is easy to do, as the difference between the offsets of two successive characters will be the width of the first of the two characters.

The loadGemFont function will set up the FONT resource passed to it and return a pointer to a buffer with the font bitmap in it. The main function might choose to override some of the values in the FONT structure, based on command line switches passed when the GEM2FONT program is run. The two objects are then combined by writeFontRes.

Assuming that you want to convert the GEM font DUTCV10N.VGA into a FONT resource using all the default GEM values, you would run GEM2FONT like this:

```
GEM2FONT DUTCV10N.VGA DUTCH10.RES
```

GEM2FONT can recognize several useful command line switches. The /F option allows you to specify a new font number, the /P allows you to specify a different point size, and the /N option allows you to specify a new name. Here's what they'd look like in use:

```
GEM2FONT DUTCV10N.VGA DUTCH10.RES /F221 /P12 /NTimes
```

If you use the /F option, make sure that you apply the same font number to all the sizes of the font family you convert. Note that the /P option doesn't change the actual size of a font—it merely changes the ostensible point size. This would be useful if you came upon a font that claimed it displayed eight point text but appeared to you as ten points.

Finally, bear in mind that, should you use the /N option, you're free to name fonts used for your own purposes anything you like. You can call the Dutch font Times Roman and the Swiss font Helvetica if you're used to these names, just as long as you don't distribute them this way.

Converting Windows FNT files

Windows 3 applications typically access fonts through Windows, which in turn deals with font resource files in its own resource format. These files have the extension .FON. The fonts in the .FON files come from individual font files with the extension .FNT. This section will discuss the latter type of files.

As with GEM/VDI font files, Windows FNT files come in convenient packages, with one font to a file. Their internal structure is a bit more peculiar, however. Because of the way the font bitmap in a Windows FNT file is structured, a Windows font will usually take up more space than a GEM font, all other things being equal.

A Windows FNT file begins with a huge, seething, twelve-eyed monster of a structure that spits sulfuric acid and is mildly radioactive. It defines everything anyone could ever want to know about a font save for the name of its designer and the temperature of the lead first used to print with it back in the nineteenth century. Even these values can probably be derived from the data provided.

Prepare yourself before you look at this beast:

```
typedef struct {
    int dfVersion;
    long dfSize;
    char dfCopyright[60];
```

```
        int dfType;
        int dfPoints;
        int dfVertRes;
        int dfHorizRes;
        int dfAscent;
        int dfIntLead;
        int dfExtLead;
        char dfItalic;
        char dfUnderline;
        char dfStrikeout;
        int dfWeight;
        char dfCharSet;
        int dfPixWidth;
        int dfPixHeight;
        char dfPitchFam;
        int dfAvgWidth;
        int dfMaxWidth;
        char dfFirstChar;
        char dfLastChar;
        char dfDefaultChar;
        char dfBreakChar;
        int dfWidthBytes;
        long dfDevice;
        long dfFace;
        long dfBitsPointer;
        long dfBitsOffset;
        char dfReserved;
        long dfFlags;
        int dfAspace;
        int dfBspace;
        int dfCspace;
        int dfColorPointer;
        long dfReserved1;
        } WINFONTHEADER;
```

As with GEMFONTHEADER, not all of WINFONTHEADER is important to this discussion. Much of it pertains to things cared about by only Windows. A complete description of the Windows 3 FNT file format can be found in the Windows Development Notes, available from Microsoft.

The dfVersion field specifies which version of Windows the font in question was created for. This will either be 0200H for Windows 2 or 0300H for Windows 3. Should you find something else in this field, chances are you've encountered one of the aforementioned clam sauce recipes.

The dfCopyright field specifies who owns the copyright for the font in question. If you subscribe to the discussion of the Copyright Office ruling from earlier in this chapter, this field will always contain the string "All of us."

The dfType field defines whether the font in question is a bitmapped font or a vector font. If the low-order bit in this field is set, the font is a vector font and you might as well give up and go home (because the WIN2FONT converter only handles bitmapped fonts).

The dfPoints field specifies the number of points in the font. The dfFirstChar and dfLastChar fields specify the first and last character codes the font represents, respectively.

The dfFace field contains the offset into the file of the name of the font it contains. The dfWidthBytes field specifies the width of the font bitmap in bytes. The dfPixHeight field defines the height of the font bitmap. The dfPixWidth field defines the width of one character if the font is monospaced and is zero if the font is proportionally spaced.

A FONT resource of the graphical user interface doesn't deal with monospaced fonts per se. A monospaced Windows font converted to a FONT resource will be treated as a proportionally spaced font with all its characters having the same width.

The dfCharSet field defines the font number, which you might want to override when you actually go to convert fonts.

The WIN2FONT program is illustrated in Fig. 9-13. It's structurally similar to GEM2FONT, except that all the GEM/VDI specific data has been replaced with corresponding Windows data.

```
/*
    WIN2FONT
*/

#include "stdio.h"
#include "alloc.h"
#include "dos.h"
#include "gui.h"

#define    CHARTABLEOFF        118

typedef struct {
    int dfVersion;
    long dfSize;
    char dfCopyright[60];
    int dfType;
    int dfPoints;
    int dfVertRes;
    int dfHorizRes;
    int dfAscent;
    int dfIntLead;
    int dfExtLead;
    char dfItalic;
    char dfUnderline;
    char dfStrikeout;
    int dfWeight;
    char dfCharSet;
    int dfPixWidth;
    int dfPixHeight;
    char dfPitchFam;
    int dfAvgWidth;
    int dfMaxWidth;
```

9-13 The WIN2FONT program.

```
        char dfFirstChar;
        char dfLastChar;
        char dfDefaultChar;
        char dfBreakChar;
        int dfWidthBytes;
        long dfDevice;
        long dfFace;
        long dfBitsPointer;
        long dfBitsOffset;
        char dfReserved;
        long dfFlags;
        int dfAspace;
        int dfBspace;
        int dfCspace;
        int dfColorPointer;
        long dfReserved1;
        } WINFONTHEADER;

char *loadWinFont(FONT *font,char *path);

int pointsize=-1;
int fontnumber=-1;
char fontname[FONTNAMESIZE+1]="";

main(argc,argv)
        int argc;
        char *argv[];
{
        FONT fh;
        char *p;
        int i,n;

        puts("WIN2FONT font converter version 1.0 - "
            "copyright (c) 1990 Alchemy Mindworks Inc.\n"
            "------------------------------------"
            "---------------------------------------");

        if(argc > 2) {
            for(i=3;i<argc;++i) {
                if(argv[i][0]=='/') {
                    switch(toupper(argv[i][1])) {
                        case 'F' :
                            n=atoi(argv[i]+2);
                            if(n>=0 && n <=255) fontnumber=n;
                            break;
                        case 'P' :
                            n=atoi(argv[i]+2);
                            pointsize=n;
                            break;
                        case 'N' :
                            if(strlen(argv[i]+2))
                              strncpy(fontname,argv[i]+2,FONTNAMESIZE);
                            fontname[FONTNAMESIZE]=0;
                            break;
                    }
                }
            }
            if((p=loadWinFont(&fh,argv[1])) != NULL) {

                if(fontnumber != -1) fh.number=fontnumber;
                if(islegalfontsize(pointsize)) fh.pointsize=pointsize;
                if(strlen(fontname)) strcpy(fh.name,fontname);
```

```
                    printf("Writing font: %s\n"
                          "         Size: %u points\n"
                          "        Number: %u\n",
                          fh.name,fh.pointsize,fh.number);

                  if(!writeFontRes(argv[2],&fh,p))
                     printf("Error creating %s\n",argv[2]);
                  free(p);
              } else printf("Error loading %s\n",argv[1]);
          } else puts("Arguments:         path to source font\n"
                      "                   path to destination resource\n"
                      "         /F<int>   font number\n"
                      "         /P<int>   point size\n"
                      "         /N<string> font name\n");

}

char *loadWinFont(font,path)
    FONT *font;
    char *path;

{

    WINFONTHEADER *win;
    FILE *fp;

long size;
char *p=NULL,*pf,*bitmap;
unsigned int i,j,entries,*word;

memset((char *)font,0,sizeof(FONT));

if((fp=fopen(path,"rb")) == NULL) return(NULL);
fseek(fp,0L,SEEK_END);
size=ftell(fp);
rewind(fp);

if(size < 0xfff0L) {
    if((pf=malloc((unsigned int)size)) != NULL) {
        if(fread(pf,1,(unsigned int)size,fp) == (unsigned int)size) {

            win=(WINFONTHEADER *)pf;

            printf("This font is %s\n",win->dfCopyright);

            if(win->dfVersion==0x0100) printf("Version 1 font\n");
            else if(win->dfVersion==0x0200) printf("Version 2 font\n");
            else if(win->dfVersion==0x0300) printf("Version 3 font\n");
            else problem("Unknown font version");

            if(win->dfType & 0x0001) problem("Vector font file");

            printf("Nominal optimum point size: %u\n",win->dfPoints);
            printf("Character set: %u\n",win->dfCharSet);

            printf("First character: %u - Last character: %u\n",
                win->dfFirstChar,win->dfLastChar);

            entries=(win->dfLastChar-win->dfFirstChar)+2;

            j=0;
            word=(unsigned int *)(((char *)win)+CHARTABLEOFF);
            for(i=0;i<entries;++i) {
                if((i+win->dfFirstChar) >= (MAXFONTCHAR-MINFONTCHAR))
                    break;
                if(win->dfVersion==0x0300) {
```

```
                     font->charoff[win->dfFirstChar+i]=j;
                     if(win->dfPixWidth) {
                          font->charwide[win->dfFirstChar+i]=
                            win->dfPixWidth;
                          j+=8*pixels2bytes(font->charwide
                            [win->dfFirstChar+i]);

                     }
                     else {
                          font->charwide[win->dfFirstChar+i]=word[i*3];
                          j+=8*pixels2bytes(font->charwide
                            [win->dfFirstChar+i]);
                     }
                }
                else {
                     font->charoff[win->dfFirstChar+i]=j;
                     if(win->dfPixWidth) {
                          font->charwide[win->dfFirstChar+i]=
                            win->dfPixWidth;
                              j+=8*pixels2bytes(font->charwide
                                [win->dfFirstChar+i]);
                     }
                     else {
                          font->charwide[win->dfFirstChar+i]=word[i*2];
                          j+=8*pixels2bytes(font->charwide
                            [win->dfFirstChar+i]);
                     }
                }
           }

           if(fontnumber == -1) font->number=win->dfCharSet;
           else font->number=fontnumber;

           if(pointsize == -1) font->pointsize=win->dfPoints;
           else font->pointsize=pointsize;

           font->padwidth=0;
           strncpy(font->name,(char *)win+(unsigned int)win->dfFace,
             FONTNAMESIZE);
           if(strlen(fontname))
             strncpy(font->name,fontname,FONTNAMESIZE);
           font->name[FONTNAMESIZE]=0;

           printf("Font name: %s\n",font->name);

           font->widestchar=win->dfMaxWidth;
           font->bitmapwidth=win->dfPixWidth;
           font->bitmapdepth=win->dfPixHeight;

           font->spacewidth=font->charwide[32];

           font->bitmapbytes=win->dfWidthBytes;

           i=font->bitmapbytes*font->bitmapdepth;

           /* convert the bitmap structure */
           if((p=malloc(i)) != NULL) {
                memset(p,0x00,i);
                bitmap=(char *)win+(unsigned int)win->dfBitsOffset;
                for(j=0;j<font->bitmapbytes;++j) {
                     for(i=0;i<font->bitmapdepth;++i) {
                          p[(i*font->bitmapbytes)+j]=*bitmap++;
```

```
                              }
                          }
                      }
                  }
              free(pf);
          }
          fclose(fp);
      }
      return(p);
}

problem(s)
    char *s;
{
    printf("ERROR: %s - aborting",s);
    exit(1);
}
```

You should note that Windows 2 font files and Windows 3 font files treat their character offset tables differently. Under Windows 2, fonts were restricted to being fairly small, and each offset into the table was defined as follows:

```
typedef struct {
    unsigned int width; /* character width */
    unsigned int offset; /* offset into bitmap */
} WIN2OFFSET;
```

Under Windows 3, immense bitmapped fonts can, in theory, be used—even if it's a bit unclear as to why anyone might want to. As such, each entry in the character offset table is defined as follows for Windows 3 fonts:

```
typedef struct {
    unsigned int width; /* character width */
    unsigned long offset; /* offset into bitmap */
} WIN3OFFSET;
```

This makes Windows 3 font character offset table entries two bytes bigger than those for Windows 2 fonts. The width values are irrelevant in both cases should dfPixWidth be non-zero, indicating a monospaced font.

The font bitmap of a Windows FNT file is structured a bit inconveniently. The characters are formed in individual bitmaps rather than in one long bitmap as has previously been the case. You might liken this arrangement to the one used by the system fonts that display text in the graphical user interface. Inasmuch as the FONT resource definition likes them in one long bitmap, they must be converted. The code at the end of the loadWinFont function takes care of this.

Windows 3 font bitmaps tend to be larger than those of other font file formats discussed here. Each character's space in the bitmap will be rounded up to the nearest eight bits. This doesn't affect the spacing of the characters when they're finally drawn, as the extra bits are simply ignored by the font manager.

The WIN2FONT program is run just like the GEM2FONT one was, and with the same three command line options.

Converting Macintosh fonts

The Macintosh offers a great wealth of fonts. If you have access to a computer bulletin board with a Macintosh conference, you'll find countless examples of public domain and shareware Macintosh fonts. Commercial Macintosh screen fonts from such companies as Cassady and Greene are often startlingly innovative. Figure 9-14 illustrates a small fraction of the available Macintosh fonts.

12 point Chicago (the Macintosh system font)

12 point Geneva

20 point Geneva

18 point London

12 point Monaco

12 point New York

20 point New York

14 point Venice

18 point San Francisco

9-14   Some Macintosh fonts.

The desirability of Macintosh fonts is matched by the difficulty involved in getting at them. The Macintosh uses a peculiar file structure. Its processor stores multiple byte numbers differently from the way PC's processor does. It handles fonts—and all its resources—in a way that's elegant for a Macintosh but very awkward anywhere else.

Clearly, it's fruitless to complain about this situation—it's a safe bet that the designers of the Macintosh weren't interested in making their system resources easy to export. You can get around all these problems, however, if you're sufficiently determined.

The first difficulty to overcome in dealing with Macintosh files in general is that of the Mac's file structure. As has been noted previously, the Macintosh uses resources in much the same way as the graphical user interface in this book. In fact, it's so fond of the notion of resources that it has wrapped the structure of its disk files around them. Every file on a Macintosh disk consists of two sections, or *forks*. One fork contains the file's data, and the other its resources. Perhaps not surprisingly, these are referred to as the *data fork* and the *resource fork*.

It's not always obvious what sort of file contents will appear in these forks. Raw data, such as a MacPaint picture or a MacWrite word processing document, would be stored in the data fork of a file. Such a file would typically have a zero length resource fork. Applications—such as MacPaint or MacWrite themselves—are stored as resources. They would have empty or nearly empty data forks. On a Macintosh, all executable code is stored as code resources.

Structured data, such as fonts, are stored in the resource forks of files. These may be dedicated font files (i.e., files to store fonts in exclusively.) However, many Macintosh applications have special purpose fonts bound to them that are also stored as resources. The fonts provided by the Macintosh for all its applications are stored as resources of the operating system.

You might want to think of the forks of a Macintosh file as being two separate files kept together transparently under one file name. If you move a Macintosh file to a PC over a local area network such as TOPS, it will actually be stored as two files, with the resource fork file being hidden. TOPS assumes that that the PC can't use Macintosh resources.

Long before there were local area networks to link Macintoshes with other computers, there were modems. Realizing the inconvenience of storing Macintosh files on non-Macintosh systems as two separate files, the authors of Macintosh telecommunications programs began to use what came to be called a *Macbinary* header to combine the two forks. A Macbinary header preserves the Macintosh-specific information about a file and provides data allowing the two forks to be combined into a single file and subsequently broken apart again when a file having a Macbinary header is ported back to a Macintosh.

A Macbinary header resembles the following struct, sort of—the longs (to be discussed momentarily) aren't quite what they seem:

```
typedef struct {
        char zerobyte;                  /* always zero */
        char name[64];                  /* name and some filler */
        char type[4];                   /* Mac file type */
        char creator[4];                /* Mac file creator */
        char filler[10];
        long datafork_size;             /* length of Mac data fork */
        long rsrcfork_size;             /* length of Mac resource fork */
        long creation_date;             /* time of file's creation */
        long modif_date;                /* time of file's modification */
        char filler2[29];
        } MACBINARY;
```

A Macbinary header is 128 bytes long, which corresponds to the block size of the XMODEM file transmission protocol. The Macbinary header serves as a "zero'th" block, telling a Macintosh telecommunications package how to name the incoming file and divide the remaining data between its data and resource forks.

Macintosh files are named differently from those on a PC. Whereas a PC is restricted to eight-character file names, the file names on a Macintosh can be up to 64 characters long, although for several reasons they're usually constrained to being no more than 32. Strings on the Macintosh are stored in Pascal format rather than as C strings. A Pascal string consists of a byte defining the length of the string followed by the text of the string itself. There is no null byte at the end of the text.

Multiple byte numbers on the Macintosh are stored in the reverse byte order to those on the PC, which affects ints and longs. The following two functions will translate Macintosh numbers into PC numbers:

```
m2inti(i)      /* translate a Macintosh integer to a PC integer */
    int i;
{
    return(((i & 0xff00) > > 8) + ((i & 0x00ff) < < 8));
}

long m2intl(l) /* translate a Macintosh long to a PC long */
    long l;
{       return(((l & 0xff000000L) > > 24) +
            ((l & 0x00ff0000L) > > 8) +
            ((l & 0x0000ff00L) < < 8) +
            ((l & 0x000000ffL) < < 24));

}
```

Macintosh numbers are stored in what's called the Motorola format, while PC numbers are stored in the Intel format—in both cases, named after the companies that created their respective processors.

All this being the case, the datafork_size element of a MACBINARY struct is not really the size of the data fork—at least, not on a PC. The real size is m2intl (datafork_size).

As an aside, the creation_date and modif_date fields of a MACBINARY struct—the creation and modification dates of the original Macintosh file respectively—also aren't in any meaningful PC format. They represent the time based on the Macintosh calendar, which begins in 1904 rather than in 1980 (the case for a PC). Both values, however, do represent the number of elapsed seconds. The difference, in seconds, can be represented as

```
#define mac2pc_date 2082830400L
```

The creation date of a Macintosh file, then, would be

```
m2intl(creation_date) + mac2pc_date.
```

Most Macintosh files found on bulletin boards are stored using a shareware archiving application called StuffIt, written by Raymond Lau. All sorts of dark, symbolic meanings might be attached to this name. Such files are usually given the extension .SIT when they appear on bulletin boards actually run on PC compatible hardware. The StuffIt application on the Mac performs the same function as the PKZIP utilities on a PC, although ZIP files and SIT files are structured differently.

There is a PC-based utility called UnStuffit that will read Macintosh SIT files ported to the PC and extract their contents. It's written by *R. Scott McGinnis* of *Caber Software, P.O. Box 3607, Mdse Mart, Chicago, IL 60654-0607.* This is a shareware program—you can usually find it on bulletin boards. UnStuffit will extract the files in a SIT file and write their forks out to normal PC files. You can have it split the forks into separate files when it encounters a file having data in both forks. Alternately, it will combine them with a Macbinary header. The MAC-2FONT converter to be discussed shortly will use them in this latter form.

With a modem and a copy of UnStuffit, you can download and work with countless megabytes of Macintosh font files. If you have a Macintosh and a local area network to connect it to your PC, you can send files directly between the two machines. Pack the fonts you want to use into a StuffIt archive—of course, you will need a copy of StuffIt. You can actually just have StuffIt write to a networked PC directly, as it will look like a Macintosh drive to Mac applications. Use UnStuffit to extract the contents of the SIT file appearing on your PC, writing each file therein to a separate PC file with a MacBinary header.

To keep things simple—at least until you get used to using the various programs discussed thus far—you should try to work exclusively with Macintosh FONT resource files rather than with applications containing FONT resources along with resources of other types. Figure 9-15 illustrates the Macintosh icon for a FONT resource file.

9-15   The Macintosh Finder   Old font file icon
icon for a font file.

New font file icon

If you want to work with fonts contained in other sorts of files—such as the Macintosh system fonts in the System file—use the Macintosh FONT/DA mover application to copy them into a new font file.

The complete source code for the MAC2FONT program is shown in Fig. 9-16. To be sure, the monstrousness of this thing makes the earlier WINFONTHEADER struct seem like a small plastic monster with day-glo fangs and a pencil sharpener in its nose by comparison.

```
/*
    MAC2FONT
    This (monsterous) program converts Macintosh FONT
    and NFNT resources into GUI FONT resource files.
*/

#include "stdio.h"
#include "alloc.h"
#include "dos.h"
#include "gui.h"

#define     max_type     128
#define     maxlist      65      /* maximum number of resources of a type */

typedef struct {
    long recdata;
    long recmap;
    long recdata_len;
    long recmap_len;
    } RECHEAD;
```

9-16   The wholly monstrous MAC2FONT program.

9-16 Continued

```
typedef struct {
     RECHEAD headcopy;
     long nexthandle;
     int refnum;
     int refattr;
     int typeoff;
     int nameoff;
     } RECMAP;

typedef struct {
     char type[4];
     int number;
     int typeoff;
     } RECTYPE;

typedef struct {
     int res_id;
     unsigned int name_offset;
     char attr;
     char data_offset[3];
     long reserved;
     } RECLIST;

typedef struct {
     int fontType;
     int firstChar;
     int lastChar;
     int widMax;
     int kernMax;
     int nDescent;
     int fRectWidth;
     int fRectHeight;
     int owTLoc;
     int ascent;
     int descent;
     int leading;
     int rowWords;
     } MACFONT;
typedef struct {
     char zerobyte;
     char name[64];
     char type[4];
     char creator[4];
     char filler[10];
     long datafork_size;
     long rsrcfork_size;
     long creation_date;
     long modif_date;
     char filler2[29];
     } MACBINARY;

typedef struct {
     int FONDflags;
     int FONDFamID;
     int FONTFirst;
     int FONDLast;
     int FONDAscent;
     int FONDDescent;
     int FONDLeading;
     int FONDWidMax;
     long FONDWTabOff;
     long FONDKernOff;
     long FONDStylOff;
```

```c
        char FONDProperty[24];
        long FONDIntl;
        int Version;
        } MACFOND;

typedef struct {
        name[65];
        unsigned int points;
        unsigned long res;
        } FONTNAME;

long fgetlong(FILE *fp);
long m2intl(long l);

RECHEAD rechead;
RECMAP recmap;

RECTYPE type_array[max_type];
char rsrc_names[maxlist][65];
RECLIST list_array[maxlist];
int list_index;

FONTNAME fontname_array[maxlist];
int fontname_index=0;

long resfork=0L;

int type_index;

int pointsize=-1;
int fontnumber=-1;
char fontname[FONTNAMESIZE+1]="";
main(argc,argv)
        int argc;
        char *argv[];
{
        puts("Mac FONT converter version 1.1 - "
                "copyright (c) 1990 Alchemy Mindworks Inc.\n"
            "---------------------------------"
              "----------------------------------------");

        if(argc > 1) {
                strupr(argv[1]);
                convertMacFonts(argv[1]);
        } else puts("Arguments:          path to source font");
}

convertMacFonts(s)
        char *s;
{
        MACBINARY macb;
        RECLIST *ls;
        MACFONT thefont;
        FONT font;
        FILE *fp;
        long l,size;
        static char macname[128];
        char *p,b[128],sb[32];
        unsigned int i,j,k,ftype,fsize,fpoints,fnumber,fcount,oldfont=0;
        unsigned int first,last;
        unsigned int locTable[258];
        unsigned int owTable[258];

        /* get a default mac name from the PC name */
```

Converting fonts from other sources   **265**

```
        fnsplit(s,NULL,NULL,macname,NULL);

        /* attempt to open the Mac resource file */
        if((fp=fopen(s,"rb")) == NULL) error("Can't open Macintosh file");

        /* look for a Macbinary header */
        if(!fgetc(fp)) {
            if(fread((char *)&macb,1,sizeof(MACBINARY),fp)==sizeof(MACBINARY))
                resfork=m2intl(macb.datafork_size)+(long)sizeof(MACBINARY);
            else error("Can't read MacBinary header");
        } else rewind(fp);

        /* get the resource header */
        if(!get_rechead(fp,&rechead)) error("Can't read resource header");

        /* get the resource map */
        if(!get_recmap(fp,&rechead,&recmap)) error("Can't read resource map");

        /* get the number of types */
        type_index=get_recmax(fp,&rechead,&recmap);

        /* get all the types into the type array */
        for(i=0;i<type_index;++i) {
            if(i >= max_type) break;
            if(!get_rectype(fp,&rechead,&recmap,&type_array[i],i))
                error("Can't read type");
        }
/* troll through the array for FONDs */
for(i=0;i<type_index;++i) {
    if(!memcmp(type_array[i].type,"FOND",4)) {
        list_index=m2inti(type_array[i].number)+1;
        for(j=0;j<list_index;++j) {
            if(j >= maxlist) break;
            if(!get_recref(fp,&rechead,&recmap,&type_array[i],
              &list_array[j],j))
                error("Can't read resource reference");

            if(!get_recname(fp,&rechead,&recmap,&list_array[j],b))
                error("Can't read resource name");

            ls=&list_array[j];

            l=(long)ls->data_offset[2]+
              ((long)ls->data_offset[1] << 8)+
              ((long)ls->data_offset[0] << 16);

            if(fseek(fp,resfork+m2intl(rechead.recdata)+1,SEEK_SET))
                error("Can't find FOND data");

            fseek(fp,0x0038L,SEEK_CUR);
            fcount=m2inti(fgetint(fp))+1;
            for(k=0;k<fcount;++k) {
                strcpy(fontname_array[fontname_index].name,b);
                fontname_array[fontname_index].points=
                  m2inti(fgetint(fp));
                fontname_array[fontname_index].res=
                  m2intl(fgetlong(fp));
                ++fontname_index;
            }
        }
    }
}
```

```
        /* if no font names found, it's an old style font resource */
        if(!fontname_index) {
            for(i=0;i<type_index;++i) {
                if(!memcmp(type_array[i].type,"FONT",4)) {
                    list_index=m2inti(type_array[i].number)+1;
                    for(j=0;j<list_index;++j) {
                        if(j >= maxlist) break;
                        if(!get_recref(fp,&rechead,&recmap,&type_array[i],
                            &list_array[j],j))
                                error("Can't read resource reference");

                        if(!get_recname(fp,&rechead,&recmap,&list_array[j],b))
                                error("Can't read resource name");

                        ls=&list_array[j];

                        l=(long)ls->data_offset[2]+
                            ((long)ls->data_offset[1] << 8)+
                            ((long)ls->data_offset[0] << 16);

                        fnumber=(m2inti(ls->res_id) >> 7) & 0x000f;
                        fpoints=m2inti(ls->res_id) & 0x007f;
                        if(!fpoints) {
                            strcpy(fontname_array[fontname_index].name,b);
                            fontname_array[fontname_index].points=fpoints;
                            fontname_array[fontname_index].res=
                                m2inti(ls->res_id);
                            ++fontname_index;
                            ++oldfont;
                        }
                    }
                }
            }
        }

        /* troll through the array for FONTs and NFNTs */
        for(i=0;i<type_index;++i) {
            if(!memcmp(type_array[i].type,"FONT",4) ||
                !memcmp(type_array[i].type,"NFNT",4)) {
                list_index=m2inti(type_array[i].number)+1;
                for(j=0;j<list_index;++j) {
                    if(j >= maxlist) break;
                    if(!get_recref(fp,&rechead,&recmap,&type_array[i],
                        &list_array[j],j))
                            error("Can't read resource reference");

                    if(!get_recname(fp,&rechead,&recmap,&list_array[j],b))
                            error("Can't read resource name");

                    ls=&list_array[j];

                    l=(long)ls->data_offset[2]+
                        ((long)ls->data_offset[1] << 8)+
                        ((long)ls->data_offset[0] << 16);

                    findFont(m2inti(ls->res_id),&fpoints,macname);
                    fnumber=(m2inti(ls->res_id) >> 7) & 0x000f;

                    if(fseek(fp,resfork+m2intl(rechead.recdata)+1,SEEK_SET))
                        error("Can't find font data");
                    size=m2intl(fgetlong(fp));
                    if(fread((char *)&thefont,1,sizeof(MACFONT),fp) !=
                        sizeof(MACFONT))
                            error("Can't read Macintosh font header");
```

```
                    ftype=m2inti(thefont.fontType) & 0xff00;

                    /* this deals with old 64K ROM font files having no FONDs */
                    if(oldfont) fpoints=m2inti(ls->res_id) & 0x007f;

                    if((ftype==0x9000 || ftype==0xb000 || ftype==0xd000) &&
                       islegalfontsize(fpoints)) {
                            printf("\nName: ");
                            getst(FONTNAMESIZE,macname,b);
                            if(strlen(b)) strcpy(macname,b);

                            sprintf(sb,"%u",fnumber);
                            printf("\nNumber for %s: ",macname);
                            getst(5,sb,b);
                            k=atoi(b);
if(k > 0 && k < 256) fnumber=k;

printf("\n%s - %d points\n",macname,fpoints);
printf("Font range from character %d to %d - "
  number %u\n",
  m2inti(thefont.firstChar),
  m2inti(thefont.lastChar),fnumber);
printf("Maximum character width: %d - ",
  m2inti(thefont.widMax));
printf("font rectangle: %d x %d\n",
  m2inti(thefont.fRectWidth),
  m2inti(thefont.fRectHeight));
printf("Save as resource file (ESC \021\304\331 "
  "to skip): ");

strcpy(sb,macname);
sb[5]=0;

strupr(sb);
sprintf(b,"%u.%s",fpoints,RESext);
strcat(sb,b);

getst(24,sb,b);

if(strlen(b)) {
     if((p=malloc(size-sizeof(MACFONT))) == NULL)
         error("Can't allocate memory");
         fsize=(2 * m2inti(thefont.rowWords) *
         m2inti(thefont.fRectHeight));
     if(fread(p,1,fsize,fp) != fsize)
         error("Can't read bit image");
     for(k=m2inti(thefont.firstChar);
       k<=(m2inti(thefont.lastChar)+2);++k)
         locTable[k]=m2inti(fgetint(fp));
     for(k=m2inti(thefont.firstChar);
       k<=(m2inti(thefont.lastChar)+2);++k)
         owTable[k]=m2inti(fgetint(fp));

     memset((char *)&font,0,sizeof(FONT));

     first=m2inti(thefont.firstChar);
     if(first < MINFONTCHAR) first=MINFONTCHAR;
     last=m2inti(thefont.lastChar);
     if(last > MAXFONTCHAR) last=MAXFONTCHAR;

     for(k=first;k<last;++k) {
             if(owTable[k] != 0xffff) {
```

```
                    font.charoff[k]=locTable[k];
                    font.charwide[k]=
                        (locTable[k+1]-locTable[k]);
            }
            else {
                    font.charoff[k]=
                        locTable[m2inti(thefont.lastChar)+1];
                    font.charwide[k]=
                        locTable[m2inti(thefont.lastChar)+2]-
                        locTable[m2inti(thefont.lastChar)+1];
            }
        }
                                font.number=fnumber;
                                font.pointsize=fpoints;
                                strncpy(font.name,macname,FONTNAMESIZE);
                                font.name[FONTNAMESIZE]=0;
                                font.widestchar=m2inti(thefont.widMax);
                                font.bitmapwidth=(m2inti(thefont.rowWords)*16);
                                font.bitmapdepth=m2inti(thefont.fRectHeight);
                                font.bitmapbytes=pixels2bytes(font.bitmapwidth);
                                font.padwidth=1;
                                font.spacewidth=owTable[32] & 0x00ff;

                                if(!writeFontRes(b,&font,p))
                                    error("Can't write font");
                                free(p);
                    }
                }
            }
        }
    }
}


findFont(n,points,name)        /* look up font resource ID in the FOND table */
    int n,*points;
    char *name;
{
    int i;

    for(i=0;i<fontname_index;++i) {
        if(fontname_array[i].res==(long)n) {
            strcpy(name,fontname_array[i].name);
            *points=fontname_array[i].points;
            break;
        }
    }
}


get_recname(fp,r,m,ls,s)               /* get resource name */
    FILE *fp;
    RECHEAD *r;
    RECMAP *m;
    RECLIST *ls;
    char *s;
{
    long l;
    int i;

    strcpy(s,"[ Untitled ]");
    if(ls->name_offset != 0xffff) {
        l=m2intl(r->recmap)+
            (long)m2inti(m->nameoff);

        if(fseek(fp,resfork+l+(long)m2inti(ls->name_offset),SEEK_SET) == 0) {
```

9-16 Continued

```
            i=fgetc(fp) % 64;
            if(fread(s,1,i,fp) == i) {
                s[i]=0;
                return(1);
            } else return(0);
        } else return(0);
    } else return(1);
}

get_recref(fp,r,m,t,ls,n)            /* get resource reference list */
    FILE *fp;
    RECHEAD *r;
    RECMAP *m;
    RECTYPE *t;
    RECLIST *ls;
    int n;
{
    long l;

    l=m2intl(r->recmap)+
       (long)m2inti(m->typeoff)+
       (long)m2inti(t->typeoff);

    if(fseek(fp,resfork+l+(n*sizeof(RECLIST)),SEEK_SET) == 0) {
        if(fread((char *)ls,1,sizeof(RECLIST),fp) == sizeof(RECLIST))
            return(1);
        else return(0);
    } else return(0);
}

get_namedrec(fp,r,m,t,s)        /* get the resource type named in s */
    FILE *fp;
    RECHEAD *r;
    RECMAP *m;
    RECTYPE *t;
    char *s;
{
    long l;
    int rt=0,i,max;

    l=m2intl(r->recmap)+(long)m2inti(m->typeoff);
    if(fseek(fp,resfork+l,SEEK_SET)==0) {
        max=m2inti(fgetint(fp))+1;
        for(i=0;i<max;++i) {
            if(fseek(fp,resfork+l+2+(i*sizeof(RECTYPE)),SEEK_SET) == 0) {
                if(fread((char *)t,1,sizeof(RECTYPE),fp) ==
                    sizeof(RECTYPE)) {
                    if(memcmp(s,t->type,4)==0) {
                        rt=i+1;
                        break;
                    }
                }
                else {
                    rt=0;
                    break;
                }
            }
            else {
                rt=0;
                break;
            }
        }
    } else rt=0;
```

```
                return(rt);
}
get_rectype(fp,r,m,t,n)          /* get resource type n */
     FILE *fp;
     RECHEAD *r;
     RECMAP *m;
     RECTYPE *t;
     int n;
{
     long l;
     int max;

     l=m2intl(r->recmap)+(long)m2inti(m->typeoff);
     if(fseek(fp,resfork+l,SEEK_SET)==0) {
          max=m2inti(fgetint(fp))+1;
          if(n < max) {
               if(fseek(fp,resfork+l+2+(n*sizeof(RECTYPE)),SEEK_SET) == 0) {
                    if(fread((char *)t,1,sizeof(RECTYPE),fp) ==
                      sizeof(RECTYPE))
                         return(1);
                    else return(0);
               } else return(0);
          } else return(0);
     } else return(0);
}

get_recmax(fp,r,m)               /* get the number of resources */
     FILE *fp;
     RECHEAD *r;
     RECMAP *m;
{
     long l;

     l=m2intl(r->recmap)+(long)m2inti(m->typeoff);
     if(!fseek(fp,resfork+l,SEEK_SET)) return(m2inti(fgetint(fp))+1);
     else return(0);
}

get_recmap(fp,r,m)               /* read in resource map */
     FILE *fp;
     RECHEAD *r;
     RECMAP *m;
{
     if(fseek(fp,resfork+m2intl(r->recmap),SEEK_SET)==0) {
          if(fread((char *)m,1,sizeof(RECMAP),fp) != sizeof(RECMAP)) return(0);
          else return(1);
     } else return(0);
}

get_rechead(fp,r)                /* read in resource header */
     FILE *fp;
     RECHEAD *r;
{
     if(fseek(fp,resfork,SEEK_SET)==0) {
          if(fread((char *)r,1,sizeof(RECHEAD),fp) == sizeof(RECHEAD)) {
          } else return(0);
     } else return(0);
}

fgetint(fp)
     FILE *fp;
{
     return(fgetc(fp) + (fgetc(fp) << 8));
}
```

```
long fgetlong(fp)
    FILE *fp;
{
    return(((long)fgetc(fp) +
            ((long)fgetc(fp) << 8) +
            ((long)fgetc(fp) << 16) +
            ((long)fgetc(fp) << 24));
}

error(s)
    char *s;
{
    puts(s);
    exit(1);
}

m2inti(i)
    int i;
{
    return(((i & 0xff00) >> 8) + ((i & 0x00ff) << 8));
}

long m2intl(l)
    long l;
{
    return(((l & 0xff000000L) >> 24) +
            ((l & 0x00ff0000L) >> 8) +
            ((l & 0x0000ff00L) << 8) +
            ((l & 0x000000ffL) << 24));
}

#define      INS        82 * 256
#define      BS         0x08
#define      CR         0x0d
#define      ESC        0x1b
#define      BLNK       '_'

getst(size,deflt,buffer)        /* get a string */
        int size;
        char *deflt,*buffer;
{
        char *p;
        int i,l,c,cursor=0,insert=0;

        *buffer = 0;
        if((p=malloc(size+1)) != NULL) {
            small_cursor();
            for(c=0;c<size;++c) putch(BLNK);
            for(c=0;c<size;++c) putch(BS);

            do {
                l = strlen(buffer);
                if(*(deflt) == 0) c = GetKey();
                else c = *deflt++;
switch(c) {
        case DEL:
            if(cursor < l) {
                memcpy(p,buffer,cursor);
                memcpy(p+cursor,buffer+cursor+1,
                    (l-cursor)+1);
                strcpy(buffer,p);
                i=printf("%s%c",buffer+cursor,BLNK);
                while(i) {
```

```
                    putch(BS);
                    --i;
                }
        }
        break;
case INS:
        if(insert) {
            insert = 0;
            small_cursor();
        }
        else {
            insert = 1;
            big_cursor();
        }
        break;
case HOME:
        while(cursor) {
            putch(BS);
            --cursor;
        }
        break;
case END:
        while(cursor < l) {
            putch(*(buffer+cursor));
             ++cursor;
        }
        break;
case CURSOR_RIGHT:
        if(cursor < l) {
            putch(*(buffer+cursor));
            ++cursor;
        }
        break;
case CURSOR_LEFT:
        if(cursor) {
            putch(BS);
            --cursor;
        }
        break;
case BS:
        if(cursor == l) {
            if(l) {
                --l;
                --cursor;
                *(buffer+l) = 0;
                putch(BS);
                putch(BLNK);
                putch(BS);
            }
        }

                else if(cursor < l && cursor > 0) {
                    --cursor;
                    memcpy(p,buffer,cursor);
                    memcpy(p+cursor,buffer+cursor+1,
                        (l-cursor)+1);
                    strcpy(buffer,p);
                    i=printf("%c%s%c",BS,buffer+cursor,BLNK)-1;
                    while(i) {
                        putch(BS);
                        --i;
                    }
                }
            break;
        case ESC:
```

```
                        while(cursor < l) {
                              putch(*(buffer+cursor));
                              ++cursor;
                        }
                        while(l--) {
                              putch(BS);
                              putch(BLNK);
                              putch(BS);
                        }
                        cursor = 0;
                        *buffer = 0;
                        break;
                  default:
                        if(c >= 0x20 && c <= 0x7f) {
                              if(cursor == l && l < size) {
                                    *(buffer + l++) = c;
                                    *(buffer + l) = 0;
                                    putch(c);
                                    ++cursor;
                              }
                              else if(cursor < l) {
                                    if(!insert) {
                                          *(buffer + cursor++) = c;
                                          putch(c);
                                    }
                                    else if(l < size){
                                          memcpy(p,buffer,cursor);
                                          *(p+cursor) = c;
                                          memcpy(p+cursor+1,
                                          buffer+cursor,(l-cursor)+1);
                                          strcpy(buffer,p);
                                          i=printf("%s",buffer+cursor)-1;
                                          while(i--) putch(BS);
                                          ++cursor;
                                    }
                              }
                        }
                        break;
            }
      } while(c != CR);
      free(p);
      small_cursor();
      return(strlen(buffer));
}
else return(-1);

}

big_cursor()      /* make the cursor big */
{
      union REGS r;

      r.h.ah = 15;
      int86(0x10,&r,&r);

      r.h.ah = 1;
      r.h.cl = 7;
      r.h.ch = 3;
      int86(0x10,&r,&r);
}

small_cursor()      /* make the cursor small */
```

```
{
    union REGS r;

    r.h.ah = 15;
    int86(0x10,&r,&r);

    r.h.ah = 1;
    r.h.cl = 6;
    r.h.ch = 5;
    int86(0x10,&r,&r);
}
```

Of necessity, the following description of the MAC2FONT program won't deal with every nuance and subtle peculiarity of Macintosh font resources. There's a five-volume set of books called *Inside Macintosh* that you might want to consult to fully understand this subject. Very few programmers will want to understand it that badly.

Three types of Macintosh resources are relevant to this discussion: FONT, FOND, and NFNT. The FONT and NFNT resources contain actual font information—bitmaps, width tables, and so on. In most cases, they're accompanied by FOND resources containing additional information about the fonts in question (such as their names).

Macintosh fonts are usually named after cities.

You can locate the resource fork of a Macintosh file with a Macbinary header by seeking past the 128-byte header and past the data fork. The data fork always comes first, and its size can be found in the datafork_size field of the header. The resource fork starts with a RECHEAD structure, as defined in Fig. 9-16. This contains a pointer to the start of the resource data and the start of the resource map. The resource map is a table of pointers into the resource data. Keep in mind that all these numbers are in the Motorola format.

The resource map allows an application reading a resource file to locate the file's "type list" (i.e., a list of all the four byte type fields defining resources in the file). In a font file, these will be FONT, NFNT, and FOND. The MAC2FONT program loads these into type_array. Each element of type_array is a RECTYPE structure.

Having loaded the type array, MAC2FONT locates all the FOND resources and loads them into fontname_array, which is an array of MACFOND structures. On a Macintosh, software needing to access fonts does so by locating the FOND in question and from there the FONT or NFNT resource specified by the FOND. This wasn't always the case—older Macs used two FONT resources for each font, with the second being a dummy resource to hold some of the information currently contained in a FOND.

Because the font files you'll find on bulletin boards can be of considerable antiquity, it's safer to work with the FONT and NFNT resources and look up the FONDs when you must. This allows for FONT resources without FONDs.

Having set up its array of FONDs, MAC2FONT looks through its type array for FONT resources first. Some of these may be from old style Macs—those having no FONDs—in which case it will revise the font name and data from the secondary FONT resources.

Finally, MAC2FONT will step through each FONT or NFNT resource and offer you the opportunity to convert it into a stand-alone graphical user interface FONT resource. It will supply default names and data from the font name array, which you can override if you want. The latter part of the program is a fairly elaborate string get function that simplifies the modification of the default data as it appears.

The PC file names of the FONT resources being written are derived from the Macintosh font names. The following is an example of what MAC2FONT displays when it's given a Macintosh FONT resource to use. In this case, the font file was called ATLANTIS.SIT, as found on a local bulletin board.

```
Name: Atlantis
Number for Atlantis: 8
Atlantis - 18 points
Font range from character 0 to 217 - number 8
Maximum character width: 12 - font rectangle: 12 × 22
Save as resource file (ESC <- to skip): ATLAN18.RES
Name: Atlantis
Number for Atlantis: 8
Atlantis - 36 points
Font range from character 0 to 217 - number 8
Maximum character width: 24 - font rectangle: 24 × 44
Save as resource file (ESC <- to skip): ATLAN36.RES
Name: Atlantis
Number for Atlantis: 8
Atlantis - 9 points
Font range from character 0 to 217 - number 8
Maximum character width: 6 - font rectangle: 6 × 11
Save as resource file (ESC <- to skip): ATLAN9.RES
```

Having converted those fonts from a Macintosh font file that you want to use, the SEEFONT program will let you look at them.

You should note that, while the first 128 characters of a font are pretty well standardized, the upper 128 vary greatly depending upon where the font came from. These "high order" character sets tend to be somewhat standardized for each of the three sources discussed in this chapter—for example, most GEM/VDI fonts designed for use with Ventura have the standard Ventura special characters.

You might want to modify SEEFONT to display an optional font chart that will associate character code values with specific characters.

Fools rush in where fools have been before.
Murphy's Laws of Computers

10

Creating dialogs

THE MACINTOSH AND MOST OF THE GRAPHICAL USER INTERFACES
that came after it—Microsoft Windows being most notable—like to promulgate the
notion of a "desktop metaphor." The idea behind this is that, in a perfect world,
you could throw away all the other objects on your real desk and get everything
done using the electronic "desktop" of your computer screen.

One thing in common between a graphical user interface purporting to be a
desktop and the top of a real desk is that neither is really big enough to hold all the
objects it's intended to support. In the case of a real desk, this usually results in
either a flurry of papers being pushed off the back of the desk from time to time or
the introduction of a perilous "Temple of Doom" made of stacked desk trays. In
time, these too will be pushed off the backs of most desks.

Virtual desktops don't allow you to push things off them. Instead, they insist
on fitting everything within the confines of your screen whether there's room or
not. In some cases, this can be arranged by having programs that only require
fairly restricted screen real estate. Most programs, however, are just crawling with
subfunctions that will want your attention—and part of your screen—from time to
time.

The usual approach to this problem—as has been dealt with informally
throughout this book—is the use of dialogs. A dialog is just a window that can pop
up when needed, do something for a while, and then go away. If you have a particularly cluttered real desk, you might equate this to pulling a sheet of paper from a
drawer, poising it on top of your monitor long enough to write on it, and then putting it away again.

This is based on the observation that the tops of most monitors remain uncluttered, despite the disarray of the desks surrounding them.

Much of the code discussed in this book involves the tools needed for the creation of dialogs. All the controls and other window paraphernalia—and windows themselves, for that matter—will usually be used in dialogs. This chapter will deal with some real world examples of effective dialog boxes.

Of necessity, the examples in this chapter will be fairly generic. You'll unquestionably have to create your own dialogs for your programs. However, the examples in this chapter will provide you with a good place to start when coming up with your own code.

The last dialog to be discussed in this chapter will also be the last thing to add to GUI.LIB. The chooseFile function, touched on in the previous chapter, is a fairly complex dialog serving as a standard way to load and save files for applications written using the graphical user interface.

The zen of dialogs

To a large extent, designing an easy and quick-to-use program is an exercise in creating a user interface. The graphical user interface in this book will handle the mechanics of a workable user interface, but it won't structure the logic of your programs for you. You still must think about how you want to deal with accessing the functions of your applications.

Most functions in a graphical user interface based program will be accessed through dialogs or as menu choices that pop up dialogs. There is a balance to be found when you have many functions to deal with or functions with complex parameters.

Consider the problem of printing something (i.e., the choices to be made if someone using your program wants to print whatever it is that your program does). Many different types of printers exist, so the first thing your program might want to know is what sort of printer is being used. It should also know which port the printer is connected to. In addition, you might need to specify the resolution of the printing to be done, or whether it will be in draft or letter quality mode. The orientation of the page can be set for some printers, as can the number of copies to be generated.

If this process is handled through a tree of individual dialogs, a user of your program would have to click his or her mouse into a coma before anything started to print. On the other hand, if you somehow squeeze all these choices into one immense dialog box, the box would be exceedingly confusing.

You do have ways to squeak by some of these problems, and these are the techniques you must keep in mind when creating a dialog. In the case of a printing dialog box, you can allow the users of your programs to set default values when the software in question is installed, thus reducing the number of choices.

It's easy to write dialogs using spaghetti logic in their layouts, and even easier still to add controls to a once simple dialog over multiple revisions of your program until it acquires the aspect of spaghetti logic. Understanding the logic of your program can make pretty convoluted dialogs look sensible to you, even if they won't to anyone else.

There are a number of zen-like axioms that can be applied to the creation of dialogs. You needn't follow any of them if you don't want to, but you might want to think about them.

To begin with, a dialog box should always have an exit. A user who gets to a box by mistake, or gets there deliberately and then changes his or her mind, should be able to return without any further action to whatever generated the dialog box. This can usually be handled by including a Cancel button in any dialog for which the Ok button would proceed with the related function.

It's been said that any program requiring a dialog box to deal with miscellaneous options hasn't been designed very well. I believe this was said by one of the authors of Ventura Publisher—Ventura Publisher has three such boxes, although (notably) none of them is called "Options." This is a good rule nonetheless, but perhaps in a modified form. A dialog box to set options should deal with options genuinely not suitable for any other dialog in the program. It should also deal with true defaults, not with things your users will probably want to change frequently throughout a session.

It's very important that all the dialogs in your program behave consistently. For example, the graphical user interface allows that hitting Enter will make a dialog react as if its "Ok" button has been clicked in. As long as you put all your dialogs together properly, this will be true for all of them.

Finally, a dialog should activate a function, not a feature. It should appear to a user as the control to change something or perform something in your program. If you keep this in mind, it's not difficult to keep extraneous controls out of your dialogs. There are few things more confusing than having to open three or four apparently unrelated dialogs to get something done.

Simple dialogs

Figure 10-1 illustrates a very simple message dialog. It has three elements and will prove to be the most frequently called sort of dialog in most programs.

 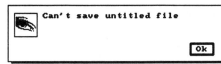

10-1   A message dialog.

The message dialog consists of a window with a bitmap, a bit of text, and a button to click in when the dialog is no longer needed. Figure 10-2 illustrates the code for this function.

```
message(s)
        char *s;
{
        TEXT t;
        BITMAP bmp;
        BUTTON ok, *bp;
```

10-2   The code to create the message dialog in Fig. 10-1.

```
WINDOW w;
RECT r;
POINT p;
unsigned int rt,a=0xff;

SetRect(&r,48,50,350,125);

arrowCursor();
if(OpenWindow(&w,&r)) {
        AddBitmap(&w,&bmp,r.left+8,r.top+10,ALERT,0x00,NULL,INACTIVE);

        SetRect(&ok.frame,r.right-40,r.bottom-23,
            r.right-8,r.bottom-8);
        AddButton(&w,&ok,Ok,ACTIVE);

        AddText(&w,&t,r.left+48,r.top+10,s,ACTIVE);

        while(a) {
                Keyboard(&w);
                if(MouseDown(&p)) {
                        rt=whereMouse(&p,&w);
                        if(rt & inButton) {
                                bp=findButton(&w,&p);
                                trackButton(bp);
                                if(bp==&ok)  a=0;
                        } else errorbeep();
                }
        }
        CloseWindow(&w);
} else errorbeep();
}
```

The message function assumes the existence of something called ALERT. This is actually a bitmap and serves as the icon in the box. In this case, the bitmap was excised from a larger image file using Desktop Paint. You can create your own small bitmap for this. Convert it to a linkable object with PCX2BIN and PRELINK and then add it to GUI.LIB.

You might want to have several different bitmaps—icons—for use in different sorts of message boxes. The Macintosh, for example, uses varying images for varying degrees of importance.

The code for message should be pretty easy to understand by now. It uses a number of standard calls into GUI.LIB. Having added its controls to its window, it will sit in its main while loop until someone clicks in the "Ok" button or hits Enter.

You'll probably find that message appears throughout your code. For example,

```
if((p = malloc(0x8000)) != NULL) {
    /* do something */
    free(p);
} else message("Error allocating memory");
```

The yesno function is nominally more involved than message. It's illustrated in its most commonly found application—asking if it's time to quit—in Fig. 10-3.

The yesno function accepts two text strings as arguments—you can pass an empty string for the second one if it's not needed. It will return a true value if the

10-3 A yes/no dialog.

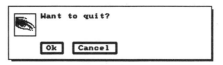

"Ok" button is clicked and a false one if the "Cancel" button is clicked (see Fig. 10-4).

```
yesno(l1,l2)
        char *l1,*l2;
{
        TEXT t1,t2;
        BITMAP bmp;
        BUTTON ok,can,*bp;
        WINDOW w;
        RECT r;
        POINT p;
        unsigned int rt,a=0xff,rv;

        SetRect(&r,48,50,350,125);

        if(OpenWindow(&w,&r)) {
                AddBitmap(&w,&bmp,r.left+8,r.top+10,ALERT,0x00,NULL,INACTIVE);

                SetRect(&ok.frame,r.left+48,r.bottom-23,r.left+80,r.bottom-8);
                AddButton(&w,&ok,Ok,ACTIVE);

                SetRect(&can.frame,r.left+96,r.bottom-23,r.left+160,r.bottom-8);
                AddButton(&w,&can,Cancel,ACTIVE);

                AddText(&w,&t1,r.left+48,r.top+10,l1,ACTIVE);
                AddText(&w,&t2,r.left+48,r.top+10+MENULINEDEEP,l2,ACTIVE);

                while(a) {
                        Keyboard(&w);
                        if(MouseDown(&p)) {
                                rt=whereMouse(&p,&w);
                                if(rt & inButton) {
                                        bp=findButton(&w,&p);
                                        trackButton(bp);
                                        if(bp==&ok) rv=1;
                                        else if(bp==&can) rv=0;
                                        a=0;
                                }
                                else errorbeep();
                        }
                }
                CloseWindow(&w);
        } else errorbeep();
        return(rv);
}
```

10-4 The code to create the yes/no dialog in Fig. 10-3.

The main loop of Desktop Paint will keep going as long as the global variable alive is true. It resembles this:

```
do {
    /* all the paint functions */
} while(alive);
```

The "Quit" item of the Desktop Paint file menu calls the function doQuit, which in turn uses yesno:

```
doQuit( )
{
    if(yesno("Want to quit?"," ")) alive = 0;
}
```

A font dialog

Dialogs that actually perform the functions of your application are among the most interesting ones to create, as well as being the most challenging. You might find the code in the some of the Desktop Paint dialogs useful, but ultimately you'll have to work out your own to suit the programs you write.

The Desktop Paint doSetFontSize dialog is one that you might be able to use in some other programs. It's interesting in that it deals with quite a few actual control objects—in this case, checkboxes. Because CHECKBOX objects really don't occupy very much memory, it's safe to allocate a reasonable size array of them on the stack.

Figure 10-5 illustrates doSetFontSize.

```
doSetFontSize()
{
    WINDOW w;
    POINT p;
    BUTTON ok,*bp;
    TEXT tx;
    CHECKBOX cb[36],*cp;
    RECT r;
    FONTENTRY *fe;
    char cbstr[36][8],title[60];
    unsigned int i,j,rt,a=0xff,count;

    count=strlen(FONTSIZEARRAY);

    SetRect(&r,48,48,400,170);
    if(OpenWindow(&w,&r)) {

        strcpy(title,"Set Font Size");
        strcat(title,fontmenu->item[currentfont].name+1);
        AddText(&w,&tx,r.left+8,r.top+10,title,ACTIVE);
        SetRect(&ok.frame,r.right-40,r.bottom-23,r.right-8,r.bottom-8);
        AddButton(&w,&ok,"Ok",ACTIVE);

        for(i=0;i<count;++i) {
            sprintf(cbstr[i],"%u",FONTSIZEARRAY[i]);

            if(i==currentfontsize)
                AddCheckbox(&w,&cb[i],r.left+8+((i%6)*56),
                    r.top+30+((i/6)*20),cbstr[i],0xff,ACTIVE);
            else
                AddCheckbox(&w,&cb[i],r.left+8+((i%6)*56),
                    r.top+30+((i/6)*20),cbstr[i],0x00,ACTIVE);
        }

        while(a) {
```

10-5 The code to create a font size dialog.

```
        Keyboard(&w);
        if(MouseDown(&p)) {
              rt=whereMouse(&p,&w);
              if(rt & inButton) {
                    bp=findButton(&w,&p);
                    trackButton(bp);
                    if(bp==&ok) a=0;
              }
              else if(rt & inCheckBox) {
                    cp=findCheckbox(&w,&p);
                    trackCheckbox(cp);
                    for(i=0;i<count;++i) {
                          if(cp==&cb[i]) {
                                for(j=0;j<count;++j) {
                                      if(cb[j].select) {
                                            cb[j].select=0x00;
                                            drawCheckbox(&cb[j]);
                                      }
                                }
                                cb[i].select=0xff;
                                drawCheckbox(&cb[i]);
                                currentfontsize=i;
                          }
                    }
              }
              else errorbeep();
        }
    }
    CloseWindow(&w);
} else errorbeep();
}
```

Actually, the definition of "reasonable size" is a bit fuzzy in doSetFontSize. As the graphical user interface stands, the number of legal font sizes isn't known at compile time. As such, this array should be big enough to allow for as many fonts as might turn up. As a rule of thumb, the largest practical size for a full font that is to fit into 64K is around 36 points. Thus, making this array 36 elements long is a pretty safe bet.

The doSetFontSize function assumes the existence of a number of global objects that are related to fonts. Specifically, these are currentfontsize—an int that serves as an index into LEGALFONTARRAY to specify the currently used point size of the current font. The fontmenu object is a MENU struct containing all the names of the available fonts. In practice, this isn't allocated as a static MENU object but rather as a dynamic buffer sized to hold a menu large enough to contain all the fonts.

This version of doSetFontSize is a bit simple-minded in that it believes that all fonts are available in all the legal sizes. If you use it, you'll want to make any check-boxes representing unsupported font sizes for your current font inactive. Desktop Paint does this but uses some complex code that would entail a significant digression into Desktop Paint's font allocation strategy to explain.

Figure 10-6 illustrates the dialog generated by the doSetFontSize function under Desktop Paint.

As an aside, Fig. 10-7 illustrates something of an oddity.

Figure 10-7 contains a 120-point commercial Macintosh font called Meow,

10-6 The font size dialog created by the code in Fig. 10-5.

10-7 A 120-point font created entirely out of cats.

from Cassady and Greene. This is a capitals-only font in which all the letters are formed from cats. Because most of its characters are missing, it does actually fit into a single 64K resource. However, 120 isn't a legal point size under the graphical user interface.

If you encounter a problem like this—an irresistible font in an unworkable size—you might want to remember that the point size of a font resource doesn't really mean anything to the code actually drawing the font. As was discussed in the previous chapter, the bitmap depth of a font determines how high it appears on your screen; the point size is just there for your reference. It's also useful in font allocation schemes such as the one that Desktop Paint uses, but it's meaningless to the font manager.

As such, you can use a huge font like Meow by changing the point size in its font resource to a legal font number, most likely 36 points for a big font like this one. It will still appear 120 points high on the screen, of course.

A printing dialog

Desktop Paint prints graphics, of course; depending upon the applications you write, you might have other printing requirements. The printing dialog you use probably won't be that much different from the one displayed by Desktop Paint if you select Print from its File menu (see Fig. 10-8).

The code that creates the Desktop Paint printing dialog is a compromise between offering users of the software too many choices to be reasonably sorted through and too many restrictions. It leaves some aspects of printing—such as the printer port—to be set when the program is initially configured.

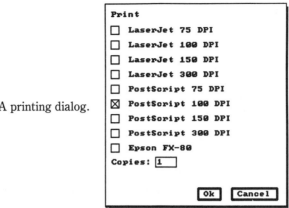

10-8 A printing dialog.

Desktop Paint has internal drivers for LaserJet and PostScript laser printers and supports other types of output devices, such as dot matrix printers, through loadable PDRV code resources. It maintains a global PRINTDRIVER pointer that will point to a PDRV resource if one was found in the program's resource file, or to NULL otherwise.

When the doPrint function is called, it sets up checkboxes for the eight printers it knows the software can deal with, these being LaserJet and PostScript printers in each of the four resolution modes they commonly support. It will set up a ninth box as active if a PDRV resource is available.

The doPrint function also uses an EDITFIELD control to allow users of the software to specify the number of copies to be printed. The printFile function that it calls does the actual printing.

Figure 10-9 illustrates the doPrint function.

```
doPrint()
{
    static char printer[9][24]= {
        "LaserJet 75 DPI",
        "LaserJet 100 DPI",
        "LaserJet 150 DPI",
        "LaserJet 300 DPI",
        "PostScript 75 DPI",
        "PostScript 100 DPI",
        "PostScript 150 DPI",
        "PostScript 300 DPI",
        "Undefined"
        };

    WINDOW w;
    POINT p;
    BUTTON ok,can,*bp;
    TEXT tx,txef;
    CHECKBOX cb[9],*cp;
    EDITFIELD ef,*ep;
    RECT r;
    char efbuf[16];
    unsigned int copies=1,i,rt,a=0xff;
```

10-9 The code that created the printing dialog in Fig. 10-8.

10-9 Continued

```
if(!isfile) return(0);

if(framechanged) {
    getdraw();
    framechanged=0x00;
}

SetRect(&r,48,48,300,320);
if(OpenWindow(&w,&r)) {

    if(printDrv != NULL) strcpy(printer[8],printDrv->name+1);

    AddText(&w,&tx,r.left+8,r.top+10,"Print",ACTIVE);

    AddText(&w,&txef,r.left+8,r.top+210,"Copies",ACTIVE);

    sprintf(efbuf,"%u",copies);
    AddEditField(&w,&ef,r.left+72,r.top+210,3,efbuf,numbertrap,ACTIVE);

    for(i=0;i<9;++i) {
        if(i==theConfig.printertype)
            AddCheckbox(&w,&cb[i],r.left+8,r.top+30+(i*20),
                printer[i],0xff,ACTIVE);
        else
            AddCheckbox(&w,&cb[i],r.left+8,r.top+30+(i*20),
                printer[i],0x00,ACTIVE);
    }

    if(printDrv==NULL) {
        cb[8].active=INACTIVE;
        drawCheckbox(&cb[8]);
    }

    SetRect(&can.frame,r.right-72,r.bottom-23,r.right-8,r.bottom-8);
AddButton(&w,&can,"Cancel",ACTIVE);

SetRect(&ok.frame,r.right-120,r.bottom-23,r.right-88,r.bottom-8);
AddButton(&w,&ok,"Ok",ACTIVE);

while(a) {
    Keyboard(&w);
    if(MouseDown(&p)) {
        rt=whereMouse(&p,&w);
        if(rt & inButton) {
            bp=findButton(&w,&p);
            trackButton(bp);
            if(bp==&ok) {
                copies=atoi(efbuf);
                if(copies < 1) copies=1;
                if(copies > 99) copies=99;
                printFile(copies);
                a=0;
            }
            else if(bp==&can) a=0;
        }
        else if(rt & inCheckBox) {
            cp=findCheckbox(&w,&p);
            trackCheckbox(cp);
            for(i=0;i<9;++i) {
                if(cp->active==ACTIVE) {
                    if(cp==&cb[i]) {
                        cb[i].select=0xff;
```

286 *Creating dialogs*

```
                                drawCheckbox(&cb[i]);
                                theConfig.printertype=i;
                            }
                            else if(cb[i].select) {
                                cb[i].select=0x00;
                                drawCheckbox(&cb[i]);
                            }
                        }
                    }
                }
                else if(rt & inEditField) {
                    ep=findEditfield(&w,&p);
                    trackEditfield(ep);
                    if(ep==&ef) {
                        copies=atoi(efbuf);
                        if(copies < 1) copies=1;
                        if(copies > 99) copies=99;
                        sprintf(efbuf,"%u",copies);
                    }
                    drawEditfield(ep);
                }
                else errorbeep();
            }
        }
        CloseWindow(&w);
        while(kbhit()) getch();
    } else errorbeep();
}
```

You'll note that when doPrint quits, it executes the following bit of code:

while(kbhit( )) getch( );

This is a quick way to empty the keyboard buffer of any pending keys that might have appeared there while the function was too busy to respond to key presses. This can happen in a function that drives a printer, as it will be busy handling the printer port and won't know much about whatever else is going on.

While Desktop Paint is busy printing, it uses a fairly handy little dialog to indicate how far along it's gotten (see Fig. 10-10 for one version).

10-10   The wait status box from Desktop Paint.

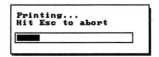

You can use the status indicator box whenever your program is busy doing something that will take a long time. It actually consists of three functions, as shown in Fig. 10-11.

```
WINDOW *openWait()
{
        char b[WAITSTEPS+1];
        WINDOW *w;
        RECT r;

        SetRect(&r,50,54,66+(WAITSTEPS*8),96);

        if((w=(WINDOW *)malloc(sizeof(WINDOW))) != NULL) {
                if(OpenWindow(w,&r)) {
```

10-11   The functions that run the wait status box.

```
                    DrawString(r.left+8,r.top+10,Black,White,
                        "Wait... hit Esc to abort");
                    memset(b,219,WAITSTEPS);
                    b[WAITSTEPS]=0;
                    DrawString(w->frame.left+8,w->frame.top+26,Dim,White,b);
                    return(w);
            }
            else {
                    free((char *)w);
                    return(NULL);
            }
        } else return(NULL);
}

void updateWait(w,n,max)
        WINDOW *w;
        int n,max;
{
        char b[WAITSTEPS+1];
        static int cur;
        unsigned int i;

        if(w != NULL && n != cur) {
                i=(n*(WAITSTEPS+1))/max;
                if(i > WAITSTEPS) i=WAITSTEPS;
                if(i != cur) {
                        memset(b,219,i);
                        b[i]=0;
                        cur=i;
                        DrawString(w->frame.left+8,w->frame.top+26,
                            Black,White,b);
                }
        }
}

void closeWait(w)
        WINDOW *w;
{
        if(w != NULL) {
                closeWindow(w);
                free((char *)w);
        }
}
```

The openWait function opens the window that the wait dialog lives in and returns a WINDOW pointer to it. Note that in this case, the memory for the WINDOW object being used must be dynamically allocated using malloc rather than being allocated on the stack, because openWait's stack variables won't stick around after it returns its pointer.

The value of WAITSTEPS is a constant. It can be anything you like, so long as it represents a value that will fit in the wait box. You might want to set it like this for the box size defined in openWait:

#define WAITSTEPS   20

The updateWait function should be called periodically throughout whatever process is causing the delay. In the case of printing a file, this would be once every line being printed, or perhaps every few lines. This function will update the bar graph in the wait window. The bar graph is really just a string of character 219, which is a solid box in the PC character set.

The w argument to updateWait is the WINDOW pointer returned by openWait. The n argument is the current value of the bar graph, while the max argument is the largest number that n might reach.

Finally, closeWait should be called when the wait is over. It closes the wait window and frees the memory used by its WINDOW object.

A Choose File dialog

The most complex, fiddly, and potentially nasty dialog you're likely to encounter in most graphical user interface applications is the chooseFile function. This dialog is used when you want to open an existing file on the disk or select a name under which to save a file. It must allow you to change drives and subdirectories, and it must be able to display files based on a file specification. The box itself is shown in Fig. 10-12; the code will prove rather more complex.

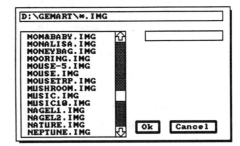

10-12 The choose file dialog box.

Unless you don't like the chooseFile function that will be described over the remainder of this chapter, you won't have to write your own. The chooseFile function and its attendant subfunctions should be added to the graphical user interface library if you've been building it up as you've worked through this book.

You can skip the rest of this chapter if you like.

A number of things conspire to make the chooseFile box complicated. To begin with, the box must handle any number of file names, with any number being pretty large if the chooseFile function happens to come upon a subdirectory with a large number of files. In moving around a complicated directory tree, it will be called upon to allocate and subsequently dump a buffer of file names multiple times. It must be able to deal in a civilized, non-fatal manner with things like a floppy drive with an open door. In addition, there are simply a lot of controls in one of these things.

The basic functioning of the chooseFile box is actually pretty simple. When it's called, it's passed a file specification to use in selecting file names. For example, if you passed it C:\DOS*.COM:, it would attempt to find all the COM files in the \DOS directory of drive C and display them. In fact, what it really does is to load all the names into a big buffer and then use a list control and a vertical scroll bar to display the buffer's contents.

If you click in a list control, the selected line will be returned by the trackList function. This makes for a pretty easy way to select a file name.

You can't safely assume that users of your programs won't want to access files in other subdirectories or even on other drives. As such, the chooseFile function requires a way to change the path of its initial file specification and troll around your system. As it's handled here, this involves adding some pseudo-file names to the buffer managed by the list control.

The pseudo-file names involved are the names of any available subdirectories in the current directory and the letters of all the available drives. As such, the code handling the name returned by trackList must be a bit smarter. It must accept a selected file name but still change both the directory or drive if a directory name or drive is selected.

Largely because it's done this way in other graphical user interfaces, selecting a name from the list control can be accomplished either by clicking on it once and then clicking in the "Ok" button of the dialog or by double clicking on the same name in the list. What this latter condition really involves is watching for the same name being returned twice in succession by trackList.

There are two particularly obscure, DOS-related things that you'll want to understand in order to make sense of the chooseFile dialog. The first deals with fetching disk file names, and the other—and far weirder—deals with handling disk hardware errors.

File names are maintained by DOS in a somewhat tricky format—for one thing, it varies between names in a root directory and those in a subdirectory. As such, there are two functions available under DOS that will allow you to fetch file names from a directory in an orderly fashion. These are accessible under Turbo C as findfirst and findnext.

The findfirst function is passed a file specification, an attribute byte, and a pointer to a struct of the type ffblk. These latter two objects will be dealt with in a moment. The file specification would usually include wild cards, such as C:\ DOS*.COM. Assuming that at least one file existed to match the file specification, findfirst would return a zero value and load the information about the file into the ffblk struct.

Calling findnext repeatedly would return all the other files matching the file specification. The findnext function would continue to return zero until no more files could be found.

This is what the ffblk struct looks like. It's defined in the DIR.H file included with Turbo C:

```
struct ffblk {
    char ff_reserved[21];
    char ff_attrib;
    unsigned ff_ftime;
    unsigned ff_fdate;
    long ff_fsize;
    char ff_name[13];
};
```

When findfirst or findnext returns a zero value, the ffblk struct passed to it will have a valid file name, size, date, and time loaded into it. It will also have a file attribute.

File attributes are actually a system of flags used by DOS to keep track of the various sorts of files appearing on a hard drive. Normal files have an attribute of zero. Subdirectories are actually treated as special files and have an attribute of sixteen. Other special files, such as hidden files, system files, volume labels, etc., have other attributes.

If you pass zero as the attribute argument to findfirst, it will only look for files having this attribute (e.g., regular DOS files). If you pass it sixteen, it will look for regular files and subdirectories. Upon each return from findfirst and findnext, you can check to see whether the file in question is a regular file or a subdirectory by seeing what value has appeared in the ff_attrib element of the ffblk struct.

Getting all the names matching a file specification into a buffer presents one with a bit of a Catch-22, actually. There's no way of knowing how big a buffer to allocate until all the names have been found. For this reason, the names must be gone through twice—once to count them and a second time to actually fetch them and put them in a buffer. Because of the internal buffering performed by DOS, this actually doesn't entail much of a speed penalty.

Alternately, you could predefine a fixed upper limit to the number of names that can be included in a chooseFile box and ignore any that exceed it. Ventura Publisher does this, much to the frustration of its users.

The getfiles function, shown in Fig. 10-13, will return a buffer with all the file names matching its file specification. This will include real file names, subdirectory names, the ".." directory name if it's present, and a list of all the available drives, as specified by its drivemap argument. A drive map is just a string with one letter for each available drive. On a system with two floppies and one hard drive, for example, the drive map would be "ABC."

```
char *getfiles(spec,count,drivemap)
        char *spec;
        int *count;
        char *drivemap;
{
        struct ffblk f;
        char *p,drive[MAXDRIVE],dir[MAXDIR],b[128];
        int i=0,j,k,dircheck();

        *count=0;

        /* start by counting the files */

        k=strlen(drivemap);
        if(!findfirst(spec,&f,0)) {
                do {
                        ++*count;
                } while(!findnext(&f));
        }

        fnsplit(spec,drive,dir,NULL,NULL);
        fnmerge(b,drive,dir,"*",".");
        if(!findfirst(b,&f,16)) {
```

10-13 The getfiles function.

```
        do {
                if((f.ff_attrib & 16) == 16 &&
                        strcmp(f.ff_name,".")) ++*count;
        } while(!findnext(&f));
}

*count+=k;
if(*count==0) return(NULL);

if((p=malloc(*count*(FILELINESIZE+1))) != NULL) {
        if(!findfirst(spec,&f,0)) {
                do {
                        sprintf(p+((FILELINESIZE+1)*i++),"%s",
                                f.ff_name);
                } while(!findnext(&f));
        }
        if(!findfirst(b,&f,16)) {
                do {
                        if((f.ff_attrib & 16) == 16 &&
                                strcmp(f.ff_name,"."))
                                sprintf(p+((FILELINESIZE+1)*i++),"\\%s",
                                        f.ff_name);
                } while(!findnext(&f));
        }

        for(j=0;j<k;++j)
                sprintf(p+((FILELINESIZE+1)*i++),"[ %c ]",drivemap[j]);
        qsort(p,*count,FILELINESIZE+1,strcmp);
}
return(p);
}
```

The getfiles function calls another somewhat obscure Turbo C function—qsort. The qsort function sorts the file names in the buffer that getfiles fills. In most cases, qsort is used to sort things into alphabetical order, but this needn't be true. It sorts based on the comparison function passed as its last argument. In this case, the standard C strcmp function is used, but the buffer has been cooked a bit to make it sort things in a more useful way. Specifically, the subdirectory names have back-slashes before them, and the drive letters have square brackets around them. Because both these characters come after the range of alphabetic characters, the subdirectory names and drive letters will be sorted to the end of the list.

The other area of the chooseFile dialog that might take a bit of explaining is the disk hardware error handler. If you attempt to access a file on a drive that isn't on line—this usually being a floppy drive with no disk in it—DOS will throw an INT 24H instruction to indicate its displeasure. By default, this is hooked to the code that prints the familiar "Abort, Retry, or Ignore" message. This would look very unprofessional indeed were it to appear in the middle of a session of a program written under the graphical user interface.

To avoid this, you must redirect this vector to something more civilized. However, because of the way DOS uses this call, you probably shouldn't leave it redirected all the time. Instead, snag the INT 24H vector, test the drive in question, and then restore the vector immediately.

Figure 10-14 illustrates the code that does this. Don't be concerned if its function isn't completely clear just yet.

```
testdisk(n)
        int n;
{
        void interrupt (*oldHarderr)();
        FILE *fp;
        char b[32];
        int diskErrorHandler();

        oldHarderr=getvect(0x24);
        harderr(diskErrorHandler);
        diskErr=0;
        getcwd(errbuf,80);
        sprintf(b,"%c:\\TEMP.DAT",n+'A');
        if((fp=fopen(b,"r")) != NULL) fclose(fp);
        setvect(0x24,oldHarderr);
        return(diskErr);
}

#pragma warn -par
int diskErrorHandler(errval,ax,bp,si)
        int errval,ax,bp,si;
{
        if(ax >=0) {
                diskErr=1;
                restoreDir(errbuf);
        }
        hardretn(2);
}

restoreDir(s)       /* restore a saved directory path */
        char *s;
{
        strupr(s);
        if(isalpha(s[0]) && s[1]==':') setdisk(s[0]-'A');
        chdir(s);
}
```

10-14 The DOS hardware error handler.

The testdisk function accepts a drive number as its argument, where drive A is 0, drive B is 1, and so on. It begins by grabbing the INT 24H vector so it can't get into any serious trouble. The old address for this vector is stored in oldHarderr so it can be restored later.

The testdisk function requires two global variables—errbuf and diskErr. The former keeps track of the current directory, to be restored should something prove to be amiss.

Having prepared itself for a leap into the unknown, the testdisk function will attempt to open a dummy file on the destination drive. If all goes well, it will then close the file immediately, restore the INT 24H vector and return 0, indicating that the drive in question is on and ready to party.

If the drive isn't actually on line, DOS will throw an INT 24H. Because it has been redirected by testdisk, it will wind up calling diskErrorHandler (also shown in Fig. 10-14). This will set diskErr to a non-zero value—indicating trouble—and restore the old directory using restoreDir, the third function in this figure.

While testdisk probably looks like a high wire act, it provides a very reliable way to work with disk drives. Unless something goes badly wrong with your hardware, it will prevent anything unexpected from crashing or disfiguring the chooseFile box.

The actual chooseFile function is shown in Fig. 10-15. Now that you understand the functions it calls, you should have little trouble working your way through it.

```
chooseFile(spec,name,x,y,drivemap)
    char *spec,*name;
    int x,y;
    char *drivemap;
{
    SCROLLBAR sb,*sp;
    LIST ls,*lp;
    TEXT errt;
    TEXTFIELD fspec;
    EDITFIELD fname,*ep;
    RECT r,errr;
    WINDOW w,errw;
    POINT p;
    BUTTON ok,can,errok,*bp;
    char *thespec,drive[MAXDRIVE],nm[24];
    char dir[MAXDIR],file[MAXFILE],ext[MAXEXT];
    unsigned int rt;
    int loc=0,a_inner,a_outer=0xff,erra,i,isname();

    r.left=x;
    r.top=y;
    r.right=r.left+300;
    r.bottom=r.top+180;

    name[0]=0;
    if(openWindow(&w,&r)) {
        SetRect(&ok.frame,r.left+168,r.bottom-25,r.left+200,r.bottom-10);
        AddButton(&w,&ok,"Ok",ACTIVE);

        SetRect(&can.frame,r.left+216,r.bottom-25,r.left+280,r.bottom-10);
        AddButton(&w,&can,"Cancel",ACTIVE);

        if(strlen(spec) <= 35) thespec=spec;
        else thespec=spec+strlen(spec)-35;
        AddTextField(&w,&fspec,r.left+8,r.top+8,35,thespec,ACTIVE);

        AddEditField(&w,&fname,r.left+184,r.top+35,13,name,isname,ACTIVE);

        AddList(&w,&ls,r.left+8,r.top+34,FILELINESIZE,14,0,loc,NULL);
        AddVertScroll(&w,&sb,ls.frame.right,ls.frame.top,
            ls.frame.bottom-ls.frame.top,0,0,0,INACTIVE);

        do {
            a_inner=0xff;
            ls.count=0;
            waitCursor();
            ls.base=getfiles(spec,&ls.count,drivemap);
            arrowcursor();
            ls.top=sb.cur=0;
            if(ls.count > 14) {
                sb.max=ls.count-14;
```

10-15 The chooseFile function.

```
                            sb.active=ACTIVE;
                        }
                    else {
                            sb.max=0;
                            sb.active=INACTIVE;
                        }
            adjustThumb(&sb,0);
            drawList(&ls);
            drawVertScroll(&sb);

            while(a_inner) {
                Keyboard(&w);
                if(MouseDown(&p)) {
                    rt=whereMouse(&p,&w);
                    if(rt & inButton) {
                        bp=findButton(&w,&p);
                        trackButton(bp);
                        if(bp==&can) {
                            name[0]=0;
                            a_inner=a_outer=0;
                        }
                        else if(bp==&ok) {
                            if(name[0] != '\\' && name[0] != '[')
                                a_outer=0;
                            a_inner=0;
                        }
                    }
                    else if(rt & inVertScroll) {
                        sp=findScrollbar(&w,&p);
                        trackScrollbar(sp,rt);
                        if(sp==&sb) {
                            ls.top=sp->cur;
                            drawList(&ls);
                        }
                    }
                    else if(rt & inList) {
                        strcpy(nm,name);
                        lp=findList(&w,&p);
                        trackList(lp,name);
                        drawEditfield(&fname);
                        if(!strcmp(name,nm)) {
                            if(name[0] != '\\' && name[0] != '[')
                                a_outer=0;
                            a_inner=0;
                        }
                    }
                    else if(rt & inEditField) {
                        ep=findEditfield(&w,&p);
                        trackEditfield(ep);
                        drawEditfield(ep);
                    }
                    else errorbeep();
                }
            }
        }
        if(ls.base != NULL) free(ls.base);
        if(name[0]=='\\') {
            /* change directory */
            fnsplit(spec,drive,dir,file,ext);
            if(strcmp(name+1,"..")) {
                /* add new directory */
                strcat(dir,name+1);
                strcat(dir,"\\");
            }
            else {
```

```
        /* back up one directory */
                        i=strlen(dir)-2;
                        while(i>0 && dir[i] != '\\') --i;
                        dir[i+1]=0;
                }
                name[0]=0;
                fnmerge(spec,drive,dir,file,ext);
                drawTextfield(&fspec);
                drawEditfield(&fname);
        }
        else if(name[0]=='[') {
                /* change drives */
                if(!testdisk(name[2]-'A')) {
                        fnsplit(spec,drive,dir,file,ext);
                        drive[0]=name[2];
                        strcpy(dir,"\\");
                        fnmerge(spec,drive,dir,file,ext);
                        name[0]=0;
                        drawEditfield(&fname);
                        drawTextfield(&fspec);
                }
                else {
                        SetRect(&errr,r.left+16,r.top+8,r.left+240,r.top+72);
                        if(OpenWindow(&errw,&errr)) {
                                AddText(&errw,&errt,errr.left+48,errr.top+10,
                                    "Error reading drive",ACTIVE);
                                SetRect(&errok.frame,errr.left+168,
                                    errr.bottom-25,
                                    errr.left+200,
                                    errr.bottom-10);
                                AddButton(&errw,&errok,"Ok",ACTIVE);
                                erra=1;
                                do {
                                    if(MouseDown(&p)) {
                                        Keyboard(&errw);
                                        rt=whereMouse(&p,&errw);
                                        if(rt & inButton) {
                                            bp=findButton(&errw,&p);
                                            trackButton(bp);
                                            if(bp==&errok) erra=0;
                                        }
                                    }
                                } while(erra);
                                CloseWindow(&errw);
                        }
                }
        } else a_outer=0;
    } while(a_outer);
    closeWindow(&w);
} else errorbeep();
return(name[0]);
}


isname(c)       /* return character for file name or false if not ok */
{
    c=toupper(c);
    if(isalpha(c) || isdigit(c) || c=='.') return(c);
    else return(0);
}
```

The arguments to chooseFile will probably be familiar by now. The spec is the file specification string. The name is a string that will contain the name chooseFile chooses. The x and y arguments are the upper left corner of the box as it will be displayed on your screen. The drivemap is a drive map string, as described previously.

There is actually one more ancillary function that chooseFile uses, albeit a small one. The isname function will decide whether a character passed to it is a legal character for use in a file name. This is necessary because chooseFile is called not only to select file names from the disk but also to enter them when you're saving a file. This function prevents people from entering file names containing illegal characters (such as backslashes).

At the moment, isname is a bit conservative. You might want to modify it a bit to allow it to accept dashes, tildes, and other legal file name punctuation.

Using the Choose File box

While it's easy to use, the chooseFile function does require a bit of preparation if it's to present itself in an optimally convenient way. Specifically, it should remember which subdirectory it has changed to between calls, such that if a user opens a file in one directory, the chooseFile box will present him or her with the same directory the next time it's called.

To properly support the chooseFile dialog, you should set up a global variable in your applications like this:

```
char filepath[129];
```

When a program initially boots up, it should load the current directory path into this buffer as a starting place for chooseFile:

```
getcwd(filepath,128);
if(filepath[strlen(filepath)-1] != ' \ \ ')
    strcat(filepath," \ \ ");
```

Alternately, if the design of your program allows users to configure the directories where files will reside, you might want to start with these as the file path. To borrow from Ventura Publisher once again, you might want to make your application really clever and have it remember the file path from session to session by writing it to a disk file when the program returns to DOS.

To use chooseFile to save a file, then, use the following code. The constant FILE_EXTENSION might be something like .PCX, .TXT, or .RES, depending upon what exactly you'll be saving, while the drivemap will be a string with legal drive letters in it.

```
doSave( )
{
    char b[129],name[16];
```

```
        char drive[MAXDRIVE],dir[MAXDIR];

    strcpy(b,filepath);
    strcat(b,"*.");
    strcat(b,FILE_EXTENSION);

    if(chooseFile(b,name,48,48,drivemap)) {
        fnsplit(b,drive,dir,NULL,NULL);
        fnsplit(name,NULL,NULL,filename,NULL);
        fnmerge(filepath,drive,dir,NULL,NULL);
        /* do whatever is needed to save the file */
    }
}
```

The doSave function will open the chooseFile box with its upper left corner at (48,48). If chooseFile returns a true value—indicating either that a name has been double clicked or that a name has been single clicked and the "Ok" button has been clicked—the file path will be updated to allow for any changes chooseFile might have made to it. The path to the actual file to be saved can be derived from filepath and name.

In a complex application, you might want to have multiple file paths for use on different occasions. For example, in a word processor, there could be one path for document files, a different one for pictures to be imported into the documents, yet another for imported tables, and so on.

The complete toolbox

Having reached the end of this chapter, you've had a chance to look at the entire graphical user interface library. You should understand all you need to know about setting up windows, using controls, and dealing with ancillary matters such as bitmaps and fonts.

There are several remaining parts of this book that you might find helpful. The first is the sample application in Chapter 11, full of real world examples for actually using the functions in the library. The second is Appendix A, which lists all the callable functions in the library by name and discusses their arguments. You'll find this to be a very handy thing to photocopy and pin to a nearby wall.

By now you'll probably have a few ideas for applications using the graphical user interface. It's quite forgivable to skip the last chapter entirely, boot up Turbo C, and get your project under way.

11

Writing an application

WRITING A PROGRAM AND WRITING AN APPLICATION DIFFER ONLY IN THE
length of what you're writing. If the instructions required to get the software up
and running occupy more space than the source code did, it's a program—and only
other programmers are likely to want to use it.

If you apply it properly, the graphical user interface discussed in this book will
make it much easier for you to turn out real applications—programs user-friendly
to the extent that they shouldn't require a great deal of instruction, on-line help, or
technical support. At least, they won't need instructions to explain their operation.
You still might have to assist your users in understanding the functions of your software.

If it's properly constructed, a user friendly program doesn't tie up a lot of its
learning curve with the simple mechanics of opening a file, changing a few toggles,
or calling for the attention of a printer.

Of course, you're free to decide whether the application to be discussed in this
chapter is truly user-friendly and intuitive. If you don't find it as such, you should
be able to use your observations of its shortcomings to improve your own software.

This chapter will feature the complete source code for Tiny Paint, a paint program using the graphical user interface library. This application is clearly distilled
from Desktop Paint, as discussed periodically throughout this book, and the distil-
lation process has been a bit savage. Tiny Paint is a very rudimentary paint program, intended to serve as a programming example rather than a useful piece of
software.

Figure 11-1 illustrates Tiny Paint in use.

11-1   The Tiny Paint program.

Comparing the screen of Tiny Paint to one of the Desktop Paint screens else-where in this book, you'll probably observe that the former is a bit thin on tools. It also lacks a few menus; when you've had a chance to try both programs for a while, you'll probably observe that much else has been lost in the translation. Tiny Paint requires fewer than 1500 lines of source code, as opposed to something over 30,000 lines of C source alone for Desktop Paint.

When you've had a chance to peruse Tiny Paint, you'll probably find that it makes a good place to start building your own applications. If you want to write a word processor based on the graphical user interface, you can begin with Tiny Paint and simply delete all the bits dealing specifically with painting.

Figure 11-2 is the complete source code for Tiny Paint. Following that code and just one other source listing, I'll discuss in detail what all the functions do. If you actually want to compile it, the code in Fig. 11-2 should be put in a file called TPAINT.C.

```
/*
        Tiny Paint
        copyright (c) 1991 Alchemy Mindworks Inc.

        This is a very simple paint program which
        illustrates the structure and approach to
        writing graphical user interface based
```

11-2   The source code for Tiny Paint—TPAINT.C.

300   *Writing an application*

```
        applications.
*/

#include "stdio.h"
#include "dos.h"
#include "dir.h"
#include "alloc.h"
#include "graphics.h"
#include "gui.h"
#include "tpaint.h"                  /* the icons */

#define MAXPAINTICONS    6          /* how many paint icons are there */

#define LEFTDRAW         88         /* the maximum offsets from the edges */
#define TOPDRAW          16         /* of the screen for the drawing area */
#define RIGHTDRAW        16
#define BOTTOMDRAW       15

#define TOOLBOXLEFT      8          /* where the toolbox goes */
#define TOOLBOXTOP       TOPDRAW

#define ODPAD            4          /* click zone around drawing rectangle */

#define toolLine         0          /* numbers for the tools */
#define toolErase        1
#define toolBox          2
#define toolEllipse      3
#define toolUndo         4
#define toolBrush        5

typedef struct {                    /* the configuration data */
        char sig[4];
        int version;
        int smalleraser;
        int bigeraser;
        int defwidth;
        int defdepth;
        char drivemap[27];
        } CONFIG;

typedef struct {                    /* bitmapped file information */
        char name[16];
        int width,depth,bytes;
        int bits_per_pixel;
        long size;
        long memory;
        } FILEINFO;

typedef struct {                    /* PCX file header */
        char manufacturer;
        char version;
        char encoding;
        char bits_per_pixel;
        int xmin,ymin;
        int xmax,ymax;
        int hres;
        int vres;
        char palette[48];
        char reserved;
        char colour_planes;
        int bytes_per_line;
        int palette_type;
        char filler[58];
        } PCXHEAD;
```

11-2 Continued

```
int doAboutBox(void);              /* prototypes for menu calls */

int doNew(void);
int doSetFiletype(void);
int doOpen(void);
int doClose(void);
int doSaveAs(void);
int doSave(void);
int doQuit(void);

int tbUndo();
char *farPtr(char *p,long l);    /* prototype for far pointer */
int putline(char *p,int n);      /* prototype for put image line */
char *getline(int n);            /* prototype for get image line */
int numbertrap(int c);           /* prototype for number trap */
void swap(int *a,int*b); /* prototype for swap */

CONFIG theConfig= {              /* the configuration data */
        "TPN",
        0x0202,
        8,
        16,
        640,
        480,
        "ABCDEFGH",
        };

MENU desk = { 1," Desk",         /* desk menu */
                " About...    ",doAboutBox,
                };

MENU file = { 7," File",         /* file menu */
                " New \004N    ",doNew,
                " Open \004O    ",doOpen,
                ".Close \004Z    ",doClose,
                ".Save \004S    ",doSave,
                ".Save as...  ",doSaveAs,
                "._____  ",idle,
                " Quit \004Q    ",doQuit,
                };

MENU edit = { 4," Edit",         /* edit menu - just for show */
                ".Cut \004X    ",idle,
                ".Copy \004C    ",idle,
                ".Paste \004V    ",idle,
                ".Clear      ",idle,
                };


RECT drawrect;         /* drawing area */
RECT outdraw;          /* area just around drawing area */
char alive=0xff;       /* flag for aliveness */
char isfile=0x00;      /* flag for a file in residence */
char framechanged=0x00; /* flag for changed frame */
char filepath[129];    /* where the file path lives */
char filename[16];     /* where the file name lives */

char *thepicture=NULL; /* buffer for picture to live in */
char *linebuf=NULL;    /* line buffer */

BITMAP painticon[MAXPAINTICONS];       /* toolbox BITMAPs */

char *p_icon[MAXPAINTICONS]={   ICON1,ICON2,    /* pointers to icons */
```

302 *Writing an application*

```
                                        ICON3,ICON4,
                                        ICON5,ICON6
                                        };

int lastTool=0,theTool=-1;              /* tool selection */
SCROLLBAR vpScroll,hpScroll;            /* main scroll bars */

unsigned int width=640,depth=480,bytes; /* picture size */
unsigned int dwidth,ddepth,dbytes;      /* display (window) size */

main()
{
        POINT thePoint;
        BITMAP *bp;
        SCROLLBAR *sp;
        int i,rt,colour;

        clrscr();

        /* initialize things */
        if(initMouse()) {

                /* do this now so the GUI module has them */
                registerbgidriver(EGAVGA_driver);
                registerbgidriver(Herc_driver);

                /* and turn on the graphics */
                if(initGraphics()) {
                        MouseOn();

                        ClearScreen();

                        /* window manager on */
                        InitWindowManager();

                        /* menu manager on */
                        InitMenuManager();

                        /* add the menus */
                        AddMenu(&desk);
                        AddMenu(&file);

AddMenu(&edit);

/* draw the menu bar */
DrawMenuBar();

/* clear the area below the menu bar */
ClearScreen();

/* get the current file path */
getcwd(filepath,128);
if(filepath[strlen(filepath)-1] != '\\')
    strcat(filepath,"\\");

do {
        /* look for an alt key pending */
        dispatchMenuItem();

        /* if there's a mouse click elsewhere... */
        if((colour=MouseDown(&thePoint)) != 0) {

                /* ...find it */
                rt=whereMouse(&thePoint,&screenwindow);
```

11-2 Continued

```
/* check for menu activity */
if(rt & inMenuBar)
    doMenu(&thePoint);

/* see if it's in the toolbox */
else if(rt & inBitmap) {

        /* find the bitmap */
        bp=findBitmap(&screenwindow,
            &thePoint);

        /* track the bitmap */
        trackBitmap(bp);

        /* compare it to all the tools */
        for(i=0;i<MAXPAINTICONS;++i) {
                if(bp==&painticon[i]) {
                        selectTool(i);
                        break;
                }
        }
}

/* see if it's in a scroll bar */
else if(rt & inVertScroll) {
        /* prpare to change drawing */
        if(framechanged) {
                getdraw();
                framechanged=0x00;
        }
        /* move the scroll */
        sp=findScrollbar(&screenwindow,
            &thePoint);
        trackScrollbar(sp,rt);
        if(sp==&vpScroll) putdraw();
}

                        /* same here for the horizontal scroll */
                        else if(rt & inHorScroll) {
                                if(framechanged) {
                                        getdraw();
                                        framechanged=0x00;
                                }
                                sp=findScrollbar(&screenwindow,
                                    &thePoint);
                                trackScrollbar(sp,rt);
                                if(sp==&hpScroll) putdraw();
                        }

                        /* see if it's in the drawing area */
                        else if(PointInRect(&thePoint,&outdraw)) {
                                dodraw(&thePoint,colour);
                                while(MouseDown(&thePoint));
                        }

                        /* it's in the grey - complain */
                        else errorbeep();
                }
        } while(alive);

        /* free the picture buffer - a formality */
        freebuffer();

        MouseOff();
```

```
                               /* graphics off */
                               deinitGraphics();
                               clrscr();
                    } else puts("Can't establish graphics mode");
          } else puts("Can't find mouse driver");
}


/* this function handles drawing with the tools. it's called any
   time a mouse click happens in the drawing area */
dodraw(start,colour)
          POINT *start;
          int colour;
{
          POINT p,oldp,endp;
          unsigned int i,n;



          switch(theTool) {
                 case toolLine:
                        /* update the picture buffer */
                        if(framechanged) getdraw();
                        /* tell BGI to XOR the lines */
                        setlinestyle(SOLID_LINE,0,NORM_WIDTH);
                        setcolor(getmaxcolor());
                        setwritemode(XOR_PUT);

                        /* keep the start within the drwing area */
                        PointLimitRect(start,&drawrect);

                        /* as long as the mouse is down, draw a
                           rubber line from start to current mouse
                           position */
                        while(MouseDown(&p)) {
                               PointLimitRect(&p,&drawrect);
                               MouseOff();
                               line(start->x,start->y,p.x,p.y);
                               MouseOn();
                               do {
                                      i=MouseDown(&oldp);
                                      PointLimitRect(&oldp,&drawrect);
                               } while(i && p.x==oldp.x && p.y==oldp.y);
                               MouseOff();
                               line(start->x,start->y,p.x,p.y);
                               MouseOn();
                        }
                        /* make sure the end point is in the drawing area */
                        PointLimitRect(&p,&drawrect);
                        /* tell BGI to draw a real line */
                        setlinestyle(SOLID_LINE,0,NORM_WIDTH);
                        if(colour & 0x0001) setcolor(BLACK);
                        else setcolor(getmaxcolor());
                        setwritemode(COPY_PUT);

                        /* draw the line */
                        MouseOff();
                        line(start->x,start->y,p.x,p.y);
                        MouseOn();

                        /* say the picture has been changed */
                        framechanged=0xff;
                        break;
                 case toolErase:
                        /* update the picture buffer */
                        if(framechanged) getdraw();
```

```
        /* set the big or small eraser, depending upon
           the mouse button pressed */
        if(colour & 0x0001) n=theConfig.smalleraser;
        else n=theConfig.bigeraser;

        /* tell BGI to draw an XOR box */
        setlinestyle(SOLID_LINE,0,NORM_WIDTH);
        setfillstyle(SOLID_FILL,getmaxcolor());
        setcolor(getmaxcolor());
        setwritemode(XOR_PUT);

        /* make sure the start is in the drawing area */
        PointLimitRect(start,&drawrect);
        MouseOff();

        /* as long as the mouse is down, draw white
           boxes with a black cursor to indicate
           the position */
        while(MouseDown(&p)) {
                PointLimitRect(&p,&drawrect);
                endp.x=p.x+n;
                endp.y=p.y+n;
                PointLimitRect(&endp,&drawrect);
                bar(p.x,p.y,endp.x,endp.y);
                rectangle(p.x,p.y,endp.x,endp.y);
                do {
                        i=MouseDown(&oldp);
                        PointLimitRect(&oldp,&drawrect);
                } while(i && p.x==oldp.x && p.y==oldp.y);
                rectangle(p.x,p.y,endp.x,endp.y);
        }
        MouseOn();

        /* say the picture has been changed */
        framechanged=0xff;
        break;
case toolBox:
        /* update the picture buffer */
        if(framechanged) getdraw();

        /* tell BGI to draw an XOR box */
        setlinestyle(SOLID_LINE,0,NORM_WIDTH);
        setcolor(getmaxcolor());
        setwritemode(XOR_PUT);

        /* make sure the start is in the drawing area */
        PointLimitRect(start,&drawrect);

        /* while the mouse is down, draw a rubber
           box from the start to the current mouse
           position */
        while(MouseDown(&p)) {
                PointLimitRect(&p,&drawrect);
                MouseOff();
                if(goodrect(start->x,start->y,p.x,p.y))
                        rectangle(start->x,start->y,p.x,p.y);
                MouseOn();
                do {
                        i=MouseDown(&oldp);
                        PointLimitRect(&oldp,&drawrect);
                } while(i && p.x==oldp.x && p.y==oldp.y);
                MouseOff();
```

```
                if(goodrect(start->x,start->y,p.x,p.y))
                        rectangle(start->x,start->y,p.x,p.y);
                MouseOn();
        }

        /* make sure there was some displacement */
        if(!goodrect(start->x,start->y,p.x,p.y)) return(0);

        /* make sure the end point is in the drawing area */
        PointLimitRect(&p,&drawrect);
        fixRectDirection(start,&p);

        /* tell BGI to draw a real box in black or white,
           depending upon the mouse button used */
        setlinestyle(SOLID_LINE,0,NORM_WIDTH);
        if(colour & 0x0001) setcolor(BLACK);
        else setcolor(getmaxcolor());
        setwritemode(COPY_PUT);
        MouseOff();
        rectangle(start->x,start->y,p.x,p.y);
        MouseOn();
        /* say the picture has been changed */
        framechanged=0xff;
        break;
case toolEllipse:
        /* update the picture buffer */
        if(framechanged) getdraw();

        /* tell BGI to draw an XOR box */
        setlinestyle(SOLID_LINE,0,NORM_WIDTH);
        setcolor(getmaxcolor());
        setwritemode(XOR_PUT);

        /* make sure start is in drawing area */
        PointLimitRect(start,&drawrect);

        /* while the mouse is down, draw a rubber
           box from the start to the current mouse
           position */
        while(MouseDown(&p)) {
                PointLimitRect(&p,&drawrect);
                MouseOff();
                if(goodrect(start->x,start->y,p.x,p.y))
                    rectangle(start->x,start->y,p.x,p.y);
                MouseOn();
                do {
                        i=MouseDown(&oldp);
                        PointLimitRect(&oldp,&drawrect);
                } while(i && p.x==oldp.x && p.y==oldp.y);
                MouseOff();
                if(goodrect(start->x,start->y,p.x,p.y))
                    rectangle(start->x,start->y,p.x,p.y);
                MouseOn();
        }

        /* make sure there was some displacement */
        if(!goodrect(start->x,start->y,p.x,p.y)) return(0);

        /* make sure the end point is in the drawing area */
        PointLimitRect(&p,&drawrect);
        fixRectDirection(start,&p);

        /* tell BGI to draw a real ellipse in black or white,
           depending upon the mouse button used */
        setlinestyle(SOLID_LINE,0,NORM_WIDTH);
```

```
                            if(colour & 0x0001) setcolor(BLACK);
                            else setcolor(getmaxcolor());
                            setwritemode(COPY_PUT);
                            MouseOff();

                            ellipse(start->x+((p.x-start->x)/2),
                                start->y+((p.y-start->y)/2),0,360,
                                (p.x-start->x)/2,(p.y-start->y)/2);

                            MouseOn();

                            /* say the picture has been changed */
                            framechanged=0xff;
                            break;
                case toolUndo:
                            /* this is handled elsewhere */
                            break;
                case toolBrush:
                            /* update the picture buffer */
                            if(framechanged) getdraw();

                            /* make sure start is in drawing area */
                            PointLimitRect(start,&drawrect);

                            /* tell BGI to draw a real line */
                            setlinestyle(SOLID_LINE,0,NORM_WIDTH);
                            if(colour & 0x0001) setcolor(BLACK);
                            else setcolor(getmaxcolor());
                            setwritemode(COPY_PUT);

                            /* while the mouse is down, draw lines */
                            while(MouseDown(&p)) {
                                    PointLimitRect(&p,&drawrect);
                                    do {
                                            i=MouseDown(&oldp);
                                            PointLimitRect(&oldp,&drawrect);
                                    } while(i && p.x==oldp.x && p.y==oldp.y);
                                    MouseOff();
                                    line(p.x,p.y,oldp.x,oldp.y);
                                    MouseOn();
                            }

                            /* say the picture has been changed */
                            framechanged=0xff;
                            break;
                }
        }
}

/* ask if it's time to leave, set alive to false if it is */
doQuit()
{
        if(yesno("Want to quit?","")) alive=0;
}

/* do the About dialog */
doAboutBox()
{
        static char ln[3][25] = { "Tiny Paint",
                                "Copyright (c) 1903",
                                "Mother Martha's Software"
                                };

        TEXT tx[3];
```

```
        BUTTON ok,*bp;
        WINDOW w;
        RECT r;
        POINT p;
        BITMAP bmp;
        unsigned int rt,i,a=0xff;

        SetRect(&r,47,56,300,220);

        /* try to open the window */
        if(OpenWindow(&w,&r)) {
                /* add the icon */
                AddBitmap(&w,&bmp,r.left+((r.right-r.left)/2)-
                    (ImageWidth(ICON6)/2),r.top+96,ICON6,0x00,NULL,INACTIVE);

                /* add the Ok button */
                SetRect(&ok.frame,r.right-40,r.bottom-23,r.right-8,r.bottom-8);
                AddButton(&w,&ok,"Ok",ACTIVE);

                /* add the text */
                for(i=0;i<3;++i)
                    AddText(&w,&tx[i],r.left+((r.right-r.left)/2)-
                        ((strlen(ln[i])*8)/2),r.top+16+(i*20),ln[i],ACTIVE);

                /* wait for some activity */
                while(a) {
                        Keyboard(&w);
                        if(MouseDown(&p)) {
                                rt=whereMouse(&p,&w);
                                if(rt & inButton) {
                                        bp=findButton(&w,&p);
                                        trackButton(bp);
                                        if(bp==&ok) a=0;
                                }
                                else errorbeep();
                        }
                }
                CloseWindow(&w);
        } else errorbeep();
}

/* do a yes/no dialog */
yesno(l1,l2)
        char *l1,*l2;
{
        TEXT t1,t2;
        BUTTON ok,can,*bp;
        WINDOW w;
        RECT r;
        POINT p;
        BITMAP bmp;
        unsigned int rt,a=0xff,rv;

        SetRect(&r,48,50,350,125);

        /* try to open the window */
        if(OpenWindow(&w,&r)) {

                /* add the bitmap */
                AddBitmap(&w,&bmp,r.left+8,r.top+10,ICON6,0x00,NULL,INACTIVE);

                /* add the Ok button */
                SetRect(&ok.frame,r.left+48,r.bottom-23,r.left+80,r.bottom-8);
                AddButton(&w,&ok,"Ok",ACTIVE);
```

```
                    /* add the Cancel button */
                    SetRect(&can.frame,r.left+96,r.bottom-23,r.left+160,r.bottom-8);
                    AddButton(&w,&can,"Cancel",ACTIVE);

                    /* add the text */
                    AddText(&w,&t1,r.left+48,r.top+10,11,ACTIVE);
                    AddText(&w,&t2,r.left+48,r.top+10+MENULINEDEEP,12,ACTIVE);

                    /* wait for some activity */
                    while(a) {
                            Keyboard(&w);
                            if(MouseDown(&p)) {
                                    rt=whereMouse(&p,&w);
                                    if(rt & inButton) {
                                            bp=findButton(&w,&p);
                                            trackButton(bp);
                                            if(bp==&ok) rv=1;
                                            else if(bp==&can) rv=0;
                                            a=0;
                                    }
                                    else errorbeep();
                            }
                    }
                    CloseWindow(&w);
            } else errorbeep();
            return(rv);
}


/* this function will ask for a file name and then call doSave
   to actually save the file */
doSaveAs()
{
        char b[129],name[16];
        char drive[MAXDRIVE],dir[MAXDIR];

        /* don't save as if there's no file to save */
        if(!isfile) return(0);

        /* make a file specification */
        strcpy(b,filepath);
        strcat(b,"*.");
        strcat(b,"PCX");

        /* call chooseFile */
        if(chooseFile(b,name,48,48,theConfig.drivemap)) {

                /* reconstruct the file path */
                fnsplit(b,drive,dir,NULL,NULL);
                fnsplit(name,NULL,NULL,filename,NULL);
                fnmerge(filepath,drive,dir,NULL,NULL);

                /* save the file */
                doSave();
        }
}

/* this function saves the picture in memory to disk as a PCX file */
doSave()
{
        FILEINFO fi;
        char b[129],fn[16];

        /* don't save if there's no file */
```

```
        if(!isfile) return(0);

        /* if the frame has been changed, update the buffer before saving */
        if(framechanged) {
                getdraw();
                framechanged=0x00;
        }

        /* make sure there's a file name to save to */
        if(!strlen(filename)) {
                message("Can't save untitled file");
                return(0);
        }

        /* construct path and name */
        strcpy(b,filepath);
        strcat(b,filename);
        strcat(b,".");
        strcat(b,"PCX");

        strcpy(fn,filename);
        strcat(fn,".");
        strcat(fn,"PCX");

        /* set up FILEINFO struct */
        fi.width=width;
        fi.depth=depth;
        fi.bytes=bytes;
        fi.bits_per_pixel=1;
        fi.memory=(long)bytes*(long)depth;

        /* attempt to save the file */
        if(access(b,0)==0) {
                if(yesno("Overwrite existing file?",fn))
                        savefile(b,&fi,getline);
        } else savefile(b,&fi,getline);
}

/* this function closes the current picture */
doClose()
{
        /* if there's no picture, there's nothing to close */
        if(!isfile) return(0);

        /* banish the drawing area and toolbox */
        ClearScreen();
        screenwindow.head.next=NULL;

        /* free the picture buffer */
        freebuffer();

        if(linebuf != NULL) free(linebuf);
        linebuf=NULL;

        isfile=0x00;                            /* say we have no file in memory */

        file.item[0].name[0]=' ';       /* enable new */
        file.item[1].name[0]=' ';       /* enable open */
        file.item[2].name[0]='.';       /* disable close */
        file.item[3].name[0]='.';       /* disable save */
        file.item[4].name[0]='.';       /* disable save as */

        /* set up tools for the next picture */
        lastTool=0;
```

```c
        theTool=-1;
}

/* this function copies the appropriate part of the picture to the screen */
putdraw()
{
        int i;

        MouseOff();
        for(i=0;i<ddepth;++i)
            memcpy(MK_FP(SCREENSEG,SCREENTBL[TOPDRAW+i]+
                    pixels2bytes(LEFTDRAW)),
                    getline(i+vpScroll.cur)+hpScroll.cur,dbytes);
        MouseOn();
}

/* this function copies the drawing area to the appropriate part
   of the picture buffer */
getdraw()
{
        int i;

        MouseOff();
        for(i=0;i<ddepth;++i) {
                memcpy(linebuf,getline(i+vpScroll.cur),bytes);
                memcpy(linebuf+hpScroll.cur,
                    MK_FP(SCREENSEG,SCREENTBL[TOPDRAW+i]+
                    pixels2bytes(LEFTDRAW)),dbytes);
                putline(linebuf,i+vpScroll.cur);
        }
        MouseOn();
}

/* write one line to the picture buffer */
putline(p,n)
        char *p;
        int n;
{
        if(thepicture != NULL)
            memcpy(farPtr(thepicture,(long)n*(long)bytes),p,bytes);
}

/* get a pointer to line n of the picture buffer */
char *getline(n)
        int n;
{
        if(thepicture != NULL) return(farPtr(thepicture,(long)n*(long)bytes));
        else return(NULL);
}

/* allocate a picture buffer n bytes long */
getbuffer(n)
        long n;
{
        thepicture=NULL;
        if((thepicture=farmalloc(n)) == NULL) return(0);
        else return(1);
}

/* free the current picture buffer */
freebuffer()
{
```

```
                if(thepicture != NULL) {
                        farfree(thepicture);
                        thepicture=NULL;
                }
        }

        /* show a message */
        message(s)
                char *s;
        {
                TEXT t;
                BUTTON ok,*bp;
                WINDOW w;
                RECT r;
                POINT p;
                BITMAP bmp;
                unsigned int rt,a=0xff;

                SetRect(&r,48,50,350,125);

                arrowCursor();

                /* open a window for the message */
                if(OpenWindow(&w,&r)) {

                        /* add an icon */
                        AddBitmap(&w,&bmp,r.left+8,r.top+10,ICON6,0x00,NULL,INACTIVE);

                        /* add the Ok button */
                        SetRect(&ok.frame,r.right-40,r.bottom-23,r.right-8,r.bottom-8);
                        AddButton(&w,&ok,"Ok",ACTIVE);

                        /* add the messafe */
                        AddText(&w,&t,r.left+48,r.top+10,s,ACTIVE);

                        /* wait for activity */
                        while(a) {
                                Keyboard(&w);
                                if(MouseDown(&p)) {
                                        rt=whereMouse(&p,&w);
                                        if(rt & inButton) {
                                                bp=findButton(&w,&p);
                                                trackButton(bp);
                                                if(bp==&ok)  a=0;
                                        } else errorbeep();
                                }
                        }
                        CloseWindow(&w);
                } else errorbeep();
        }
        char *farPtr(p,l) /* return a far pointer p + l */
                char *p;
                long l;
        {
                unsigned int seg,off;

                seg = FP_SEG(p);
                off = FP_OFF(p);
                seg += (off / 16);
                off &= 0x000f;
                off += (unsigned int)(l & 0x000fL);
                seg += (l / 16L);
                p = MK_FP(seg,off);
                return(p);
```

```
}

/* return true if the rectangle has some volume */
goodrect(l,t,r,b)
        int l,t,r,b;
{
        if(l != r && t != b) return(1);
        else return(0);
}

/* swap two integers */
void swap(a,b)
        int *a,*b;
{
        int t;

        t=*a;
        *a=*b;
        *b=t;
}

/* displace RECT r by POINT p */
DisplaceRect(r,p)
        RECT *r;
        POINT *p;
{
        r->left+=p->x;
        r->right+=p->x;
        r->top+=p->y;
        r->bottom+=p->y;
}

/* make sure POINT r1 is above and to the left of POINT r2 */
fixRectDirection(r1,r2)
        POINT *r1,*r2;
{
        if(r1->x > r2->x) swap(&r1->x,&r2->x);
        if(r1->y > r2->y) swap(&r1->y,&r2->y);
}

/* restrict POINT p to RECT r */
PointLimitRect(p,r)
        POINT *p;
        RECT *r;
{
        if(p->x < r->left) p->x=r->left;
        if(p->x >= r->right) p->x=r->right;
        if(p->y < r->top) p->y=r->top;
        if(p->y >= r->bottom) p->y=r->bottom;
}

/* this function creates a new (blank) picture */
doNew()
{
        WINDOW w;
        POINT p;
        BUTTON ok,can,*bp;
        TEXT tx,vertx,hortx;
        EDITFIELD ver,hor,*ep;
        RECT r;
        char verstr[8],horstr[8];
        unsigned int rt,a=0xff;
```

```
/* there's currently an open picture, return */
if(isfile) return(0);

SetRect(&r,48,48,270,140);

/* open a window to get parameters with */
if(OpenWindow(&w,&r)) {

        /* start width default dimensions */
        width=theConfig.defwidth;
        depth=theConfig.defdepth;

        /* put them in buffers */
        sprintf(horstr,"%d",width);
        sprintf(verstr,"%d",depth);

        /* add a title */
        AddText(&w,&tx,r.left+8,r.top+10,"New File",ACTIVE);

        /* add the EDITFIELD names */
        AddText(&w,&hortx,r.left+8,r.top+30,"Horizontal",ACTIVE);
        AddText(&w,&vertx,r.left+8,r.top+46,"Vertical",ACTIVE);

        /* add the EDITFIELDs */
        AddEditField(&w,&hor,r.left+104,r.top+30,5,horstr,
            numbertrap,ACTIVE);
        AddEditField(&w,&ver,r.left+104,r.top+46,5,verstr,
            numbertrap,ACTIVE);

        /* add Ok button */
        SetRect(&ok.frame,r.right-40,r.bottom-23,r.right-8,r.bottom-8);
        AddButton(&w,&ok,"Ok",ACTIVE);

        /* add Cancel button */
        SetRect(&can.frame,r.right-120,r.bottom-23,r.right-56,r.bottom-8);
        AddButton(&w,&can,"Cancel",ACTIVE);

        /* wait for activity */
        while(a) {
                Keyboard(&w);
                if(MouseDown(&p)) {

                        rt=whereMouse(&p,&w);
                        if(rt & inButton) {
                                bp=findButton(&w,&p);
                                trackButton(bp);
                                if(bp==&ok) a=0;
                                else if(bp==&can) a=0;
                        }
                        else if(rt & inEditField) {
                                ep=findEditfield(&w,&p);

                                trackEditfield(ep);
                                drawEditfield(ep);
                        }
                        else errorbeep();
                }
        }
        CloseWindow(&w);

        /* if the Ok button was clicked... */
        if(bp==&ok) {

                /* round width up to nearest byte */
                width=pixels2bytes(atoi(horstr))<<3;
```

```
                                /* get depth */
                                depth=atoi(verstr);

                                /* check limits */
                                if(width > 31 && width < 32767 &&
                                    depth > 31 && depth < 32767) {
                                        bytes=pixels2bytes(width);

                                        /* ask for memory to hold the picture */
                                        if(getbuffer((long)bytes*(long)depth)) {

                                                /* set up for a loaded picture */
                                                if(setopen()) {
                                                        isfile=0xff;
                                                        filename[0]=0;
                                                        clearbuffer();
                                                        putdraw();
                                                }
                                                else {
                                                        doClose();
                                                        message("Error allocating memory");
                                                }
                                        } else message("Error allocationg buffer");
                                } else message("Bad size values");
                        }
                } else errorbeep();
}

/* return true if c is a digit */
numbertrap(c)
        int c;
{
        if(c < '0' || c > '9') return(0);
        else return(c);
}
/* fill the current picture with white - used by doNew */
clearbuffer()
{
        char *p;
        int i;

        if(isfile) {
                if((p=malloc(bytes)) != NULL) {
                        memset(p,0xff,bytes);
                        for(i=0;i<depth;++i) putline(p,i);
                        free(p);
                }
        }
}

/* this function attempts to open a picture */
doOpen()
{
        char b[129],name[16];
        char drive[MAXDRIVE],dir[MAXDIR],ext[MAXEXT];

        /* if a picture is already open, return */
        if(isfile) return(0);

        /* construct a file path */
        strcpy(b,filepath);
        strcat(b,"*.");
```

```
                strcat(b,"PCX");
                setwritemode(COPY_PUT);

                /* get a file name */
                if(chooseFile(b,name,48,48,theConfig.drivemap)) {

                        /* reconstruct the file path */
                        fnsplit(b,drive,dir,NULL,NULL);
                        fnsplit(name,NULL,NULL,filename,ext);
                        fnmerge(b,drive,dir,filename,ext);

                        fnmerge(filepath,drive,dir,NULL,NULL);

                        /* get the picture */
                        if(loadfile(b,putline)) {

                                /* set up for an open picture */
                                if(setopen()) {
                                        isfile=0xff; /* say file in memory */
                                        putdraw();
                                }
                                else {
                                        doClose();
                                        message("Error allocating memory");
                                }
                        } else message("Error loading file");
                }
        }

/* handle everything to say a file is open */
setopen()
{
int i;

/* allocate the line buffer */
if((linebuf=malloc(bytes*2)) == NULL) return(0);

file.item[0].name[0]='.';       /* disable new */
file.item[1].name[0]='.';       /* disable open */
file.item[2].name[0]=' ';       /* enable close */
file.item[3].name[0]=' ';       /* enable save */
file.item[4].name[0]=' ';       /* enable save as */

/* get the drawing area width */
dwidth=1+getmaxx()-(LEFTDRAW+RIGHTDRAW);
if(dwidth > width) dwidth=width;

/* get the drawing area depth */
ddepth=getmaxy()-(TOPDRAW+BOTTOMDRAW);
if(ddepth > depth) ddepth=depth;

/* clear the SCROLLBARs - quick 'n nasty */
memset((char *)&vpScroll,0,sizeof(SCROLLBAR));
memset((char *)&hpScroll,0,sizeof(SCROLLBAR));

/* if there's a vertical scrollbar needed, add it
   to the screen */
if(ddepth < depth)
        AddVertScroll(&screenwindow,&vpScroll,
                LEFTDRAW+dwidth,TOPDRAW-1,ddepth+1,
                0,depth-ddepth,0,ACTIVE);

/* if there's a horizontal scrollbar needed, add it
   to the screen */
```

```
if(dwidth < width)
        AddHorScroll(&screenwindow,&hpScroll,
                LEFTDRAW-1,TOPDRAW+ddepth,dwidth/*+2*/+1,
                0,pixels2bytes(width-dwidth)/*-1*/,0,ACTIVE);

/* if both scroll bars are visible, put a white box in
   the corner where they meet */
if(ddepth < depth && dwidth < width) {
        setfillstyle(SOLID_FILL,getmaxcolor());
        setlinestyle(SOLID_LINE,0,NORM_WIDTH);
        setcolor(BLACK);
        bar(vpScroll.frame.left,vpScroll.frame.bottom,
                vpScroll.frame.left+15,vpScroll.frame.bottom+15);
        rectangle(vpScroll.frame.left,vpScroll.frame.bottom,
                vpScroll.frame.left+15,vpScroll.frame.bottom+15);
}

/* work out the number of bytes in a line of the drawing area */
dbytes=pixels2bytes(dwidth);

/* set up the drawing rectangle and draw a frame
   around the drawing area */
MouseOff();
setlinestyle(SOLID_LINE,0,NORM_WIDTH);
setcolor(BLACK);
SetRect(&drawrect,LEFTDRAW,TOPDRAW,LEFTDRAW+dwidth-1,
    TOPDRAW+ddepth-1);
        SetRect(&outdraw,drawrect.left-ODPAD,drawrect.top-ODPAD,
                drawrect.right+ODPAD,drawrect.bottom+ODPAD);
        rectangle(drawrect.left-1,drawrect.top-1,drawrect.right+1,
                drawrect.bottom+1);
        MouseOn();

        /* add the BITMAP objects (the toolbox) to the screen */
        for(i=0;i<MAXPAINTICONS;++i)
                AddBitmap(&screenwindow,&painticon[i],
                        TOOLBOXLEFT+((ImageWidth(p_icon[i]))*(i&1)),
                        TOOLBOXTOP+ ((ImageDepth(p_icon[i]))*(i/2)),
                        p_icon[i],0x00,NULL,ACTIVE);

        /* draw a box around the tools */
        MouseOff();
        rectangle(TOOLBOXLEFT-1,TOOLBOXTOP-1,
                TOOLBOXLEFT+(2*ImageWidth(p_icon[0])),
                        TOOLBOXTOP+((MAXPAINTICONS/2)*ImageWidth(p_icon[0])));
        MouseOn();

        /* select the first tool */
        selectTool(0);

        /* say the frame does not need updating right away */
        framechanged=0x00;
        return(1);
}

/* handle the undo function */
tbUndo()
{
        putdraw();
        selectTool(lastTool);
}
```

```
/* select one of the paint box tools */
selectTool(n)
        int n;
{
        /* unselect the previous tool */
        if(theTool != -1) {
                painticon[theTool].select=0x00;
                drawBitmap(&painticon[theTool]);
                lastTool=theTool;
        }

        /* select the new tool */
        theTool=n;
        painticon[theTool].select=0xff;
        drawBitmap(&painticon[theTool]);

        /* if the tool is undo, reselect the previous tool */
        if(theTool==toolUndo) tbUndo();
}

loadfile(s,putl)    /* load a PCX file. call putl to stash the lines */
        char *s;
        int (*putl)();
{
        FILEINFO f;
        int r=0;

        waitCursor();

        /* get the file information */
        if(getFileInfo(&f,s) && f.bits_per_pixel==1) {

                /* set the global picture variables. note that
                   the width is tounded up to the nearest byte */
                width=pixels2bytes(f.width)<<3;
                depth=f.depth;
                bytes=f.bytes;

                /* get a buffer and load the file */
                if(getBuffer(f.memory)) r=loadPcxfile(s,&f,putl);
        }

        if(!r) freebuffer();
        arrowCursor();
        return(r);
}

/* load PCX data into memory */
loadPcxfile(s,fi,putl)
        char *s;
        FILEINFO *fi;
        int (*putl)();
{
        FILE *fp;
        PCXHEAD h;
        char *lb;
        int i,r=1;

        /* allocate a scratch line buffer */
        if((lb=malloc(fi->bytes*4)) == NULL) return(0);

        /* open the file */
        if((fp=fopen(s,"rb")) != NULL) {
```

```
                          /* read the header */
                          if(fread((char *)&h,1,sizeof(PCXHEAD),fp)==sizeof(PCXHEAD)) {

                                  /* check its authenticity */
                                  if(h.manufacturer==0x0a) {

                                          /* read each line... */
                                          for(i=0;i<fi->depth;++i) {
                                                  if(readPcxLine(lb,fp,fi->bytes)
                                                      != fi->bytes) {
                                                          r=0;
                                                          break;
                                                  }

                                                  /* ...clear off any stray bits... */
                                                  cleanline(lb,fi->bytes,fi->width);

                                                  /* ...and save it in memory */
                                                  (putl)(lb,i);
                                          }
                                  } else r=0;
                          } else r=0;
                          fclose(fp);
                  } else r=0;

                  /* free the scratch buffer */
                  free(lb);

                  return(r);
        }

/* read and decode a PCX line into p */
ReadPcxLine(p,fp,bytes)
        char *p;
        FILE *fp;
        int bytes;
{
        int n=0,c,i;

        memset(p,0,bytes);
        do {
                c=fgetc(fp) & 0xff;
                if((c & 0xc0) == 0xc0) {
                        i=c & 0x3f;
                        c=fgetc(fp);
                        while(i--) p[n++]=c;
                }
                else p[n++]=c;
        } while(n < bytes);
        return(n);
}

/* clear off any stray bits at the right end of a line of
   bitmap data */
cleanline(p,bytes,width)
        char *p;
        int bytes,width;
{
        int i,n;

        n=bytes<<3;
```

```
                        for(i=width;i<n;++i) p[i>>3] |= (0x80 >> (i & 0x0007));
        }

        /* get information about a PCX file */
        getFileInfo(f,s)
                FILEINFO *f;
                char *s;
        {
                FILE *fp;
                PCXHEAD pcx;
                int r=0;

                /* clear out the FILEINFO */
                memset((char *)f,0,sizeof(FILEINFO));

                /* open the file */
                if((fp=fopen(s,"rb")) != NULL) {

                        /* read the header and check it */
                        if(fread((char *)&pcx,1,128,fp)==128 &&
                           pcx.manufacturer==0x0a) {

                                /* extract the information for the header */
                                f->width = (pcx.xmax-pcx.xmin)+1;
                                f->depth = (pcx.ymax-pcx.ymin)+1;
                                f->bytes = pcx.bytes_per_line;

                                if(pcx.bits_per_pixel==1)
                                        f->bits_per_pixel=pcx.colour_planes;
                                else f->bits_per_pixel=pcx.bits_per_pixel;
                                if(f->bits_per_pixel==8)
                                        f->memory=(long)f->width*(long)f->depth;
                                else f->memory=(long)f->bytes*(long)f->depth*
                                        (long)f->bits_per_pixel;
                                r=1;
                        }
                        fclose(fp);
                }
                return(r);
        }

        /* save a picture to a PCX file */
        savefile(s,fi,getl)
                char *s;
                FILEINFO *fi;
                char *(*getl)();
        {
                PCXHEAD h;
                FILE *fp;
                char *p;
                int i,r=0;

                /* attempt to create the file */
                if((fp=fopen(s,"wb")) == NULL) return(0);

                waitCursor();

                /* clear out the PCX header */
                memset((char *)&h,0,sizeof(PCXHEAD));

                /* fill it in */
                h.manufacturer=0x0a;
                h.encoding=1;
```

```
           h.xmin=h.ymin=0;
           h.xmax=fi->width-1;
           h.ymax=fi->depth-1;
           h.palette_type=1;
           h.bits_per_pixel=1;
           h.version=2;
           h.colour_planes=1;
           h.bytes_per_line=fi->bytes;


           /* write the header */
           fwrite((char *)&h,1,sizeof(PCXHEAD),fp);
           /* write each line of the picture */
           for(i=0;i<fi->depth;++i) {
                   p=(getl)(i);
                   if(p != NULL) {
                           invert(p,fi->bytes);
                           if(writePcxLine(p,fp,fi->bytes) != 0) {
                                   r=0;
                                   break;
                           } else r=1;
                           invert(p,fi->bytes);
                   }
                   else {
                           r=0;
                           break;
                   }
           }

           arrowCursor();
           fclose(fp);
           return(r);
}


/* compress one line of raw bitmapped information with PCX encoding */
writePcxLine(p,fp,n)
           char *p;
           FILE *fp;
           int n;
{
           unsigned int i=0,j=0,t=0;

           do {
                   i=0;
                   while((p[t+i]==p[t+i+1]) && ((t+i) < n) && (i<63))++i;
                   if(i>0) {
                           fputc(i | 0xc0,fp);
                           fputc(~p[t],fp);
                           t+=i;
                           j+=2;
                   }
                   else {
                           if(((~p[t]) & 0xc0)==0xc0) {
                                   fputc(0xc1,fp);
                                   ++j;
                           }
                           fputc(~p[t++],fp);
                           ++j;
                   }
           } while(t<n);
           return(ferror(fp));
}
```

```
/* invert n bytes starting at p */
invert(p,n)
        char *p;
        int n;
{
        int i;

        for(i=0;i<n;++i) *p++^=0xff;
}
```

The source code in Fig. 11-2 is complete save for one element. The six icons forming Tiny Paint's albeit abbreviated toolbox aren't contained in the basic source file. They're awkward enough to require a header of their own. The source for Tiny Paint expects to find them in TPAINT.H (see Fig. 11-3).

In the actual Desktop Paint package, the small bitmaps aren't dealt with as C source at all. As I've discussed earlier, they're handled as linkable object module files. It's a bit tricky to print an object module in a book, however. If you decide to type TPAINT.C in from the foregoing two listings, you'll require the icons in their C language form.

As an aside, having to type in Fig. 11-3 is among the best arguments for ordering the companion source code disk for this book.

```
char ICON1[] = {
0x20,0x00,0x20,0x00,0xff,0xff,0xff,0xff,
0xfd,0x80,0x00,0x00,0x00,0xcc,0x80,0x00,
0x70,0x00,0xfb,0x80,0x00,0x78,0x00,0x8f,
0x80,0x00,0x7c,0x00,0x86,0x80,0x00,0x7e,
0x00,0xff,0x80,0x00,0x3f,0x00,0x95,0x80,
0x00,0x1f,0x80,0x80,0x90,0x80,0x0f,0xc0,
0xfd,0x88,0x40,0x07,0xe0,0xcc,0x84,0x20,
0x03,0xf0,0xfb,0x82,0x10,0x01,0xf0,0x8f,
0x81,0x08,0x00,0xf0,0x86,0x90,0x84,0x00,
0x00,0xff,0x88,0x42,0x00,0x00,0x95,0x84,
0x21,0x00,0x00,0x80,0x82,0x10,0x80,0x00,
0xfd,0x81,0x08,0x40,0x00,0xcc,0x80,0x84,
0x20,0x00,0xfb,0x80,0x42,0x10,0x00,0x8f,
0x80,0x21,0x08,0x00,0x86,0x80,0x10,0x84,
0x00,0xff,0x80,0x08,0x42,0x00,0x95,0x80,
0x04,0x21,0x00,0x80,0x80,0x02,0x10,0x80,
0xfd,0x80,0x01,0x08,0x40,0xcc,0x80,0x00,
0x04,0x20,0xfb,0x80,0x00,0x00,0x10,0x8f,
0x80,0x00,0x00,0x00,0x86,0x80,0x00,0x00,
0x00,0xff,0x80,0x00,0x00,0x00,0x95,0x80,
0x00,0x00,0x00,0x80,0xff,0xff,0xff,0xff,
0xfd
};

char ICON2[] = {
0x20,0x00,0x20,0x00,0xff,0xff,0xff,0xff,
0xfd,0x80,0x40,0x00,0xd5,0xcc,0x80,0x20,
0x01,0xaa,0xfb,0x80,0x10,0x03,0x55,0x8f,
0x80,0x08,0x06,0xab,0x86,0x80,0x04,0x0d,
0x57,0xff,0x80,0x02,0x1a,0xaf,0x95,0x80,
0x01,0x35,0x5f,0x80,0x80,0x02,0x9a,0xbf,
0xfd,0xc0,0x05,0x4d,0x7f,0xcc,0xa0,0x0a,
0xa6,0xff,0xfb,0xd4,0x15,0x13,0xff,0x8f,
```

11-3 The icons for Tiny Paint—TPAINT.H.

```
0xaa,0xaa,0x09,0xff,0x86,0x95,0x54,0x04,
0xff,0xff,0x8a,0xac,0x04,0x7f,0x95,0x85,
0x5c,0x02,0x3e,0x80,0x82,0xbc,0x02,0x1c,
0xfd,0x81,0x78,0x04,0x08,0xcc,0x80,0xf8,
0x04,0x04,0xfb,0x82,0x78,0x08,0x02,0x8f,
0x87,0x3e,0x08,0x01,0x86,0x8d,0x9f,0xf0,
0x00,0xff,0x9a,0xcf,0xc0,0x00,0x95,0xb5,
0x63,0x00,0x00,0x80,0xea,0xb0,0x00,0x00,
0xfd,0xd5,0x78,0x00,0x00,0xcc,0xaa,0xfc,
0x00,0x00,0xfb,0xd5,0xfe,0x00,0x00,0x8f,
0xab,0xff,0x00,0x00,0x86,0xd7,0xff,0x80,
0x00,0xff,0xaf,0xff,0x40,0x00,0x95,0xdf,
0xfe,0x20,0x00,0x80,0xff,0xff,0xff,0xff,
0xfd,
};

char ICON3[] = {
0x20,0x00,0x20,0x00,0xff,0xff,0xff,0xff,
0xfd,0x80,0x00,0x00,0x00,0xcb,0x80,0x00,
0x00,0x00,0xfb,0x80,0x00,0x00,0x00,0x8f,
0x80,0x00,0x00,0x00,0x86,0x80,0x00,0x00,
0x00,0xff,0x80,0x00,0x00,0x00,0x95,0x81,
0xff,0xff,0xc0,0x80,0x81,0x00,0x00,0x40,
0xfd,0x81,0x00,0x00,0x40,0xcb,0x81,0x00,
0x00,0x40,0xfb,0x81,0x00,0x00,0x40,0x8f,
0x81,0x00,0x00,0x40,0x86,0x81,0x00,0x00,
0x40,0xff,0x81,0x00,0x00,0x40,0x95,0x81,
0x00,0x00,0x40,0x80,0x81,0x00,0x00,0x40,
0xfd,0x81,0x00,0x00,0x40,0xcb,0x81,0x00,
0x00,0x40,0xfb,0x81,0x00,0x00,0x40,0x8f,
0x81,0x00,0x00,0x40,0x86,0x81,0x00,0x00,
0x40,0xff,0x81,0x00,0x00,0x40,0x95,0x81,
0x00,0x00,0x40,0x80,0x81,0x00,0x00,0x40,
0xfd,0x81,0xff,0xff,0xc0,0xcb,0x80,0x00,
0x00,0x00,0xfb,0x80,0x00,0x00,0x00,0x8f,
0x80,0x00,0x00,0x00,0x86,0x80,0x00,0x00,
0x00,0xff,0x80,0x00,0x00,0x00,0x95,0x80,
0x00,0x00,0x00,0x80,0xff,0xff,0xff,0xff,
0xfd
};

char ICON4[]={
0x20,0x00,0x20,0x00,0xff,0xff,0xff,0xff,
0xfd,0x80,0x00,0x00,0x00,0xca,0x80,0x00,
0x00,0x00,0xfb,0x80,0x00,0x00,0x00,0x8f,
0x80,0x07,0xf0,0x00,0x86,0x80,0x18,0x0c,
0x00,0xff,0x80,0x60,0x03,0x00,0x95,0x80,
0x80,0x00,0x80,0x80,0x81,0x00,0x00,0x40,
0xfd,0x82,0x00,0x00,0x20,0xca,0x82,0x00,
0x00,0x20,0xfb,0x84,0x00,0x00,0x10,0x8f,
0x84,0x00,0x00,0x10,0x86,0x88,0x00,0x00,
0x08,0xff,0x88,0x00,0x00,0x08,0x95,0x88,
0x00,0x00,0x08,0x80,0x88,0x00,0x00,0x08,
0xfd,0x88,0x00,0x00,0x08,0xca,0x88,0x00,
0x00,0x08,0xfb,0x88,0x00,0x00,0x08,0x8f,
0x84,0x00,0x00,0x10,0x86,0x84,0x00,0x00,
0x10,0xff,0x82,0x00,0x00,0x20,0x95,0x82,
0x00,0x00,0x20,0x80,0x81,0x00,0x00,0x40,
0xfd,0x80,0x80,0x00,0x80,0xca,0x80,0x60,
0x03,0x00,0xfb,0x80,0x18,0x0c,0x00,0x8f,
0x80,0x07,0xf0,0x00,0x86,0x80,0x00,0x00,
0x00,0xff,0x80,0x00,0x00,0x00,0x95,0x80,
```

```
0x00,0x00,0x00,0x80,0xff,0xff,0xff,0xff,
0xfd
};

char ICON5[]= {
0x20,0x00,0x20,0x00,0xff,0xff,0xff,0xff,
0xfd,0x80,0x00,0x00,0x00,0xc9,0x80,0x00,
0x00,0x00,0xfb,0x80,0x00,0x00,0x00,0x8f,
0x80,0x00,0x00,0x00,0x86,0xb8,0x0e,0x70,
0x1c,0xff,0xb8,0x0e,0x78,0x1c,0x95,0xb8,
0x0e,0x7c,0x1c,0x80,0xb8,0x0e,0x7e,0x1c,
0xfd,0xb8,0x0e,0x7f,0x1c,0xc9,0xb8,0x0e,
0x77,0x9c,0xfb,0xb8,0x0e,0x73,0xdc,0x8f,
0xb8,0x0e,0x71,0xfc,0x86,0xb8,0x0e,0x70,
0xfc,0xff,0xbc,0x1e,0x70,0x7c,0x95,0x9f,
0xfc,0x70,0x3c,0x80,0x8f,0xf8,0x70,0x1c,
0xfd,0x80,0x00,0x00,0x00,0xc9,0xbf,0xf0,
0x3f,0xf0,0xfb,0xbf,0xf8,0x7f,0xf8,0x8f,
0xb8,0x3c,0xf0,0x3c,0x86,0xb8,0x1c,0xe0,
0x1c,0xff,0xb8,0x1c,0xe0,0x1c,0x95,0xb8,
0x1c,0xe0,0x1c,0x80,0xb8,0x1c,0xe0,0x1c,
0xfd,0xb8,0x1c,0xe0,0x1c,0xc9,0xb8,0x1c,
0xe0,0x1c,0xfb,0xb8,0x3c,0xf0,0x3c,0x8f,
0xbf,0xf8,0x7f,0xf8,0x86,0xbf,0xf0,0x3f,
0xf0,0xff,0x80,0x00,0x00,0x00,0x95,0x80,
0x00,0x00,0x00,0x80,0xff,0xff,0xff,0xff,
0xfd
};

char ICON6[] = {
0x20,0x00,0x20,0x00,0xff,0xff,0xff,0xff,
0xfd,0x80,0x00,0x00,0x00,0xc9,0x80,0x00,
0x60,0x00,0xfb,0x80,0x00,0x90,0x00,0x8f,
0x80,0x00,0x90,0x00,0x86,0x80,0x00,0x90,
0x00,0xff,0x80,0x00,0x90,0x00,0x95,0x80,
0x00,0xa0,0x00,0x80,0x80,0x00,0x50,0x00,
0xfd,0x80,0x00,0xa0,0x00,0xc9,0x80,0x00,
0x50,0x00,0xfb,0x80,0x00,0xa0,0x00,0x8f,
0x80,0x00,0xa0,0x00,0x86,0x80,0x01,0x50,
0x00,0xff,0x80,0x02,0xa8,0x00,0x95,0x80,
0x05,0x54,0x00,0x80,0x80,0x0a,0xaa,0x00,
0xfd,0x80,0x10,0x01,0x00,0xc9,0x80,0x10,
0x01,0x00,0xfb,0x80,0x1f,0xff,0x00,0x8f,
0x80,0x10,0x01,0x00,0x86,0x80,0x1f,0xff,
0x00,0xff,0x80,0x1b,0xff,0x00,0x95,0x80,
0x1a,0xff,0x00,0x80,0x80,0x1e,0xbf,0x00,
0xfd,0x80,0x1e,0xbf,0x00,0xc9,0x80,0x37,
0xff,0x00,0xfb,0x80,0x3f,0xfe,0x00,0x8f,
0x80,0x55,0x54,0x00,0x86,0x80,0xaa,0xa8,
0x00,0xff,0x80,0x00,0x00,0x00,0x95,0x80,
0x00,0x00,0x00,0x80,0xff,0xff,0xff,0xff,
0xfd
};
```

Once you get all the source code for Tiny Paint into its respective files, you will need a project file to compile and link it, as it must be linked to GUI.LIB.

Basic program structures

The functions of Tiny Paint are few enough to be easily comprehensible with only a brief glance at the toolbox and menus. It will allow you to load and save monochrome PCX files. You can scroll the files around if you load pictures bigger than the drawing area. You can draw lines, rectangles, ellipses, and free-form curves in the drawing area, and these will become part of the picture. There's also an undo tool that will remove the effects of your most recent drawing from your picture.

Paint programs are actually a lot less clever than they seem. The process of drawing on the screen and having the things you draw become part of an image file is really just a fairly crude bit of memory manipulation. Much of the process involves moving data between two buffers—the drawing area of the screen, and the buffer holding the lines of image data composing the picture being worked on.

Whenever you draw something in the drawing area of Tiny Paint, the drawing function sets a flag to say that the screen has been changed. If you go to draw something else, if you scroll the screen, or if you save the file, the contents of the drawing area are copied from the screen into the image buffer holding the picture. As such, the new data overwrites the existing data, and your recent bit of drawing becomes part of the picture.

The undo function works in reverse. If you click on the Undo icon, the appropriate portion of the image is copied from the image buffer back to the screen, wiping out the most recent thing you've drawn.

The code copying the lines of image data between the screen and the image buffer must work very quickly such that its operation doesn't cause a noticeable wait between drawing actions. This isn't actually all that hard to arrange so long as everything can be handled using bytes rather than being done one bit at a time. The screen buffer can be addressed using the SCREENTBL array discussed in Chapter 2. The image buffer can be addressed as a series of offsets from the pointer defining it.

This can be a bit of a problem if you go to paint pictures that unpack into more than 64K. This isn't something dealt with in Chapter 6 during the discussion of bitmaps because large bitmaps aren't suitable for use with the Turbo C putimage function. The drawing area of the screen isn't handled with putimage for reasons of speed; and, as such, it's possible to work with any picture you have enough memory to contain.

The farPtr function (look at Fig. 11-2) deals with the problem of working with pictures occupying more than 64K of memory. It adds a long to a pointer, something not supposed to be done under C. (I'll discuss it a bit later in this chapter.)

Note that Tiny Paint always rounds the horizontal dimensions of files up to the nearest byte to allow all the image data read from or written to the screen to be handled in full bytes.

There are several important data structures used in Tiny Paint. The PCX-HEAD structure was discussed in detail in Chapter 6. The CONFIG structure is an example of a very useful practice—putting all the configurable values in an application in one struct. If you want to allow your users to configure the software you write—in this case, to change things like the drive map or the default new image dimensions—it's a great deal easier to handle if they're all in one place.

The FILEINFO structure is a standardized way of representing the pertinent information about an image file. Having come up with a FILEINFO structure describing a file you want to load, it's fairly easy to allocate a buffer for it. If fi is a FILEINFO, the size of the buffer needed to contain the picture is (long)fi. bytes*(long)fi.depth. It's important to cast these values to long before they're multiplied together such that the result won't be truncated into an int if it turns out to be bigger than 64K.

Many of the functions comprising Tiny Paint have prototypes. There are several good reasons for doing this, even if you don't usually bother with them. All the functions called by menus must be defined somewhere before their addresses can be used in the menu definitions. This is also true of functions passed around as function pointers. Finally, a few functions (such as the venerable swap) might crash your system pretty colorfully if you pass them the wrong sorts of argument. Calling swap(a,b) rather than swap(&a,&b) is a nearly foolproof way to bring DOS to its knees.

A few objects are referred to throughout Tiny Paint. For example, thePicture points to the current image buffer, as allocated by farmalloc. The linebuf pointer points to a buffer long enough to contain one line of the image.

The drawrect is a RECT defining the periphery of the screen area where drawing is permitted. The size of this area will vary; it can be quite small if the image you're working with is smaller than the screen dimensions, and it will be almost as large as the screen—allowing for the toolbox, the menu bar, and two scroll bars—if the image is larger than the screen.

A second RECT object called outdraw defines an area four pixels larger in each direction than the area contained by drawrect. It's used when Tiny Paint wants to decide whether a mouse click is intended to begin a drawing operation. Someone trying to draw a rectangle from the upper left corner of the drawing area, for example, might actually start a pixel or two outside the area defined by drawrect.

The six bitmaps ICON1 through ICON6 are the small icons forming the toolbox. The ICON6 bitmap also serves as an alert icon and a bit of window dressing around the program. This saves typing in another large swath of hex data in TPAINT.H.

The alive value is true so long as the program is running. Setting alive false is the correct way to have Tiny Paint return to DOS.

The main function

The main function of Tiny Paint does pretty well what it has done in the other examples in this book. It initializes the graphical user interface, clears the graphics screen, and sets up the menus. It also sets up a filepath buffer for use with chooseFile, as discussed in Chapter 10. With everything ready to roll, it falls into a do loop from which all subsequent painting will spring.

The do loop of main repeatedly calls dispatchMenuItem from GUI.LIB to handle any pending Alt-key combinations. It then uses MouseDown to check for activity from the mouse's buttons. Under Tiny Paint, the left button draws in black and the right button draws in white, so the value returned by MouseDown is retained. The POINT that MouseDown fills is passed to whereMouse to determine where on the screen the mouse has been clicked. The return value lives in rt.

If the rt value indicates that the mouse was clicked in the menu bar, calling doMenu from GUI.LIB will handle the click. The doMenu function will dispatch the appropriate menu function if one is called for.

If the rt value specifies that the mouse click occurred in a bitmap, this really means that it took place in one of the toolbox icons, as these are the only BITMAP objects on the main screen. Note that findBitmap uses screenWindow as its window pointer argument, specifying the main screen rather than a specific window.

Trolling through the painticon array will determine which BITMAP object (i.e., tool icon) has been selected. The selectTool function, to be discussed presently, handles the actual selection.

The rt value can reflect mouse action in one of two scroll bars should they be present. Because scrolling the image will affect the relationship of the picture in the drawing area to the overall picture in the image buffer, the contents of the drawing area must be replaced in the image buffer before any scrolling is done. The framechanged flag will be true if this needs to be done (i.e., if some drawing has occurred since the last time it happened). The getdraw function—discussed later in this chapter—does the actual work.

The putdraw function paints a new part of the image buffer in the drawing area.

Finally, if none of the foregoing conditions is true, the do loop checks for a mouse click within the drawing area of the screen, drawrect. If this is the case, it passes the point and the button flag word colour to dodraw, which handles the actual drawing.

The line following the call to dodraw,

```
while(MouseDown(&thePoint));
```

simply forces everything to wait should a mouse button still be down when dodraw finishes. This is a very useful bit of code—you'll find it solves many problems if you tack it onto the ends of functions in which people might tend to lean on their mice.

When the do loop finally gives up the ghost—because alive has become false— the main function will free the image buffer, de-initialize the graphical user interface, and return to DOS.

The dodraw function

The dodraw function of Tiny Paint is the longest single function in the program. If it seems daunting, consider that the one for Desktop Paint runs about five times longer still.

The action of the dodraw function will be based on the current tool, as defined by theTool. The selectTool function will be discussed later on, although its call appeared back up in main. The main switch statement of dodraw selects which tool to use.

The Turbo C BGI graphics library allows lines and rectangles to be drawn either normally or using an XOR function. In the latter case, rather than actually drawing pixels, the graphic functions invert them black for white.

You can draw a "rubber" line or box—one that moves across the screen to track the movement of a mouse cursor—by using the XOR drawing mode. To begin with, an initial line or rectangle is inverted. Each time the mouse cursor moves, the old line or rectangle is inverted, restoring the screen to its original state because inverting a pixel twice returns it to normal. A new line or rectangle is then inverted in the new location.

You'll note that no mention of ellipses was made in the foregoing discussion. The Turbo C BGI library doesn't allow you to use the ellipse function in XOR mode. As such, Tiny Paint draws ellipses using a moving rectangle to define the area of the ellipse and then the ellipse function to do the final drawing.

The toolLine case of the dodraw function's switch uses the XOR mode to draw a moving line from the start point to the current mouse location. If the mouse moves outside the drawing area, the end point of the line is constrained to the nearest point within the drawing area by PointLimitRect. The while loop handles repeatedly erasing and drawing the line until the mouse button is released, at which point the line is drawn "for real" using the normal COPY_PUT drawing mode.

The framechanged flag is set after a line has been drawn, as is the case for all the other tools that actually draw something. You'll also note that each of the five drawing tools—line, box, ellipse, erase, and brush—also has a call at the beginning of its case to getdraw if this flag has been set true. The getdraw function will set it false after it has updated the image buffer.

The toolErase case works very much like the toolLine case except that it draws a white box every place the mouse goes for as long as it's held down. This has the effect of erasing things to white on the screen.

The toolBox and toolEllipse cases both work in the same way save that in the latter case an ellipse is drawn inside the framing rectangle. The process begins by setting the BGI drawing mode to XOR. The while loop repeatedly draws and erases a box from the start point to the current mouse location. The goodrect function is used to ensure that some area is contained within the box (i.e., that the upper left and lower right corners are displaced by at least one pixel in each direction). The PointLimitRect function constrains the end point of the rectangle to be within the drawing area.

The toolUndo case isn't handled in dodraw. The undo function isn't really a drawing tool—it's just convenient to have the undo control in the toolbox, rather than in a menu.

The toolBrush case represents the simplest of the drawing tools. It simply draws lines between the points where the mouse cursor appears for as long as one of the buttons is held down.

The doAboutBox, yesno, and message functions

The doAboutBox function is a pretty typical dialog. It has somewhat more text in it than most and includes a bitmap, but the structure of its controls and code are easily understood. Figure 11-4 illustrates what this box should look like.

As with any dialog, doAboutBox begins by defining the area it will occupy with

Tiny Paint
Copyright (o) 1983
Mother Martha's Software

Ok

11-4 The Tiny Paint About box.

a RECT—r—loading the values into r with SetRect. It then calls OpenWindow to actually display the window on the screen.

The call to AddBitmap and the subsequent calls to AddText involve a fair amount of calculation because they automatically center their respective objects within the dialog window. Allowing that r is the RECT defining the window, r.left + ((r.right-r.left)/2) will be the center of the window, and this value minus half the width of a text string or bitmap will be the left edge of the object in question if it's to be centered. The width of a text string drawn in the system font is strlen(text)*8, while the width of a bitmap is ImageWidth(p), where p is a pointer to the bitmap fragment to be displayed.

As with the other dialogs in Tiny Paint, the doAboutBox function uses the paintbrush icon—ICON6—for dialog decoration.

Note that the Ok button is defined relative to the lower right corner of the window. This will keep it in place if you decide to enlarge the window later on. Alternately, you might want to adjust the code defining its RECT to automatically center it.

The while loop in the doAboutBox function waits for a click in the Ok button or for some activity from the keyboard. The Keyboard function will make it appear that the Ok button has been clicked if the Enter key is pressed. Alternately, if MouseDown returns a true value, the whereMouse function will locate the click and the findButton function will decide which button it's in. As there is only one button, the results should be fairly predictable.

The yesno function is a much smaller and somewhat simpler dialog than doAboutBox. It's structured in much the same way except that in this case there are two buttons to click; and, as such, the findButton function in its while loop actually gets to do some work.

The message function is the simplest of these three dialogs. It's essentially the yesno function with one button missing.

(See Chapter 10 for detailed information on both yesno and message.)

The doSaveAs and doSave functions

You will probably find that the combination of doSaveAs and doSave will port easily into most of your own applications. The doSaveAs function doesn't do any saving per se—it just gets a file name. The doSave function handles most of the mechanics of actually saving a file. In this case, the file in question is a PCX file. You would have to change this if you wanted to write a different sort of application.

Both these functions are called from their respective File menu items.

The doSaveAs function begins by constructing a file specification path in b based on the current file path and the wild card *.PCX, which it then passes to chooseFile. If chooseFile returns a true value—indicating that a name has been selected—doSaveAs will reconstruct the file path and then call doSave. It must reconstruct the file path in case chooseFile has changed drives or directories in the process of selecting a file name.

The doSave function begins by checking to make sure that the drawing area doesn't contain anything that hasn't been copied back into the image buffer, correcting this situation if it exists with a call to getdraw. It then constructs a path to the file to be saved to in b and the name itself in fn.

The FILEINFO object fi is required by the savefile function that actually writes a PCX file. It defines the image in memory.

The doSave function checks to make sure that the file it's being asked to save to doesn't currently exist, calling yesno to inquire about overwriting it if it does.

The doClose function

The doClose function handles the housekeeping involved in closing a file. This will vary among different sorts of applications. In this case, it returns the screen below the menu bar to grey with a call to ClearScreen and abandons any objects added to screenwindow by setting its OBJECTHEAD pointer to NULL. It frees the memory for the picture and line buffers and tidies up the menus. In Tiny Paint, opening a file disables the Open item of the File menu and enables the Close item. Closing a file reverses this process. The doClose function is also responsible for disabling menu items representing functions that would be inappropriate when no file exists in memory, such as Save.

The doNew function

Most of the doNew function is code to manage the dialog box shown in Fig. 11-5. This requests the dimensions of the new file to create.

11-5 The Tiny Paint New box.

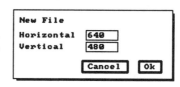

The doNew dialog begins by defining a rectangle for its window to occupy and then opening the window. It fetches its default width and depth values from the theConfig object. In a real application, these would have been defined by the user of the software. It creates strings based on these values in horstr and verstr, as EDIT-FIELDs can only allow for editing strings.

There are three TEXT objects to be added to the doNew dialog—the title of the window and the names of the EDITFIELDs. The EDITFIELDs themselves are added using the numbertrap function as a filter for typed characters.

This dialog has two buttons—Ok and Cancel.

The main while loop of doNew is by now a familiar structure to wait for activity. The only new thing in it is a section dealing with a click in an EDITFIELD. These objects are tracked and handled in pretty well the same way as other controls are.

When the main while loop finishes, the bp BUTTON pointer will point to one of the two button objects. If it points to the ok object, a new picture is to be created. The function multiplies the width and depth values together to determine the amount of memory required for the new picture. If getbuffer is able to allocate the required memory, the buffer is cleared to white with a call to clearbuffer and all or part of it is written to the drawing area with putdraw. The setopen function does all the housekeeping for an open file. Tiny Paint won't actually know that the picture in memory is a new one, rather than one that has been loaded from a disk file.

The numbertrap function immediately below doNew is only used by the afore-mentioned EDITFIELDs. It tests keyboard input to make sure it only contains dig-its. The clearbuffer function initializes a newly allocated buffer by writing a white line to each line of the new image.

The doOpen and setopen functions

The doOpen does much of the same file path manipulation as doSave and doSaveAs. It also uses chooseFile to select the file name to be opened. The loadfile function—to be discussed shortly—does the actual work in unpacking and loading a PCX file into memory.

Most of the housekeeping required to tell Tiny Paint that a file has been loaded is performed by setopen. This function was also called by doNew.

The setopen function is really a catch-all to set up defaults and such that exist when a file has just been created or loaded into memory. It begins by allocating line-buf, used by several of the drawing area manipulation functions to stash screen lines in while they're being moved on and off the screen. It then adjusts the file menu items pertaining to loading and saving files, such that the ones that create and open files are disabled and the ones that save and close files are enabled. You might recall that doClose performed the opposite function.

The dwidth, ddepth, and dbytes values specify the width, depth, and bytes in a line of the drawing area. They're calculated by setopen, which subtracts the padding around the drawing area from the screen dimensions as returned by the Turbo C get-maxx and getmaxy functions. If these values prove to be inadequate to allow the whole picture in memory to be displayed at once, one or both of the drawing area scroll bars will be set up and added to the screen. If both scroll bars are present, a white box is drawn below and to the right of the drawing area to make them look a little neater.

It's dreadfully tempting to have something unusual happen if someone clicks in this box.

Having set up the drawing area dimensions and the scroll bars if they're required, the setopen function draws a box around the drawing area and adds the toolbox BITMAP objects to the screen. It then draws a box around the toolbox and selects the first tool.

The selectTool and tbUndo functions

The selectTool function is used to unselect the current toolbox item and select a new one. It's called when the main function detects a mouse click in the toolbox area.

In fact, selectTool doesn't really have very much work to do because most of the graphics involved in inverting the icons in question are handled by the GUI.LIB functions maintaining BITMAP objects. The whole process really involves toggling the select elements of the two BITMAP objects in question and then redrawing the icons.

The only thing that makes this function even slightly involved is the existence of the Undo tool. Not actually a drawing tool, the Undo button is included in the tool-box more because it's handy to have there than because it really qualifies as a tool. As such, it must be treated differently. Specifically, if it's clicked, the putdraw function must be called and then the previously selected tool re-selected. Both these operations are performed by tbUndo.

The drawing window management functions

The picture in Tiny Paint's drawing area is managed by four functions. The putdraw function copies part of the image buffer to the drawing area and calls getline to fetch lines from the buffer. The getdraw function copies the contents of the drawing area back into the image buffer and uses putline to place lines in the image buffer. In fact, because putline works with whole lines and getdraw might well be asked to copy to part of the imagebuffer if the image is bigger than the Tiny Paint drawing area, get-draw actually calls getline to fetch each line, inserts the new data into it, and then calls putline to replace it.

You probably won't need these functions unless you write an application that makes use of large bitmaps. However, they're a useful illustration of how to deal with the screen buffer directly using SCREENTBL. The for loops in putdraw and getdraw use the entries in this table to create pointers into the screen memory.

Note that these functions decide where in the image buffer the part of the picture in the drawing area resides by referring to the two scroll bars hpScroll and vpScroll. These are the same scroll bars checked back up in the main function. The thumb positions of the scroll bars reflect offsets into the image buffer for the upper left corner of the drawing area if the picture being edited by Tiny Paint is bigger than the drawing area.

The image memory management functions

The getbuffer function works out to being a call to farmalloc under Tiny Paint. Under Desktop Paint it's much more elaborate, as it will allocate extended or expanded memory if not enough conventional memory exists to contain the picture being loaded. You should handle the allocation of large buffers with this sort of top-down approach. A part of your program calling for memory needn't know what sort of memory it will be getting, and a function like getbuffer can include the logic to parcel out memory in an optimum way.

The freebuffer function in Tiny Paint is just a call to farfree; but, again, it would contain the code to de-allocate extended or expanded memory in a more elaborate application.

The farmalloc and farfree functions use the DOS memory manager to parcel out memory. You should note that DOS gets exceedingly cranky if you attempt to de-allocate memory that it didn't allocate in the first place. When you pass farfree a pointer, DOS expects to find that the sixteen bytes immediately below it contain some internal notation to itself about the memory block in question; if it doesn't find this, it's liable to crash.

Because large applications can allocate and de-allocate memory in multiple ways, you should keep track of whether a pointer really points to an allocated buffer. Arguably, good programming logic should keep you from attempting to free the same pointer twice, for example, but it's worth having a safety net as well. As such, getbuffer will set the pointer it handles to NULL if there isn't enough memory and freebuffer will only de-allocate it if it doesn't point to NULL, setting it to NULL thereafter. Forcing all unused pointers to NULL is a quick way to keep track of what they're up to.

The farPtr function, mentioned earlier in this chapter, is a way to fool Turbo C into addressing data objects bigger than 64K. In "pure" C, you can only add pointers and integers, not pointers and longs. As such, on a machine with sixteen-bit integers—such as a PC—the biggest area a pointer can address will be what can be defined in sixteen bits—65535 bytes.

Addressing larger blocks of memory involves being able to add a long integer to a pointer. It's possible to write a hardware-dependent function to do this if the internal structure of a large model pointer is known, which it is under Turbo C's large memory model. Pointers in this case are just segment and offset values. The farPtr function works by splitting the number of bytes in its l argument into the equivalent of segment and offset values and adding them to the segment and offset values of the pointer passed to it in p.

The PCX file functions

The last part of Tiny Paint is the code dealing specifically with monochrome PCX files. If you're interested in knowing more about these files, or if you want a more complete description than given here of the code working with them, you might want to check out my book *Bitmapped Graphics*. The discussion of PCX files herein will be limited to those aspects of them pertaining to Tiny Paint.

The loadfile function begins by calling getFileInfo to find out the size of the PCX file it's been asked to load and how many colors it uses. Files with more than one bit per pixel (i.e., color files) can't be loaded into Tiny Paint. Confronted with such a file, loadfile will refuse to proceed and the calling function doOpen will display an error message.

Having decided to load a file, loadfile will call getbuffer to allocate some memory and then loadPcxFile to actually unpack the file.

The getFileInfo function reads the header of a PCX file passed to it and decodes the information therein, as was discussed in Chapter 7. It loads the results of its deliberations into a struct of the type FILEINFO, which is defined at the top of Fig. 11-2.

The loadPcxFile function has been discussed in detail in Chapter 7. The only thing a bit different about this version of it is the putl argument—rather than being written with a hard-wired function to store image lines in a buffer, it accepts a pointer to a suitable function as one of its arguments. This allows more complex programs to use the same loadPcxFile function to load file into different buffers for different applications. Under Desktop Paint, for example, it gets used to load both the main image file being edited and smaller image fragments being imported into the clipboard.

The cleanline function tidies up one of the undocumented messy aspects of PCX files. In a monochrome PCX file having a horizontal dimension that's not an even multiple of eight, there can be a number of unused bits at the end of each line. These usually contain something meaningless, which will appear as random black and white pixels along the right edge of a picture being displayed in Tiny Paint, as Tiny Paint rounds the horizontal dimensions of images up to even eight bit values. As such, cleanline sets all the unused bits to white.

The savefile function does exactly the opposite of what the loadfile function did. It fills a PCXHEAD structure with all the relevant data and writes it to a new file. It then packs each line in the image into a PCX encoded string by calling writePcxLine and writes the result to the new file. Finally, it closes the file.

The writePcxLine implements PCX encoding. The theory behind this is a bit involved, although you can work it out if you like by considering how these lines are unpacked (see Chapter 7).

Ready to interface

Having dealt with the internal mysteries of Tiny Paint, you should be pretty well armed to do battle with an original application of your own devising. Despite the complexity of a graphical user interface based application, you'll find that they're pretty easy to put together when you're absolved of the need to deal with the user interface. The SeeFont application in Chapter 9, for example, took less than half an hour to write from scratch.

Tiny Paint took even less time, but admittedly it was distilled down from Desktop Paint, so most of the work had already been done.

A

GUI library functions reference

This appendix lists the names and arguments for the library functions in GUI.LIB. Note that this includes the externally callable functions only—it doesn't list those functions existing in the library but only used by other library functions.

The Choose File function
chooseFile

```
chooseFile(spec,name,x,y,drivemap)
    char *spec,*name;
        int x,y;
    char *drivemap;
```

The chooseFile function will display a dialog either to select an existing file name for opening or to accept a new file name to save to. It allows for changes of drives and directories in the process of selecting a name. Also, it returns a true value if the name argument contains a selected file name (i.e., if a name has been double-clicked or if the Ok button was selected).

The spec argument is a char string conforming to a standard DOS path and wild card to specify the names to be included in the selection list.

The name argument is a char string that will be long enough to contain the returned name (i.e., at least 13 bytes long).

The x and y arguments are integers and specify the coordinates of the upper left corner of the choose file box when it's displayed.

The drivemap argument is a char string that specifies all the available disk drives.

General dialog functions
Keyboard

```
Keyboard(w)
    WINDOW *w;
```

The Keyboard function checks for waiting keyboard characters, directing them to those controls capable of responding to them. Specifically, it will simulate a click in the first and second button controls in the window specified if Enter or Esc, respectively, are hit. It will direct all printable characters and other editing key codes to the currently selected editfield control if one exists. Keyboard should be called frequently from the main loop of any dialog using controls.

The w argument is a pointer to a WINDOW object containing the controls to be dealt with.

Editfield functions
addEditfield

```
addEditfield(w,t,x,y,l,p,proc,a)
    WINDOW *w;
    EDITFIELD *t;
    int x,y;
    int l;
    char *p;
    int (*proc)( );
    int a;
```

The addEditfield function adds an editfield control to a window.

The w argument is a pointer to a WINDOW object that will contain the new editfield control.

The t argument is a pointer to the new EDITFIELD object.

The x and y arguments are integers specifying the coordinates of the upper left corner of the new editfield control.

The l argument is an integer specifying the maximum length of the text string the editfield will deal with.

The p argument is a pointer to a char string long enough to contain the text of the new editfield. It must be at least l + 1 bytes long.

The proc argument is a pointer to a function that will determine whether a character typed into the editfield is acceptable for inclusion in the text string. The function should either return the character if it's acceptable or a zero value if it isn't.

The a argument is an integer specifying whether the editfield is active or not. It should contain one of the constants ACTIVE or INACTIVE.

drawEditfield

```
drawEditfield(t)
    EDITFIELD *t;
```

The drawEditfield function will draw or redraw an editfield control previously added to a window.

The t argument should be a pointer to the EDITFIELD object to be drawn.

findEditfield

```
EDITFIELD *findEditfield(w,p)
    WINDOW *w;
    POINT *p;
```

The findEditfield function locates an editfield that has been clicked and returns a pointer to the appropriate EDITFIELD object.

The w argument is a pointer to the WINDOW object containing the editfields in question.

The p argument is a pointer to a POINT object containing the coordinates of the mouse click.

trackEditfield

```
trackEditfield(f)
    EDITFIELD *f;
```

The trackEditfield function performs the actions required to indicate that clicking in an editfield has been noticed by the system. It sets the select flag in the editfield in question.

The f argument is a pointer to an EDITFIELD object.

Checkbox functions
addCheckbox

```
addCheckbox(w,cb,x,y,text,select,active)
    WINDOW *w;
    CHECKBOX *cb;
    int x,y;
    char *text;
    int select;
    int active;
```

The addCheckbox function adds a checkbox control to a window.

The w argument is a pointer to a WINDOW object that will contain the new checkbox control.

The cb argument is a pointer to the new CHECKBOX object.

The x and y arguments are integers specifying the coordinates of the upper left corner of the new checkbox control.

The text argument is a pointer to a char string containing the text to be associated with the new checkbox.

The select argument should be true if the checkbox is to be drawn initially selected (i.e., with a cross through it) or false if it's to be drawn unselected.

The active argument is an integer specifying whether the checkbox is active or not. It should contain one of the constants ACTIVE or INACTIVE.

drawCheckbox

```
drawCheckbox(cb)
    CHECKBOX *cb;
```

The drawCheckbox function will draw or redraw a checkbox control previously added to a window.

The cb argument is a pointer to the CHECKBOX object to be drawn.

findCheckbox

```
CHECKBOX *findCheckbox(w,p)
    WINDOW *w;
    POINT *p;
```

The findCheckbox function locates a checkbox that has been clicked and returns a pointer to the appropriate CHECKBOX object.

The w argument is a pointer to the WINDOW object containing the checkboxes in question.

The p argument is a pointer to a POINT object containing the coordinates of the mouse click.

trackCheckbox

```
trackCheckbox(cb)
    CHECKBOX *cb;
```

The trackCheckbox function performs the actions required to indicate that clicking in a checkbox has been noticed by the system.

The cb argument is a pointer to a CHECKBOX object.

Scroll bar functions
addHorScroll

```
addHorScroll(w,sb,x,y,len,min,max,cur,active)
    WINDOW *w;
    SCROLLBAR *sb;
    int x,y;
    int len;
    int min,max;
    int cur;
    int active;
```

The addHorScroll function adds a horizontal scroll bar control to a window.

The w argument is a pointer to a WINDOW object that will contain the new scroll bar control.

The sb argument is a pointer to the new SCROLLBAR object.

The x and y arguments are integers specifying the coordinates of the upper left corner of the new scroll bar control.

The len argument is an integer specifying the length in pixels of the new scroll bar.

The min, max, and cur arguments specify the minimum, maximum, and current numeric values of the new scroll bar.

The active argument is an integer specifying whether the scroll bar is active or not. It should contain one of the constants ACTIVE or INACTIVE.

addVertScroll

```
addVertScroll(w,sb,x,y,len,min,max,cur,active)
    WINDOW *w;
    SCROLLBAR *sb;
    int x,y;
    int len;
    int min,max;
    int cur;
    int active;
```

The addVertScroll function adds a vertical scroll bar control to a window.

The w argument is a pointer to a WINDOW object that will contain the new scroll bar control.

The sb argument is a pointer to the new SCROLLBAR object.

The x and y arguments are integers specifying the coordinates of the upper left corner of the new scroll bar control.

The len argument is an integer specifying the length in pixels of the new scroll bar.

The min, max, and cur arguments specify the minimum, maximum, and current numeric values of the new scroll bar.

The active argument is an integer specifying whether the scroll bar is active or not. It should contain one of the constants ACTIVE or INACTIVE.

drawHorScroll

```
drawHorScroll(sb)
    SCROLLBAR *sb;
```

The drawHorScroll function will draw or redraw a horizontal scroll bar control previously added to a window.

The sb argument is a pointer to the SCROLLBAR object to be drawn.

drawVertScroll

```
drawVertScroll(sb)
```

```
SCROLLBAR *sb;
```

The drawVertScroll function will draw or redraw a vertical scroll bar control that was previously added to a window.

The sb argument is a pointer to the SCROLLBAR object to be drawn.

findScrollbar

```
SCROLLBAR *findScrollbar(w,p)
    WINDOW *w;
    POINT *p;
```

The findScrollbar function locates a scroll bar that has been clicked in and returns a pointer to the appropriate SCROLLBAR object.

The w argument is a pointer to the WINDOW object containing the scroll bars in question.

The p argument is a pointer to a POINT object containing the coordinates of the mouse click.

trackScrollbar

```
trackScrollbar(sb,rt)
    SCROLLBAR *sb;
    int rt;
```

The trackScrollbar function performs the actions required to indicate that clicking in a scroll bar has been noticed by the system. Specifically, it performs the animation to move the scroll bar's thumb.

The sb argument is a pointer to a SCROLLBAR object.

The rt argument is an integer returned by whereMouse containing the part flags indicating the area of the scroll bar in which the mouse click occurred.

List functions
addList

```
addList(w,l,x,y,width,depth,count,top,base)
    WINDOW *w;
    LIST *l;
    int x,y;
    int width,depth;
    int count;
    int top;
    char *base;
```

The addList function adds a list control to a window.

The w argument is a pointer to a WINDOW object that will contain the new list control.

The l argument is a pointer to the new LIST object.

The x and y arguments are integers specifying the coordinates of the upper left corner of the new list control.

The width and depth arguments are integers specifying the width and depth of the list in characters.

The count argument is an integer containing the number of lines in the list's buffer.

The top argument is an integer specifying the number of lines from the base of the buffer to begin displaying the list's contents.

The base argument is a pointer to a char buffer containing the list's contents. Each line in the buffer should be width + 1 bytes wide.

drawList

```
drawList(l)
    LIST *l;
```

The drawList function will draw or redraw a list control previously added to a window.

The l argument is a pointer to the LIST object to be drawn.

findList

```
LIST *findList(w,p)
    WINDOW *w;
    POINT *p;
```

The findList function locates a list control that has been clicked in. It returns a pointer to the appropriate LIST object.

The w argument is a pointer to the WINDOW object containing the lists in question.

The p argument is a pointer to a POINT object containing the coordinates of the mouse click.

trackList

```
trackList(lp,s)
    LIST *lp;
    char *s;
```

The trackList function performs the actions required to indicate that clicking in a list has been noticed by the system. It inverts the clicked line for as long as the mouse is held down and also returns the text of the selected line.

The lp argument is a pointer to a LIST object.

The s argument is a pointer to a char string long enough to contain the returned line.

Text and Textfield functions
addText

```
addText(w,t,x,y,p,a)
    WINDOW *w;
```

```
    TEXT *t;
    int x,y;
    char *p;
    int a;
```

The addText function adds a text control to a window.

The w argument is a pointer to a WINDOW object that will contain the new text control.

The t argument is a pointer to the new TEXT object.

The x and y arguments are integers specifying the coordinates of the upper left corner of the new text control.

The p argument is a pointer to a char string containing the text for the control.

The active argument is an integer specifying whether the text is active or not. It should contain one of the constants ACTIVE or INACTIVE.

addTextfield

```
    addTextfield(w,t,x,y,l,p,a)
        WINDOW *w;
        TEXTFIELD *t;
        int x,y;
        int l;
        char *p;
        int a;
```

The addTextfield function adds a textfield control to a window.

The w argument is a pointer to a WINDOW object that will contain the new textfield control.

The t argument is a pointer to the new TEXTFIELD object.

The x and y arguments are integers specifying the coordinates of the upper left corner of the new textfield control.

The l argument is an integer specifying the maximum length of the text string the textfield will deal with.

The p argument is a pointer to a char string long enough to contain the text of the new textfield.

The a argument is an integer specifying whether the textfield is active or not. It should contain one of the constants ACTIVE or INACTIVE.

drawText

```
    drawText(t)
        TEXT *t;
```

The drawText function will draw or redraw a text control previously added to a window.

The t argument is a pointer to the TEXT object to be drawn.

drawTextfield

```
drawTextfield(t)
    TEXTFIELD *t;
```

The drawTextfield function will draw or redraw a textfield control previously added to a window.

The t argument is a pointer to the TEXTFIELD object to be drawn.

Bitmap functions
addBitmap

```
addBitmap(w,b,x,y,p,select,proc,active)
    WINDOW *w;
    BITMAP *b;
    int x,y;
    char *p;
    int select;
    int (*proc)( );
    int active;
```

The addBitmap function adds a bitmap control to a window.

The w argument is a pointer to a WINDOW object that will contain the new bitmap control.

The b argument is a pointer to the new BITMAP object.

The x and y arguments are integers specifying the coordinates of the upper left corner of the new bitmap control.

The p argument is a pointer to a char buffer containing a monochrome bitmap fragment.

The select argument is an integer that will be true if the bitmap will be drawn as selected or false if won't.

The proc argument is a pointer to a function to be called when the bitmap is clicked in or to NULL if no function is applicable.

The active argument is an integer specifying whether the bitmap is active or not. It should contain one of the constants ACTIVE or INACTIVE.

drawBitmap

```
drawBitmap(b)
    BITMAP *b;
```

The drawBitmap function will draw or redraw a bitmap control previously added to a window.

The b argument is a pointer to the BITMAP object to be drawn.

findBitmap

```
BITMAP *findBitmap(w,p)
    WINDOW *w;
```

```
    POINT *p;
```

The findBitmap function locates a bitmap control that has been clicked in and returns a pointer to the appropriate BITMAP object.

The w argument is a pointer to the WINDOW object containing the bitmaps in question.

The p argument is a pointer to a POINT object containing the coordinates of the mouse click.

trackBitmap

```
    trackBitmap(b)
        BITMAP *b;
```

The trackBitmap function performs the actions required to indicate that clicking in a bitmap has been noticed by the system. It inverts the clicked bitmap for as long as the mouse is held down.

The b argument is a pointer to a BITMAP object.

Button functions
addButton

```
    addButton(w,b,tx,active)
        WINDOW *w;
        BUTTON *b;
        char *tx;
        int active;
```

The addButton function adds a button control to a window.

The w argument is a pointer to a WINDOW object that will contain the new button control.

The b argument is a pointer to the new BUTTON object. The location of the button will have been previously stored in the frame element of the BUTTON object.

The tx argument is a pointer to a char string containing the button's text.

The active argument is an integer specifying whether the button is active or not. It should contain one of the constants ACTIVE or INACTIVE.

drawButton

```
    drawButton(b)
        BUTTON *b;
```

The drawButton function will draw or redraw a button control previously added to a window.

The b argument is a pointer to the BUTTON object to be drawn.

findButton

```
    BUTTON *findButton(w,p)
```

```
WINDOW *w;
POINT *p;
```

The findButton function locates a button control that has been clicked in and returns a pointer to the appropriate BUTTON object.

The w argument is a pointer to the WINDOW object containing the buttons in question.

The p argument is a pointer to a POINT object containing the coordinates of the mouse click.

trackButton

```
trackButton(b)
    BUTTON *b;
```

The trackButton function performs the actions required to indicate that clicking in a button has been noticed by the system. It inverts the clicked button for as long as the mouse is held down.

The b argument is a pointer to a BUTTON object.

Menu functions

addMenu

```
addMenu(m)
    MENU *m;
```

The addMenu function adds a menu to the menu array of the menu manager.

The m argument is a pointer to a MENU object. It returns a true value if the menu was added or a false value if no more room exists in the menu array.

dispatchMenuItem

```
void dispatchMenuItem(void)
```

The dispatchMenuItem function checks for alternate key combinations and attempts to call menu functions corresponding with them. It should be called frequently in the main loop of any application using menus.

doMenu

```
doMenu(p)
    POINT *p;
```

The doMenu function will display a menu, perform the animation of selecting items based on the mouse location, and dispatch a menu item function if it must. It returns a true value if the menu was opened or a false value if there wasn't enough memory to display it.

The p argument is a pointer to a MENU object.

drawMenuBar

> DrawMenuBar(void)

The drawMenuBar function draws the menu bar at the top of the screen based on the current contents of the menu array.

idle

> idle( )

The idle function does nothing. It just serves as a place holder in MENU objects.

InitMenuManager

> void InitMenuManager(void)

The InitMenuManager function sets up the menu manager for use and should be called at the beginning of a program.

Window functions
closeWindow

> closeWindow(w)
>   WINDOW *w;

The closeWindow function removes a window by replacing its screen contents and then de-allocating its buffer.

The w argument is the pointer to a previously opened WINDOW object.

InitWindowManager

> InitWindowManager( )

The InitWindowManager function sets up the window manager for use and should be called at the beginning of a program.

openWindow

> openWindow(w,r)
>   WINDOW *w;
>   RECT *r;

The openWindow function attempts to open a window on the screen. It allocates memory to preserve the area behind the window, copies the appropriate screen image area to its allocated buffer, and then draws the window. OpenWindow returns a true value if the window opened successfully or a false value if there wasn't enough memory to allocate a buffer for it.

The w argument is a pointer to a WINDOW object.

The r argument is a pointer to a RECT object specifying the area the window is to occupy.

Graphic functions

deinitGraphics

    deinitGraphics( )

The deinitGraphics function turns off the graphics mode of your display card and should be called prior to exiting from an application using the graphical user interface.

ega2mono

    char *ega2mono(source)
        char *source;

The ega2mono function creates a monochrome putimage image fragment based on the four-plane fragment passed to it. It allocates a buffer for the new image fragment and returns a pointer to it.

    The source argument is a pointer to a char buffer containing the four-plane image fragment to be converted. Note that the latter three planes of the source image will be ignored.

initGraphics

    initGraphics( )

The initGraphics function turns on the graphics mode of your display card and should be called before using the graphical user interface. It returns a true value if the graphics mode has been established or a false value if it hasn't.

InvertRect

    InvertRect(r)
        RECT *r;

The InvertRect function inverts an area on the screen black for white.

    The r argument is a pointer to a RECT object specifying the area to be inverted.

mono2ega

    char *mono2ega(source)
        char *source;

The mono2ega function creates a four-plane putimage image fragment based on the monochrome fragment passed to it. It allocates a buffer for the new image fragment and returns a pointer to it.

    The source argument is a pointer to a char buffer containing the monochrome image fragment to be converted.

PointInRect

```
PointInRect(p,r)
    POINT *p;
    RECT *r;
```

The PointInRect function will return a true value if the coordinates in the point argument passed to it lie within the area specified by the rectangle argument and a false value otherwise.

The p argument should be a pointer to a POINT object.

The r argument should be a pointer to a RECT argument.

SetRect

```
SetRect(r,left,top,right,bottom)
    RECT *r;
    int left,top,right,bottom;
```

The SetRect function serves as a convenient way to initialize the values of a RECT object.

The r argument is a pointer to a RECT object.

The left, top, right, and bottom arguments are integers.

Mouse functions

GetKey

```
GetKey( )
```

The GetKey function will return the next keyboard character. If the next character is extended, the low order byte of the return value will be zero and the high order byte will contain the scan code.

InitMouse

```
InitMouse( )
```

The InitMouse function initializes the mouse in graphics mode. It returns a true value if a Microsoft compatible mouse driver has been located or a false value if a driver cannot be found.

MouseButton

```
MouseButton( )
```

The MouseButton function returns an integer containing the current button status of the mouse. The first bit of the return value will be set if the left button is currently depressed, the second bit indicates the state of the middle or right button, and so on.

MouseDown

    MouseDown(p)
        POINT *p;

The MouseDown function returns the button status of the mouse and its location.

The p argument is a pointer to a POINT object that will be loaded with the current mouse coordinates. The return value will be an integer as described under MouseButton.

Note that MouseDown might return a true value even if a button hasn't been clicked should the Keyboard function have signaled a false mouse click.

MouseLoc

    MouseLoc(p)
        POINT *p;

The MouseLoc function returns the location of the mouse.

The p argument is a pointer to a POINT object that will be loaded with the current mouse coordinates.

MouseOff

    MouseOff( )

The MouseOff function hides the mouse cursor.

MouseOn

    MouseOn( )

The MouseOn function shows the mouse cursor.

MoveMouse

    MoveMouse(p)
        POINT *p;

The MoveMouse function repositions the mouse cursor.

The p argument is a pointer to a POINT object containing the new coordinates for the cursor.

SetupMouse

    SetupMouse(mx,my,x,y,n)
        int mx,my,x,y,n;

The SetupMouse function sets the boundary of the mouse travel.

arrowCursor

    void arrowCursor(void)

The arrowCursor function will make the mouse cursor appear as a normal pointer, indicating that the system will respond to clicks.

waitCursor

```
void waitCursor(void)
```

The waitCursor function will make the mouse cursor appear as an hour glass, indicating that the system is busy.

whereMouse

```
whereMouse(p,w)
    POINT *p;
    WINDOW *w;
```

The whereMouse function returns a constant indicating the nature of the area a mouse click has occurred in.

The p argument is a pointer to a POINT object containing the mouse coordinates.

The w argument is a pointer to the WINDOW object the click occurred in.

Font functions

bitmapstringFM

```
char *bitmapstringFN(s,font)
    char *s;
    FONT *font;
```

The bitmapstringFN function will create a monochrome putimage fragment containing the text passed to it drawn in the specified font. It will return NULL if insufficient memory exists to allocate a buffer for the image fragment.

The s argument is a pointer to the string to be drawn.

The font argument is a pointer to a FONT object.

charwidthFN

```
charwidthFN(n,font)
    int n;
    FONT *font;
```

The charwidthFN function returns the width in pixels of a specific character.

The n argument is the ASCII value of the character to be measured.

The font argument is a pointer to a FONT object.

drawstringFN

```
drawstringFN(s,font,x,y)
    char *s;
    FONT *font;
    int x,y;
```

The drawstringFN function will draw the text passed to it in the specified font.

The s argument is a pointer to the string to be drawn.

The font argument is a pointer to a FONT object.

The x and y arguments are integers specifying the upper left corner of the rectangle that will contain the drawn text.

fontdepthFN

    fontdepthFN(font)

The fontdepthFN function returns the maximum depth in pixels of a specified font.

The font argument is a pointer to a FONT object.

islegalfontsize

    islegalfontsize(n)

The islegalfontsize function will return a true value if its argument is a legal font size.

The n argument is an integer containing the font size value to be checked.

stringwidthFN

    stringwidthFN(s,font)
        char *s;
        FONT *font;

The stringwidthFN function returns the width in pixels of a string of text.

The s argument is a pointer to the string to be measured.

The font argument is a pointer to a FONT object.

writeFontRes

    writeFontRes(path,font,bitmap)
        char *path;
        FONT *font;
        char *bitmap;

The writeFontRes function will create a resource file having one FONT resource in it.

The path argument specifies the DOS path and name for the file.

The font argument is a pointer to a FONT object.

The bitmap argument is a pointer to the font bitmap data.

Resource functions
addRF

    addRF(fh,type,number,size,res)
        RFILE fh;
        char *type;
        unsigned long number;
        unsigned int size;
        char *res;

The addRF function adds a resource to an open resource file. It will return a true value if the resource was successfully added to the file or a false value if it couldn't be written.

The fh argument is the RFILE for the resource file to be added to.

The type argument is a pointer to a four-byte resource type string.

The number argument is a long integer containing a unique resource number for the specified type in this file.

The size argument is an integer specifying the size of the resource data in bytes.

The res argument is a pointer to the resource data.

countRF

```
countRF(fh,type)
    RFILE fh;
    char *type;
```

The countRF function returns either the number of resources of a type in an open resource file or a zero if no resources of the specified type can be found.

The fh function is the RFILE of the resource file to be scanned.

The type argument is a pointer to a four-byte resource type string.

createRF

```
createRF(name,description)
    char *name,*description;
```

The createRF will create a new and empty resource file, returning a true value if the file is created or a false value if it isn't.

The name argument is a DOS path and name for the file to be created.

The description argument is a text string describing the eventual contents of the file and should be no more than 64 bytes long.

closeRF

```
void closeRF(fh)
```

The closeRF function closes a previously opened resource file.

The fh argument is the RFILE for an open resource file.

freenumberRF

```
long freenumberRF(fh,type)
    RFILE fh;
    char *type;
```

The freenumberRF function will return either a resource number not currently in use for the type specified or BADRECNUM if no unused numbers can be found.

The fh argument is the RFILE of the resource file in question.

The type argument is a pointer to a four-byte resource type string.

getallRF

```
getallRF(fh,proc)
    RFILE fh;
    int (*proc)( );
```

The getallRF function will step through all the resources in a resource file and call a function to deal with each.

The fh argument is the RFILE of the resource file in question.

The proc argument is a pointer to the function to be called. The function will be passed three arguments: a pointer to the found RESOURCE object, the RFILE of the resource file, and an integer specifying the position of the resource in the file.

getdataRF

```
getdataRF(p,fh,size)
    char *p;
    RFILE fh;
    unsigned int size;
```

The getdataRF function will load the data from a previously located resource into a previously allocated buffer. It will return true if the read was successful or false if it wasn't.

The p argument is a pointer to the buffer to contain the resource data.

The fh argument is the RFILE of the resource file in question.

The size argument is an integer specifying the number of bytes of data to be read.

getinfoRF

```
getinfoRF(rh,fh)
    RESHEAD *rh;
    RFILE fh;
```

The getinfoRF function will return the resource header information of a resource file, with the return value being true if the data in rh is valid or false if it isn't.

The rh argument is a pointer to a RESHEAD object to contain the data.

The fh argument is the RFILE of the resource file in question.

getnumberedRF

```
getnumberedRF(fh,type,n,rc)
    RFILE fh;
    char *type;
    int n;
    RESOURCE *rc;
```

The getnumberedRF function will locate a resource of a specific type and position in a resource file, returning true if the specified resource is found or false if it isn't.

The fh argument is the RFILE of the resource file in question.

The type argument is a pointer to a four-byte resource type string.

The n argument is an integer containing the position of the resource you want to locate.

The rc argument is a pointer to a RESOURCE object to contain the resource when it's found.

getRF

```
getRF(fh,type,n,rc)
    RFILE fh;
    char *type;
    long n;
    RESOURCE *rc;
```

The getRF function will locate a resource of a specific type and number, returning true if the specified resource is found or false if it isn't.

The fh argument is the RFILE of the resource file in question.

The type argument is a pointer to a four-byte resource type string.

The n argument is a long integer containing the number of the resource you want to locate.

The rc argument is a pointer to a RESOURCE object to contain the resource when it's found.

openRF

```
RFILE openRF(name)
    char *name;
```

The openRF function attempts to open a resource file. It will return the RFILE for the opened resource file or a zero if the file couldn't be opened.

The name argument is a DOS path and name for the file to be opened.

removeresRF

```
removeresRF(fh,rc)
    RFILE fh;
    RESOURCE *rc;
```

The removeresRF function will remove a specified resource from a resource file, returning true if the resource was removed or false if it couldn't be removed.

The fh argument is the RFILE of the resource file to be edited.

The rc argument is a pointer to a RESOURCE object.

B

The GUI library header

Appendix B contains the complete listing for the GUI.H header file. This file should be included in both GUI.C when you compile it and in any C language files that make calls into the graphical user interface library. Note that when GUI.H is used by GUI.C, the __GUIDATA constant is set true, causing the library's data objects to be generated. If this constant isn't true or isn't defined—the case for all other uses of GUI.H—all the data objects will be declared as *extern*.

```
/*
        gui.h
*/

#define ISREGDRIVER     1       /* set true for registered BGI drivers */
#define FASTWINDOW      1       /* set true for fast window image handlers */

#define MAXMENUITEM     16      /* maximum number of menu items */
#define MENULINESIZE    13      /* maximum length of menu item */
#define MENULINEDEEP    10      /* depth of menu line */
#define MENUCOUNT       9       /* number of menus */
#define MENUTITLESIZE   8       /* maximum length of menu title */
#define MENUBARDEEP     10      /* depth of menu bar */
#define FONTDEEP        8       /* depth of system font */
#define DROPSHADOW      4       /* size of window drop shadows */
#define FILELINESIZE    14      /* size of one file line */

/* some extended keyboard characters */

#define DEL             83 * 256
#define HOME            71 * 256
```

B-1 The complete listing for the GUI.H header.

```
#define CURSOR_LEFT      75 * 256
#define CURSOR_RIGHT     77 * 256
#define END              79 * 256

#define ALT_Q            0x1000
#define ALT_W            0x1100
#define ALT_E            0x1200
#define ALT_R            0x1300
#define ALT_T            0x1400
#define ALT_Y            0x1500
#define ALT_U            0x1600
#define ALT_I            0x1700
#define ALT_O            0x1800
#define ALT_P            0x1900

#define ALT_A            0x1E00
#define ALT_S            0x1F00
#define ALT_D            0x2000
#define ALT_F            0x2100
#define ALT_G            0x2200
#define ALT_H            0x2300
#define ALT_J            0x2400
#define ALT_K            0x2500
#define ALT_L            0x2600

#define ALT_Z            0x2C00
#define ALT_X            0x2D00
#define ALT_C            0x2E00
#define ALT_V            0x2F00
#define ALT_B            0x3000
#define ALT_N            0x3100
#define ALT_M            0x3200

#define ALT_1            0x7800
#define ALT_2            0x7900
#define ALT_3            0x7a00
#define ALT_4            0x7b00
#define ALT_5            0x7c00
#define ALT_6            0x7d00
#define ALT_7            0x7e00
#define ALT_8            0x7f00
#define ALT_9            0x8000
#define ALT_0            0x8100

/*** object masks ***/

#define inNothing        0x0000
#define inWindow         0x0001
#define inMenuBar        0x0002
#define inButton         0x0004
#define inBitmap         0x0008
#define inText           0x0010
#define inTextfield      0x0020
#define inList           0x0040
#define inVertScroll     0x0080
#define inHorScroll      0x0100
#define inUpArrow        0x0200
#define inDownArrow      0x0400
#define inJumpUp         0x0800
#define inJumpDown       0x1000
#define inThumb          0x2000
#define inCheckBox       0x4000
```

```
#define inEditField      0x8000
#define CHECKMARK        251

/* state flags */

#define ACTIVE           0xffff
#define INACTIVE         0xaa55

/* character to indicate keyboard equivalent in menus */
#define KEYMENUCHAR      4

/* useful macros */

#define pixels2bytes(n)   ((n+7)/8)
#define pixels2words(n)   ((n+15)/16)
#define ImageWidth(p)     (1+p[0]+(p[1] << 8))
#define ImageDepth(p)     (1+p[2]+(p[3] << 8))
#define ImageBytes(p)     (pixels2bytes((1+p[0]+(p[1] << 8))))

#define errorbeep()       putchar(7)

#define MINFONTCHAR      0        /* lowest number font character */
#define MAXFONTCHAR      255      /* highest number font character */

#define FONTNAMESIZE     32       /* maximum size of a font name */
#define FONTid           "FONT"   /* resource type for fonts */

#define TIMES            14       /* standard type face numbers */
#define HELVETICA        2

#define resourceID       "ALCHRSRC"
#define BADRECNUM        0xffffffffL           /* illegal resource number */
#define BADRECTYPE       "\000\000\000\000"    /* illegal resource type */
#define RESext           "RES"                 /* resource file extension */
typedef struct {
        unsigned int type;
        void *next;
        } OBJECTHEAD;

typedef struct {
        int x,y;
        } POINT;

typedef struct {
        int left,top,right,bottom;
        } RECT;

typedef struct {
        char name[MENULINESIZE+1];
        int (*proc)();
        } MENUITEM;

typedef struct {
        int count;
        char title[MENUTITLESIZE+1];
        } MENUHEAD;

typedef struct {
        int count;
        char title[MENUTITLESIZE+1];
        MENUITEM item[MAXMENUITEM];
        } MENU;

typedef struct {
```

```
        OBJECTHEAD head;
        RECT frame;
        char *back;
        } WINDOW;

typedef struct {
        OBJECTHEAD head;
        RECT frame;
        char *text;
        unsigned int active;
        } BUTTON;

typedef struct {
        OBJECTHEAD head;
        int x,y;
        RECT frame;
        char select;
        unsigned int active;
        char *bitmap;
        int (*proc)();
        } BITMAP;

typedef struct {
        OBJECTHEAD head;
        int x,y;
        char *text;
        unsigned int active;
        } TEXT;

typedef struct {
        OBJECTHEAD head;
        int x,y;
        int length;
        RECT frame;
        char *text;
        unsigned int active;
        } TEXTFIELD;

typedef struct {
        OBJECTHEAD head;
        int x,y;
        int length,depth;
        int count;
        int top;
        RECT frame;
        char *base;
        } LIST;

typedef struct {
        OBJECTHEAD head;
        int x,y;
        int size;
        RECT frame,uparr,dnarr,thumb,jump;
        unsigned int active;
        int min,max,cur;
        } SCROLLBAR;

typedef struct {
        OBJECTHEAD head;
        int x,y;
        RECT frame;
        unsigned int active;
        char *text;
```

```
                char select;
                } CHECKBOX;

        typedef struct {
                OBJECTHEAD head;
                int x,y;
                int length;
                int curpos;
                int (*proc)();
                char select;
                RECT frame;
                char *text;
                unsigned int active;
                } EDITFIELD;

        typedef struct {
                char name[FONTNAMESIZE+1];
                char number;
                char pointsize;
                char charwide[(MAXFONTCHAR-MINFONTCHAR)+1];
                unsigned int charoff[(MAXFONTCHAR-MINFONTCHAR)+1];
                unsigned int bitmapwidth;
                unsigned int bitmapdepth;
                unsigned int bitmapbytes;
                unsigned int widestchar;
                unsigned int padwidth;
                unsigned int spacewidth;
                } FONT;

        typedef int     RFILE;

        typedef struct {
                char id[8];
                char description[65];
                unsigned int count;
                } RESHEAD;

        typedef struct {
                char type[4];
                unsigned long number;
                unsigned int size;
                } RESOURCE;

        typedef struct {
                int (*init_printer)();
                int (*print_line)();
                int (*deinit_printer)();
                int (*print_text)();
                int (*null_one);
                int (*null_two);
                int (*null_three);
                int (*null_four);
                int page_wide;
                int page_deep;
                int line_deep;
                int colours;
                int driver_version;
                int driver_subversion;
                char name[25];
                } PRINTDRIVER;

extern unsigned int SCREENTBL[];
extern unsigned int SCREENSEG,SCREENBYTES;      /* variables in */
extern unsigned int SCREENWIDE,SCREENDEEP;      /* GUIASM.OBJ   */
```

```
char *getfiles(char *spec,int *count,char *drivemap);

void DrawString(int x,int y,char *p,int mask);

int OpenWindow(WINDOW *w,RECT *r);
int PointInRect(POINT *p,RECT *r);
int whereMouse(POINT *p,WINDOW *w);

int trackCheckbox(CHECKBOX *cb);
CHECKBOX *findCheckbox(WINDOW *w,POINT *p);
addCheckbox(WINDOW *w,CHECKBOX *cb,int x,int y,char *text,int select,int active);
drawCheckbox(CHECKBOX *cb);

chooseFile(char *spec,char *name,int x,int y,char *drivemap);
putFile(char *spec,char *name,int x,int y,char *drivemap);

trackScrollbar(SCROLLBAR *sb,int rt);
adjustThumb(SCROLLBAR *sb,int n);
eraseThumb(SCROLLBAR *sb);
drawThumb(SCROLLBAR *sb);
SCROLLBAR *findScrollbar(WINDOW *w,POINT *p);
addVertScroll(WINDOW *w,SCROLLBAR *sb,int x,int y,int len, \
    int min,int max,int cur,int active);
drawVertScroll(SCROLLBAR *sb);

trackList(LIST *lp,char *s);
LIST *findList(WINDOW *w,POINT *p);
addList(WINDOW *w,LIST *l,int x,int y,int width,int depth, \
    int count,int top,char *base);
drawList(LIST *l);

addText(WINDOW *w,TEXT *t,int x,int y,char *p,int a);
drawText(TEXT *t);

addTextField(WINDOW *w,TEXTFIELD *t,int x,int y,int l,char *p,int a);
drawTextfield(TEXTFIELD *t);

addEditField(WINDOW *w,EDITFIELD *t,int x,int y,int l,char *p, \
    int (*proc)(),int a);
drawEditfield(EDITFIELD *t);
trackEditfield(EDITFIELD *f);
EDITFIELD *findEditfield(WINDOW *w,POINT *p);
Keyboard(WINDOW *w);

trackBitmap(BITMAP *b);
BITMAP *findBitmap(WINDOW *w,POINT *p);
addBitmap(WINDOW *w,BITMAP *b,int x,int y,char *p,int select,\
    int (*proc)(),int active);
drawBitmap(BITMAP *b);

addButton(WINDOW *w,BUTTON *b,char *tx,int active);
drawButton(BUTTON *b);
trackButton(BUTTON *b);
BUTTON *findButton(WINDOW *w,POINT *p);

InitMenuManager(void);
int addMenu(MENU *m);
DrawMenuBar(void);
doMenu(POINT *p);

InitWindowManager(void);
openWindow(WINDOW *w,RECT *r);
```

```
        closeWindow(WINDOW *w);

        whereMouse(POINT *p,WINDOW *w);

        deinitGraphics(void);
        initGraphics(void);

        MouseOff(void);
        MouseOn(void);
        MoveMouse(POINT *p);
        MouseButton(void);
        MouseDown(POINT *p);
        MouseLoc(POINT *p);
        InitMouse(void);
        whichCard(void);
        long tick(void);
        isHerc(void);
        isRam(unsigned int n);
        SetupMouse(int mx,int my,int x,int y,int n);
        RestoreHercDivet(void);

        PointInRect(POINT *p,RECT *r);
        SetRect(RECT *r,int left,int top,int right,int bottom);
        InvertRect(RECT *r);

        int idle(void);
        int buffersize(RECT *r);
        char *mono2ega(char *source);
        char *ega2mono(char *source);

        int ismonomode(void);
        void arrowCursor(void);
        void waitCursor(void);

        /* font related prototypes */
        int islegalfontsize(int n);
        int writeFontRes(char *path,FONT *font,char *bitmap);
        int charwidthFN(int n,FONT *font);
        int stringwidthFN(char *s,FONT *font);
        int fontdepthFN(FONT *font);
        char *bitmapstringFN(char *s,FONT *font);
        int drawstringFN(char *s,FONT *font,int x,int y);

        /* resource related prototypes */
        int createRF(char *name,char *description);
        RFILE openRF(char *name);
        void closeRF(RFILE fh);
        int addRF(RFILE fh,char *type,unsigned long number, \
            unsigned int size,char *res);
        int countRF(RFILE fh,char *type);
        int getdataRF(char *p,RFILE fh,unsigned int size);
        int getRF(RFILE fh,char *type,long n,RESOURCE *rc);
        int getnumberedRF(RFILE fh,char *type,int n,RESOURCE *rc);
        int getallRF(RFILE fh,int (*proc)());
        int getinfoRF(RESHEAD *rh,RFILE fh);
        long freenumberRF(RFILE fh,char *type);
        int removeresRF(RFILE fh,RESOURCE *rc);
        int dcreate(char *s);
        int dopen(char *s);
        void dclose(RFILE h);
        int dread(char *p,unsigned int n,RFILE h);
        int dwrite(char *p,unsigned int,RFILE h);
        long dseek(RFILE h,long l,int m);
        long dtell(RFILE h);
```

B-1 Continued

```
#if _GUIDATA
int graphicmode,hercdivet,menuindex=0;

POINT fakeMouseDown={-1,-1};

MENU *menuarray[MENUCOUNT];
WINDOW screenwindow;
RECT menubarRect;          /* where the menu bar is */
int diskErr;               /* disk error value */
char errbuf[129];          /* place to store valid directory for error */

char scrollbarfill[]="\063\314\063\314\063\314\063\314";

unsigned int altkeytable[]= {
        ALT_Q,'Q',ALT_W,'W',ALT_E,'E',ALT_R,'R',
        ALT_T,'T',ALT_Y,'Y',ALT_U,'U',ALT_I,'I',
        ALT_O,'O',ALT_P,'P',ALT_A,'A',ALT_S,'S',
        ALT_D,'D',ALT_F,'F',ALT_G,'G',ALT_H,'H',
        ALT_J,'J',ALT_K,'K',ALT_L,'L',ALT_Z,'Z',
        ALT_X,'X',ALT_C,'C',ALT_V,'V',ALT_B,'B',
        ALT_N,'N',ALT_M,'M',ALT_1,'1',ALT_2,'2',
        ALT_3,'3',ALT_4,'4',ALT_5,'5',ALT_6,'6',
        ALT_7,'7',ALT_8,'8',ALT_9,'9',ALT_0,'0',
        0xffff
                };

char FONTSIZEARRAY[]={6,7,8,9,10,11,12,14,16,18,20,22,24,28,30,32,36,0};
char masktable[8]={0x80,0x40,0x20,0x10,0x08,0x04,0x02,0x01};

#else
extern int graphicmode,hercdivet,menuindex;

extern POINT fakeMouseDown;
extern MENU *menuarray[MENUCOUNT];
extern WINDOW screenwindow;

extern RECT menubarRect;
extern int diskErr;
extern char errbuf[129];
extern char scrollbarfill[];
extern unsigned int altkeytable[];
extern char FONTSIZEARRAY[];
extern char masktable[];
#endif
```

C

The GUI C source code

Appendix C contains the complete source code for the graphical user interface library, GUI.C. In order to avoid spurious warnings and complaints from Turbo C, make sure you set its compiler and linker defaults appropriately when you compile and subsequently use this library. Specifically, turn off the ANSI extensions, make sure that characters are unsigned, and use case-insensitive linking.

```
/*
     Alchemy paint version 1.0
     copyright (c) 1990 Alchemy Mindworks Inc.
*/

#include "stdio.h"
#include "dos.h"
#include "dir.h"
#include "alloc.h"
#include "ctype.h"
#include "string.h"
#include "graphics.h"
#define    _GUIDATA       1
#include "gui.h"

#if FASTWINDOW

/* return the size of a buffer for fastgetimage */
fastbuffersize(r)
     RECT *r;
{
     int left,right;
```

C-1 The complete source code for GUI.C, the graphical user interface library.

```
        left=r->left & 0xfff8;
        right=r->right;
        if(right & 0x0007) right=(right | 0x0007)+1;
        return(4+(pixels2bytes(right-left)*((r->bottom-r->top)+1)));
}

/* get a fast image fragment to the buffer p */
fastgetimage(left,top,right,bottom,p)
        int left,top,right,bottom;
        char *p;
{
        int i,width,depth,bleft,bytes;

        left &= 0xfff8;
        if(right & 0x0007) right=(right | 0x0007)+1;
        width=right-left;
        depth=bottom-top;
        bleft=left>>3;
        bytes=pixels2bytes(width);

        *p++=(width-1);
        *p++=((width-1)>>8);
        *p++=(depth-1);
        *p++=((depth-1)>>8);

        for(i=0;i<depth;++i) {
             memcpy(p,MK_FP(SCREENSEG,SCREENTBL[top+i]+bleft),bytes);
             p+=bytes;
        }
}


/* place a fast image on the screen */
fastputimage(left,top,p)
        int left,top;
        char *p;
{
        int i,width,depth,bleft,bytes;

        width=ImageWidth(p);
        depth=ImageDepth(p);
        bleft=left>>3;
        bytes=pixels2bytes(width);
        p+=4;

        fourplanes();
        for(i=0;i<depth;++i) {
             memcpy(MK_FP(SCREENSEG,SCREENTBL[top+i]+bleft),p,bytes);
             p+=bytes;
        }
}
#endif        FASTWINDOW

/* do a choose file dialog */
chooseFile(spec,name,x,y,drivemap)
        char *spec,*name;
        int x,y;
        char *drivemap;
{
        SCROLLBAR sb,*sp;
        LIST ls,*lp;
        TEXT errt;
        TEXTFIELD fspec;
        EDITFIELD fname,*ep;
```

```
        RECT r,errr;
        WINDOW w,errw;
        POINT p;
        BUTTON ok,can,errok,*bp;
        char *thespec,drive[MAXDRIVE],nm[24];
        char dir[MAXDIR],file[MAXFILE],ext[MAXEXT];
        unsigned int rt;
        int loc=0,a_inner,a_outer=0xff,erra,i,isname();

        r.left=x;
        r.top=y;
        r.right=r.left+300;
        r.bottom=r.top+180;

        name[0]=0;
        if(openWindow(&w,&r)) {
            SetRect(&ok.frame,r.left+168,r.bottom-25,r.left+200,r.bottom-10);
            AddButton(&w,&ok,"Ok",ACTIVE);

            SetRect(&can.frame,r.left+216,r.bottom-25,r.left+280,r.bottom-10);
            AddButton(&w,&can,"Cancel",ACTIVE);

            if(strlen(spec) <= 35) thespec=spec;
            else thespec=spec+strlen(spec)-35;
            AddTextField(&w,&fspec,r.left+8,r.top+8,35,thespec,ACTIVE);

            AddEditField(&w,&fname,r.left+184,r.top+35,13,name,isname,ACTIVE);

            AddList(&w,&ls,r.left+8,r.top+34,FILELINESIZE,14,0,loc,NULL);
            AddVertScroll(&w,&sb,ls.frame.right,ls.frame.top,
                ls.frame.bottom-ls.frame.top,0,0,0,INACTIVE);

do {
        a_inner=0xff;
        ls.count=0;
        waitCursor();
        ls.base=getfiles(spec,&ls.count,drivemap);
        arrowcursor();
        ls.top=sb.cur=0;
        if(ls.count > 14) {
                sb.max=ls.count-14;
                sb.active=ACTIVE;
        }
        else {
                sb.max=0;
                sb.active=INACTIVE;
        }
        adjustThumb(&sb,0);
        drawList(&ls);
        drawVertScroll(&sb);

        while(a_inner) {
                Keyboard(&w);
                if(MouseDown(&p)) {
                        rt=whereMouse(&p,&w);
                        if(rt & inButton) {
                                bp=findButton(&w,&p);
                                trackButton(bp);
                                if(bp==&can) {
                                        name[0]=0;
                                        a_inner=a_outer=0;
                                }
                                else if(bp==&ok) {
                                        if(name[0] != '\\' && name[0] != '[')
                                                a_outer=0;
```

```
                            a_inner=0;
                }
        }
        else if(rt & inVertScroll) {
                sp=findScrollbar(&w,&p);
                trackScrollbar(sp,rt);
                if(sp==&sb) {
                        ls.top=sp->cur;
                        drawList(&ls);
                }
        }
        else if(rt & inList) {
                strcpy(nm,name);
                lp=findList(&w,&p);
                trackList(lp,name);
                drawEditfield(&fname);
                if(!strcmp(name,nm)) {
                        if(name[0] != '\\' && name[0] != '[')
                                a_outer=0;
                        a_inner=0;
                }
        }
        else if(rt & inEditField) {
                ep=findEditfield(&w,&p);
                trackEditfield(ep);
                drawEditfield(ep);
        }
        else errorbeep();
    }
}
if(ls.base != NULL) free(ls.base);
if(name[0]=='\\') {
    /* change directory */
    fnsplit(spec,drive,dir,file,ext);
    if(strcmp(name+1,"..")) {
        /* add new directory */
        strcat(dir,name+1);
        strcat(dir,"\\");
    }
    else {
        /* back up one directory */
        i=strlen(dir)-2;
        while(i>0 && dir[i] != '\\') --i;
        dir[i+1]=0;
    }
    name[0]=0;
    fnmerge(spec,drive,dir,file,ext);
    drawTextfield(&fspec);
    drawEditfield(&fname);
}
else if(name[0]=='[') {
    /* change drives */
    if(!testdisk(name[2]-'A')) {
        fnsplit(spec,drive,dir,file,ext);
        drive[0]=name[2];
        strcpy(dir,"\\");
        fnmerge(spec,drive,dir,file,ext);
        name[0]=0;
        drawEditfield(&fname);
        drawTextfield(&fspec);
    }
    else {
        SetRect(&errr,r.left+16,r.top+8,r.left+240,r.top+72);
        if(OpenWindow(&errw,&errr)) {
```

```
                    AddText(&errw,&errt,errr.left+48,errr.top+10,
                        "Error reading drive",ACTIVE);
                    SetRect(&errok.frame,errr.left+168,
                            errr.bottom-25,
                            errr.left+200,
                            errr.bottom-10);
                    AddButton(&errw,&errok,"Ok",ACTIVE);
                    erra=1;
                    do {
                        if(MouseDown(&p)) {
                            Keyboard(&errw);
                            rt=whereMouse(&p,&errw);
                            if(rt & inButton) {
                                bp=findButton(&errw,&p);
                                trackButton(bp);
                                if(bp==&errok) erra=0;
                            }
                        }
                    } while(erra);
                    CloseWindow(&errw);
                }
            }
            } else a_outer=0;
        } while(a_outer);
        closeWindow(&w);
    } else errorbeep();
    return(name[0]);
}

/* return a buffer with file names in it - used by chooseFile */
char *getfiles(spec,count,drivemap)
    char *spec;
    int *count;
    char *drivemap;
{
    struct ffblk f;
    char *p,drive[MAXDRIVE],dir[MAXDIR],b[128];
    int i=0,j,k,dircheck();

    *count=0;

    /* start by counting the files */

    k=strlen(drivemap);
    if(!findfirst(spec,&f,0)) {
        do {
            ++*count;
        } while(!findnext(&f));
    }

    fnsplit(spec,drive,dir,NULL,NULL);
    fnmerge(b,drive,dir,"*",".");
    if(!findfirst(b,&f,16)) {
        do {
            if((f.ff_attrib & 16) == 16 && strcmp(f.ff_name,".")) ++*count;
        } while(!findnext(&f));
    }

    *count+=k;
    if(*count==0) return(NULL);

    if((p=malloc(*count*(FILELINESIZE+1))) != NULL) {
        if(!findfirst(spec,&f,0)) {
            do {
```

```
                        sprintf(p+((FILELINESIZE+1)*i++),"%s",f.ff_name);
                } while(!findnext(&f));
        }
        if(!findfirst(b,&f,16)) {
                do {
                    if((f.ff_attrib & 16) == 16 && strcmp(f.ff_name,"."))
                            sprintf(p+((FILELINESIZE+1)*i++),"\\%s",f.ff_name);
                } while(!findnext(&f));
        }

        for(j=0;j<k;++j)
                sprintf(p+((FILELINESIZE+1)*i++),"[ %c ]",drivemap[j]);
        qsort(p,*count,FILELINESIZE+1,strcmp);
    }
    return(p);
}
/* see if drive n is on line - used by chooseFile */
testdisk(n)
    int n;
{
    void interrupt (*oldHarderr)();
    FILE *fp;
    char b[32];
    int diskErrorHandler();

    oldHarderr=getvect(0x24);
        harderr(diskErrorHandler);
    diskErr=0;
    getcwd(errbuf,80);
    sprintf(b,"%c:\\TEMP.DAT",n+'A');
    if((fp=fopen(b,"r")) != NULL) fclose(fp);
    setvect(0x24,oldHarderr);
    return(diskErr);
}

/* handle a disk hardware error - used by chooseFile */
#pragma warn -par
int diskErrorHandler(errval,ax,bp,si)
    int errval,ax,bp,si;
{
    if(ax >=0) {
        diskErr=1;
        restoreDir(errbuf);
    }
    hardretn(2);
}

/* restore a saved directory path - used by chooseFile */
restoreDir(s)
    char *s;
{
    strupr(s);
    if(isalpha(s[0]) && s[1]==':') setdisk(s[0]-'A');
    chdir(s);
}

/* return character for file name or false if not ok - used by chooseFile */
isname(c)
{
    c=toupper(c);
    if(isalpha(c) || isdigit(c) || c=='.') return(c);
    else return(0);
```

```
    }

/* handle an alternate key press and dispatch a menu command */
dispatchMenuItem()
{
    char *p;
    unsigned int c,ca=0,i=0,menu,item,rt=0;

    if(kbhit()) {
        if(!(bioskey(1) & 0x00ff)) {
            c=GetKey();
            while(altkeytable[i] != 0xffff) {
                if(altkeytable[i]==c) {
                    ca=altkeytable[i+1];
                    break;
                }
                i+=2;
            }
            if(!ca) return(0);

            for(menu=0;menu<menuindex;++menu) {
                if(rt) break;
                for(item=0;item<menuarray[menu]->count;++item) {
                    if(rt) break;
                    if((p=strchr(menuarray[menu]->item[item].name,KEYMENUCHAR))
                       != NULL) {
                        if(ca==(unsigned int)p[1]) {
                            (menuarray[menu]->item[item].proc)(item);
                            rt=1;
                        }
                    }
                }
            }
        }
    }
}

/* check for keyboard activity if edit fields are in use */
Keyboard(w)
    WINDOW *w;
{
    OBJECTHEAD *oh;
    BUTTON *bp;
    EDITFIELD *f;
    int c,len,i,bcount=0;

    /* if there's a key waiting... */

    if(kbhit()) {
        c=GetKey();
        oh=(OBJECTHEAD *)w;
        while(oh != NULL) {
            if(oh->type==inButton) {
                bp=(BUTTON *)oh;
                ++bcount;
                if(bcount==1 && c==13) {
                    fakeMouseDown.x=bp->frame.left+1;
                    fakeMouseDown.y=bp->frame.top+1;
                }
                else if(bcount==2 && c==27) {
                    fakeMouseDown.x=bp->frame.left+1;
                    fakeMouseDown.y=bp->frame.top+1;
                }
            }
```

```
          if(oh->type==inEditField) {
              f=(EDITFIELD *)oh;
              if(f->select) {
                  len=strlen(f->text);
                  switch(c) {
                      case DEL:
                          if(f->curpos < len) {
                                  for(i=f->curpos;i<=len;++i)
                                      f->text[i]=f->text[i+1];
                          }
                          break;
                      case HOME:
                          f->curpos=0;
                          break;
                      case END:
                          f->curpos=len;
                          break;
                      case CURSOR_LEFT:
                          if(f->curpos) --f->curpos;
                          break;
                      case CURSOR_RIGHT:
                          if(f->curpos < len) ++f->curpos;
                          break;
                      case 'X'-0x40:
                          f->curpos=0;
                          f->text[0]=0;
                          break;
                      case 8:
                          if(f->curpos && len) {
                              if(f->curpos < len) {
                                  for(i=f->curpos;i<=len;++i)
                                      f->text[i-1]=f->text[i];
                                  --f->curpos;
                              }
                              else {
                                  --f->curpos;
                                  f->text[len-1]=0;
                              }
                          }
                          break;
                      default:
                          if(f->proc != NULL) c=(f->proc)(c);
                          else {
                              if(!isprint(c)) c=0;
                          }
                          if(c && (len+1) < f->length) {
                              for(i=(len+1);i>f->curpos;--i)
                                  f->text[i]=f->text[i-1];
                              f->text[f->curpos]=c;
                              ++f->curpos;
                          }
                          break;
                  }
                  drawEditfield(f);
              }
          }
          oh=oh->next;
      }
  }
}

/* track an editfield control */
```

```
        trackEditfield(f)
            EDITFIELD *f;
        {
            POINT p;
            MouseLoc(&p);
            if(PointInRect(&p,&f->frame)) f->select=0xff;
        }

        /* return a pointer to the selected editfield */
        EDITFIELD *findEditfield(w,p)
            WINDOW *w;
            POINT *p;
        {
            OBJECTHEAD *oh;
            EDITFIELD *f;

            oh=(OBJECTHEAD *)w;
            while(oh != NULL) {
                if(oh->type == inEditField) {
                    f=(EDITFIELD *)oh;
                    if(PointInRect(p,&f->frame) && f->active==ACTIVE) return(f);
                }
                oh=oh->next;
            }
            return(NULL);
        }

        /* add an edit field to the window object w */
        addEditField(w,t,x,y,l,p,proc,a)
            WINDOW *w;          /* the window */
            EDITFIELD *t;       /* the TEXT */
            int x,y;            /* the location */
            int l;              /* the maximum length */
            char *p;            /* the words */
            int (*proc)();      /* character filter procedure */
            int a;              /* active */
        {
            OBJECTHEAD *oh;
            /* start by finding end of chain */

            oh=(OBJECTHEAD *)w;
            while(oh->next != NULL) oh=oh->next;

            oh->next=(OBJECTHEAD *)t;
            t->x=x;
            t->y=y;
            t->text=p;
            t->active=a;
            t->length=l;
            t->select=0x00;
            t->curpos=0;
            t->proc=proc;
            t->frame.left=x-3;
            t->frame.top=y-3;
            t->frame.right=x+(8*l)+2;
            t->frame.bottom=y+FONTDEEP+2;
            t->head.type=inEditField;
            t->head.next=NULL;
            drawEditfield(t);
        }

        /* draw an edit field */
        drawEditfield(t)
            EDITFIELD *t;
```

```
{
    MouseOff();
    setwritemode(COPY_PUT);
    setfillstyle(SOLID_FILL,getmaxcolor());
    setlinestyle(SOLID_LINE,0,NORM_WIDTH);
    setcolor(BLACK);
    bar(t->frame.left,t->frame.top,t->frame.right,t->frame.bottom);
    rectangle(t->frame.left,t->frame.top,t->frame.right,t->frame.bottom);
    DrawString(t->x,t->y,t->text,t->active);
    if(t->active==ACTIVE && t->select) {
        setcolor(getmaxcolor());
        setwritemode(XOR_PUT);
        line(t->frame.left+(8*t->curpos)+2,t->frame.top+2,
            t->frame.left+(8*t->curpos)+2,t->frame.bottom-2);
    }
    MouseOn();
}

/* track a check box */
trackCheckbox(cb)
    CHECKBOX *cb;
{
    POINT p;

    MouseLoc(&p);
    if(PointInRect(&p,&cb->frame)) {
        InvertRect(&cb->frame);
        while(MouseDown(&p));
        InvertRect(&cb->frame);
    }
}

/* return a pointer to the selected checkbox */
CHECKBOX *findCheckbox(w,p)
    WINDOW *w;
    POINT *p;
{
    OBJECTHEAD *oh;
    CHECKBOX *cb;

    oh=(OBJECTHEAD *)w;
    while(oh != NULL) {
        if(oh->type == inCheckBox) {
            cb=(CHECKBOX *)oh;
            if(PointInRect(p,&cb->frame) && cb->active==ACTIVE) return(cb);
        }
        oh=oh->next;
    }
    return(NULL);
}

/* add a checkbox object to the window w */
addCheckbox(w,cb,x,y,text,select,active)
    WINDOW *w;          /* the window */
    CHECKBOX *cb;       /* the checkbox */
    int x,y;            /* the upper left corner */
    char *text;         /* the items */
    int select;         /* true if selected */
    int active;         /* active */
{
    OBJECTHEAD *oh;
    /* start by finding end of chain */

    oh=(OBJECTHEAD *)w;
```

```
        while(oh->next != NULL) oh=oh->next;

        oh->next=(OBJECTHEAD *)cb;

        cb->x=x;
        cb->y=y;
        cb->text=text;
        cb->select=select;
        cb->active=active;
        cb->frame.left=x-1;
        cb->frame.top=y-1;
        cb->frame.right=x+10;
        cb->frame.bottom=y+10;
        cb->head.type=inCheckBox;
        cb->head.next=NULL;
        drawCheckbox(cb);
}

/* draw a checkbox */
drawCheckbox(cb)
        CHECKBOX *cb;
{
        MouseOff();
        setwritemode(COPY_PUT);
        setfillstyle(SOLID_FILL,getmaxcolor());
        setlinestyle(SOLID_LINE,0,NORM_WIDTH);
        setcolor(BLACK);
        bar(cb->frame.left,cb->frame.top,cb->frame.right,cb->frame.bottom);
        rectangle(cb->frame.left,cb->frame.top,cb->frame.right,cb->frame.bottom);
        DrawString(cb->frame.right+16,cb->frame.top+2,cb->text,cb->active);
        if(cb->select) {
                line(cb->frame.left,cb->frame.top,cb->frame.right,cb->frame.bottom);
                line(cb->frame.left,cb->frame.bottom,cb->frame.right,cb->frame.top);
        }
        MouseOn();
}

/* track a scroll bar - rt is mouse return for part flag */
trackScrollbar(sb,rt)
        SCROLLBAR *sb;
        int rt;
{
        POINT p,oldp;
        int i,n;

        if(sb != NULL && (sb->head.type==inVertScroll ||
                        sb->head.type==inHorScroll) && sb->active==ACTIVE) {
                if(rt & inUpArrow) {
                        InvertRect(&sb->uparr);
                        n=250;
                        while(sb->cur > sb->min && MouseDown(&p) &&
                                PointInRect(&p,&sb->uparr)) {
                eraseThumb(sb);
                adjustThumb(sb,-1);
                drawThumb(sb);
                delay(n);
                n=25;
        }
        InvertRect(&sb->uparr);
}
else if(rt & inDownArrow) {
        InvertRect(&sb->dnarr);
        n=250;
        while(sb->cur < (sb->max-1) && MouseDown(&p) &&
```

```
            PointInRect(&p,&sb->dnarr)) {
        eraseThumb(sb);
        adjustThumb(sb,1);
        drawThumb(sb);
        delay(n);
        n=25;
    }
    InvertRect(&sb->dnarr);

    if(sb->head.type==inVertScroll) {
        eraseThumb(sb);
        if(sb->thumb.top==sb->jump.top) sb->cur=sb->min;
        else if(sb->thumb.bottom==sb->jump.bottom)
            sb->cur=sb->max;
        else sb->cur=(int)((float)(sb->max-sb->min)/
            ((float)(sb->size-48)/(sb->thumb.top-sb->jump.top)));
        drawThumb(sb);
    }
    else {
        eraseThumb(sb);
        if(sb->thumb.left==sb->jump.left) sb->cur=sb->min;
        else if(sb->thumb.right==sb->jump.right)
            sb->cur=sb->max;
        else sb->cur=(int)((float)(sb->max-sb->min)/
            ((float)(sb->size-48)/(sb->thumb.left-sb->jump.left)));
        drawThumb(sb);
    }
}
else if(rt & inJumpUp) {
    eraseThumb(sb);
    adjustThumb(sb,-8);
    drawThumb(sb);
}
else if(rt & inJumpDown) {
    eraseThumb(sb);
    adjustThumb(sb,8);
    drawThumb(sb);
    if(sb->head.type==inVertScroll) {
        eraseThumb(sb);
        if(sb->thumb.top==sb->jump.top) sb->cur=sb->min;
        else if(sb->thumb.bottom==sb->jump.bottom)
            sb->cur=sb->max;
        else sb->cur=(int)((float)(sb->max-sb->min)/
            ((float)(sb->size-48)/(sb->thumb.top-sb->jump.top)));
        drawThumb(sb);
    }
    else {
            eraseThumb(sb);
            if(sb->thumb.left==sb->jump.left) sb->cur=sb->min;
            else if(sb->thumb.right==sb->jump.right)
                sb->cur=sb->max;
            else sb->cur=(int)((float)(sb->max-sb->min)/
                ((float)(sb->size-48)/(sb->thumb.left-sb->jump.left)));
            drawThumb(sb);
        }
    }
    else if(rt & inThumb) {
        if(sb->head.type==inVertScroll) {
            MouseDown(&oldp);
            while(MouseDown(&p)) {
                if(oldp.y != p.y && PointInRect(&p,&sb->jump)) {
                    eraseThumb(sb);
```

```
                              i=p.y-oldp.y;
                              if((sb->thumb.top+i) <= sb->jump.top ||
                                  (sb->thumb.bottom+i) >sb->jump.bottom) i=0;
                              sb->thumb.top+=i;
                              sb->thumb.bottom+=i;
                              drawThumb(sb);
                              memcpy((char *)&oldp,(char *)&p,sizeof(POINT));
                          }
                      }
                      eraseThumb(sb);
                      if(sb->thumb.top==sb->jump.top) sb->cur=sb->min;
                      else if(sb->thumb.bottom==sb->jump.bottom)
                          sb->cur=sb->max;
                      else sb->cur=(int)((float)(sb->max-sb->min)/
                          ((float)(sb->size-48)/(sb->thumb.top-sb->jump.top)));
                      drawThumb(sb);
                  }
              else if(sb->head.type==inHorScroll) {
                  MouseDown(&oldp);
                  while(MouseDown(&p)) {
                      if(oldp.x != p.x && PointInRect(&p,&sb->jump)) {
                          eraseThumb(sb);
                          i=p.x-oldp.x;
                          if((sb->thumb.left+i) <= sb->jump.left ||
                              (sb->thumb.right+i) > sb->jump.right) i=0;
                          sb->thumb.left+=i;
                          sb->thumb.right+=i;
                          drawThumb(sb);
                          memcpy((char *)&oldp,(char *)&p,sizeof(POINT));
                      }
                  }
                  eraseThumb(sb);
                  if(sb->thumb.left==sb->jump.left) sb->cur=sb->min;
                  else if(sb->thumb.right==sb->jump.right)
                      sb->cur=sb->max;
                  else sb->cur=(int)((float)(sb->max-sb->min)/
                      ((float)(sb->size-48)/(sb->thumb.left-sb->jump.left)));
                  drawThumb(sb);
              }
          }
      while(MouseDown(&p));
  }
}
/* internal routine - adjust the scroll bar thumb */
adjustThumb(sb,n)
    SCROLLBAR *sb;
    int n;
{
    int i,rn,f;

    i=sb->cur+n;
    if(i < sb->min) i=sb->min;
    else if(i >= sb->max) i=sb->max-1;
    sb->cur=i;
    rn=sb->size-48;
    if(sb->cur==sb->min) f=0;
    else if(sb->cur==(sb->max-1)) f=rn;
    else f=(int)((float)rn/((float)(sb->max-sb->min)/(float)sb->cur));

    if(sb->head.type==inVertScroll) {
        if(f==rn) sb->thumb.top=sb->dnarr.top-16;
        else sb->thumb.top=sb->uparr.bottom+f+1;
        sb->thumb.bottom=sb->thumb.top+16;
    }
```

```
    else if(sb->head.type==inHorScroll) {
        if(f==rn) sb->thumb.left=sb->dnarr.left-16;
        else sb->thumb.left=sb->uparr.right+f+1;
        sb->thumb.right=sb->thumb.left+16;
    }
}

/* internal routine - erase the scroll bar thumb */
eraseThumb(sb)
    SCROLLBAR *sb;
{
    MouseOff();
    setcolor(BLACK);
    setfillpattern(scrollbarfill,getmaxcolor());
    if(sb->head.type==inVertScroll)
        bar(sb->thumb.left+1,sb->thumb.top,
            sb->thumb.right-1,sb->thumb.bottom-1);
    else bar(sb->thumb.left,sb->thumb.top+1,
            sb->thumb.right-1,sb->thumb.bottom-1);
    MouseOn();
}

/* internal routine - draw the scroll bar thumb */
drawThumb(sb)
    SCROLLBAR *sb;
{
    static char thumb2[]={ 0x0f,0x00,0x0f,0x00,
        0x00,0x00,0x7F,0xFE,0x7F,0xFE,0x7F,0xFE,
        0x7F,0xFE,0x7F,0xFE,0x7F,0xFE,0x7F,0xFE,
        0x7F,0xFE,0x7F,0xFE,0x7F,0xFE,0x7F,0xFE,
        0x7F,0xFE,0x7F,0xFE,0x7F,0xFE,0x00,0x00 };

    static char thumb16[]={ 0x0f,0x00,0x0f,0x00,
        0x00,0x00,0x00,0x00,0x00,0x00,0x00,0x00,
        0x7F,0xFE,0x7F,0xFE,0x7F,0xFE,0x7F,0xFE,
        0x7F,0xFE,0x7F,0xFE,0x7F,0xFE,0x7F,0xFE,
        0x7F,0xFE,0x7F,0xFE,0x7F,0xFE,0x7F,0xFE,
        0x7F,0xFE,0x7F,0xFE,0x7F,0xFE,0x7F,0xFE,
        0x7F,0xFE,0x7F,0xFE,0x7F,0xFE,0x7F,0xFE,
        0x7F,0xFE,0x7F,0xFE,0x7F,0xFE,0x7F,0xFE,
        0x7F,0xFE,0x7F,0xFE,0x7F,0xFE,0x7F,0xFE,
        0x7F,0xFE,0x7F,0xFE,0x7F,0xFE,0x7F,0xFE,
        0x7F,0xFE,0x7F,0xFE,0x7F,0xFE,0x7F,0xFE,
        0x7F,0xFE,0x7F,0xFE,0x7F,0xFE,0x7F,0xFE,
        0x7F,0xFE,0x7F,0xFE,0x7F,0xFE,0x7F,0xFE,
        0x7F,0xFE,0x7F,0xFE,0x7F,0xFE,0x7F,0xFE,
        0x7F,0xFE,0x7F,0xFE,0x7F,0xFE,0x7F,0xFE,
        0x00,0x00,0x00,0x00,0x00,0x00,0x00,0x00 };

    if(sb->active==ACTIVE) {
        MouseOff();
        if(ismonomode())
            putimage(sb->thumb.left,sb->thumb.top,thumb2,COPY_PUT);
        else putimage(sb->thumb.left,sb->thumb.top,thumb16,COPY_PUT);
        MouseOn();
    }
}

/* return a pointer to the selected scrollbar */
SCROLLBAR *findScrollbar(w,p)
    WINDOW *w;
```

```
        POINT *p;
{
    OBJECTHEAD *oh;
    SCROLLBAR *b;

    oh=(OBJECTHEAD *)w;
    while(oh != NULL) {
        if(oh->type == inVertScroll || oh->type == inHorScroll) {
            b=(SCROLLBAR *)oh;
            if(PointInRect(p,&b->frame) && b->active==ACTIVE) return(b);
        }
        oh=oh->next;
    }
    return(NULL);
}

/* add a vertical scroll object to the window w */
addVertScroll(w,sb,x,y,len,min,max,cur,active)
    WINDOW *w;              /* the window */
    SCROLLBAR *sb;          /* the scroll bar */
    int x,y;                /* the upper left corner */
    int len;                /* the depth of the bar */
    int min,max;            /* the returned values of the bar */
    int cur;                /* where the bar is at the moment */
    int active;             /* is the scroll bar active */
{
    OBJECTHEAD *oh;
    /* start by finding end of chain */

    oh=(OBJECTHEAD *)w;
    while(oh->next != NULL) oh=oh->next;

    oh->next=(OBJECTHEAD *)sb;

    sb->x=x;
    sb->y=y;
    sb->size=len;
    sb->min=min;
    sb->max=max;
    sb->cur=cur;
    sb->active=active;
    sb->frame.left=x;
    sb->frame.top=y;
    sb->frame.right=x+15;
    sb->frame.bottom=y+len;
    SetRect(&sb->uparr,sb->frame.left,sb->frame.top,
                    sb->frame.right,sb->frame.top+15);
    SetRect(&sb->dnarr,sb->frame.left,sb->frame.bottom-15,
                    sb->frame.right,sb->frame.bottom);
    SetRect(&sb->thumb,sb->frame.left,sb->frame.top+16,
                    sb->frame.right,sb->frame.top+32);
    SetRect(&sb->jump, sb->frame.left,sb->uparr.bottom,
                    sb->frame.right,sb->dnarr.top);
    sb->head.type=inVertScroll;
    sb->head.next=NULL;
    drawVertScroll(sb);
}

/* draw a vertical scroll bar */
drawVertScroll(sb)
    SCROLLBAR *sb;
{
    static char uparrow[]={ 0x0f,0x00,0x0f,0x00,
        0x00,0x00,0x7E,0x7E,0x7D,0xBE,0x7B,0xDE,
```

```
            0x77,0xEE,0x6F,0xF6,0x5F,0xFA,0x03,0xC0,
            0x7B,0xDE,0x7B,0xDE,0x7B,0xDE,0x7B,0xDE,
            0x78,0x1E,0x7F,0xFE,0x7F,0xFE,0x00,0x00 };

    static char downarrow[]={ 0x0f,0x00,0x0f,0x00,
            0x00,0x00,0x7F,0xFE,0x7F,0xFE,0x78,0x1E,
            0x7B,0xDE,0x7B,0xDE,0x7B,0xDE,0x7B,0xDE,
            0x03,0xC0,0x5F,0xFA,0x6F,0xF6,0x77,0xEE,
            0x7B,0xDE,0x7D,0xBE,0x7E,0x7E,0x00,0x00 };

    char *p;

    MouseOff();
    if(sb->active==ACTIVE) setfillpattern(scrollbarfill,getmaxcolor());
    else setfillstyle(SOLID_FILL,getmaxcolor());

    setwritemode(COPY_PUT);
    setlinestyle(SOLID_LINE,0,NORM_WIDTH);
    setcolor(BLACK);
    bar(sb->frame.left,sb->frame.top,sb->frame.right,sb->frame.bottom);
    rectangle(sb->frame.left,sb->frame.top,sb->frame.right,sb->frame.bottom);

    if(ismonomode()) putimage(sb->uparr.left,sb->uparr.top,uparrow,COPY_PUT);
    else {
        if((p=mono2ega(uparrow)) != NULL) {
            putimage(sb->uparr.left,sb->uparr.top,p,COPY_PUT);
            free(p);
        } else errorbeep();
    }
    if(ismonomode())
        putimage(sb->dnarr.left,sb->dnarr.bottom-15,downarrow,COPY_PUT);
    else {
        if((p=mono2ega(downarrow)) != NULL) {
            putimage(sb->dnarr.left,sb->dnarr.bottom-15,p,COPY_PUT);
            free(p);
        } else errorbeep();
    }

    drawThumb(sb);

    MouseOn();
}

/* add a horizontal scroll object to the window w */
addHorScroll(w,sb,x,y,len,min,max,cur,active)
    WINDOW *w;              /* the window */
    SCROLLBAR *sb;          /* the scroll bar */
    int x,y;                /* the upper left corner */
    int len;                /* the depth of the bar */
    int min,max;            /* the returned values of the bar */
    int cur;                /* where the bar is at the moment */
    int active;             /* is the scroll bar active */
{
    OBJECTHEAD *oh;
    /* start by finding end of chain */

    oh=(OBJECTHEAD *)w;
    while(oh->next != NULL) oh=oh->next;

    oh->next=(OBJECTHEAD *)sb;

    sb->x=x;
```

```
        sb->y=y;
        sb->size=len;
        sb->min=min;
        sb->max=max;
        sb->cur=cur;
        sb->active=active;
        sb->frame.left=x;
        sb->frame.top=y;
        sb->frame.right=x+len;
        sb->frame.bottom=y+15;
        SetRect(&sb->uparr,sb->frame.left,sb->frame.top,
                        sb->frame.left+15,sb->frame.bottom);
        SetRect(&sb->dnarr,sb->frame.right-15,sb->frame.top,
                        sb->frame.right,sb->frame.bottom);
        SetRect(&sb->thumb,sb->frame.left+16,sb->frame.top,
                        sb->frame.left+32,sb->frame.bottom);
        SetRect(&sb->jump, sb->uparr.right,sb->frame.top,
                        sb->dnarr.left,sb->frame.bottom);
        sb->head.type=inHorScroll;
        sb->head.next=NULL;
        drawHorScroll(sb);
}


drawHorScroll(sb)
        SCROLLBAR *sb;
{
        static char leftarrow[]={ 0x0f,0x00,0x0f,0x00,
            0x00,0x00,0x7E,0x7E,0x7D,0x7E,0x7B,0x7E,
            0x77,0x7E,0x6F,0x06,0x5F,0xF6,0x3F,0xF6,
            0x3F,0xF6,0x5F,0xF6,0x6F,0x06,0x77,0x7E,
            0x7B,0x7E,0x7D,0x7E,0x7E,0x7E,0x00,0x00 };

        static char rightarrow[]={ 0x0f,0x00,0x0f,0x00,
            0x00,0x00,0x7E,0x7E,0xBE,0x7E,0xDE,
            0x7E,0xEE,0x60,0xF6,0x6F,0xFA,0x6F,0xFC,
            0x6F,0xFC,0x6F,0xFA,0x60,0xF6,0x7E,0xEE,
            0x7E,0xDE,0x7E,0xBE,0x7E,0x7E,0x00,0x00 };

        char *p;

        MouseOff();
        if(sb->active==ACTIVE) setfillpattern(scrollbarfill,getmaxcolor());
        else setfillstyle(SOLID_FILL,getmaxcolor());

        setwritemode(COPY_PUT);
        setlinestyle(SOLID_LINE,0,NORM_WIDTH);
        setcolor(BLACK);
        bar(sb->frame.left,sb->frame.top,sb->frame.right,sb->frame.bottom);
        rectangle(sb->frame.left,sb->frame.top,sb->frame.right,sb->frame.bottom);

        if(ismonomode()) putimage(sb->uparr.left,sb->uparr.top,leftarrow,COPY_PUT);
        else {
            if((p=mono2ega(leftarrow)) != NULL) {
                putimage(sb->uparr.left,sb->uparr.top,p,COPY_PUT);
                free(p);
            } else errorbeep();
        }

        if(ismonomode())
            putimage(sb->dnarr.left,sb->dnarr.bottom-15,rightarrow,COPY_PUT);
        else {
            if((p=mono2ega(rightarrow)) != NULL) {
                putimage(sb->dnarr.left,sb->dnarr.bottom-15,p,COPY_PUT);
                free(p);
```

```
            } else errorbeep();
    }

    drawThumb(sb);

    MouseOn();
}

/* track a list control */
trackList(lp,s)
    LIST *lp;
    char *s;
{
    RECT r;
    POINT p;
    int n;

    MouseLoc(&p);
    if(PointInRect(&p,&lp->frame)) {
        if((n=((p.y-lp->frame.top)/MENULINEDEEP)) < lp->depth &&
            n < lp->count) {
            SetRect(&r,lp->frame.left+1,
                        lp->frame.top+(n*MENULINEDEEP)+1,
                        lp->frame.right-1,
                        lp->frame.top+((n+1)*MENULINEDEEP)+3);
            InvertRect(&r);
            while(MouseDown(&p));
            InvertRect(&r);
            strcpy(s,lp->base+((n+lp->top)*(lp->length+1)));
        }
    }
}

/* return a pointer to the selected list */
LIST *findList(w,p)
    WINDOW *w;
    POINT *p;
{
    OBJECTHEAD *oh;
    LIST *b;

    oh=(OBJECTHEAD *)w;
    while(oh != NULL) {
        if(oh->type == inList) {
            b=(LIST *)oh;
            if(PointInRect(p,&b->frame)) return(b);
        }
        oh=oh->next;
    }
    return(NULL);
}

/* add a list object to the window w */
addList(w,l,x,y,width,depth,count,top,base)
    WINDOW *w;              /* the window */
    LIST *l;                /* the list */
    int x,y;                /* the upper left corner */
    int width,depth;        /* the width and depth in characters */
    int count;              /* the number of items in the list */
    int top;                /* the first visible item */
    char *base;             /* the items */
{
```

```
        OBJECTHEAD *oh;
        /* start by finding end of chain */

        oh=(OBJECTHEAD *)w;
        while(oh->next != NULL) oh=oh->next;

        oh->next=(OBJECTHEAD *)l;

        x &= 0xfff8;

        l->x=x;
        l->y=y;
        l->length=width;
        l->depth=depth;
        l->count=count;
        l->top=top;
        l->base=base;
        l->frame.left=x-2;
        l->frame.top=y-2;
        l->frame.right=x+((width+2)*8)+2;
        l->frame.bottom=y+(depth*MENULINEDEEP)+2;
        l->head.type=inList;
        l->head.next=NULL;
        drawList(l);
}

/* draw a list object */
drawList(l)
        LIST *l;
{
        int i;
        MouseOff();
        setwritemode(COPY_PUT);
        setfillstyle(SOLID_FILL,getmaxcolor());
        setlinestyle(SOLID_LINE,0,NORM_WIDTH);
        setcolor(BLACK);
        bar(l->frame.left,l->frame.top,l->frame.right,l->frame.bottom);
        rectangle(l->frame.left,l->frame.top,l->frame.right,l->frame.bottom);

        if(l->base != NULL) {
            for(i=0;i<l->depth;++i) {
                if((l->top+i) >= l->count) break;
                DrawString(l->x+8,l->y+(i*MENULINEDEEP)+2,
                           l->base+((l->top+i)*(l->length+1)),ACTIVE);
            }
        }
        MouseOn();
}

/* add a text object to the window w */
addText(w,t,x,y,p,a)
        WINDOW *w;    /* the window */
        TEXT *t;      /* the TEXT */
        int x,y;      /* the location */
        char *p;      /* the words */
        int a;        /* active */
{
        OBJECTHEAD *oh;
        /* start by finding end of chain */

        oh=(OBJECTHEAD *)w;
        while(oh->next != NULL) oh=oh->next;

        oh->next=(OBJECTHEAD *)t;
```

```
        t->x=x;
        t->y=y;
        t->text=p;
        t->active=a;
        t->head.type=inText;
        t->head.next=NULL;
        drawText(t);
}

/* draw a text object */
drawText(t)
        TEXT *t;
{
        MouseOff();
        DrawString(t->x,t->y,t->text,t->active);
        MouseOn();
}

/* add a textfield object to the window w */
addTextField(w,t,x,y,l,p,a)
        WINDOW *w;              /* the window */
        TEXTFIELD *t;           /* the TEXT */
        int x,y;                /* the location */
        int l;                  /* the maximum length */
        char *p;                /* the words */
        int a;                  /* active */
{
        OBJECTHEAD *oh;
        /* start by finding end of chain */

        oh=(OBJECTHEAD *)w;
        while(oh->next != NULL) oh=oh->next;

        oh->next=(OBJECTHEAD *)t;
        t->x=x;
        t->y=y;
        t->text=p;
        t->active=a;
        t->length=l;
        t->frame.left=x-3;
        t->frame.top=y-3;
        t->frame.right=x+(8*l)+2;
        t->frame.bottom=y+FONTDEEP+2;
        t->head.type=inTextfield;
        t->head.next=NULL;
        drawTextfield(t);
}

/* draw a textfield object */
drawTextfield(t)
        TEXTFIELD *t;
{
        MouseOff();
        setwritemode(COPY_PUT);
        setfillstyle(SOLID_FILL,getmaxcolor());
        setlinestyle(SOLID_LINE,0,NORM_WIDTH);
        setcolor(BLACK);
        bar(t->frame.left,t->frame.top,t->frame.right,t->frame.bottom);
        rectangle(t->frame.left,t->frame.top,t->frame.right,t->frame.bottom);
        DrawString(t->x,t->y,t->text,t->active);
        MouseOn();
}
```

```
/* track a bitmap object */
trackBitmap(b)
    BITMAP *b;
{
    POINT p;

    MouseLoc(&p);
    if(PointInRect(&p,&b->frame) && b->active==ACTIVE) {
        InvertRect(&b->frame);
        while(MouseDown(&p));
        InvertRect(&b->frame);
            if(b->proc != NULL) (b->proc)();
    }
}

/* return a pointer to the selected bitmap */
BITMAP *findBitmap(w,p)
    WINDOW *w;
    POINT *p;
{
    OBJECTHEAD *oh;
    BITMAP *b;

    oh=(OBJECTHEAD *)w;
    while(oh != NULL) {
        if(oh->type == inBitmap) {
            b=(BITMAP *)oh;
            if(PointInRect(p,&b->frame) && b->active==ACTIVE) return(b);
        }
        oh=oh->next;
    }
    return(NULL);
}

/* add a bitmap object to the window w */
addBitmap(w,b,x,y,p,select,proc,active)
    WINDOW *w;      /* the window */
    BITMAP *b;      /* the BITMAP */
    int x,y;        /* the location */
    char *p;        /* the image */
    int select;     /* is it selected */
    int (*proc)();  /* function to call when it's selected */
    int active;     /* can it be selected? */
{
    OBJECTHEAD *oh;
    /* start by finding end of chain */

    oh=(OBJECTHEAD *)w;
    while(oh->next != NULL) oh=oh->next;

    oh->next=(OBJECTHEAD *)b;
    b->x=x;
    b->y=y;
    b->bitmap=p;
    b->select=select;
    b->proc=proc;
    b->active=active;
    b->head.type=inBitmap;
    b->head.next=NULL;
    b->frame.left=b->x;
    b->frame.top=b->y;
    b->frame.right=b->frame.left+ImageWidth(b->bitmap);
    b->frame.bottom=b->frame.top+ImageDepth(b->bitmap);
    drawBitmap(b);
```

```
}

/* draw a bitmap object */
drawBitmap(b)
     BITMAP *b;
{
     char *p;
     int n;

     if(b->select) n=COPY_PUT;
     else n=NOT_PUT;
     if(b->active==INACTIVE) n=NOT_PUT;
     MouseOff();
     if(ismonomode()) putimage(b->x,b->y,b->bitmap,n);
     else {
          if((p=mono2ega(b->bitmap)) != NULL) {
               putimage(b->x,b->y,p,n);
               free(p);
          } else errorbeep();
     }
     MouseOn();
}

/* add a button to the window w */
addButton(w,b,tx,active)
     WINDOW *w;          /* the window */
     BUTTON *b;          /* the button */
     char *tx;           /* the text */
     int active;         /* the active flag */
{
     OBJECTHEAD *oh;
     /* start by finding end of chain */

     oh=(OBJECTHEAD *)w;
     while(oh->next != NULL) oh=oh->next;

     oh->next=(OBJECTHEAD *)b;
     b->text=tx;
     b->active=active;
     b->head.type=inButton;
     b->head.next=NULL;
     b->frame.left &= 0xfff8;
     b->frame.right &= 0xfff8;
     drawButton(b);
}

/* draw a button */
drawButton(b)
     BUTTON *b;
{
     MouseOff();
     setwritemode(COPY_PUT);
     setfillstyle(SOLID_FILL,getmaxcolor());
     setlinestyle(SOLID_LINE,0,THICK_WIDTH);
     setcolor(BLACK);
     bar(b->frame.left,b->frame.top,b->frame.right,b->frame.bottom);
     rectangle(b->frame.left,b->frame.top,b->frame.right,b->frame.bottom);

     DrawString(b->frame.left+8,b->frame.top+4,b->text,b->active);
     MouseOn();
}
```

```
/* track a button */
trackButton(b)
     BUTTON *b;
{
     POINT p;

     if(b != NULL && b->head.type==inButton && b->active==ACTIVE) {
          InvertRect(&b->frame);
          while(MouseDown(&p));
          InvertRect(&b->frame);
     } else errorbeep();
}

/* return a pointer to the selected button */
BUTTON *findButton(w,p)
     WINDOW *w;
     POINT *p;
{
     OBJECTHEAD *oh;
     BUTTON *b;

     oh=(OBJECTHEAD *)w;
     while(oh != NULL) {
          if(oh->type == inButton) {
               b=(BUTTON *)oh;
               if(PointInRect(p,&b->frame) && b->active==ACTIVE) return(b);
          }
          oh=oh->next;
     }
     return(NULL);
}

/* initialize the menu manager */
InitMenuManager()
{
     int i;

     for(i=0;i<MENUCOUNT;++i) menuarray[i]=NULL;
     SetRect(&menubarRect,0,0,SCREENWIDE,MENUBARDEEP);
}

/* add a menu to the menu array */
addMenu(m)
     MENU *m;
{
     if(menuindex < MENUCOUNT) {
          menuarray[menuindex++]=m;
          return(1);
     } else return(0);

}

/* draw the menu bar */
DrawMenuBar(void)
{
     int i;

     WhiteRule(MENUBARDEEP,0);
     BlackRule(2,10);
     for(i=0;i<menuindex;++i)
          DrawString(i*(8*MENUTITLESIZE),1,menuarray[i]->title,ACTIVE);
}

/* handle a menu */
```

```
doMenu(p)
     POINT *p;
{
     WINDOW w;
     RECT r,lr;
     POINT pn;
     int m,n,i;

     m=p->x / (MENUTITLESIZE<<3);
     if(m >= menuindex) return(0);

     r.left=(m*(MENUTITLESIZE<<3))+16;
     r.top=menubarRect.bottom+1;
     r.right=r.left+(MENULINESIZE<<3);
     r.bottom=r.top+(menuarray[m]->count*MENULINEDEEP);

     if(openWindow(&w,&r)) {
          for(i=0;i<menuarray[m]->count;++i) {
               if(menuarray[m]->item[i].name[0]==' ')
                    DrawString(r.left+8,r.top+(i*MENULINEDEEP)+1,
                      menuarray[m]->item[i].name+1,ACTIVE);
               else if(menuarray[m]->item[i].name[0]==CHECKMARK)
                    DrawString(r.left,r.top+(i*MENULINEDEEP)+1,
                      menuarray[m]->item[i].name,ACTIVE);
               else
                    DrawString(r.left+8,r.top+(i*MENULINEDEEP)+1,
                      menuarray[m]->item[i].name+1,INACTIVE);
          }
          i=-1;
          while(MouseDown(&pn)) {
               if(PointInRect(&pn,&r)) {
                    n=(pn.y-r.top)/MENULINEDEEP;
                    if(n != i) {
                         if(i != -1) {
                              SetRect(&lr,r.left,r.top+(i*MENULINEDEEP),
                                r.right,r.top+(i*MENULINEDEEP)+MENULINEDEEP)
                              if(menuarray[m]->item[i].name[0]==' ')
                                   InvertRect(&lr);
                         }
                         SetRect(&lr,r.left,r.top+(n*MENULINEDEEP),
                           r.right,r.top+(n*MENULINEDEEP)+MENULINEDEEP);
                         if(menuarray[m]->item[n].name[0]==' ')
                              InvertRect(&lr);
                         i=n;
                    }
               }
          }
          closeWindow(&w);
          if(PointInRect(&pn,&r) && menuarray[m]->item[n].name[0]==' ') {
               n=(pn.y-r.top)/MENULINEDEEP;
               (menuarray[m]->item[n].proc)(n);
          }
          return(1);
     } else return(0);
}
/* initialize the window manager */
InitWindowManager()
{
     screenwindow.head.type=inWindow;
     screenwindow.head.next=NULL;
     SetRect(&screenwindow.frame,0,0,getmaxx(),getmaxy());
     screenwindow.back=NULL;
```

```
            arrowCursor();
}

/* open a window */
openWindow(w,r)
      WINDOW *w;
      RECT *r;
{
      int size;

      w->frame.left   = r->left-1;
      w->frame.top    = r->top-1;
      w->frame.right  = r->right+DROPSHADOW+1;
      w->frame.bottom = r->bottom+DROPSHADOW+1;

      #if FASTWINDOW
      if((size=fastbuffersize(&w->frame))== -1) return(0);
      #else
      if((size=buffersize(&w->frame))== -1) return(0);
      #endif

      w->head.next=NULL;
      w->head.type=inWindow;
      if((w->back=malloc(size)) != NULL) {
            MouseOff();
            #if FASTWINDOW
            fastgetimage(w->frame.left,w->frame.top,
                         w->frame.right,w->frame.bottom,w->back);
            #else
            getimage(w->frame.left,w->frame.top,
                     w->frame.right,w->frame.bottom,w->back);
            #endif
            setwritemode(COPY_PUT);
            setfillstyle(SOLID_FILL,getmaxcolor());
            setlinestyle(SOLID_LINE,0,NORM_WIDTH);
            setcolor(BLACK);
            bar(r->left-1,r->top-1,r->right+1,r->bottom+1);
            rectangle(r->left-1,r->top-1,r->right+1,r->bottom+1);
            setlinestyle(SOLID_LINE,0,THICK_WIDTH);
            line(r->right+2,r->top+DROPSHADOW,r->right+2,r->bottom+3);
            line(r->left+DROPSHADOW,r->bottom+2,r->right,r->bottom+2);
            MouseOn();
            return(1);
      } else return(0);
}

/* close a window */
closeWindow(w)
      WINDOW *w;
{
      MouseOff();
      if(w->back != NULL) {
            #if FASTWINDOW
            fastputimage(w->frame.left,w->frame.top,w->back);
            #else
            putimage(w->frame.left,w->frame.top,w->back,COPY_PUT);
            #endif
            free(w->back);
      }
      MouseOn();
}

/* return a constant to indicate where the mouse is */
whereMouse(p,w)
```

```
    POINT *p;
    WINDOW *w;
{
    EDITFIELD *f;
    CHECKBOX *cb;
    SCROLLBAR *sb;
    TEXTFIELD *tf;
    LIST *ls;
    BITMAP *bmp;
    BUTTON *b;
    OBJECTHEAD *oh;
    int r=inNothing,i;

    if(PointInRect(p,&menubarRect)) return(inMenuBar);
    else {
        oh=(OBJECTHEAD *)w;
        if(!PointInRect(p,&w->frame)) return(inNothing);
        else {
            while(oh != NULL) {
                switch(oh->type) {
                    case inButton:
                        b=(BUTTON *)oh;
                        if(PointInRect(p,&b->frame)) r |= inButton;
                        break;
                    case inWindow:
                        r &= inWindow;
                        break;
                    case inBitmap:
                        bmp=(BITMAP *)oh;
                        if(PointInRect(p,&bmp->frame)) r |= inBitmap;
                        break;
                    case inList:
                        ls=(LIST *)oh;
                        if(PointInRect(p,&ls->frame)) r |= inList;
                        break;
                    case inTextfield:
                        tf=(TEXTFIELD *)oh;
                        if(PointInRect(p,&tf->frame)) r |= inTextfield;
                        break;
                    case inVertScroll:
                        sb=(SCROLLBAR *)oh;
                        if(PointInRect(p,&sb->frame)) {
                            r |= inVertScroll;
                            if(PointInRect(p,&sb->uparr))
                                r |= inUpArrow;
                            else if(PointInRect(p,&sb->dnarr))
                                r |= inDownArrow;
                            else if(PointInRect(p,&sb->thumb))
                                r |= inThumb;
                            else {
                                /* it's in a jump zone */
                                if(p->y < sb->thumb.top)
                                    r |= inJumpUp;
                                else r |= inJumpDown;
                            }
                        }
                        break;
                    case inHorScroll:
                        sb=(SCROLLBAR *)oh;
                        if(PointInRect(p,&sb->frame)) {
                            r |= inHorScroll;
                            if(PointInRect(p,&sb->uparr))
```

```
                                                     r |= inUpArrow;
                                      else if(PointInRect(p,&sb->dnarr))
                                          r |= inDownArrow;
                                      else if(PointInRect(p,&sb->thumb))
                                          r |= inThumb;
                                      else {
                                          /* it's in a jump zone */
                                          if(p->x < sb->thumb.left)
                                              r |= inJumpUp;
                                          else r |= inJumpDown;
                                      }
                                  }
                                  break;
                            case inCheckBox:
                                  cb=(CHECKBOX *)oh;
                                  if(PointInRect(p,&cb->frame)) r |= inCheckBox;
                                  break;
                            case inEditField:
                                  f=(EDITFIELD *)oh;
                                  if(f->select) {
                                          f->select=0x00;
                                          drawEditfield(f);
                                  }
                                  if(PointInRect(p,&f->frame)) {
                                          r |= inEditField;
                                          f->curpos=(p->x-f->frame.left)/8;
                                          if(f->curpos > (i=strlen(f->text)))
                                              f->curpos=i;
                                  }
                                  break;
                      }
                      oh=oh->next;
                  }
                  return(r);
            }
      }
}

/* turn off graphics */
deinitGraphics()
{
      closegraph();
      if(graphicmode==HERCMONO) RestoreHercDivet();
      while(kbhit()) getch();
}

/* turn on graphics */
initGraphics()
{
      int d,m;

      detectgraph(&d,&m);

      if(d<0) return(0);
          initgraph(&d,&m,"");
      if(graphresult() < 0) return(0);
      setcolor(getmaxcolor());
      graphicmode=d;
      if(graphicmode==VGA) graphicmode=MCGA;
      DoTable(graphicmode);
      SetupMouse(2,2,SCREENWIDE-8,SCREENDEEP-8,graphicmode);
}

/* hide the mouse cursor */
```

```
MouseOff()
{
     union REGS r;

     r.x.ax=2;
     int86(0x33,&r,&r);
}

/* show the mouse cursor */
MouseOn()
{
     union REGS r;

     r.x.ax=1;
     int86(0x33,&r,&r);
}

/* move the mouse cursor */
MoveMouse(p)
     POINT *p;
{
     union REGS r;

     r.x.ax=4;
     r.x.cx=p->x;
     r.x.dx=p->y;
     int86(0x33,&r,&r);
}

/* return the mouse button status */
MouseButton()
{
     union REGS r;

     r.x.ax=3;
     int86(0x33,&r,&r);

     return(r.x.bx & 0x03);
}

/* return button status and location */
MouseDown(p)
     POINT *p;
{
     union REGS r;

     if(fakeMouseDown.x != -1 && fakeMouseDown.y != -1) {
          memcpy((char *)p,(char *)&fakeMouseDown,sizeof(POINT));
          fakeMouseDown.x=-1;
          fakeMouseDown.y=-1;
          return(1);
     }

     r.x.ax=3;
     int86(0x33,&r,&r);

     p->x=r.x.cx;
     p->y=r.x.dx;
     return(r.x.bx & 0x03);
}

/* return mouse location */
```

```
MouseLoc(p)
     POINT *p;
{
     union REGS r;

     r.x.ax=3;
     int86(0x33,&r,&r);

     p->x=r.x.cx;
     p->y=r.x.dx;
}

/* initialize the mouse, return true if driver is present */
InitMouse()
{
     union REGS r;

     r.x.ax=0;
     int86(0x33,&r,&r);
     return(r.x.ax);
}

/* set up the mouse */
SetupMouse(mx,my,x,y,n)
     int mx,my,x,y,n;
{
     char *p;
     union REGS r;

     if(n==HERCMONO) {
          p=MK_FP(0x0040,0x0049);
          hercdivet=*p;
          *p=6;
          r.x.ax=0;
          int86(0x33,&r,&r);
     }

     r.x.ax=0x0007;
     r.x.cx=mx;
     r.x.dx=x;
     int86(0x33,&r,&r);

     r.x.ax=0x0008;
     r.x.cx=my;
     r.x.dx=y;
     int86(0x33,&r,&r);
}

RestoreHercDivet()
{
     char *p;

     p=MK_FP(0x0040,0x0049);
     *p=hercdivet;
}


/* return true if point is in rect */
PointInRect(p,r)
     POINT *p;
     RECT *r;
{
     if(p->x > r->left && p->x < r->right &&
        p->y > r->top  && p->y < r->bottom) return(1);
```

```
        else return(0);
}

/* set a rectangle */
SetRect(r,left,top,right,bottom)
      RECT *r;
      int left,top,right,bottom;
{
      r->left=left;
      r->top=top;
      r->right=right;
      r->bottom=bottom;
}

/* invert a rectangle */
InvertRect(r)
      RECT *r;
{
      char *p,b[81];
      int i,j,width,depth,bleft,bytes,left,right,pleft,pright;

      left=r->left & 0xfff8;
      right=r->right;
      if(right & 0x0007) right=(right | 0x0007)+1;
      width=right-left;
      depth=r->bottom-r->top;
      bleft=left>>3;
      pleft=r->left-left;
      pright=pleft+(r->right-r->left);
      bytes=pixels2bytes(width)+1;
      memset(b,0,bytes);

      for(i=pleft;i<=pright;++i) b[i>>3] |= masktable[i & 0x0007];

      fourplanes();
      MouseOff();
      for(i=0;i<=depth;++i) {
            p=MK_FP(SCREENSEG,SCREENTBL[r->top+i]+bleft);
            for(j=0;j<bytes;++j) p[j] ^= b[j];
      }
      MouseOn();
}

/* do nothing */
idle()
{
      return(0);
}

/* return the size of a buffer based on a RECT */
buffersize(r)
      RECT *r;
{
      return(imagesize(r->left,r->top,r->right,r->bottom));
}

/* return an EGA version of a monochrome bitmap */
char *mono2ega(source)
      char *source;
{
      char *p;
      int x,y,j,ls,sz;
```

```
                x=1+source[0]+(source[1] << 8);
                y=1+source[2]+(source[3] << 8);
                if((sz=imagesize(0,0,x,y)) != -1) {
                    if((p=malloc(sz)) != NULL) {
                        memcpy(p,source,4);
                        ls=pixels2bytes(x);
                        for(j=0;j<y;++j) {
                            memcpy(p+4+((j*4)*ls),source+4+(j*ls),ls);
                            memcpy(p+4+ls+((j*4)*ls),source+4+(j*ls),ls);
                            memcpy(p+4+(ls*2)+((j*4)*ls),source+4+(j*ls),ls);
                            memcpy(p+4+(ls*3)+((j*4)*ls),source+4+(j*ls),ls);
                        }
                        return(p);
                    }
                } else return(NULL);
        }

        /* return a mono version of an EGA bitmap */
        char *ega2mono(source)
                char *source;
        {
                char *p;
                int x,y,j,ls,sz;

                x=1+source[0]+(source[1] << 8);
                y=1+source[2]+(source[3] << 8);

                ls=pixels2bytes(x);
                sz=(ls*y)+4;
                if((p=malloc(sz)) != NULL) {
                    memcpy(p,source,4);
                    for(j=0;j<y;++j) memcpy(p+4+(j*ls),source+4+((j*4)*ls),ls);
                    return(p);
                } else return(NULL);
        }

        /* get a key */
        GetKey()
        {
                int c;

                c = getch();
                if(!(c & 0x00ff)) c = getch() << 8;
                return(c);
        }

        /* set the wait cursor */
        void waitCursor(void)
        {
                union REGS r;
                struct SREGS sr;

                static char cursor[] = {
                    0x00,0x00,0x00,0x00,
                    0x00,0x00,0x01,0x80,
                    0x03,0xC0,0x07,0xE0,
                    0x0F,0xF0,0x07,0xE0,
                    0x03,0xC0,0x01,0x80,
                    0x00,0x00,0x00,0x00,
                    0x00,0x00,0x00,0x00,
                    0xFF,0xFF,0xFF,0xFF,

                    0x00,0x00,0xFE,0x7F,
                    0x06,0x60,0x0C,0x30,
```

```
          0x18,0x18,0x30,0x0C,
          0x60,0x06,0xC0,0x03,
          0x60,0x06,0x30,0x0C,
          0x98,0x19,0xCC,0x33,
          0xE6,0x67,0xFE,0x7F,
          0x00,0x00,0x00,0x00 };

     r.x.ax=0x0009;
     r.x.bx=7;
     r.x.cx=7;
     r.x.dx=FP_OFF(cursor);
     sr.es=FP_SEG(cursor);
     int86x(0x33,&r,&r,&sr);
}

/* set the normal cursor */
void arrowCursor(void)
{
     union REGS r;
     struct SREGS sr;
     static char cursor[] = {
          0xFF,0x3F,0xFF,0x1F,
          0xFF,0x0F,0xFF,0x07,
          0xFF,0x03,0xFF,0x01,
          0xFF,0x00,0x7F,0x00,
          0x3F,0x00,0x1F,0x00,
          0xFF,0x01,0xFF,0x10,
          0xFF,0x30,0x7F,0xF8,
          0x7F,0xF8,0x7F,0xFC,
          0x00,0x00,0x00,0x40,
          0x00,0x60,0x00,0x70,
          0x00,0x78,0x00,0x7C,
          0x00,0x7E,0x00,0x7F,
          0x80,0x7F,0x00,0x7C,
          0x00,0x6C,0x00,0x46,
          0x00,0x06,0x00,0x03,
          0x00,0x03,0x00,0x00 };

     r.x.ax=0x0009;
     r.x.bx=/*-1*/0;
     r.x.cx=/*-1*/0;
     r.x.dx=FP_OFF(cursor);
     sr.es=FP_SEG(cursor);
     int86x(0x33,&r,&r,&sr);
}

/* return true if the screen is in a monochrome mode */
ismonomode()
{
     if(getmaxcolor()==1) return(1);
     else return(0);
}

/* return true if n is a legal font size */
islegalfontsize(n)
     int n;
{
     if(strchr(FONTSIZEARRAY,n)==NULL) return(0);
     else return(1);
}

/* write a font resource */
```

```
writeFontRes(path,font,bitmap)
     char *path;
     FONT *font;
     char *bitmap;
{
     char *p,b[FONTNAMESIZE+32];
     RFILE fh;
     unsigned int size,rt=0;

     size=sizeof(FONT)+(font->bitmapbytes*font->bitmapdepth);
     if((p=malloc(size)) != NULL) {
          memcpy(p,(char *)font,sizeof(FONT));
          memcpy(p+sizeof(FONT),bitmap,font->bitmapbytes*font->bitmapdepth);
          sprintf(b,"%u point %s",font->pointsize,font->name);
          if(createRF(path,b)) {
               if((fh=openRF(path)) != 0) {
                    if(addRF(fh,FONTid,0L,size,p)) rt=1;
                    closeRF(fh);
               }
          }
          free(p);
     }
     return(rt);
}

/* return the width of char n in font */
charwidthFN(n,font)
     int n;
     FONT *font;
{
     if(n==32) return(font->spacewidth+font->padwidth);
     else if(!font->charwide[n]) return(0);
     else return((unsigned int)font->charwide[n]+font->padwidth);
}

/* return the width of string s in font */
stringwidthFN(s,font)
     char *s;
     FONT *font;
{
     unsigned int a=0;

     while(*s) a+=(unsigned int)charwidthFN(*s++,font);
     return(a);
}

/* return the depth of font */
fontdepthFN(font)
     FONT *font;
{
     return(font->bitmapdepth);
}

/* create a bitmap of string s in font */
char *bitmapstringFN(s,font)
     char *s;
     FONT *font;
{
     char *p,*pr,*bmp;
     int n,bytes,width,i,j,k,kl,cp,cb,bsize;

     n=strlen(s);
     width=stringwidthFN(s,font);
     bytes=pixels2bytes(width);
```

```
      bmp=((char *)font)+sizeof(FONT);
      bsize=4+(bytes*font->bitmapdepth);

      if((p=malloc(bsize)) != NULL) {
          memset(p,0xff,bsize);
          p[0]=width-1;
          p[1]=(width-1)>>8;
          p[2]=font->bitmapdepth-1;
          p[3]=(font->bitmapdepth-1)>>8;

          pr=p+4;
          for(i=0;i<font->bitmapdepth;++i) {
              cb=0;
              for(j=0;j<n;++j) {
                  if(s[j] != 32) {
                      kl=font->charwide[s[j]];
                      cp=font->charoff[s[j]];
                      for(k=0;k<kl;++k) {
                          if(bmp[cp>>3] & masktable[cp & 0x0007])
                              pr[cb>>3] &= ~masktable[cb & 0x0007];
                          ++cb;
                          ++cp;
                      }
                      cb+=font->padwidth;
                  } else cb+=(font->spacewidth+font->padwidth);
              }
              bmp+=font->bitmapbytes;
              pr+=bytes;
          }
          return(p);
      } else return(NULL);
}

/* draw string s in font at (x,y) */
drawstringFN(s,font,x,y)
      char *s;
      FONT *font;
      int x,y;
{
      char *pr,*bmp;
      int n,i,j,k,kl,cp,cb;

      n=strlen(s);
      bmp=((char *)font)+sizeof(FONT);

      fourplanes();
      MouseOff();
      for(i=0;i<font->bitmapdepth;++i) {
          if((y+i) >=SCREENDEEP) break;
          pr=(char *)MK_FP(SCREENSEG,SCREENTBL[y+i]);
          cb=x;
          for(j=0;j<n;++j) {
              if(s[j]!=32) {
                  kl=font->charwide[s[j]];
                  cp=font->charoff[s[j]];
                  for(k=0;k<kl;++k) {
                      if(bmp[cp>>3] & masktable[cp & 0x0007])
                          pr[cb>>3] &= ~masktable[cb & 0x0007];
                      ++cb;
                      ++cp;
                  }
                  cb+=font->padwidth;
```

```
                } else cb+=(font->spacewidth+font->padwidth);
            }
            bmp+=font->bitmapbytes;
        }
        MouseOn();
}

/* create a resource file and leave it unopened */
createRF(name,description)
    char *name,*description;
{
    RESHEAD rh;
    int fh,r=0;

    if((fh=dcreate(name)) != NULL) {
        memset((char *)&rh,0,sizeof(RESHEAD));
        memcpy(rh.id,resourceID,8);
        strcpy(rh.description,description);
        if(dwrite((char *)&rh,sizeof(RESHEAD),fh) == sizeof(RESHEAD)) r=1;
        dclose(fh);
    }
    return(r);
}

/* open a resource file and return its handle */
RFILE openRF(name)
    char *name;
{
    RESHEAD rh;
    int fh;

    if((fh=dopen(name)) != NULL) {
        if(dread((char *)&rh,sizeof(RESHEAD),fh) == sizeof(RESHEAD)) {
            if(memcmp(rh.id,resourceID,8)) {
                dclose(fh);
                return(0);
            }
            return((RFILE )fh);
        }
        else {
            dclose(fh);
            return(0);
        }
    } else return(0);
}

/* close a resource file */
void closeRF(fh)
    RFILE fh;
{
    dclose(fh);
}

/* add a resource to a resource file */
addRF(fh,type,number,size,res)
    RFILE fh;
    char *type;
    unsigned long number;
    unsigned int size;
    char *res;
{
    RESHEAD rh;
    RESOURCE rc;
    unsigned int i;
```

```
        if(getinfoRF(&rh,fh) && number != BADRECNUM) {
            for(i=0;i<rh.count;++i) {
                if(dread((char *)&rc,sizeof(RESOURCE),fh)!=sizeof(RESOURCE))
                  return(0);
                dseek(fh,(long)rc.size,SEEK_CUR);
            }
            memset((char *)&rc,0,sizeof(RESOURCE));
            memcpy(rc.type,type,4);
            rc.number=number;
            rc.size=size;
            if(dwrite((char *)&rc,sizeof(RESOURCE),fh) != sizeof(RESOURCE))
              return(0);
            if(dwrite(res,size,fh) != size) return(0);
            ++rh.count;
            dseek(fh,0L,SEEK_SET);
            if(dwrite((char *)&rh,sizeof(RESHEAD),fh) != sizeof(RESHEAD))
              return(0);
            return(1);
        } else return(0);
}


/* count the resources of type in a resource file */
countRF(fh,type)
    RFILE fh;
    char *type;
{

    RESOURCE rc;
    RESHEAD rh;
    unsigned int i,count=0;

    if(getinfoRF(&rh,fh)) {
        for(i=0;i<rh.count;++i) {
            if(dread((char *)&rc,sizeof(RESOURCE),fh)!=sizeof(RESOURCE))
              return(0);
            if(!memcmp(rc.type,type,4)) ++count;
            dseek(fh,(long)rc.size,SEEK_CUR);
        }
        return(count);
    } else return(0);
}


/* remove a resource */
removeresRF(fh,rc)
    RFILE fh;
    RESOURCE *rc;
{

    RESHEAD rh;
    RESOURCE lrc;
    long source,dest;
    char *p;
    int i,r=0;
    unsigned int size,dsize;

    if(!getinfoRF(&rh,fh)) return(0);
    for(i=0;i<rh.count;++i) {
        if(dread((char *)&lrc,sizeof(RESOURCE),fh) != sizeof(RESOURCE))
          return(0);
        if(!memcmp(rc->type,lrc.type,4) && rc->number==lrc.number) {
            r=1;
            break;
        }
        dseek(fh,(long)lrc.size,SEEK_CUR);
```

```
            }
        if(!r) return(0);
        size=lrc.size+sizeof(RESOURCE);
        if((p=malloc(size)) == NULL) return(0);
        source=dtell(fh)+lrc.size;
        dest=source-(long)(lrc.size+sizeof(RESOURCE));

        do {
            dseek(fh,source,SEEK_SET);
            if((dsize=dread(p,size,fh)) > 0) {
                dseek(fh,dest,SEEK_SET);
                dwrite(p,dsize,fh);
            }
            source+=(long)size;
            dest+=(long)size;
        } while(dsize==size);

        free(p);

        --rh.count;
        dseek(fh,0L,SEEK_SET);
        if(dwrite((char *)&rh,sizeof(RESHEAD),fh) != sizeof(RESHEAD)) return(0);
        return(1);
}

/* get the resource data from a file */
getdataRF(p,fh,size)
    char *p;
    RFILE fh;
    unsigned int size;
{
    if(dread(p,size,fh) == size) return(1);
    else return(0);
}

/* get a resource */
getRF(fh,type,n,rc)
    RFILE fh;
    char *type;
    long n;
    RESOURCE *rc;
{

    RESHEAD rh;
    unsigned int i;

    if(getinfoRF(&rh,fh)) {
        for(i=0;i<rh.count;++i) {
            if(dread((char *)rc,sizeof(RESOURCE),fh)!=sizeof(RESOURCE))
                return(0);
            if(!memcmp(rc->type,type,4)) {
                if(rc->number==n) return(1);
            }
            dseek(fh,(long)rc->size,SEEK_CUR);
        }
        return(0);
    } else return(0);
}
/* get a numbered resource */
getnumberedRF(fh,type,n,rc)
    RFILE fh;
    char *type;
    int n;
    RESOURCE *rc;
{
```

```
        RESHEAD rh;
        unsigned int i,count=0;

        if(getinfoRF(&rh,fh)) {
            for(i=0;i<rh.count;++i) {
                if(dread((char *)rc,sizeof(RESOURCE),fh)!=sizeof(RESOURCE))
                  return(0);
                if(!memcmp(rc->type,type,4)) {
                    if(count++==n) return(1);
                }
                dseek(fh,(long)rc->size,SEEK_CUR);
            }
            return(0);
        } else return(0);
}

/* get each resource in the file. call proc for each.
   abort if proc returns zero */
getallRF(fh,proc)
        RFILE fh;
        int (*proc)();
{
        RESHEAD rh;
        RESOURCE rc;
        unsigned long pos;
        unsigned int i;

        if(getinfoRF(&rh,fh)) {
            for(i=0;i<rh.count;++i) {
                if(dread((char *)&rc,sizeof(RESOURCE),fh) != sizeof(RESOURCE))
                  return(0);
                pos=dtell(fh);
                if(!(proc)(&rc,fh,i)) return(0);
                dseek(fh,pos+(long)rc.size,SEEK_SET);
            }
            return(1);
        } else return(0);
}

/* get the data about a resource file */
getinfoRF(rh,fh)
        RESHEAD *rh;
        RFILE fh;
{
        dseek(fh,0L,SEEK_SET);
        if(dread((char *)rh,sizeof(RESHEAD),fh)==sizeof(RESHEAD)) return(1);
        else return(0);
}

/* find a free number in a resource file */
long freenumberRF(fh,type)
        RFILE fh;
        char *type;
{
        RESOURCE rc;
        long i,rt=BADRECNUM;
        long pos;

        pos=dtell(fh);

        for(i=0;i<BADRECNUM;++i) {
            if(!getRF(fh,type,i,&rc)) {
```

```
                    rt=i;
                    break;
              }
       }
       dseek(fh,pos,SEEK_SET);
       return(rt);
}

dcreate(s)            /* direct DOS file create */
       char *s;
{
       union REGS r;
       struct SREGS sg;

       r.x.ax=0x3c00;
       r.x.cx=0;
       r.x.dx=FP_OFF(s);
       sg.ds=FP_SEG(s);
       int86x(0x21,&r,&r,&sg);
       if(r.x.cflag) return(0);
       else return(r.x.ax);
}

dopen(s)              /* direct DOS file open */
       char *s;
{
       union REGS r;
       struct SREGS sg;

       r.x.ax=0x3d02;
       r.x.cx=0;
       r.x.dx=FP_OFF(s);
       sg.ds=FP_SEG(s);
       int86x(0x21,&r,&r,&sg);
       if(r.x.cflag) return(0);
       else return(r.x.ax);
}

void dclose(h)
       RFILE h;
{
       union REGS r;

       r.x.ax=0x3e00;
       r.x.bx=h;
       int86(0x21,&r,&r);
       if(r.x.cflag) return(r.x.ax);
       else return(0);
}
dread(p,n,h)              /* direct DOS file read */
       char *p;
       unsigned int n;
       RFILE h;
{
       union REGS r;
       struct SREGS sg;

       r.x.ax=0x3f00;
       r.x.bx=h;
       r.x.cx=n;
       r.x.dx=FP_OFF(p);
       sg.ds=FP_SEG(p);
       int86x(0x21,&r,&r,&sg);
       if(r.x.cflag) return(0);
```

```
          else return(r.x.ax);
}

dwrite(p,n,h)              /* direct DOS file write */
      char *p;
      unsigned int n;
      RFILE h;
{
      union REGS r;
      struct SREGS sg;

      r.x.ax=0x4000;
      r.x.bx=h;
      r.x.cx=n;
      r.x.dx=FP_OFF(p);
      sg.ds=FP_SEG(p);
      int86x(0x21,&r,&r,&sg);
      if(r.x.cflag) return(0);
      else return(r.x.ax);
}

long dseek(h,l,m)          /* direct DOS file read */
      int h,m;
      long l;
{
      union REGS r;
      struct SREGS sg;

      r.h.ah=0x42;
      r.h.al=m;
      r.x.bx=h;
      r.x.cx=(unsigned int)(l >> 16);
      r.x.dx=(unsigned int)l;
      int86x(0x21,&r,&r,&sg);
      if(r.x.cflag) return(-1L);
      else return(((long)r.x.dx << 16)+ (long)r.x.ax);
}

long dtell(h)              /* direct DOS file read */
      RFILE h;
{
      union REGS r;
      struct SREGS sg;
      r.h.ah=0x42;
      r.h.al=0x01;
      r.x.bx=h;
      r.x.cx=0;
      r.x.dx=0;
      int86x(0x21,&r,&r,&sg);
      if(r.x.cflag) return(-1L);
      else return(((long)r.x.dx << 16)+ (long)r.x.ax);
}

fourplanes()               /* select all four EGA/VGA planes */
{
      if(ismonomode()) return(0);

      outportb(0x3c4,0x02);
      outportb(0x3c5,0x0f);
}
```

D

The GUI
assembler source code

Appendix D contains the source code for GUIASM.ASM. This file will assemble with any recent version of MASM or TASM. The resulting OBJ file—GUI-ASM.OBJ—will link with GUI.OBJ to complete the set of library functions.

```
                COMMENT +

                machine language module for the graphical user interface

                          +

_AOFF           EQU     6               ;STACK OFFSET TO FIRST ARG

CGA             EQU     1               ;THESE EQUATES ARE EQUIVALENT TO
MCGA            EQU     2               ;THE VALUES RETURNED BY THE
EGA             EQU     3               ;TURBO C DetectGraph FUNCTION
HERCMONO        EQU     7

_AOFF           EQU     6               ;FAR STACK OFFSET

FONTDEPTH       EQU     8
MENULINEDEPTH   EQU     12

;SET ALL FOUR PLANES ON AN EGA OR VGA DISPLAY
FOURPLANES      MACRO
                LOCAL   FPEXIT
                CMP     DS:[_SCREENSEG],0A000H
                JNE     FPEXIT
                MOV     AL,2
                MOV     DX,03C4H
                OUT     DX,AL
```

D-1 The source code for GUIASM.ASM.

```
                    INC     DX
                    MOV     AL,0FH
                    OUT     DX,AL
FPEXIT:
                    ENDM

;THIS MACRO FETCHES THE DATA SEGEMENT
DATASEG             MACRO
                    PUSH    AX
                    MOV     AX,_DATA
                    MOV     DS,AX
                    POP     AX
                    ENDM


;DISPLAY THE MQUSE CURSOR
MOUSEON             MACRO
                    MOV     AX,0001H
                    INT     33H
                    ENDM


;HIDE THE MOUSE CURSOR
MOUSEOFF            MACRO
                    MOV     AX,0002H
                    INT     33H
                    ENDM


;TRANSLATE PIXELS TO BYTES IN AX
PIXELS2BYTES        MACRO
                    ADD     AX,0007H
                    SHR     AX,1
                    SHR     AX,1
                    SHR     AX,1
                    ENDM
  TRANSLATE PIXELS TO WORDS IN AX
PIXELS2WORDS        MACRO
                    ADD     AX,000FH
                    SHR     AX,1
                    SHR     AX,1
                    SHR     AX,1
                    SHR     AX,1
                    ENDM


APASM_TEXT          SEGMENT BYTE PUBLIC 'CODE'
                    ASSUME  CS:APASM_TEXT,DS:_DATA


;DRAW A WHITE RULE ACROSS THE SCREEN
;                   ARG1 = DEPTH
;                   ARG2 = TOPLINE
                    PUBLIC  _WhiteRule
_WhiteRule          PROC    FAR
                    PUSH    BP
                    MOV     BP,SP

                    DATASEG
                    FOURPLANES
                    MOUSEOFF
                    MOV     AX,DS:[_SCREENSEG]
                    MOV     ES,AX

                    MOV     CX,[BP + _AOFF + 0]
                    MOV     BX,[BP + _AOFF + 2]
                    SHL     BX,1
```

```
                        MOV     DX,DS:[_SCREENBYTES]
        WR1:            PUSH    CX
                        MOV     DI,DS:[_SCREENTBL+BX]
                        ADD     BX,2
                        MOV     CX,DX
                        CLD
                        MOV     AL,0FFH
                REPNE   STOSB
                        POP     CX
                        LOOP    WR1
                        MOUSEON
                        POP     BP
                        RET
        _WhiteRule      ENDP

        ;DRAW A BLACK RULE ACROSS THE SCREEN
        ;               ARG1 = DEPTH
        ;               ARG2 = TOPLINE
                        PUBLIC  _BlackRule
        _BlackRule      PROC    FAR
                        PUSH    BP
                        MOV     BP,SP

                        DATASEG
                        FOURPLANES
                        MOUSEOFF
                        MOV     AX,DS:[_SCREENSEG]
                        MOV     ES,AX
                        MOV     CX,[BP + _AOFF + 0]
                        MOV     BX,[BP + _AOFF + 2]
                        SHL     BX,1
                        MOV     DX,DS:[_SCREENBYTES]
        BR1:            PUSH    CX
                        MOV     DI,DS:[_SCREENTBL+BX]
                        ADD     BX,2
                        MOV     CX,DX
                        CLD
                        MOV     AL,00H
                REPNE   STOSB
                        POP     CX
                        LOOP    BR1
                        MOUSEON
                        POP     BP
                        RET
        _BlackRule      ENDP

        ;DRAW A TEXT STRING
        ;               ARG1 = X
        ;               ARG2 = Y
        ;               ARG3 = STRING
        ;               ARG4 = MASK
                        PUBLIC  _DrawString
        _DrawString     PROC    FAR
                        PUSH    BP
                        MOV     BP,SP

                        DATASEG
                        FOURPLANES
                        MOUSEOFF
                        MOV     AX,DS:[_SCREENSEG]
                        MOV     ES,AX

                        MOV     CL,3
                        SHR     WORD PTR [BP + _AOFF + 0],CL
```

```
                MOV     CX,FONTDEPTH
DS1:            PUSH    CX
                DEC     CX

                MOV     AX,[BP + _AOFF + 8]
                XCHG    AH,AL
                MOV     [BP + _AOFF + 8],AX

                MOV     BX,[BP + _AOFF + 2]
                ADD     BX,CX
                SHL     BX,1

                DATASEG
                MOV     DI,DS:[_SCREENTBL+BX]
                ADD     DI,[BP + _AOFF + 0]

                MOV     SI,[BP + _AOFF + 4]
                MOV     DS,[BP + _AOFF + 6]

DS2:            MOV     BH,00H
                MOV     BL,DS:[SI]
                CMP     BL,0
                JE      DS3

                PUSH    DS
                SHL     BX,1
                SHL     BX,1
                SHL     BX,1

                ADD     BX,CX

                DATASEG
                MOV     AL,DS:[_THEFONT+BX]
                AND     AX,[BP + _AOFF + 8]
                NOT     AL
                STOSB

                POP     DS
                INC     SI
                JMP     DS2

DS3:            POP     CX
                LOOP    DS1

DSX:            DATASEG
                MOUSEON
                POP     BP
                RET
_DrawString     ENDP

;CLEAR THE SCREEN TO GREY
                PUBLIC  _ClearScreen
_ClearScreen    PROC    FAR

                MOV     AX,_DATA
                MOV     DS,AX

                MOV     AX,_SCREENSEG
                MOV     ES,AX

                FOURPLANES
                MOUSEOFF
```

```
                     MOV      CX,_SCREENDEEP
                     SUB      CX,MENULINEDEPTH
                     MOV      BX, (MENULINEDEPTH*2)

CLS1:                PUSH     CX
                     TEST     CX,1
                     MOV      AL,0AAH
                     JZ       CLS2
                     MOV      AL,055H
CLS2:                MOV      DI,[_SCREENTBL+BX]
                     MOV      CX,_SCREENBYTES
                     CLD
          REPNE      STOSB
                     POP      CX
                     ADD      BX,2
                     LOOP     CLS1

                     MOUSEON
                     RET
_ClearScreen         ENDP

;SET UP THE SCREEN TABLE
;                    ARG1 = CARD TYPE
                     PUBLIC   _DoTable
_DoTable             PROC     FAR
                     PUSH     BP
                     MOV      BP,SP

                     DATASEG

                     CMP      WORD PTR [BP + _AOFF + 0],CGA
                     JNE      NOT_CGA                ;CHECK CARD TYPE

                     ;IT'S A CGA CARD
                     MOV      _SCREENSEG,0B800H
                     MOV      _SCREENBYTES,80
                     MOV      _SCREENWIDE,640
                     MOV      _SCREENDEEP,200

                     MOV      CX,_SCREENDEEP
                     SUB      DX,DX
                     MOV      SI,OFFSET _SCREENTBL

CTB0:                PUSH     CX
                     PUSH     DX
                     MOV      AX,_SCREENBYTES ;AX = WIDTH OF TUBE
                     MOV      BX,DX            ;BX =
                     MOV      CL,1             ;
                     SHR      BX,CL            ; ... LINE NUMBER DIV 4
                     PUSH     DX
                     MUL      BX               ;MUL WIDTH OF SCREEN
                     MOV      DI,AX            ;DI IS NOW THE PARTIAL OFFSET
                     POP      DX

                     SUB      DH,DH            ;
                     MOV      AX,2000H         ;MULTIPLY DX MOD 4 BY 2000H
                     AND      DX,1
                     MUL      DX
                     ADD      DI,AX            ;ADD TO THE OFFSET
                     POP      DX
                     POP      CX

                     MOV      BX,DX            ;AND PUT IT IN THE TABLE
                     SHL      BX,1
```

```
                MOV     [SI+BX],DI
                INC     DX
                LOOP    CTB0
                SUB     AX,AX               ;EVERYTHING'S FINE
                JMP     TABLE_OK

NOT_CGA:        CMP     WORD PTR [BP + _AOFF + 0],EGA
                JNE     NOT_EGA

                ;IT'S AN EGA CARD
                MOV     _SCREENSEG,0A000H
                MOV     _SCREENBYTES,80
                MOV     _SCREENWIDE,640
                MOV     _SCREENDEEP,350

                MOV     CX,_SCREENDEEP
                SUB     DX,DX
                MOV     SI,OFFSET _SCREENTBL

ETB0:           PUSH    DX
                MOV     AX,_SCREENBYTES
                MUL     DX
                MOV     [SI],AX
                ADD     SI,2
                POP     DX
                INC     DX
                LOOP    ETB0
                SUB     AX,AX               ;EVERYTHING'S FINE
                JMP     TABLE_OK

NOT_EGA:        CMP     WORD PTR [BP + _AOFF + 0],MCGA
                JNE     NOT_MCGA

                ;IT'S AN MCGA CARD
                MOV     _SCREENSEG,0A000H
                MOV     _SCREENBYTES,80
                MOV     _SCREENWIDE,640
                MOV     _SCREENDEEP,480

                MOV     CX,_SCREENDEEP
                SUB     DX,DX
                MOV     SI,OFFSET _SCREENTBL

MTB0:           PUSH    DX
                MOV     AX,_SCREENBYTES
                MUL     DX
                MOV     [SI],AX
                ADD     SI,2
                POP     DX
                INC     DX
                LOOP    MTB0
                SUB     AX,AX               ;EVERYTHING'S FINE
                JMP     TABLE_OK

NOT_MCGA:       CMP     WORD PTR [BP + _AOFF + 0],HERCMONO
                JNE     NOT_HERCMONO

                ;IT'S A HERCULES CARD
                MOV     _SCREENSEG,0B000H
                MOV     _SCREENBYTES,90
                MOV     _SCREENWIDE,720
                MOV     _SCREENDEEP,348
```

```
                    MOV         CX,_SCREENDEEP
                    SUB         DX,DX
                    MOV         SI,OFFSET _SCREENTBL

HTB0:               PUSH        CX
                    PUSH        DX
                    MOV         AX,_SCREENBYTES ;AX = WIDTH OF TUBE
                    MOV         BX,DX           ;BX =
                    MOV         CL,2            ;
                    SHR         BX,CL           ; ... LINE NUMBER DIV 4
                    PUSH        DX
                    MUL         BX              ;MUL WIDTH OF SCREEN
                    MOV         DI,AX           ;DI IS NOW THE PARTIAL OFFSET
                    POP         DX

                    SUB         DH,DH           ;
                    MOV         AX,2000H        ;MULTIPLY DX MOD 4 BY 2000H
                    AND         DX,3
                    MUL         DX
                    ADD         DI,AX           ;ADD TO THE OFFSET
                    POP         DX
                    POP         CX

                    MOV         SI,OFFSET _SCREENTBL
                    MOV         BX,DX
                    SHL         BX,1
                    MOV         [SI+BX],DI
                    INC         DX
                    LOOP        HTB0
                    SUB         AX,AX           ;EVERYTHING'S FINE
                    JMP         TABLE_OK

NOT_HERCMONO:       MOV         AX,-1

TABLE_OK:           POP         BP
                    RET
_DoTable            ENDP

;SWITCH TO GRAPHICS MODE
;                   ARG1 = CARD TYPE
                    PUBLIC      _GraphicsMode
_GraphicsMode       PROC        FAR
                    PUSH        BP
                    MOV         BP,SP

                    DATASEG

                    MOV         AX,[BP + _AOFF + 0]
                    MOV         GMODE,AX

                    CMP         GMODE,CGA
                    JNE         NOT_GCGA

                    MOV         AX,0006H
                    INT         10H
                    JMP         GRAF_OK

NOT_GCGA:           CMP         GMODE,EGA
                    JNE         NOT_GEGA

                    MOV         AX,0010H
                    INT         10H
                    JMP         GRAF_OK
```

```
NOT_GEGA:       CMP     GMODE,MCGA
                JNE     NOT_GMCGA
                MOV     AX,0011H
                INT     10H
                JMP     GRAF_OK

NOT_GMCGA:      MOV     DX,03BFH
                MOV     AL,1
                OUT     DX,AL

                MOV     AL,2
                MOV     SI,OFFSET GTABLE
                MOV     BX,0
                MOV     CX,4000H
                CALL    HERC_MODE

GRAF_OK:        POP     BP
                RET
_GraphicsMode   ENDP

;SWITCH TO TEXT MODE
                PUBLIC  _TextMode
_TextMode       PROC    FAR
                PUSH    BP
                MOV     BP,SP

                DATASEG

                CMP     GMODE,HERCMONO
                JE      TEXT_HERC

                MOV     AX,0003H
                INT     10H
                JMP     TEXT_OK

TEXT_HERC:      MOV     DX,03BFH
                XOR     AL,AL
                OUT     DX,AL

                MOV     AX,20H
                MOV     SI,OFFSET TTABLE
                MOV     BX,720H
                MOV     CX,2000H
                CALL    HERC_MODE

TEXT_OK:        POP     BP
                RET
_TextMode       ENDP

;THIS ROUTINE SETS UP THE MODE FOR THE HERCULES CARD
HERC_MODE       PROC    NEAR
                PUSH    DS
                PUSH    ES

                PUSH    AX
                PUSH    BX
                PUSH    CX

                MOV     DX,3B8H
                OUT     DX,AL
                MOV     DX,3B4H
                MOV     CX,12
```

```
                        XOR      AH,AH

                        CLI
                        CLD
        HERC_MODE1:     MOV      AL,AH
                        OUT      DX,AL
                        INC      DX
                        LODSB
                        OUT      DX,AL

                        INC      AH
                        DEC      DX
                        LOOP     HERC_MODE1

                        POP      CX
                        MOV      AX,0B000H
                        CLD

                        MOV      ES,AX
                        XOR      DI,DI
                        POP      AX
                        REP      STOSW

                        MOV      DX,03BAH          ;WAIT FOR VERTICAL RETRACE
        HERC_MODE2:     IN       AL,DX
                        SHL      AL,1
                        JNC      HERC_MODE2

        HERC_MODE3:     IN       AL,DX
                        SHL      AL,1
                        JC       HERC_MODE3

                        MOV      DX,3B8H
                        POP      AX
                        ADD      AL,8
                        OUT      DX,AL
                        STI
                        POP      ES
                        POP      DS
                        RET
        HERC_MODE       ENDP

        APASM_TEXT      ENDS

        DGROUP          GROUP    _DATA,_BSS
        _DATA           SEGMENT  WORD PUBLIC 'DATA'

                        PUBLIC   _SCREENTBL
                        PUBLIC   _SCREENSEG,_SCREENBYTES
                        PUBLIC   _SCREENWIDE,_SCREENDEEP

        EXTRN                    _THEFONT:BYTE

        _SCREENTBL      DW       480 DUP(0)        ;MAXIMUM LINE COUNT
        _SCREENSEG      DW       ?                 ;POINTER TO SCREEN
        _SCREENBYTES    DW       ?                 ;WIDTH OF SCREEN IN BYTES
        _SCREENWIDE     DW       ?                 ;WIDTH OF SCREEN IN PIXELS
_SCREENDEEP     DW       ?                         ;DEPTH OF SCREEN IN PIXELS

;GRAPHICS CARD INITIALIZATION DATA
TTABLE          DB       61H,50H,52H,0FH,19H,06H,19H,19H,02H,0DH,0BH,0CH
GTABLE          DB       35H,2DH,2EH,07H,5BH,02H,57H,57H,02H,03H,00H,00H
GMODE           DW       ?
```

```
_DATA          ENDS

_BSS           SEGMENT WORD PUBLIC 'BSS'

_BSS           ENDS

               END
```

Index

font management (*cont.*)
putimage function use, 232
resource files, adding a font,
237-238
resource files, creating font
resource file, SYS2FONT
program, 238-239
size limitations, 237
software packages for fonts,
15-16
spacewidth element, 234
stringwidthFN function,
236-237, 353
Ventura, screen fonts, 248
viewing FONT resources,
SEEFONT program, 239-247
widestchar element, 234
Windows FNT font
conversion, WIN2FONT
program, 253-259
writeFontRes function,
237-238, 353
fontdepthFN function, 236-237,
353
forks, 17
Macintosh, font management,
260
fourplanes function, 49-50
FOURPLANES macro, 49-50
frames, 10, 63
freebuffer function, 333-334
freenumberRF function,
203-204, 354
function pointers, menu
management, 78-79
function programming
techniques, assembly vs. C,
39-42
Future font, 229, 241

G

GALLERY.RES files, resource
file management, 195-196
GEM packaged GUI, 4-5
font conversion, GEM2FONT
program, 247-253
GEM2FONT program, 247-253
Geneva font, 260
getallRF function, 202, 213, 355
getbuffer function, 333-334
getdataRF function, 355
getdraw function, 333
getFileInfo function, 334
getfiles function, 291-292

getimage function, 11, 17, 65-71,
167
getinfoRF function, 203, 355
GetKey function, 350
getline function, 333
getnumberedRF function,
191-192, 355
getRF function, 191-192, 356
graphical user interfaces (GUI)
defined, 1-5
graphics display management,
349-350
assembly language vs. C,
39-42, 49-50
BGI drivers, 48-49
BGIOBJ.EXE, 49
BlackRule function, 48
CGA, 33
ClearScreen function, 42, 48
deinitGraphics function, 38,
349
DoTable function, 38-39, 40, 42
EGA modes, 7, 34-35, 36-50
ega2mono function, 349
Hercules graphics card, 7,
34-37
initGraphics function, 38, 40,
49, 349
InvertRect function, 349
line start tables, 38-39, 42-48
modes, 33-50
monochrome graphics cards
(*see also* Hercules), 7, 35
mono2ega function, 349
patching, 50
PointInRect function, 350
screen drivers, 39-42
screen drivers, high-speed, 36,
38-39
SCREENBYTES global
element, 39, 40
SCREENDEEP global
element, 39, 40
SCREENSEG global element,
39, 40
SCREENTBL global element,
39, 40
SCREENWIDE global
element, 39, 40
SetRect function, 350
VGA mode, 7, 34-35, 36-50
WhiteRule function, 48
GUI.C source code listing, 31,
365-404

GUI.H header file, 31, 357-364
GUI.LIB, 20, 31-32
GUIASM.ASM assembler
source code listing, 31,
405-413

H

Hacker font, 241
handleRec function, resource file
management, 202-203
handleRF function, 202-203
handles, memory management,
12-13
hardware requirements, 5-7
header files
GUI.H code listing, 357-364
resource files, 18
Tiny Paint, TPAINT.H,
323-325
Helvetica font, 229
Hercules graphics cards (*see also*
graphics display
management), 7, 35-37
BGI screen drivers, 48-49
mouse compatibility, 14, 51
mouse compatibility,
SetupMouse function, 57-58
window management, 65
hieroglyphics as GUIs, 1-2
hotspots, mouse cursor, 54-55
hpScroll function, 333
huge memory model, 30

I

icons
bitmaps vs., 163-164
menu management, 107
Tiny Paint, 327
idle function, 79, 348
image boundaries, window
management, 66
ImageBytes function, 70
ImageDepth function, 69-70
imagesize function, 70
ImageWidth function, 69-70
INACTIVE, menu management,
81
initGraphics function, 38, 40, 49,
349
InitMenuManager function,
81-82, 348
InitMouse function, 51, 350
InitWindowManager function,
348

RF